CHANGING
us for
GLORY

CHANGING
us for
GLORY

Daily Readings on God's Transforming Power

DAVID GOODING

EDITED BY HELEN CROOKES

Changing Us for Glory: Daily Readings on God's Transforming Power

Copyright © 2024 The Myrtlefield Trust

All rights reserved. No part of this publication may be reproduced, stored in a retrieval system, or transmitted, in any form or by any means, electronic, mechanical, photocopying, recording or otherwise, without the prior permission of the publisher or a license permitting restricted copying. In the UK such licenses are issued by the Copyright Licensing Agency Ltd., 1 St Katharine's Way, London, E1W 1UN.

Scripture quotations, unless otherwise indicated, are from the ESV® Bible (The Holy Bible, English Standard Version®), copyright © 2001 by Crossway, a publishing ministry of Good News Publishers. Used by permission. All rights reserved.
Scripture quotations marked DWG are the author's own translation.
Scripture quotations marked KJV are from The Authorized (King James) Version. Rights in the Authorized Version in the United Kingdom are vested in the Crown. Reproduced by permission of the Crown's patentee, Cambridge University Press.
Scripture quotations marked RV are from the English Revised Version of the Holy Bible (1885).
Scripture quotations marked NIV are taken from the Holy Bible, New International Version®, NIV®. Copyright © 1973, 1978, 1984, 2011 by Biblica, Inc.™ Used by permission of Zondervan. All rights reserved worldwide.
Scripture quotations marked NKJV are taken from the New King James Version®. Copyright © 1982 by Thomas Nelson. Used by permission. All rights reserved.
Scripture quotations marked NASB are from the New American Standard Bible®, Copyright © 1960, 1962, 1963, 1968, 1971, 1972, 1973, 1975, 1977, 1995 by The Lockman Foundation. Used by permission.

Cover design, interior design and composition: Matthew Craig
Cover image: Shutterstock

First published 2024
Published by The Myrtlefield Trust
PO BOX 2216
Belfast
N Ireland
BT1 9YR

w: www.myrtlefieldhouse.com
e: info@myrtlefieldhouse.com

ISBN: 978-1-912721-91-7 (hbk.)
ISBN: 978-1-874584-96-4 (pbk.)
ISBN: 978-1-874584-97-1 (PDF)
ISBN: 978-1-874584-98-8 (Kindle)
ISBN: 978-1-874584-99-5 (EPUB without DRM)

29 28 27 26 25 24   10 9 8 7 6 5 4 3 2 1

Contents

Preface		ix
Detailed Contents		xi

PART

1.	The Triune God who has Always Been the God of Relationships	1
2.	The God who Calls us into Fellowship with Himself	15
3.	The God who Calls us into Fellowship with One Another	37
4.	The Eternal Living and Transcendent Creator	49
5.	The Sovereign Lord's Use of Power	63
6.	The Sovereign Lord's Government and Guidance in our Lives	79
7.	The God of Love and Grace	111
8.	The God who is Loyal and Humble	143
9.	The Only Wise God	169
10.	The God of Truth	189
11.	The God of Revival and Restoration	213
12.	The Eternal God whose Purposes are Fulfilled in History	233
13.	The God who Makes our Lives Part of his Grand Story	263
14.	The God who Saves	291
15.	The God whose Great Salvation Changes our Thinking	331
16.	The Holy God who Makes us Holy	355
17.	The God of Revelation who Wants to be Known	387
18.	The True God who is the God of Joy	399

Index of Daily Readings and Key Verses	409
Publications by David Gooding	419

Preface

It has been said that we become like what we worship, and that genuine worship presupposes knowledge and understanding of its object. This second volume of daily readings edited from the works of David Gooding has as its premise the words of 2 Corinthians 3:

> And we all, with unveiled face, beholding the glory of the Lord, are being transformed into the same image from one degree of glory to another. (v. 18)

That is to say, the more we truly see the glories of the character of God in his triune majesty, the more we become like him. It is the aim of this volume to deepen our understanding of some characteristics of our God in the hope and belief that such understanding will renew our minds and, consequently, shape the way we live our lives. It is not comprehensive of course. How, indeed, could it be? And you will doubtless have many thoughts of your own about aspects of God's character that could or should have been included; but it is our hope that these extracts will inspire in us a more fervent appreciation of our God and Saviour, enriching our worship and transforming us on a daily basis to become more like our Lord Jesus Christ.

Helen Crookes
Belfast, 2024

Detailed Contents

PART 1   THE TRIUNE GOD WHO HAS ALWAYS BEEN THE GOD OF RELATIONSHIPS

Jan			
	1	The communion of the holy Trinity (John 1:1–9)	3
	2	The relationship of the Father to the Son (John 5:16–20)	4
	3	The Father gives the Son the right to give life (John 5:21–30)	5
	4	His only begotten Son (Matt 17:1–5)	6
	5	The revelation of the Trinity at Christ's baptism (Matt 3:13–17)	7
	6	The submission of the Messiah (Isa 50:4–8)	8
	7	The submission of the Messiah and all things to God (1 Cor 15:20–28)	9
	8	We beheld his glory (Exod 40:17–38)	10
	9	Infinity contained in the finite (2 Chron 6:18–21 & 7:1–4)	11
	10	The Holy Spirit is a person (John 14:15–22)	12
	11	Becoming like Christ through the Holy Spirit (2 Cor 3:12–18)	13
	12	Discovering the fullness of God (Isa 53:1–5)	14

PART 2   THE GOD WHO CALLS US INTO FELLOWSHIP WITH HIMSELF

Jan	13	Oneness with the divine persons (John 17:20–26)	17
	14	True spirituality (Ps 42)	18
	15	The heart of the matter (John 7:37–44)	19
	16	Fasting and spiritual exercises (Luke 5:33–39)	20
	17	Sacrifice and true worship (Gen 22:1–8)	21
	18	Discovering Christ's identity and experiencing true worship (Matt 14:22–36)	22
	19	The motivating power of Christ's redemption (Matt 17:24–27)	23
	20	Indwelt by the Father and the Son (John 17:6–12)	24
	21	Christ baptizes his people in the Holy Spirit (1 Cor 12:11–13)	25
	22	What true fellowship is (1 John 1:1–4)	26
	23	The life we share with the Father and with the Son (John 14:23–27)	27
	24	Children of the Father and members of the family (1 John 3:1–3)	28
	25	The family likeness (1 John 3:4–10)	29
	26	The world will not recognize God's children (John 8:42–47)	30
	27	How we know that God abides in us (Gal 4:1–7)	31
	28	Abiding in Christ (John 15:1–8)	32
	29	Called into the fellowship of his Son (Luke 12:35–40)	33
	30	The fellowship that changes and sustains us (1 Cor 1:4–17)	34
	31	Enjoying fellowship as a taste of things to come (Jude 20–25)	35
Feb	1	The new regime (Col 1:18–20)	36

PART 3		**THE GOD WHO CALLS US INTO FELLOWSHIP WITH ONE ANOTHER**	
Feb	2	Unity through loyalty to Christ (Luke 22:19–23)	39
	3	Our unity as fellow members of the eternal city (1 Chr 11:1–9)	40
	4	You are God's dwelling place (Rom 8:9–11)	41
	5	Built together into a dwelling place for God (Eph 2:19–22)	42
	6	The secret of Christian unity (1 Kgs 8:1–10)	43
	7	God: the walls around us and the glory in our midst (Acts 5:1–16)	44
	8	Coming together to meet with God (John 1:14–18)	45
	9	Only one house (1 Kgs 12:25–33)	46
	10	Peace in famine and trouble: Jehovah Shalom (Judg 6:11–24)	47
	11	Comfort amidst strife (2 Cor 1:3–11)	48
PART 4		**THE ETERNAL LIVING AND TRANSCENDENT CREATOR**	
Feb	12	Resting in the knowledge that God is our creator (Isa 43:1–4)	51
	13	The dangers of the universe point to a supreme creator (Exod 4:1–19)	52
	14	The living God (1 Kgs 18:18–39)	53
	15	The fear of the living God (2 Sam 6:1–7)	54
	16	The living God will carry and he will save (Isa 46:1–7)	55
	17	God and nature (Acts 27:13–38)	56
	18	The Son of God and the maintenance of the universe (Isa 65:17–25)	57
	19	Being interested in God's universe (Col 1:12–17)	58
	20	Nature and the believer (Acts 28:1–10)	59
	21	What is man? (Ps 8)	60
	22	Man's position in God's universe (Gen 1:26–31)	61
	23	The source of light comes from outside of us (Job 38:12–21)	62
PART 5		**THE SOVEREIGN LORD'S USE OF POWER**	
Feb	24	God's sovereignty is good news (Isa 51:12–16)	65
	25	God takes responsibility for his universe (John 9:1–12)	66
	26	The Lamb, the Shepherd-King (Rev 5:11–14)	67
	27	The nature of true kingship (Mark 10:41–45)	68
	28	True kingship and the great restoration to come (Zech 12:10–13:3)	69
	29	God does not play games with our lives (2 Sam 2:10–28)	70
Mar	1	What the blind beggar saw (Luke 18:35–43)	71
	2	Gethsemane and the authority we can trust (Matt 26:47–56)	72
	3	God's tactics in winning the jailer (Acts 16:16–40)	73
	4	Covenant kindness (2 Sam 9:1–11)	74
	5	The rainbow round the throne (Gen 8:15–22)	75
	6	The sea of glass (Titus 3:1–8)	76
	7	The power of the Lamb (1 Peter 3:13–21)	77
PART 6		**THE SOVEREIGN LORD'S GOVERNMENT AND GUIDANCE IN OUR LIVES**	
Mar	8	The easy yoke (2 Chr 10:1–11)	81
	9	Not the yoke of the law (Luke 13:10–17)	82
	10	Don't replace one yoke with another (Acts 15:1–11)	83

Mar	11	False liberty (2 Pet 2:12–16)	84
	12	How shall we escape the authority of God's Word? (Heb 2:1–4)	85
	13	The house of God (Gen 28:10–22)	86
	14	The source of power (2 Sam 1:5–16)	87
	15	The use and abuse of authority (Luke 12:42–48)	88
	16	Power for those who see the true value of God's people (Eph 1:15–23)	89
	17	God's signet ring (Hag 2:20–23)	90
	18	The church is Christ's body and functions as his civil service (Col 1:24–29)	91
	19	The church and the kingdom of God (Matt 16:13–20)	92
	20	Being trained to govern (Luke 19:11–19)	93
	21	The absent Christ who comes to meet his people in their need (Matt 14:22–36)	94
	22	Growing up together in the church (Eph 4:11–16)	95
	23	Governing for God (1 Pet 2:9–12)	96
	24	Being a true priest (1 Sam 2:1–10)	97
	25	Obedience is the path to reigning with Christ (Heb 5:7–10)	98
	26	Saul's training in God's guidance (1 Sam 9:1–24)	99
	27	Saul's failure to wait (1 Sam 13:8–14)	100
	28	Saul's failure to listen and obey (1 Sam 15:1–23)	101
	29	Frustrating God's government in our lives (1 Cor 11:27–32)	102
	30	The Lord will judge (Jas 2:8–13)	103
	31	The principle of mercy (2 Tim 1:13–18)	104
Apr	1	The spirit of sonship (Gal 4:8–11, 28–31)	105
	2	The principle of private property (2 Sam 12:1–14)	106
	3	God's providence (Job 1:6–12)	107
	4	God's guidance (Ezek 34:11–16)	108
	5	God's leading in Lydia's life (Acts 16:11–15)	109
	6	God's guidance of Eliezer's way (Gen 24:10–27)	110
PART 7		**THE GOD OF LOVE AND GRACE**	
Apr	7	God commended his love to us while we were still sinners (Rom 5:6–11)	113
	8	Love made manifest (1 John 4:7–12)	114
	9	Christ came down (John 6:25–40)	115
	10	Christ announces the acceptable year of the Lord (Matt 11:1–10)	116
	11	The true God is known in sacrifice (Ps 94:3–11)	117
	12	Propitiation (Lev 16)	118
	13	Love and punishment (2 Sam 14:12–21)	119
	14	Love one another (1 John 4:7–21)	120
	15	The principle of love (1 Cor 13)	121
	16	Seeking spiritual gifts (1 Cor 12:27–31)	122
	17	Greater love has no one than this (John 15:9–17)	123
	18	A two-way friendship (2 John 4–11)	124
	19	Devotion to God's people and to Christ (Ruth 2)	125
	20	Loving one another helps us to understand God's love (1 John 4:7–17)	126
	21	Love is a source of confidence before God (1 John 3:16–24)	127
	22	God accepts us as we are (Rom 5:6–11)	128
	23	Zacchaeus and the results of being accepted (Luke 19:1–10)	129

Apr	24	The Father loves you (John 16:19–28)	130
	25	Love gives us security to face the future (Luke 10:17–23)	131
	26	Jesus himself drew near (Luke 24:13–27)	132
	27	An attitude toward God that is not good enough (Rev 3:14–22)	133
	28	Putting God first (Judg 6:25–32)	134
	29	A sweet-smelling offering to God (Phil 4:14–20)	135
	30	The slippery slope (Mal 1:6–14)	136
May	1	Worldliness is a matter of the heart (Matt 6:26–34)	137
	2	Worldliness is a matter of desire (1 Cor 4:6–13)	138
	3	Worldliness is a matter of fellowship (Rom 14:5–8)	139
	4	Reasons for not loving the world (1 John 2:12–17)	140
	5	The supreme joy of Paul's life in this world (Acts 20:17–27)	141

PART 8 THE GOD WHO IS LOYAL AND HUMBLE

May	6	Who is like Jehovah? (Mic 6:1–8)	145
	7	The humility of God (Phil 2:5–12)	146
	8	God was content to dwell in a tent (2 Sam 7:1–16)	147
	9	How the Lord responded to rejection by Jerusalem (Luke 13:31–35)	148
	10	God's loyalty to the end (Rev 4)	149
	11	Christ stands between us and the foe (Exod 14:10–28)	150
	12	The victorious king is one of us (Col 2:13–19)	151
	13	The risen and ascended man (Acts 1:1–11)	152
	14	Taking humanity into the very presence of God (Acts 7:40–56)	153
	15	Doing things God's way (2 Sam 6:13–23)	154
	16	True love and loyalty in the life of Rahab (Josh 2:12–21)	155
	17	The Gibeonites and evidence of genuine conversion (Josh 9:3–27)	156
	18	Who is on the Lord's side? (Exod 32)	157
	19	Being on the right side when the king returns (2 Sam 19:9–24)	158
	20	Those who will have status in the kingdom of God (Luke 18:15–17)	159
	21	Status in the kingdom for those Christ calls his friends (2 Thess 2:13–17)	160
	22	The status of leaders in the kingdom is that of servants (Mark 10:35–45)	161
	23	Status in the kingdom does not allow for partiality (Jas 2:1–4)	162
	24	Status in the kingdom and the dignity of bearing Christ's name (Jas 2:5–9)	163
	25	Status in the kingdom and those God uses to reveal himself (1 Cor 3:1–9)	164
	26	Carrying light in jars of clay (Judg 7:15–25)	165
	27	David's pride and the danger of serving for our own glory (1 Chr 21:1–17)	166
	28	The answer to pride (1 Chr 21:18–22:1)	167

PART 9 THE ONLY WISE GOD

May	29	Redemption displays God's wisdom to the angels (Eph 3:7–13)	171
	30	God's strategy in winning hearts (Rev 13:1–17)	172
	31	The wisdom of God (Judg 5)	173
Jun	1	God's tactics in destroying faith in man (Rev 12)	174
	2	The cross exposes the folly of trusting in man (1 Cor 1:10–20)	175
	3	God's strategy of destroying false confidence in the flesh (1 Cor 4:1–7)	176
	4	Exposing our need and commanding us to repent (Col 1:21–23)	177

Jun	5	How far the Lord's anointed must go to overcome rebel hearts (1 Sam 20:5–23)	178
	6	The kind of wisdom that leads man to refuse a saviour (1 Sam 17:4–24)	179
	7	The wisdom of the cross and the house God is building (Eph 2:19–22; 1 Cor 1:18–31)	180
	8	Suffering is not meaningless (Jas 5:7–11)	181
	9	The suffering will be worth it (2 Cor 4:13–18)	182
	10	The offering of cooked food (Lev 2:4–13)	183
	11	Paul's wise attitude to suffering (Acts 21:10–14)	184
	12	Leading us in his triumph (2 Cor 2:12–17)	185
	13	The deep things of God (1 Cor 2:9–16)	186
	14	Unwise kindness (2 Sam 10:1–6)	187

PART 10 — THE GOD OF TRUTH

Jun	15	Truth or power and the character of the Messiah (Ps 45:1–9)	191
	16	God cannot lie (Josh 6:15–25)	192
	17	God's covenant promises are sure (Heb 8:7–13)	193
	18	The truth about the Father (Ps 103:13–22)	194
	19	The objective historical truth of the gospel (Acts 7:44–53)	195
	20	The second coming and our Lord's stand for the truth (Rev 19:11–16)	196
	21	He will destroy the lie (2 Thess 2:1–4)	197
	22	Standing for the truth (2 Kgs 18:9–16, 32–35)	198
	23	Loving his appearing means standing for the truth (2 Tim 4:1–5)	199
	24	The spirit of antichrist (1 John 2:18–21)	200
	25	Test the spirits (1 John 4:1–6)	201
	26	An example of heresy (1 John 2:22–27)	202
	27	The audience for false teachers (2 Pet 2:1–10)	203
	28	The Christian's response to idolatry (Acts 19:23–37)	204
	29	True and false disciples (John 13:16–20)	205
	30	Saul discovers the truth about God (Acts 26:12–23)	206
Jul	1	Evidence of true repentance and belief (Acts 9:10–22)	207
	2	Knowing that we are true believers (1 John 2:1–6)	208
	3	True faith as opposed to superstition (Acts 19:13–20)	209
	4	Carnality masquerading as spirituality (John 16:1–4)	210
	5	Don't be double-minded (Jas 1:5–8)	211
	6	Facing the truth about ourselves (Jas 4:1–4)	212

PART 11 — THE GOD OF REVIVAL AND RESTORATION

Jul	7	God is a God of restoration (Zech 8:11–13)	215
	8	Restoration in Israel's history (Zech 7:8–14)	216
	9	Future restoration (Zech 14:5–11)	217
	10	Keeping on going in times of uncertainty (Isa 6:1–8)	218
	11	Worship restored (Zech 3:1–4)	219
	12	The high priest restored (Zech 3:5–10)	220
	13	Our great high priest (Heb 7:11–18)	221
	14	The restoration of our walk (1 Sam 2:22–25)	222
	15	Restoration by the Holy Spirit (Zech 4:1–10)	223

Jul	16	The balance of rebuke and encouragement (Hag 1:1–15)	224
	17	Peter's restoration (John 13:36–14:3)	225
	18	The way back (Jas 4:6–10)	226
	19	Restoration can be tough (Ezra 3:11–4:4)	227
	20	Perseverance in restoration (Neh 2:17–20)	228
	21	Remembering past failures (Zech 1:1–6)	229
	22	Setting our own houses right (Zech 5:1–4)	230
	23	Mothers lead the revival (1 Sam 1:21–28)	231

PART 12		**THE ETERNAL GOD WHOSE PURPOSES ARE FULFILLED IN HISTORY**	
Jul	24	Christ the Lord of time (Isa 46:5–13)	235
	25	God's original plan for mankind (Heb 2:5–9)	236
	26	Prototype and fulfilment (Heb 9:23–10:7)	237
	27	Abraham and the royal road of redemption (Gen 12:1–9)	238
	28	Isaac: the child of promise (Rom 4:4–25)	239
	29	Our debt to Judaism (Isa 45:20–25)	240
	30	The significance of Jerusalem (Dan 11:28–35)	241
	31	The incarnation and the fulfilment of God's plan for mankind (Ps 110)	242
Aug	1	Greater things foreshadowed in the healing of Jairus' daughter (Luke 8:40–56)	243
	2	Greater things foreshadowed in the feeding of the five thousand (Luke 9:10–17)	244
	3	The sacrifice of Christ was planned as the turning point in history (Luke 9:28–36)	245
	4	The once-for-all Passover (Heb 9:11–14)	246
	5	The risen Christ brings us to God (John 20:10–18)	247
	6	How the risen Lord Jesus maintains our faith (Luke 22:28–34)	248
	7	Our perfect high priest's oath of appointment (Heb 7:20–28)	249
	8	Baptism in the Holy Spirit at Pentecost (Acts 2:1–13)	250
	9	Abraham and Paul chosen in God's redemptive plan (Acts 9:1–19)	251
	10	The significance of Peter's deliverance from prison (Acts 12:1–18)	252
	11	The ark comes to Jerusalem (1 Chr 15:16–28)	253
	12	The Lord's return (Heb 10:19–25)	254
	13	The coming of Elijah (Jas 5:13–20)	255
	14	Building the eternal tabernacle (1 Chr 29:1–9)	256
	15	Antichrists now and the antichrist to come (Jude 11–23)	257
	16	Satan's big man (Rev 13:1–18)	258
	17	The end result of mankind's rebellion (2 Thess 2:5–12)	259
	18	The new Jerusalem (Rev 21:1–4, 15–20)	260
	19	The death of the unsaved (Eph 2:1–5)	261
	20	Part of an eternal plan (Hag 2:1–9)	262

PART 13		**THE GOD WHO MAKES OUR LIVES PART OF HIS GRAND STORY**	
Aug	21	An enlarged concept of history (Matt 16:24–17:9)	265
	22	Our personal significance in history (1 Chr 6:31–50)	266

Aug	23	The significance in history of our present activities (Rev 5:1–10)	267
	24	The hope and purpose of our calling is to bring God satisfaction (Eph 1:3–10)	268
	25	The hope and purpose of our calling is to be prepared for the world to come (Rom 8:18–22)	269
	26	Believing that there is a world to come (Luke 16:19–31)	270
	27	The road to fruitfulness (Gen 37:1–11)	271
	28	Growing in spirituality (Phil 3:12–21)	272
	29	A permanent home (1 Chr 6:1–11)	273
	30	Building work in progress (Phil 2:12–18)	274
	31	That we may not be ashamed (1 Kgs 1:38–53)	275
Sep	1	What shall we spend our souls on? (Matt 6:19–24)	276
	2	Rewards (Matt 19:27–30)	277
	3	Assessing a human being from a spiritual perspective (Exod 2:1–10)	278
	4	Life's thorn bushes (Exod 3:1–6)	279
	5	The significance of our lives (Ruth 4:13–22)	280
	6	Five enemies that must be destroyed (Josh 10:16–28)	281
	7	Encouragement to persevere (Dan 12:5–13)	282
	8	A living sacrifice (Dan 3:16–30)	283
	9	Reigning with Christ: the parable of the minas (Luke 19:11–19)	284
	10	The unfaithful servant (Luke 19:20–27)	285
	11	The end of life: the unjust steward (Luke 16:1–13)	286
	12	Measuring Jerusalem (Zech 2:1–13)	287
	13	Future glory (Numb 14:39–15:2)	288
	14	Crown him (Zech 6:9–14)	289
	15	Preparing for the future (2 Tim 2:8–13)	290

PART 14   THE GOD WHO SAVES

Sep	16	Our moral sense demands judgment (Ps 96)	293
	17	The dilemma of a just forgiveness (Rom 3:21–31)	294
	18	The basis of salvation (Gal 3:10–14)	295
	19	Judgment that fell on the sacrifice (Isa 53:5–12)	296
	20	The sacrifice that cleanses (1 Cor 6:9–11)	297
	21	The perfect sacrifice (Ps 40:6–8)	298
	22	Faith's basic doctrine of sacrifice (Gen 4:1–16)	299
	23	Justification by faith apart from the law (Acts 13:26–43)	300
	24	Pentecost and the parable of the vineyard (Acts 2:14–36)	301
	25	Trying to earn God's salvation at the expense of others (Luke 14:1–6)	302
	26	Christ's refusal to retaliate brings us to repentance (1 Pet 2:21–24)	303
	27	Deliverance from a greater bondage than Israel's (John 8:14–29)	304
	28	Deliverance from this world (Exod 5:1–9)	305
	29	The beauty of forgiveness (Isa 44:21–23)	306
	30	True forgiveness means that we know we are forgiven (Luke 24:44–49)	307
Oct	1	God's offer of forgiveness draws us to him (Luke 7:36–38)	308
	2	Love follows forgiveness, not the other way round (Luke 7:39–50)	309
	3	The results of forgiveness (Luke 8:1–3)	310
	4	Deliverance even for the oppressors (Luke 4:16–21)	311

Oct	5	Forgiveness and perfection (Heb 8:8–12)	312
	6	God's law within (Ezek 11:16–20)	313
	7	The new covenant (Jer 31:31–36)	314
	8	God can justly forgive and forget (Heb 9:15–22)	315
	9	New life as a gift (Eph 2:6–18)	316
	10	The certainty of eternal life (1 John 5:13–21)	317
	11	God himself witnesses to us that we have eternal life (1 John 5:6–12)	318
	12	Assurance of salvation (Josh 6:8–14)	319
	13	The certainty of our inheritance (Josh 4:15–24)	320
	14	The conquest of the fear of death (Heb 2:10–18)	321
	15	What happens when a believer dies? (Phil 1:19–26)	322
	16	A greater than Joshua brings us into our inheritance (Heb 4:1–10)	323
	17	Christ sustains our faith (John 21:15–19)	324
	18	The growth of Peter's faith after his failure (Luke 22:54–62)	325
	19	Sealed with the Holy Spirit (Eph 1:11–14)	326
	20	The sealed (Rev 7:1–8)	327
	21	The saved (Rev 7:9–17)	328
	22	The gospel to the Gentiles (Ruth 3:8–18)	329
	23	The scope of our salvation (Gen 41:37–57)	330

PART 15   THE GOD WHOSE GREAT SALVATION CHANGES OUR THINKING

Oct	24	The path to salvation (1 Tim 1:12–16)	333
	25	The wrong way—through our own efforts (Gen 16)	334
	26	Our prayers reveal how we think about salvation (Luke 18:9–14)	335
	27	Faith's reasons and commitment (Luke 4:22–29)	336
	28	Evidence for our faith (John 20:24–29)	337
	29	Trusting in what cannot save (Exod 12:33–36)	338
	30	Security in God alone (Gen 22:15–19)	339
	31	The right way—through trusting in the living Christ (Col 2:8–12)	340
Nov	1	Christ is not ashamed to be known as one of Rahab's descendants (Matt 1:1–6)	341
	2	Repentance and conversion (Acts 2:36–42)	342
	3	Salvation may involve struggle (Luke 14:25–33)	343
	4	Our claim to be forgiven requires the evidence of a Christian walk (Mark 2:1–12)	344
	5	The basis of our forgiveness requires us to forgive others (1 John 2:7–12)	345
	6	The faith that overcomes the world (1 John 5:1–5)	346
	7	Faith without works (Jas 2:14–24)	347
	8	Faith evidenced by a willingness to sacrifice (Gen 22:9–14)	348
	9	The Messiah's faith in Jehovah (Isa 49:1–7)	349
	10	Paul's response of faith to the Lord's call on his life (Acts 9:20–31)	350
	11	Faith in Christ's entire programme of salvation (Luke 7:18–23)	351
	12	Fear of making our faith known (Luke 12:4–12)	352
	13	The serious business God calls us to do (Isa 55:1–5)	353

PART 16		**THE HOLY GOD WHO MAKES US HOLY**	
Nov	14	The beauty of holiness (Exod 40:1–5)	357
	15	Holiness and sincerity (Matt 26:17–29)	358
	16	The perfect balance of the holiness of the Lord Jesus (Lev 4:14–17)	359
	17	Preparing for us a place of perfect holiness (1 Thess 4:14–17)	360
	18	The bread of the Presence (Exod 25:23–30)	361
	19	The foundation of holiness (Acts 10:34–48)	362
	20	Holiness requires a new nature (2 Pet 2:17–22)	363
	21	The assurance of God's love enables us to face our failings (Rom 5:1–5)	364
	22	The Holy Spirit changes our desires (Rom 8:1–5)	365
	23	The constant battle between the spirit and the flesh (Gal 5:16–23)	366
	24	The necessity of growth (Eph 4:7–16)	367
	25	Trials bring us closer to our destination (Exod 15:22–27)	368
	26	Discipline through trials (Heb 12:4–12)	369
	27	Focusing on Christ's perfections rather than on our sin ((Heb 12:1–3)	370
	28	We are to be imitators of Christ (Eph 5:1–20)	371
	29	Overcoming the lure of the forces around us (Eph 4:7–13)	372
	30	The right attitude to evil powers (Matt 5:17–20)	373
Dec	1	Accepting Christ as Lord (Rom 14:5–9)	374
	2	The motivating power for Christian behaviour (John 13:1–15)	375
	3	Live in love and walk in the light (1 John 2:9–11)	376
	4	Recognizing the source of temptation (Jas 1:13–18)	377
	5	Defining worldliness (John 12:4–11)	378
	6	A Gentile attitude to our work (1 Thess 2:6–12)	379
	7	The beauty of our Lord's perfect self-control (Matt 26:36–46)	380
	8	Bringing our emotions under God's control (Mark 14:32–36)	381
	9	Control of the will (Luke 22:47–53)	382
	10	Bringing the gift of speech under the control of Christ (Jas 3:1–6)	383
	11	How do we control the tongue? (Jas 3:7–12)	384
	12	When and how to speak (1 Pet 3:10–12)	385
	13	How we should pray for our fellow Christians (Eph 3:14–19)	386
PART 17		**THE GOD OF REVELATION WHO WANTS TO BE KNOWN**	
Dec	14	God is his own evidence (John 5:31–47)	389
	15	God's revelation of himself culminating in Christ (Heb 1:1–5)	390
	16	Manifesting God's name (Deut 32:1–4)	391
	17	The Lord manifests himself to us (John 21:1–14)	392
	18	Knowing God (John 10:1–16)	393
	19	Knowing the 'I AM' is the secret of deliverance (Exod 3:7–15)	394
	20	Real worship requires knowledge of God (Phil 3:7–11)	395
	21	Mysteries revealed to children (Luke 10:21–24)	396
	22	How the Lord made himself known after his resurrection (Luke 24:28–35)	397
	23	Making Christ known to others (Luke 9:46–50)	398

PART 18	**THE TRUE GOD WHO IS THE GOD OF JOY**	
Dec 24	The Lord's joy (Luke 15:1–7)	401
25	Where we find the secret of joy (John 2:1–11)	402
26	The secret of joy and the knowledge of God's acceptance (Ps 103:1–12)	403
27	Joy that death is not the end and adventure awaits (Rev 21:15–27)	404
28	Why some people miss the joy (Matt 11:11–19)	405
29	The older brother standing away from the celebration (Luke 15:11–32)	406
30	Facing trials with joy (Matt 13:3–9, 18–23)	407
31	A never failing source of joy (John 14:28–31)	408

CHANGING *us for* GLORY

PART 1

The Triune God who has Always Been the God of Relationships

1st January

THE COMMUNION OF THE HOLY TRINITY

Reading: John 1:1–9

In the beginning was the Word, and the Word was with God, and the Word was God. (John 1:1)

There was a time when the Son of God was not human. What was he then?

We learn of his eternal existence from the opening words of John's Gospel: 'In the beginning was the Word'. He existed with an eternal, timeless beginning—without beginning of life nor end of days. We learn that he was with the Father, and therefore in some sense distinct from him. But he was with the Father, which indicates that they enjoyed an intimate, living, glorious and marvellous fellowship. He was 'that eternal life, which was with the Father' for the Father's eternal enjoyment.

And so we learn from that same clause of Scripture that God—the supreme God, the Holy Trinity—is not a monolith but a fellowship, a communion. And our hearts are warmed when we read that this life has been manifested for the very purpose that we might have fellowship with God—'and indeed our fellowship is with the Father and with his Son Jesus Christ' (1 John 1:1–3). That is a thing to be pondered, my fellow believers. As we live here on this planet we can, and do, have fellowship in the very intimate things of God. We have fellowship with the Father and share with him this eternal life which is his Son.

Then we are told that the Word 'was God'. Though the Word can be viewed as distinct from the Father, we must try to apprehend that there are not two Gods, nor three Gods, there is only one God. For the Word of God—the Son of God—shares the very basic essential life and being of God. The Son is as much God as the Father is God, and that is true also of the Holy Spirit. The Holy Spirit is as much God as the Son is, or as the Father is—all three persons of the Godhead being equally God.

David Gooding, *Understanding the Trinity: Six Studies on God's Revelation of Himself*, 13–14

2nd January

THE RELATIONSHIP OF THE FATHER TO THE SON

Reading: John 5:16–20

No man has seen God at any time; the only begotten Son,
who is in the bosom of the Father, he has declared him. (John 1:18 DWG)

Notice what he is called: 'the one and only Son, who is in the bosom of the Father.' When we read those words we shouldn't think of a place. No, it is a metaphorical term meaning that the one and only Son of the Father dwelt in such intimate communion with the Father that you could say he was in the bosom of the Father. Knowing the Father's heartbeat and all the secrets of the heart and being of God, he came down here in human form and expounded God to the full. Marvellous, is it not? But let's go further.

Listen to what he says, 'Verily, verily I say unto you, the Son can do nothing of himself, but only what he sees the Father doing. Whatever the Father does, the Son does also' (John 5:19 DWG).

He says the Son can do nothing of himself. 'From himself' is the literal translation. In this, our Lord is saying he is not independent. He is in fact asserting that he does nothing *from* himself. He simply does what he sees the Father doing. The Son of God is equal with the Father but not independent of the Father. Secondly, it is always the Father within the Godhead who takes the initiative. The Son doesn't take the initiative, nor the Holy Spirit either. It's the Father who takes the initiative.

Just ponder these very terms with me for a moment: *Father and Son*.

It doesn't say *brother* and *brother*, does it? It's 'Father' and 'Son', and the two terms are not interchangeable. For instance, you will find Scripture saying 'the Father sent the Son to be the Saviour of the world' (1 John 4:14 KJV). You will never read that the Son sent the Father, will you? Our blessed Lord, the Son of God, obeyed the Father, but you will never find it said that the Father obeyed the Son.

Here our Lord is telling us of the relationship between the Son and the Father. He's claiming to be equal with God: he's just as much God as the Father is God. But within the persons of the Trinity there is this relationship, and the Father is the Father. He takes the initiative; and the Son does not act from himself but he does whatever he sees the Father doing. That's interesting, isn't it?

David Gooding, *Understanding the Trinity: Six Studies on God's Revelation of Himself*, 19–20

3rd January

THE FATHER GIVES THE SON THE RIGHT TO GIVE LIFE

Reading: John 5:21–30

*'Whatever the Son sees the Father doing,
the Son does it in like manner.' (John 5:19 DWG)*

Our Lord has been telling us of relations within the Trinity. But in case you think that he is less than the Father, look what he goes on to say: 'For what things soever the Father does, these does the Son also *in like manner*.' Do consider what that means. Whatever the Son sees the Father doing, the Son does it (as well as the Father doing it), and the Son does it *in like manner*. You just imagine that. Does the Father cause the sun to rise on the godly and the ungodly (see Matt 5:45)? Well then the Son of God causes the sun to rise. Is God Creator? Then the Son is Creator. Whatever he sees the Father doing, he does in exactly the same way and to the same extent. How could he do that if he were not God himself?

So, in the verses that follow, our blessed Lord tells us how the Father has committed to him the divine functions in two respects. First, 'For as the Father raises the dead and gives them life, so also the Son gives life to whom he will . . . For as the Father has life in himself, so has he granted the Son to have life in himself' (John 5:21, 26). And then, 'The Father judges no one, but has given all judgment to the Son, that all may honour the Son, just as they honour the Father' (vv. 22–23).

Let's pause again. Because the Father has given the Son to have life in himself, he can give life to whom he will, and he is the judge. Ponder it, my dear brothers and sisters. When you came to Christ and received forgiveness and eternal life from him, from whom were you receiving it? Does it matter to you who he was?

Well you say, 'Of course it matters. How could Christ give me life, eternal life—the very life of God—if he were not God himself?'

Amen. That's how it is. Oh, shout Hallelujah in your heart, even if you're afraid to do it in public! You have the word of God incarnate; you have the word of the final judge. I trust you'll rest easy in your bed tonight, though the final judgment were to be tomorrow, because you have the word of the incarnate Son of God. If you trust him and believe him who sent him, you have eternal life and shall not come into condemnation (v. 24).

David Gooding, *Understanding the Trinity: Six Studies on God's Revelation of Himself*, 20–1

4th January

HIS ONLY BEGOTTEN SON

Reading: Matthew 17:1–5

In this was manifested the love of God toward us, because that God sent his only begotten Son into the world, that we might live through him. (1 John 4:9 KJV)

Notice that John says not merely that God has sent his Son into the world, but that he has sent his only begotten Son into the world. The relations that subsist through the persons of the Godhead are mysterious indeed and go beyond our understanding. Men have tried to explain the Godhead and have not realized that it is so far beyond our understanding and description that we cannot possibly reduce it to our formulae, but must learn to believe what we are told and worship.

And yet what we have been told is for our reverent study. The Son of God is described as 'the only begotten of the Father' (John 1:14 KJV). You may choose to believe that those words, 'only begotten', mean nothing more than 'only'. For my part, I think there is something deeper involved. The ties that bind the members of the Godhead together are ties of life, one life with the Father. God has sent us someone who was his very vitals, his only begotten Son. How wonderful this is. How should we measure, then, the love of God to us?

'Ah,' says somebody, 'if God gave me a little bit more cash, if life were easier, then I could think that God loves me.'

So would you be mightily pleased if one of these days God gave you a whole planet? Mars, for instance: how would you like to have Mars? Or perhaps Pluto? Or a constellation or two? Would that be a bit too much? Would you be impressed by the love of God if he gave you a whole planet to yourself?

Think again. God could give you a whole spiral nebula and not miss it, so to speak. He's got plenty of them. When he thought to give you an expression of his love, he gave you nothing so cheap as a spiral nebula with all its millions of stars. He gave you something that was unique: he gave his only Son. And I say again, 'his only begotten Son'. It was his very vitals being given to you. What for? 'That we might live through him.' Don't you see the point? It was God giving us the very vitals of his life, so that we might have that life and share it with God.

David Gooding, *Love is from God: One Study on 1 John 4:7–21*, 6–7

5th January

THE REVELATION OF THE TRINITY AT CHRIST'S BAPTISM

Reading: Matthew 3:13–17

The Holy Spirit descended on him in bodily form, like a dove; and a voice came from heaven, 'You are my beloved Son; with you I am well pleased.' (Luke 3:22)

Three facts are thus told us, and for a while three persons only, in their solitary divine splendour, are allowed to fill our vision. Two things are said to come out of the opened heaven, the Holy Spirit and the voice. Both are directed to Christ. The Holy Spirit comes down upon him in bodily form as a dove. Why a dove? Perhaps it was meant to recall Noah's dove, which 'found no rest for the sole of her foot' (Gen 8:9 KJV) on the flood waters, and to emphasize by contrast that the Son of God, having come through Jordan's baptismal waters, was a fit resting place for the Spirit of God.

Whatever the truth of the matter, the main thing we must grasp is Luke's insistence that the Holy Spirit came down in bodily form, that is, visibly. We are not dealing here with some private experience within Christ's inner consciousness, invisible to others, and only known about because Christ later on told his disciples about it. The express point of Luke's narrative is that the procession of the Holy Spirit from the Father to the Son was on this occasion deliberately made visible. In John 1:32–34, John the Baptist is on record as claiming to have seen it.

And with the Holy Spirit's presence made visible the Father's presence is made audible as he declares 'You are my beloved Son: in you I have found delight'. The words were addressed to the Son: 'You are . . .'. According to Matthew 3:17 other people heard them and rightly interpreted the voice as giving them to understand 'This is my beloved Son'. But for his part Luke is content to concentrate our attention solely on the three persons so that we might see Jesus as the Son of God in his unique relationship with the Father and with the Holy Spirit. This is no doctrine of the Trinity in complicated philosophical-theological terminology, appropriate and necessary as that would later become. Here is a revelation from an open heaven and a demonstration, divine in its sublime simplicity, of the delightful relationships of the three persons of the Trinity. It points to the unique sense in which Jesus is the Son of God.

David Gooding, According to Luke: The Third Gospel's Ordered Historical Narrative, 76–7

6th January

THE SUBMISSION OF THE MESSIAH

Reading: Isaiah 50:4–8

The head of Christ is God. (1 Corinthians 11:3)

This is the basic fact, and it takes us in one stride to the heart of the wonder of our Christian gospel: 'the head of Christ is God'. Just imagine what this verse is saying—the head of the Messiah, the head of the Christ, is God.

Who is this Messiah, otherwise known as the Son of God—the second person of the Trinity, as the theologians call him? When we remember this we shall immediately remember that the blessed Son of God, Son of the Father, the second person of the eternal Trinity, was not always the Messiah. There were uncharted ages of eternity before he became Messiah. He became that Messiah for God's sake, and for our sakes so that he might redeem us and bring us back to God. 'I want you to understand that,' says Paul, 'lest salvation should become to you a thin little thing, an arbitrary matter of a few regulations that could be ignored.' Let the wonder of this grip our hearts just now. For your sake and for mine, as for God's sake, he who is God and stood on equality with God, for our sakes became Messiah to bring us back to God. And becoming Messiah meant for him knowing God as head.

The wonder of it is beautifully expressed in the early Christian hymn that Paul quotes in his letter to the Philippians: '. . . Christ Jesus, who, though he was in the form of God, did not count equality with God a thing to be grasped' (Phil 2:5–6). He never ceased to be God, but what he gladly surrendered for our sakes was to be on equal terms with God. He thought it not a prize; something to be grasped and held on to. The marvellous wonder of it is that he did not cling to his outward dignities. He whom angels worshipped on an equality with God gave up being on equal terms with God. While God was forever as God was in his unsullied presence, this blessed one was born in a stable among some of the humblest of his little creatures. 'He emptied himself' (RV)—'poured himself out' the word means, and took the form of a servant. Though he was and remained God, he became a servant (2:7). That's what it means for him to be Messiah: grasp it if you can.

David Gooding, *Symbols of Headship and Remembrance: Two Studies on Major Themes in 1 Corinthians*, 6–7

7th January

THE SUBMISSION OF THE MESSIAH
AND ALL THINGS TO GOD

Reading: 1 Corinthians 15:20–28

Then the Son himself will also be subjected to him who put all things in subjection under him, that God may be all in all. (1 Corinthians 15:28)

It is wonderful to think what happened when the Son of God was born and laid in a manger, and then for our sakes he went to Calvary. But for a moment, let's remember God's great scheme in appointing him: 'For God has put all things in subjection under his feet' (1 Cor 15:27).

> What is man that you are mindful of him, and the son of man that you care for him? Yet you have made him a little lower than the heavenly beings and crowned him with glory and honour. You have given him dominion over the works of your hands; you have put all things under his feet. (Psalm 8:4–6)

That's God's word about the Messiah. Notice then what Paul adds: 'But when it says, "all things are put in subjection", it is plain that he is excepted who put all things in subjection under him. When all things are subjected to him, then the Son himself will also be subjected to him who put all things in subjection under him, that God may be all in all' (1 Cor 15:27–28).

That's a very complicated sentence in modern English. It means that God, who subjected all things to Christ and put them under Christ's feet, still remains above the Messiah. When confronted with a whole universe gone astray, and the world of men and women gone astray, how should God bring back his great empire? He appointed his own Son as the Messiah and his viceroy, who for our sakes became man. God's plan was that the Lord Jesus should redeem mankind by 'becoming obedient to the point of death, even death on a cross' (see Phil 2:7–8). God has ordained that not only in this age, but also in that which is to come, one day everything in heaven, earth and hell will bow the knee and admit Christ's right to rule (see Eph 1:20–23); 'and through him to reconcile to himself all things, whether on earth or in heaven' (Col 1:20).

And when the blessed Lord Jesus has brought that vast empire, including you and me, back to the Father, the Son himself shall bow at the Father's footstool and be subject to the Father eternally. What a magnificent role our blessed Lord Jesus carries.

David Gooding, *Symbols of Headship and Remembrance: Two Studies on Major Themes in 1 Corinthians*, 8

8th January

WE BEHELD HIS GLORY

Reading: Exodus 40:17–38

And the Word became flesh, and dwelt among us (and we beheld his glory, glory as of the only begotten from the Father), full of grace and truth. (John 1:14 RV)

This is a lovely verse. But many scholars, and I among them, believe that when John uses the verb 'dwelt among us', it is a deliberate allusion to the book of Exodus, for it is an unusual verb to use in this context. It reminds us of the tent that God commanded Moses and the Israelites to build as a sanctuary for him to dwell in.

They made the tabernacle in the course of their journey from Egypt to Canaan, and with great excitement, eagerness and interest the historian records how they built it. The women worked the wool and the skins and made the curtains, while the men worked with the wood and the gold. They made it all exactly as God had said and as Moses commanded. They brought it to Moses, and Moses inspected all the material, and then he erected it. And when they had done so, then we are told that the glory of God descended and filled the tabernacle.

I wonder if you can imagine it. Can you visualize all those thousands of Israelites: the men, their hands now a bit calloused with hard skin from doing all that work; the women seeing the curtains they had made? All has now been put into place, and with trepidation, awe and wonder they see the very glory of God in the cloud of his presence come and fill that tabernacle and dwell among them!

Says John, 'It was like that when we saw the blessed Lord Jesus, and it dawned on us who he was—the one and only Son of the Father. He came and dwelt in a human body and we saw his glory, glory as of the only begotten from the Father, full of grace and truth.'

Now consider the words, he is the glory of God. As the Epistle to the Hebrews puts it: 'God has spoken unto us in his Son, . . . who is the effulgence of his glory', meaning the outshining, the radiance of his glory (see Heb 1:2–3). Just as a sunbeam is of the same substance as the sun, so is the Son of God of the same substance as the Father and was able to tell out his glory.

David Gooding, *Understanding the Trinity: Six Studies on God's Revelation of Himself*, 18

9th January

INFINITY CONTAINED IN THE FINITE

Reading: 2 Chronicles 6:18–21 & 7:1–4

For in him the whole fullness of deity dwells bodily. (Colossians 2:9)

When the temple was built, Solomon had a little bit of a problem, and he said to God, 'Now I've built you a house, Lord, but will God indeed dwell on earth with men? The whole of the heavens cannot contain you. How much less this house that I have built!' And it is a very big theological problem. How will the transcendent God come and dwell in a house like that? And you say, 'How can he come, therefore, and live in our hearts?' How can you get God inside you when the highest heavens cannot contain him?

The answer to that problem is to be found in this—the man who built the house was not just any ordinary man. This is what God said about David's son, 'I will be to him a father, and he shall be to me a son' (1 Chr 17:13). The house was built by the son; not merely the son of David, but the son who stood in this special relationship with God. God will be a father to him and he will be a son to God. When we turn to the New Testament, we discover that Solomon was but the prototype. When the reality came, it would be fulfilled in a far higher sense.

The builder of this house, this unique house, was to be literally the Son of the Father: God his Father, in the absolute sense, and he the Son of God, in the absolute sense. Paul reminds us that when Jesus Christ was born as a man, his body formed a temple of God. This was the wonderful mystery. This was God coming inside his creation in the person of his Son, who was human and divine at the same time, and all the fullness of the Godhead dwelled in him bodily (Col 2:9).

Here was God's answer. The house was to be built by the one who is the very Son of God, and God is his Father in the fuller sense of that term. The wonder is that God has solved the great problems concerned with his purposes. He wants to dwell in us. First of all, he sent his Son, and all the fullness of the Godhead dwells in him. Now he joins us to his Son, and in his Son God can dwell in us as well. What a wonder it is!

David Gooding, *Visions of Eternity: Five Studies on Major Themes in 1–2 Chronicles*, 44–5

10th January

THE HOLY SPIRIT IS A PERSON

Reading: John 14:15–22

And I will pray the Father, and he shall give you another Comforter, that he may be with you for ever, even the Spirit of truth. (John 14:16–17 RV)

Just as the Father and the Son are persons, so the Holy Spirit is a person.

This is a lovely title of the Holy Spirit—'the other Comforter'. But that immediately asks us to enquire: If the Holy Spirit is another comforter, who was the first comforter? And the first comforter, of course, was our blessed Lord himself. And he was about to leave them, as he was telling his disciples on this occasion (14:3), but he wouldn't leave them orphans (14:18). He wouldn't leave them worse off than they had been when he was with him, for he would send another comforter, a comforter like himself who would be with them.

The very fact that the Holy Spirit is the second comforter shows us at once that he is a person just as our Lord was. For if our Lord went away from his apostles and only sent an impersonal force in his place, then certainly they would have been in a worse state than they were when the Lord Jesus was with them. But, no, he is the other Comforter. In that sense, like the Lord Jesus, he is a person.

Talking about the Spirit, our Lord says, 'When he, the Spirit of truth, is come, he shall guide you into all the truth, for he shall not speak from himself, but whatever things he hears, these shall he speak' (16:13 DWG). Now notice that verb, if you will: 'whatever things he *hears*'. An impersonal force couldn't hear anything, could it? Have a go at speaking to the lightning or the thunder. The thunder won't hear you, nor the lightning either. Watch an atomic bomb explode, if you dare, and speak to it. It won't hear you; it is just an impersonal force. But the Holy Spirit 'will not speak from himself'—he'll not take the initiative—but 'what he hears, he speaks'. The very verb shows that the Holy Spirit is a person who can, of course, hear.

Somebody will say, 'What does he hear and from whom does he hear it?' Well, from our blessed ascended Lord, of course: 'He shall take of my things and show them to you' (16:14 DWG).

David Gooding, *Understanding the Trinity: Six Studies on God's Revelation of Himself*, 35–6

11th January

BECOMING LIKE CHRIST THROUGH THE HOLY SPIRIT

Reading: 2 Corinthians 3:12–18

Now the Lord is the Spirit, and where the Spirit of the Lord is, there is freedom. (2 Corinthians 3:17)

I pause to think what could be happening even in these humble studies, but it is happening daily as well. God has shown us his dear Son and revealed him in the world, and we have the record of it. But how shall I ever be like him? Where can I turn so that my character may begin to glow with the very glory of the Lord?

Well, you can get preachers to help you and pray for you, but our resource is here: whenever we turn to the Lord the Spirit. It is the Spirit who will take the veil from our hearts and our eyes and reveal the glory of the Lord to us as we 'behold' it (v. 18). The Greek word here can be translated two ways: 'beholding as in a mirror', or 'reflecting as in a mirror'. If you get a mirror and turn it to the light, the mirror beholds the light. At the same time it reflects the light; the two are joined. And if we behold the glory of the Lord, at the same time we shall reflect the glory of the Lord, and in that process be transformed from glory to glory as by the Lord the Spirit.

Oh, let's pause here to worship, because the Holy Spirit is not just a force; he is a person.

Consider the wonder that God has done, the extreme to which God has gone! God wanted to manifest himself so he sent his dear Son, because 'no one has seen God at any time'. Nonetheless, 'the only begotten Son, who is in the bosom of the Father, he has told him out' (see John 1:18).

How shall I take it in? How shall I bear the sight of it? How shall I be turned into that same glory and become like the Lord Jesus? It's good that I read of him in the Scriptures and contemplate him, but God has done more for us than that. God has given us his Spirit, and that Spirit is God himself. The Son came to reveal God, and I see that glory. Yes, but God has given me his Holy Spirit, and when I turn to the Holy Spirit for his illumination, then he reveals to me the glory of God and helps me to see it.

David Gooding, *Understanding the Trinity: Six Studies on God's Revelation of Himself*, 40

12th January

DISCOVERING THE FULLNESS OF GOD

Reading: Isaiah 53:1–5

They shall look on me, on him whom they have pierced, and they shall mourn for him as one mourns for an only child. (Zechariah 12:10)

One day Israel shall discover again, not only God but they shall discover, some of them for the first time, the person of the Son. They shall see the one whom the nation despised, whom the kings rejected, and they shall say in their consternation, 'But we esteemed him stricken, smitten of God and afflicted. We thought he was afflicted for his own sins, we held that he was a blasphemer.' When they shall see him whom they pierced, there shall be a day of great mourning and contrition, and they shall say, 'But he was wounded for our transgressions; he was crushed for our iniquities; upon him was the chastisement that brought us peace, and with his stripes we are healed' (Isa 53:5).

What a day it will be when Israel discovers the person of the Son. When he was here on earth they rejected him. They thought they knew all there was to know about God. There was one God, that was perfectly true; but their concept of one God was very limited.

It's possible for us, too, to think we know everything about God; but we shall never do that. Because Israel had got one part of the truth that God is one, they weren't prepared to open their minds to consider what that oneness might be: a blessed Trinity in one. One plus one plus one is three, but one times one times one is one, isn't it? One day Israel shall come with amazement to see that God is far bigger than they imagined him to be.

God help us, who already know him and know the Son of God. In the days to come, may God grant us the spirit of wisdom and revelation in the knowledge of him, to discover that God is bigger than we thought, and so is Jesus his Son. We have the gospel, don't we? The Jewish people nowadays have no gospel, for they have no suffering servant to proclaim to the nations, no sacrifice to proclaim. Therefore all they can do is to preach the law and tell you to behave.

What our weary world needs more than anything else is the gospel. He was wounded for our transgressions, bruised for our iniquities, the chastisement of our peace was upon him and with his stripes we are healed.

David Gooding, *The Restoration of Israel: One Study on Prophetic Lessons from Isaiah 43, 53 and 59*, 5

Part 2

The God who Calls us into Fellowship with Himself

13th January

ONENESS WITH THE DIVINE PERSONS

Reading: John 17:20–26

'That they may all be one, just as you, Father, are in me,
and I in you, that they also may be in us.' (John 17:21)

What a wonderful thing it would have been if our salvation had simply amounted to the cancelling of all our debts and the forgiveness of our sins. That alone would have merited ten million Hallelujahs, undying to eternity. In addition to forgiveness, it would have been wonderful if salvation had secured for us some little collapsible seat round some murky little corner of the celestial courts, (except of course there are no murky corners, nor any collapsible seats). But who can grasp this? It is not just forgiveness, not just a place in God's heaven, but oneness with the divine persons themselves! What a staggering concept, what awesome reality Jesus Christ our Lord talks to us about in these simple words: a unity between us and the very persons of the Godhead, modelled on that glorious unity between the Father and the Son. Within the holy Trinity, each person is and remains distinct. As the theologians tell us, the Father is not the Son, nor is the Son the Father.

So it is with the redeemed. We shall never be God: there will no blurring of our human personality nor any merging with the absolute, in the Hindu sense. And yet there is a *oneness*, and I should require more than the archangel's voice to explain it. May God save me from one extreme or the other. But how can I hear it without being moved? He speaks of a oneness between you and me, my brother, and you, my sister, and all of us, with the persons of the Godhead. A oneness in mind, love, purpose and moral character. We are heirs of God and joint heirs with Christ, sons and daughters of the living God and one with him.

It is modelled on the relationship between Christ and his Father. First of all, it is oneness within the divine persons, the mutual indwelling of the Father and the Son, who prays, 'that they may all be one, . . . even as we are one, I in them and you in me' (John 17:21–23). This is the mutual inter-communion and inter-penetration of the persons of the deity. He is saying, 'I wish them to be one like that, not merely among themselves, but one in us.' Who can bear the weight of glory that such words express?

David Gooding, *Back to the Gospel: Three Studies on True Progress in Spirituality, Freedom, and Church Life*, 8

14th January

TRUE SPIRITUALITY

Reading: Psalm 42

*As the deer pants after the water brooks,
so my soul longs after you, O God. (Psalm 42:1 DWG)*

Spirituality is the soul's hunger and thirst after God. It springs from the realization that God is more important than all else. God is more important than his universe, more important than his gifts. God himself is more important than even our work for God. Sometimes, in the hustle and bustle of our busy world, the fires of our spirituality burn low. God grant us above all else that we might find time for God, so that from our redeemed hearts there might rise up to the blessed Saviour and Son of God the longing to know him, and the discovery that he is more important and more wonderful and more beautiful than all else.

Spirituality, then, is the desire for a deeper, more personal, more real relationship with God, involving our innermost heart's affections. It is the desire to know God, to behold his glory—granted that now we see it as in a mirror, yet we may behold it, 'with open face' (2 Cor 3:18 KJV), that is, with the veil removed from our faces. It is a desire to behold the beauty of God until our own characters are transformed inch by inch from glory to glory, to grow more like the blessed Lord Jesus.

It is our hope for eternity that when we see him we shall be like the Saviour. But, as the Apostle John so practically observed, 'Everyone who has this hope in him purifies himself as he is pure' (1 John 3:3 DWG). None shall say, 'Well that's it! I can wait until I see him and it will all be done for me in a second—why should I bother to be like him now?' No, no! If the hope is real, that one day on seeing the blessed Saviour I shall be like him, it burns within me the desire to purify myself now so that I shall be progressively more like him. Spirituality is not just to know God, nor just to behold the glory of God and to be like him, but it is the longing of my spirit to be ever more closely united with the Lord and one with him, for 'whoever abides in love abides in God, and God abides in him' (1 John 4:16).

David Gooding, *Back to the Gospel: Three Studies on True Progress in Spirituality, Freedom, and Church Life*, 5

15th January

THE HEART OF THE MATTER

Reading: John 7:37–44

On the last day of the feast, the great day, Jesus stood up and cried out, 'If anyone thirsts, let him come to me and drink.' (John 7:37)

If you are thinking of your duty to your fellow man or woman, it is obvious that religion by itself will not be enough. It is not enough to sing hymns and attend church; you must cross the road and help to lift that fallen person and minister to his physical as well as to his spiritual needs. But it is an altogether more serious charge that religion is not enough even when it comes to our relationship with God. We commonly use religious ceremonies as a means of cultivating what we might call our personal relationship with God. Therefore it is a serious matter to have our Lord suggesting that religion—in the sense of all those ceremonies, symbols and festivals which people have invented—is totally inadequate.

In his Gospel John records one illustration to the point. The Jews had been celebrating one of their most colourful religious festivals of the whole year, the Feast of Tabernacles. It was a beautiful ceremony and, what is more, God himself had ordained a large portion of it. Yet we are told that towards the end of the last great day of this festival, a rather loud voice was heard in the temple court, saying, 'If anyone thirsts, let him come to me and drink' (7:37).

Caiaphas and the chief priests generally were absolutely livid. They'd put on the show of the year and they counted it as a stunning insult to have one of these trumped up street preachers daring to suggest that the ceremonies that had been offered were not everything a person could possibly wish for.

'If anyone thirsts,' he said, deliberately implying that the whole week's round of religious ceremonies could leave many feeling unsatisfied. Our Lord was saying that there is a better way to God; a nearer approach than symbol and ceremony. If that is so, then our Lord would not hesitate to tell the people. He wasn't saying that symbol and ceremony were wrong, for he believed that both had been appointed by God. He was saying that it is possible for someone to imagine that the performance of the ceremony is all there is. In that case people would inevitably be left unfilled and unsatisfied, because only a person to person relationship can possibly satisfy.

David Gooding, The Unexpected Christ: Four Studies on the Person and Character of Jesus, 15–16

16th January

FASTING AND SPIRITUAL EXERCISES

Reading: Luke 5:33–39

'The disciples of John frequently fast and engage in solemn prayers, and so do the Pharisees' disciples; but yours eat and drink.' (Luke 5:33 DWG)

So Christ's critics had another problem. They found such laxity disturbing in Jesus' disciples: it seemed to take the seriousness out of true religion.

Christ replied with an analogy: 'Can you make wedding guests fast while the bridegroom is with them?' (5:34). No, of course not. To try to enforce fasting on such an occasion would be absurdly inappropriate.

'On the other hand,' said Christ, 'the days will come when the bridegroom is taken away from them, and then they will fast' (5:35). But by now the analogy had begun to merge into a metaphor: Christ was the bridegroom, and for his disciples his presence, his forgiveness, their release from spiritual bondage and the new vistas he opened up before them made their joy like that of a wedding banquet. To have imposed fasting on them at that stage in their spiritual experience would have been highly incongruous and artificial. There is no point in fasting just for the sake of fasting. To be of any use, it must be related to the spiritual realities of any given situation.

It didn't mean that they would never fast. They would, when the bridegroom was taken away. Historically that happened at the crucifixion; though their sorrow was soon overtaken by the joy of the resurrection, the ascension, and the coming of the Holy Spirit (see John 16:19–22). Spiritually, it can happen with believers. They will not lose the Lord's presence with them, but if they should find themselves in the thick of some spiritual battle they may lose a sense of the unclouded joy of his presence, and fasting could well be appropriate then.

Two things must strike us about Christ's answer to this criticism. The first is its plain common sense: there was obviously no trace of religiosity about him. The second is a matter of much greater importance, as so often it is at this stage: Christ puts himself forward as the key, the controlling factor, the regulator of true spirituality. His disciples' lives are ordered not so much by rules and regulations as by the practical realities of a living relationship with a living Lord. For them, forgiveness and salvation, morality, ethics and religious discipline all hinge upon a personal relationship with Christ.

David Gooding, *According to Luke: The Third Gospel's Ordered Historical Narrative*, 111–12

17th January

SACRIFICE AND TRUE WORSHIP

Reading: Genesis 22:1–8

'I and the boy will go over there and worship . . .' (Genesis 22:5)

'Worship? Are you going to have a thanksgiving meeting up on the mountain and rehearse before God all the wonders of the benefits he has given you?'

'No, not today.'

Abraham had sheep and oxen, servants and wealth beyond computation, and doubtless he had thanked God many times for these gifts. Today God had asked him to take the sublimest gift: the gift that made sense of all the other gifts, without which life was empty and nothing, apart from God. God had asked Abraham to give it back to God.

'Abraham, what kind of a God would give you a gift one day and take it away the next?'

Says Abraham, 'I am giving my all to God; I go to worship him. What are all his gifts, if I do not have God? Let me tell God what I think of him. If I had all heaven and ten thousand galaxies and not God, how poverty-stricken I should be. Let God take all, so long as he is mine. That's what I am going to tell him.

'Furthermore, God has said that through Isaac shall my offspring be named. I cannot tell you how he will do it—but I am going there to offer my son as he tells me to. I believe he's not a God who says "Yes" today and "No" tomorrow. I believe he is a God of utter consistency, true to his word, though heaven and hell fall apart. If he has said he will bless me and Isaac, he will; though I put Isaac on this altar.

'That's what I'll be telling God now. I shall not wait until he gives me Isaac back, but now in this dark moment, in the flood of the trial, I want to tell God that he is my all. It will be easy to tell him in the sunshine of heaven when it's all come right in the end, but I should be ashamed to join the worship at that late stage. I'll do it now.'

So he took his all, put it on the altar, and Abraham and his son together worshipped God. May God induce in our hearts such appreciation of himself that in this vale of tears we too might be found as those who think as Abraham did.

David Gooding, *The Adoration of Christ: Six Studies on the Nature and Practice of Worship*, 8

18th January

DISCOVERING CHRIST'S IDENTITY AND EXPERIENCING TRUE WORSHIP

Reading: Matthew 14:22–36

And those in the boat worshipped him, saying, 'Truly you are the Son of God.' (Matthew 14:33)

This was the famous occasion on the storm-tossed lake when Peter, taking faith in both hands, got out of the ship and walked towards the Lord Jesus. In the process, however, he took fright and began to sink, and the Lord saved him. Doubtless, when he got back into the boat, Peter's heart would be beating full of gratitude that he had been saved from a possibly terrible fate in the depths of that lake. But the predominant atmosphere was not so much of gratitude for Peter's salvation, for in the dark of that night they had caught a glimpse of who Jesus Christ was.

Soon the clouds of human limitation closed in again and they forgot, and failed to work out its implication. But in that moment, like a sunray coming through the cloud, they had caught a glimpse that this Jesus of Nazareth was no mere carpenter's son. Catching sight of who he was, as they knelt in the boat in the swamp of the bilge water they had discovered a bit of eternity. They saw God manifest in flesh and bowed their hearts in worship.

From time to time during the forty days before his ascension the apostles had spent some hours with Jesus Christ our Lord. By God's wisdom they had begun to grow accustomed to the realities of that other world in which Jesus Christ already stood. They were growing accustomed to a way of life that lives with both feet on this earth, yet has discovered the reality of that other world. Presently, on the last day he raised his hands in blessing and was parted from them and the cloud received him out of their sight.

> Then he led them out as far as Bethany, and lifting up his hands he blessed them. While he blessed them, he parted from them and was carried up into heaven. And they worshipped him and returned to Jerusalem with great joy. (Luke 24:50–52)

As they saw him rise to sit at the right hand of God on high, his exceeding majesty dawned on them as never before and they bowed their hearts in worship.

David Gooding, *The Adoration of Christ: Six Studies on the Nature and Practice of Worship*, 10–11

19th January

THE MOTIVATING POWER OF CHRIST'S REDEMPTION

Reading: Matthew 17:24–27

He himself bore our sins in his own body on the tree, that we might die to sin and live to righteousness. (1 Peter 2:24 DWG)

Jesus and his disciples came to Capernaum. Those who received the temple tax came to Peter and said, 'Does your teacher not pay the tax?' (Matt 17:24).

Peter replied, 'Yes'. When he came back to the house, our Lord spoke to him. 'What do you think, Simon? From whom do kings of the earth take toll or tax? From their sons or from others?'

'From others,' said Peter.

'Yes,' said our Lord, 'then the children are free, aren't they? Would the king demand that the prince should pay tribute to live in the palace?'

How like Peter we are. He believed in the deity of Christ, but he hadn't worked out its logical implications. We too believe in it with all our hearts and then five minutes down the road we discover that we haven't worked out the implications either. 'I don't have to pay taxes to enter my father's house, Peter. I'm the Son of the Father, and as for paying redemption money I don't need to be redeemed.'

So what was Peter to do? 'However, not to give offence to them,' said our Lord, 'go to the sea and cast a hook and take the first fish that comes up, and when you open its mouth you will find a shekel. Take that and give it to them for me and for yourself' (17:27). He didn't have to pay it, but if he refused the crowd wouldn't understand and they would think that he was insulting God. That magnificent discovery was going to revolutionize Peter's life. He discovered that the Son of God loved him and paid the redemption price for him when he didn't have to.

What practical difference does it make in the life of the church? If my brother sins against me, what shall I do? (18:15). How can I refuse to forgive him when he comes and asks for forgiveness? Since Christ has paid the redemption money for me, how then can I in my turn refuse to forgive my brother?

Christ forgave me all my debt, but then I turn round and refuse to forgive someone who has repented and asked for my forgiveness. The discovery of the deity of Christ ought to bring a new motivation into our behaviour.

David Gooding, The Son of the Living God: One Study on the Implications of the Deity of Christ, 14–15

20th January

INDWELT BY THE FATHER AND THE SON

Reading: John 17:6–12

'that they may be one, even as we are one.' (John 17:11)

You may recall the buzz, when it began to dawn on the apostolic minds that across the table there sat not just a rabbi but God himself! 'You asked me,' said our blessed Lord to Philip, 'to show you the Father. Whoever has seen me *has* seen the Father. And the words that I say, I do not speak from myself, but from the Father who is in me' (see John 14:8–10). That is marvellous; but how will the biggest theologian who was ever invented begin to explain this mystery? God is in Christ, yes. But God in Christ is in *me*!

And then our Lord goes on to talk about the need for oneness, and that this oneness shall constantly be perfected, for it is not yet perfected. He says, 'I have already given them the glory which you gave me, that they may be one' (see 17:22–23). But as yet our hearts are not fully open, are they? They need to be opened for this wonderful oneness between us and the Saviour to be expanded and developed, so that the world shall see, not what good Christians we are (they'll be a long while seeing that), but that God has loved us even as he loved his Son. How wealthy I should appear to you, if you began to catch the faintest glimmer that God has loved me as he has loved his Son.

Nor is that enough for Christ. 'Father, I will,' he says, 'that those whom you have given me may be with me where I am, so that they may behold my glory, the glory I had with you before the world was, for you loved me then' (see 17:24). And now words must fail us, and become cheap little empty tin cans, as we try to express the reality. What shall it be, my brother and sister, when at last we see him?

> *Face to face with Christ, my Saviour;*
> *Face to face—what will it be*
> *When with rapture I behold Him,*
> *Jesus Christ who died for me?*

What shall it be when we behold him and see his face, to see that which is the chief purpose for which we were created? There will be no higher glory, and though there were ten thousand occupations there will be none higher than to see his face. His desire for us to see his glory was the purpose of our making.

David Gooding, *Back to the Gospel: Three Studies on True Progress in Spirituality, Freedom, and Church Life*, 6–7

21st January

CHRIST BAPTIZES HIS PEOPLE IN THE HOLY SPIRIT

Reading: 1 Corinthians 12:11–13

'I have baptized you [in] water, but he [the Lord Jesus] will baptize you [in] the Holy Spirit.' (Mark 1:8)

You will notice: It's not the Holy Spirit who baptizes, it's the Lord Jesus who baptizes you. Just as John baptized people in water, so the Lord Jesus baptizes people in the Spirit. That is, when you come to Christ, Christ gets you and he puts you in his Spirit. He makes you drink of the Spirit—he puts the Spirit in you. That is indeed the only way you could have a spiritual body. Marvellous, isn't it? And you have to have both things at the same time, of course.

You say, 'Well then, what is it that keeps all these members together and makes them one body?'

The simple fact is that I'm standing here in the air, and as I breathe the air is in me. Isn't that so? As the air goes into me, it carries the oxygen through my blood stream, right down to the tips of my little fingers, and keeps it all together. If you were to cut off that supply of air to my little finger, it would go gangrenous and fall off.

So, in order to have a human body, I must have two things at once—I must be in the air and the air must be in me. It's no good having one at a time, is it? Suppose you tie something round my throat, I'm in the air but the air isn't in me. I'd go blue in the face!

Try it the other way round. Shoot me off into space, and say, 'Take a deep breath, old boy!' So the air goes into me and then you shoot me out into space. But because I'm not in the air, then I'd go *pop*.

No, I've got to have both things, and I must have both at once.

And, my dear Christian friends, so it is with this matter. How are we made into the body of Christ? Christ baptizes us in his Spirit—he puts us in the Holy Spirit. And at the same time he puts his Spirit in us and makes us drink of the Holy Spirit. I am in the Spirit and the Spirit is in me.

Oh, what a glorious thing it is. Every believer is baptized in the Holy Spirit and made to drink of that Spirit. Let the wonder of it grip our souls.

David Gooding, *Christ Living in You: One Study on the Gift and Gifts of the Holy Spirit*, 10–11

22nd January

WHAT TRUE FELLOWSHIP IS

Reading: 1 John 1:1–4

And indeed our fellowship is with the Father and with his Son Jesus Christ. (1 John 1:3)

Just let's pause for a moment on that familiar phrase, 'have fellowship with', and ask ourselves how we're to understand it. The word fellowship in Greek can mean to have a close relationship with somebody. But it can be used in another sense—to have a share in something with somebody else. So, here you're not merely thinking of two people, and between them there's some invisible but very real current flowing that you might call communion or friendship, but there's a very concrete third thing: something which the two of them share together.

In modern terms you could talk of people who have bought shares in British Airways, and all these people have this in common, that they have shares in this great corporation. The New Testament uses it in that sense in Luke 5:10, where it is describing Peter in his boat and we read of James and John who were his partners in the operation. They were partners and therefore having fellowship together, which meant enjoying common possessions—a boat and nets, and common experience in the activity of fishing.

And John writes that we may have fellowship with him and the other apostles, and our fellowship is with the Father and with his Son Jesus Christ. In what sense? Well, doubtless, when we're born again a fellowship is set up in the sense of communion between our hearts. But it seems to me that the word implies something more than that here. John is telling us about this eternal life, so that we may enjoy the common possession of life with God. It's a fact, isn't it, that while believers sleep at night, not thinking about anything in particular, they still share the life of God?

You've got your new shares in British Airways and locked them away in your strongbox. Now you've gone to bed, but you still have your shares, don't you? And this eternal life isn't just something I have when I'm in communion with God and enjoying his fellowship; it's something that's permanent. When you believe on the Lord Jesus Christ you receive a life that you didn't have before. And for all eternity you will share that life with all God's people, and with the Father and the Son, for having fellowship means that you have a common share in the very life of God himself.

David Gooding, Unity, Origin and Victory: Fourteen Studies from 1 John on Life in the Family of God, 14–15

23rd January

THE LIFE WE SHARE WITH THE FATHER AND WITH THE SON

Reading: John 14:23–27

'Because I live, you also will live.' (John 14:19)

Your pet dog can understand quite a bit about you. When he sees you eating some beef he understands perfectly what is going on and the delightful sensations you are enjoying, because he has a stomach like human beings have. He knows what hunger is and the delights of satisfying that hunger with food. But show your dog a beautiful oil painting and the dog will be completely bemused. He will not be able to make any sense of the thing whatsoever. He may try to smell the painting, lick it, or even chew it, if you let him, for these are the only means he has of getting to know things. He does not possess a human spirit such as you have, and therefore he will never understand your picture. That part of your life, which you enjoy by means of your human spirit, lies forever beyond the dog's limited experience of life. So the artist reveals his thoughts and sense of beauty to you by his painting; but even though the dog can see the painting, he does not receive the artist's revelation.

In giving us his Holy Spirit, Christ has opened our eyes to see a world of meaning, significance and delight to which unregenerate men and women are completely dead. They do not possess the kind of life that is necessary for the enjoyment of these things. That is why you can read words out of Scripture, which for you are living and vibrant and convey the very heartbeat of God, whereas an unregenerate person can read those same words and find them lifeless and dull. The reason is that the Lord is manifesting himself to you through his word and through the life that he shares with you.

There is this practical fellowship of life between you and him. You love the Lord and you keep his commandments. You feel the joy of pleasing him, and he feels the joy of being pleased in you. And because you love him, the Father will love you and the Lord will love you, and that mutual love will widen and deepen the channel of communication between you until both the Father and the Son will come and make their dwelling place in your heart (see 14:21, 23).

David Gooding, *In The School of Christ: Lessons on Holiness in John 13–17*, 99–100

24th January

CHILDREN OF THE FATHER AND MEMBERS OF THE FAMILY

Reading: 1 John 3:1–3

Behold, what manner of love the Father has bestowed upon us, that we should be called children of God. (1 John 3:1 DWG)

The first part of John's Epistle referred to the people of God as children, as young men and as fathers, by referring to God as our Father; so already the idea of family was explicit. But notice at the beginning of chapter 3 how gloriously it is added to now.

We have the status of children, and we're rightly called children of God. This is not some empty epithet, some courteous description that isn't really true. It really is true; and not because we've arrogated it to ourselves and in our sentimentality say, 'All people must be children of God.' No, we've had that status conferred upon us, and what tremendous love of God it shows. And not only 'called', but some of the manuscripts add, 'and so we are'—in my judgment and in the judgment of many others, rightly so. We not only have the status of being called children of God, but in actual fact, as to our nature we are his children.

So now we come to the heart of the matter. This fellowship that we're in is not just superficially called a family, it's a real family. Consider then the origin of why we are called 'children of God':

> If you know that he is righteous, you know that everyone also that practises righteousness is begotten of him. (2:29 DWG)

It isn't merely that we've some mutual interest, like two people might be brought together because they share an interest in amateur photography, and we've come together with God because we share an interest in theology. No, it's infinitely deeper than that. We're brought together in fellowship because, in actual fact, every believer has been begotten of God. Just as my father and I had a common interest because I had his life—he begat me; so every believer in the Lord Jesus has fellowship with the Father because we actually share the life of the Father—we have been begotten of the Father.

David Gooding, *Unity, Origin and Victory: Fourteen Studies from 1 John on Life in the Family of God*, 47

25th January

THE FAMILY LIKENESS

Reading: 1 John 3:4–10

No one who is born of God will continue to sin, because
God's seed remains in them. (1 John 3:9 NIV)

They cannot go on practising sin, which is the force of the Greek word, because they are begotten of God; and what's more, the seed of God abides in them. That's an interesting term. As medicine has increased we've come more and more to consider the wonders of our human physical life. I'm told by those who knew my esteemed father that I resemble him in lots of things; not only in the shape of my face, but in the colour of my eyes, for instance, and in the thinness of my hair, and in all sorts of funny little mannerisms. The learned medics tell me that in great part it's because with the life of my father came my father's genes. And with those genes that abide in me come all sorts of things that control my nature and behaviour.

And the wonder is that the believer in Christ not only has the life of God, but with it the seed of God—his very nature. This is no cheap salvation, my dear friends. It isn't that Jesus has been kind and loving, and now he says 'try and behave like children of God'. It's a glorious fact of divine regeneration that when we were born again we received the very nature of God. Let's hug that gospel to our hearts and then go out and preach it! There are many religious folks who are trying to do like Israel had to do in Egypt, make bricks without straw. They try to behave like children of God without first of all being born again as children of God. They need to be told not merely to imitate the Lord Jesus, but that there is this great regeneration available to them. They can be born again; they can receive the life of God and the very nature of God. 'God's seed abides in them', says 1 John 3:9.

It doesn't mean that we're already perfect. Verse 3 tells us that we still have the need to purify ourselves, but in spite of that we're already children of God. When the Lord Jesus is manifested we'll be transformed completely, and we shall be like him. So you can see that the family is not merely a fellowship: it's a real family in which the members have the very life of the Father.

David Gooding, *Unity, Origin and Victory: Fourteen Studies from 1 John on Life in the Family of God*, 48

26th January

THE WORLD WILL NOT RECOGNIZE GOD'S CHILDREN

Reading: John 8:42–47

The reason the world does not know us is that it did not know him. (1 John 3:1 NIV)

Let's come then to family likeness. We are told that true children of God will of necessity bear the likeness of the Father because they have the Father's life, but notice how John keeps these ideas in true balance. He tells us that there's a sense in which the children of God aren't yet manifest, and the world doesn't know us. You can't tell which is which by just looking at us (see 1 John 3:1–2). But then he tells us that there's another sense in which the children of God are manifest: 'By this it is evident who are the children of God' (v. 10). Oh yes, you can tell them, as plain as eggs are eggs!

In the one place we're told that the world doesn't recognize the children of God. This is a ground of some encouragement to us, for we remember that when the Lord Jesus was here the world didn't recognize him either. It's not only that they said he wasn't the Son of God and the Messiah, but when they watched him they actually found his behaviour shocking. Some of the religious people were the ones who were most offended, and they said that he couldn't possibly be the Christ of God. 'Look at the company he keeps! He's to be found with prostitutes and tax gatherers.' They didn't recognize him because he didn't seem to be a true portrayal of the God they knew.

If the Lord Jesus wasn't recognized, it's understandable that sometimes the world fails to recognize the true children of God, and they will think that we're wrong. On the other hand, we mustn't make that an excuse for lax behaviour. Sometimes the reason the world doesn't recognize us as Christians is because we're not behaving as Christians. We're doing all sorts of horrible things to one another and to our unconverted friends, misbehaving in business and showing evil temper and worldly standards of life. So there must be a balance. Although in one sense it's not yet manifest what we shall be, already it's as plain as a pikestaff!

Says John, 'By this it is evident who are the children of God, and who are the children of the devil' (3:10). John's view is that if someone is to be found constantly practising unrighteousness, he can say what he likes, he's not a child of God: he is of the devil.

David Gooding, *Unity, Origin and Victory: Fourteen Studies from 1 John on Life in the Family of God*, 51–2

27th January

HOW WE KNOW THAT GOD ABIDES IN US

Reading: Galatians 4:1–7

*By this we know that we abide in him and he in us,
because he has given us of his Spirit. (1 John 4:13)*

Let me remind you of a similar observation that Paul makes in Galatians. He says, 'And because you are sons, God has sent forth the Spirit of his Son into our hearts, crying Abba! Father!' (Gal 4:6 DWG).

Let me tell you a silly story. Once there was a devoted man and wife who had their first child. They were sincere believers, and they were determined that the first word this infant should ever speak would be 'Jesus'. So, at suitable hours in the day the infant was propped on Dad's knee and he said to the infant, 'Jesus, Jesus, Jesus', and the infant looked at him—as they look, you know. Eventually the infant responded, 'Dada!' Why was that? Well, 'Dada' is the natural thing for a child to say—it's simply their nature coming out.

'And because you are sons, God has sent the Spirit of his Son into our hearts', and naturally the believer says, 'Abba!' The Holy Spirit is within him, and from that expression to his Father you will perceive that God has given him of his Spirit in the same way.

How do we know that God abides in us and we in God? The answer is that, though God himself is invisible, we have come to perceive him and to perceive what God is like. At Calvary multitudes went by as our blessed Lord hung, beaten, scourged and naked, on that terrible cross. They saw him hanging there, but they saw nothing in it. To them he was just one more criminal coming to his end.

But a wonderful thing has been true of you. As you stood by the same cross and looked upon that crucified form, your eyes were opened and you said to yourself, 'That is the Son of God; why is he hanging there? Is that what God is like?' The Holy Spirit opened your eyes to see what the invisible God is like, and the stunning realization came home, 'He's hanging there for me. That's what God is like, and I've seen it.' Your eyes have seen what multitudes of eyes don't see, and you can say with Paul, 'The Son of God loved me and gave himself for me' (Gal 2:20).

'Whosoever shall confess that Jesus is the Son of God, God abides in him, and he in God' (1 John 4:15 DWG).

David Gooding, *Unity, Origin and Victory: Fourteen Studies from 1 John on Life in the Family of God*, 69–70

28th January

ABIDING IN CHRIST

Reading: John 15:1–8

'If you abide in me, and my words abide in you, ask whatever you wish, and it will be done for you.' (John 15:7)

The invitation to ask whatever we wish, and the promise that it shall be done to us, is clearly not an open ended invitation to ask for just anything we might happen to desire—a new car, a larger house and so forth. The invitation is limited by two conditions. Firstly, 'If you abide in me'; that is, remain in close and intimate fellowship and communion with the Lord. Secondly, 'and my words abide in you'.

If we enjoy intimate communion with the Lord in our private devotions we shall become increasingly aware of his love for us, and his love will certainly give us confidence to bring him our requests. But what shall we ask for? In order to ask aright, we must let his words abide in us, correcting our misconceived desires; opening up to us what God's purposes and objectives are for us and for others, so that we can shape our requests accordingly. But granted that, the wonderful thing is that we are invited to cooperate with the vinedresser in accomplishing his desires. After all, while metaphorically speaking we are vine branches, literally we are not passive pieces of vine wood. We are redeemed personalities. As we abide in Christ, and his words abiding in us begin to renew our minds, we shall soon become aware of faults in our personalities—hard knots in the vine branch, so to speak—that limit our fruitfulness and impede our growth. And when that happens, then we are invited to cooperate with the vinedresser and ask for these things to be removed, so that more fruit shall result for his glory.

We are not allowed to dictate to him how he shall do it. We may well find that he chooses unexpected and sometimes painful methods. Nor are we allowed to dictate how long he shall take over it. We are not to suppose that habits and complexes ingrained over many years will necessarily be removed instantaneously. But we may ask, and go on asking, in the God given assurance that our asking is not in vain, and he will do for us what we ask. When the resultant fruit brings him the credit we shall have the joy of knowing that we cooperated with him in achieving his glory, and the added joy of realizing that our fruit bearing demonstrates that we are genuine disciples of Christ.

David Gooding, *In The School of Christ: Lessons on Holiness in John 13–17*, 148–50

29th January

CALLED INTO THE FELLOWSHIP OF HIS SON

Reading: Luke 12:35–40

God is faithful, by whom you were called into the fellowship of his Son, Jesus Christ our Lord. (1 Corinthians 1:9)

Being the Son of God, this Lord Jesus Christ into whose fellowship we are called, is the author of the universe. If you should ask, 'What is the universe for?', the answer is that it was made for Jesus Christ our Lord. And we have been called into his fellowship! Does it even seem realistic to you, or is this a little bit of Paul's enthusiasm running away with him? Indeed, it is not. God has called you into the fellowship of his dear Son, and it is God who is going to provide the necessary resources all the way home until we are with him and like him for ever.

In Hebrews 1 the writer quotes Psalm 45, which is modelled on songs that were sung at the weddings of ancient kings. And you will notice there that almighty God addresses the Son as God:

> But of the Son he says, 'Your throne, O God, is for ever and ever, the sceptre of uprightness is the sceptre of your kingdom. You have loved righteousness and hated wickedness; therefore God, your God, has anointed you with the oil of gladness beyond your companions.' (Heb 1:8–9)

So here is the New Testament referring to our blessed Lord, enthroned by God and supreme among his companions. And who are the companions? The Greek word *metochos* means someone who shares in something with somebody—a partaker or partner. I believe that the princes of the ruling house, who will surround our blessed Lord when he is enthroned in his kingdom, will be his redeemed people such as you and me. My brothers and sisters, if it is true may God help us to grasp it. We shall be companions of the Messiah, companions of the King.

When our Lord was getting tired of the disciples' discussion in the Upper Room, as to who should be the greatest among them, he turned the subject and said to them, 'I assign to you, as my Father assigned to me, a kingdom, that you may eat and drink at my table in my kingdom' (Luke 22:29–30). What a magnificent assignment, my dear Christian friend, to be taken into glory and invited to sit down as one of the companions of the King himself, to eat and drink with him at his royal table eternally. God is faithful, who has called you into the fellowship of his Son.

David Gooding, *When You Gather Together: Two Studies on the Significance of Fellowship and Headship in the Church*, 5–6

30th January

THE FELLOWSHIP THAT CHANGES AND SUSTAINS US

Reading: 1 Corinthians 1:4–17

[He] will sustain you to the end, guiltless in the day of our Lord Jesus Christ. (1 Corinthians 1:8)

You say, 'They must have been an exceptional assembly there in Corinth to have things like that said about them.' Well they were exceptional, but not in your sense. They were exceptionally perverse. You could scarcely think of a sin that they didn't commit.

From the very first chapter Paul has to start rebuking them for the strife in their assembly. They were prosecuting each other in the law courts. There was immorality among them, such as would shock Greeks—and Greeks took some shocking when it came to immorality. They had some strange doctrines. Some of them had decided that there was no such thing as a resurrection; apparently oblivious to the fact that if the resurrection is not true and if Christ has not risen, they were yet in their sins and there was no salvation.

As Paul starts to write to this assembly with all its manifold troubles, arguments and boastful rebellions, he changes the subject and refocuses their vision. If only these dear Corinthians could get their eyes on the indescribable majesty of the fellowship into which they have been called, their petty jealousies and superiorities, their careless living and false teaching, so dishonouring to Christ, would all disappear. We cannot run out of this world, but sometimes we are so engrossed with all the failures, not only of the world, but of the believers, that we lose the true focus of the majesty of the fellowship into which we're called.

You say, 'It sounds exciting. But it's not really practical, is it?'

'It is indeed practical,' says Paul, 'because it is God who has called you into his fellowship. When I came, God confirmed the testimony about Christ among you, and you were brought to repentance and faith' (see 1:6).

Something happened as they believed—the great miracle of the new birth and the entry of the Holy Spirit into their hearts. And with his presence came the gifts of the Holy Spirit to provide for their further learning and spiritual education, so that they had the confirmation of God in their hearts.

And then Paul says, 'It is not merely that God has called you into the fellowship of his Son, but God is determined to sustain you right to the end, as you wait for the appearing of our Lord Jesus Christ' (see 1:7–9).

David Gooding, *When You Gather Together: Two Studies on the Significance of Fellowship and Headship in the Church*, 6–7

31st January

ENJOYING FELLOWSHIP AS A TASTE OF THINGS TO COME

Reading: Jude 20–25

We know that when he appears we shall be like him, because we shall see him as he is. (1 John 3:2)

In the book of Revelation the Apostle John relates how, when he came across an angel, his immediate reaction was to fall down at his feet to worship him. And the angel said, 'John, get up, man. I'm merely a fellow servant like you' (see Rev 19:10).

Likewise, you and I are servants of the King. We shall see him in all his majesty, and when we see him we shall be like him (see 1 John 3:2). Be careful how you treat those dear believers, won't you? I know they can be a bit exasperating. I specialize in being exasperating myself! But if we could see our fellow believers as they will be, away above angels and like the blessed Lord, it would temper our reactions to them.

'I don't feel worthy,' you say. Well you're not, we can settle that right now! You never will be; but God is determined to sustain you to the end, so that he may present you blameless—that is, without charge, and no case proved against you (see Jude 24).

This is no licence for us to sin, but think of it: 'Who shall lay anything to the charge of God's elect, when it is God who justifies?' And supposing a charge were laid and the evidence allowed to be cited, 'who would condemn?' (Rom 8:33–34). All judgment is given to the Son, and that same Son gave himself for us. He died for us and is risen again. He is at the right hand of God and makes intercession for us.

It's realistic. This is God's idea for our future, and already it is beginning to happen. We have been introduced into the fellowship of his Son. Fellowship is when two people have something in common that they share. What is this fellowship that we share with the Father and with his Son, with the apostles and with our fellow believers? The answer is this: 'It was the eternal life, which was with the Father and was made manifest to us' (1 John 1:2). It is the life without beginning that has fed the love and heart of God from all eternity, and has been manifested to us.

We have been brought into the fellowship of his dear Son—to be enjoyed in heaven but also to be enjoyed now.

David Gooding, *When You Gather Together: Two Studies on the Significance of Fellowship and Headship in the Church*, 8–9

1st February

THE NEW REGIME

Reading: Colossians 1:18–20

For it became him, for whom are all things, and by whom are all things, in bringing many sons unto glory, to make the captain of their salvation perfect through sufferings. (Hebrews 2:10 KJV)

In the New Testament we find a new regime where, as well as God the Father to whom we are ultimately responsible, God has appointed us a Christ, a messiah, a sovereign, a leader, a shepherd—call him what you will—to be the Lord to whom we are immediately responsible.

Abraham didn't have that. We do, and it's part of what it means for each of us to be a redeemed man or woman. I say it's new, but you might perceive some early prototypes of this in the Old Testament. Come to Moses for instance, who was used of God to bring Israel out of slavery in Egypt. Moses came to reveal the name of God to the Israelites in Egypt and get them to put their faith in God. But for the exodus to be a success, it was necessary not only that the Israelites believed God; they had to believe Moses. God gave him all kinds of miracles to do so that the people would believe Moses. Eventually it came to the critical moment on which their very fate hung. When they stood on the banks of the Red Sea and looked back to hear what the noise was coming behind them, they saw Pharaoh and all his chariots and they cried out in panic to God. God told Moses to take his rod and the waters parted. As Moses stood there, Israel had their choice—would they go back to Pharaoh, or get baptized to Moses? Believing in God meant believing in Moses. If you were a true Israelite, you couldn't believe in God without accepting Moses as the captain and leader of your salvation.

It's not enough nowadays to believe in God. If you would be saved, you must believe in the Lord Jesus. 'Believe in God; believe also in me,' said Jesus (John 14:1). He stands unique. Neither Moses nor David was a new kind of human being, and Israel was never called 'the Body of Moses'. These shadowy prototypes fall into the background and leave us with the extraordinary wonder of our blessed redeemer.

What is man—what are redeemed men and redeemed women? All something magnificently wonderful. Part of this new race; already part of the new entity which is the Body of Christ, and willing subjects in a new regime under the blessed Lord Jesus as head.

David Gooding, *Symbols of Headship and Remembrance: Two Studies on Major Themes in 1 Corinthians*, 5–6

Part 3

The God who Calls us into Fellowship with One Another

2nd February

UNITY THROUGH LOYALTY TO CHRIST

Reading: Luke 22:19–23

*So all the elders of Israel came to the king at Hebron, and David made a covenant with them at Hebron before the L*ORD*. (1 Chronicles 11:3)*

This will remind us straightaway that our blessed Lord Jesus has done the same for us: he has made a covenant with his people. In that lovely simple ceremony that he himself ordained on the night before he was betrayed, he took the bread and said, 'This is my body'. Holding up the cup and passing it to his people, he said, 'This cup . . . is the new covenant in my blood'. In response to his request—indeed, his command—we meet as the people of God to celebrate the new covenant and think not only of that gracious promise, 'I will put my laws into their hearts, and in their minds will I write them', but we think also of its glorious provision, 'And their sins and iniquities will I remember no more' (Heb 10:16–17 KJV).

My brothers and sisters, here is the genius of the King: his power to bring his squabbling little children together, all willing to obey him. Hear him: 'This cup is the new covenant in my blood. Take it, drink it. I grant you forgiveness, and I propose to write my laws on your heart.'

Is there a man or a woman in Christ who would rise up and say, 'No, no! Forgiveness is what I want; but I'm not prepared to obey his commandments'?

We don't say that, do we? But we behave like it sometimes; hence the wisdom of our Lord that calls us to constantly celebrate that central festival of Christianity, the covenant that the Lord Jesus has made with us, his people. There is perhaps no place on earth more calculated to unite God's people as when they take bread and wine in remembrance of the Lord Jesus. Being many, we are one body, for we all partake of the same loaf (see 1 Cor 10:17).

> *We would remember we are one*
> *With every saint that loves Thy Name;*
> *United to Thee on the throne,*
> *Our life, our hope, our Lord the same.*[1]

---

1 James G. Deck (1802–84), 'Lord, we would ne'er forget Thy love'.

David Gooding, *Mankind's Pathway to the Coming Age of Peace: Six Studies on the Overall Message of 1 Chronicles*, 28–9

3rd February

OUR UNITY AS FELLOW MEMBERS OF THE ETERNAL CITY

Reading: 1 Chronicles 11:1–9

Here there is not Greek and Jew, circumcised and uncircumcised, barbarian, Scythian, slave, free; but Christ is all, and in all. (Colossians 3:11)

David did something that was a stroke of genius to unite his people. He knew the difficulty that some of them had in coming to Hebron, with all its historical associations, so he united the armies of all Israel and led them to a town occupied by the Jebusites, called Jebus. They took Jebus and David made it the capital city for all the people of God, whether they came from the north in Dan or from the south in Beersheba. All the people could now rejoice in Jerusalem—it belonged to Dan, it belonged to Judah, it belonged to Ephraim.

What do you suppose they called it? What would we have called it, do you suppose, if we had been in charge? Named it after doctrines; named it after anything but the name of Christ—shame on us. They called it 'the city of David'. That was his headquarters. It was the city of the great king, and all the tribes came and felt at home. It became their very heart.

The New Testament makes use of this idea of the city of Jerusalem, in its moral and spiritual and heavenly aspects. Writing in Ephesians, Paul is wanting to enhance our Gentile estimate of the superb grace of God. He talks bluntly, 'And you were dead in the trespasses and sins in which you once walked, following the course of this world' (Eph 2:1–2).

'You were once,' says he, 'a lot of hopeless Gentiles. We Israelites are the true Jews. This is our covenant and promise; the Messiah is coming to us.' Then he says,

> But now in Christ Jesus you who once were far off have been brought near by the blood of Christ. For he himself is our peace, who has made us both one and has broken down in his flesh the dividing wall of hostility by abolishing the law of commandments expressed in ordinances, that he might create in himself one new man in place of the two, so making peace. (2:13–15)

It has been God's great pleasure to take Jews and Gentiles, and not just put them together but of the two to make one new man, thus making peace. Gentiles in Christ and Jews in Christ—fellow citizens of that eternal city.

David Gooding, *Mankind's Pathway to the Coming Age of Peace: Six Studies on the Overall Message of 1 Chronicles*, 29–31

4th February

YOU ARE GOD'S DWELLING PLACE

Reading: Romans 8:9–11

Christ in you, the hope of glory. (Colossians 1:27)

God didn't need the universe as a place to live in. Pantheism says that the universe is part of God, but that isn't true. God remains the transcendent Lord, outside and independent of his universe. The marvellous thing is that God's purpose in creating it would be that one day the transcendent God might come and enter his own universe, live inside it, and be approachable to his creatures. Isn't that stupendous?

And I've something else to tell you, so listen carefully. It was God's plan, not only to get inside this universe but to get inside some of his creatures. You say that you can hardly believe it! You're a Christian, and don't you believe that already God has been active in his plans of redemption? Since you trusted Christ, Christ has come and he dwells in you—'Christ in you, the hope of glory'. Frail little me, a creature of God, and yet, in God's great redemption plan, Christ the very Son of God has come and entered me, and he lives within me.

Suppose you had the ability to make robotic lions or monkeys, or such things. It would be interesting, manipulating the robots and getting them roaring and prancing around. But you wouldn't know what they feel—what it's like to be a robotic lion or monkey. It would be fantastic if somehow you could get into their world, and into them. 'I wouldn't want to do that,' you say. 'I'm a human being and I wouldn't want to descend to that level and be a robotic lion, and get inside it.'

No, I don't suppose you would. But can you take it in that the transcendent Lord not only made you as a creature, but made you so that one day he might live in you? That God's own Son should come from heaven to die for you and pay the debt of your guilt? That the Son of God should become human, and remain human, so that he might save human beings, and that he might live in them, and they in him? One of the great goals of creation is this: 'the dwelling place of God is with man. He will dwell with them' (Rev 21:3). And what is the dwelling place made up of? Redeemed men and women—such a magnificent thing!

David Gooding, *Visions of Eternity: Five Studies on Major Themes in 1–2 Chronicles*, 40–1

5th February

BUILT TOGETHER INTO A DWELLING PLACE FOR GOD

Reading: Ephesians 2:19–22

The dwelling place of God is with man. He will dwell with them, and they will be his people, and God himself will be with them as their God. (Revelation 21:3)

The scheme is this: God is going to have this eternal dwelling place and one day the great city, the New Jerusalem, shall come down out of heaven. The voice shall proclaim, 'Behold, the dwelling place of God is with man. He will dwell with them, and they will be his people and God himself will be with them as their God.'

But we don't have to wait until the great eternity dawns. As you meet as a church here on earth, God by his Spirit comes and dwells among you. We are being prepared for great glory, and for our tasks in eternity. What is more, Paul prays like this for his fellow believers, so that we shall grasp it: 'that . . . he may grant you to be strengthened with power through his Spirit in your inner being, so that Christ may dwell in your hearts through faith' (Eph 3:16–17). Doesn't he dwell in all our hearts as believers? Yes, he does. But he wants to have more room in your heart—to dwell in every nook and cranny, in every department of your life. He wants life to be an ongoing, ever more vivid experience of Christ dwelling in your heart. While he was in prison, that is what Paul was praying for the Ephesians, and also for us today.

What will that do to us? First of all, it will root and ground us in the love of God. The more the Saviour dwells in our hearts, the more secure we are in the face of life's storms. Instead of the storms blowing us over, we will be rooted and grounded in his love.

And it has another effect. If the Lord Jesus comes and dwells in our hearts like that, it will change our outlook on life.

The next thing it will do is to make us aware that, just as he is dwelling in our hearts, he is dwelling in our brothers' and sisters' hearts. The same Lord is dwelling in all of us, so we can say together with all the saints that together we are being formed into a dwelling place for God by the Spirit (see Eph 2:22). It comes down to practical things, and one of the great goals for which we should pray every day is that Christ might increasingly dwell in our hearts by faith.

David Gooding, *Where Does God Dwell Today? Two Studies on the Purpose and Nature of the Church*, 9

6th February

THE SECRET OF CHRISTIAN UNITY

Reading: 1 Kings 8:1–10

Do you not know that you are God's temple and that
God's Spirit dwells in you? (1 Corinthians 3:16)

Christ dwelling within—it's so wonderful as to be beyond words, that Christ would be prepared to come and dwell in my heart.

Would you have the Lord's people join together and have unity in the church and in the home? How shall we achieve it?

One of the secrets of the unification of God's people under King David was to bring up the ark of the covenant. What a magnificent idea, and if you've got any concept of what that ark stood for, your pulse will race along a little bit more just now. It was the ark of God, the Lord of the whole earth, 'who sits enthroned above the cherubim' (1 Chr 13:6). Wasn't it a magnificent suggestion that they should invite, so to speak, the very God of heaven into the centre of their city?

How shall we achieve unity among the Lord's people? By 'bringing up the ark,' my dear brother! Not just into the church, but into the heart. Listen to Paul's prayer: 'So that Christ may dwell in your hearts through faith—that you, being rooted and grounded in love, may have strength to comprehend with all the saints what is the breadth and length and height and depth, and to know the love of Christ that surpasses knowledge' (Eph 3:17–19).

Mark it well. If we would have cohesion amongst the people of God, then it starts with the Lord Jesus dwelling in my heart. And when I have opened my eyes to see the stupendous grace of the Lord of heaven coming to dwell in my heart—the very 'ark of God' in my person—presently I shall discover that you've had that experience too. He dwells in you, and in that woman over there, and him, and him, and him, and him. And being in our hearts, the blessed Lord will unite us. Those awkward personality difficulties that all of us suffer from, and I more than anyone, that keep us jarring with one another, will gradually be resolved by the grace of his presence and they'll disappear, won't they? If we can take our personality difficulties and our sins to the Lord Jesus to sort them out, and as he lives in me and he lives in you and in each believer, we come to realize with all the people of God what is the breadth and length and height and depth of the love of Christ, and are drawn by the sheer reality of his life within us, filling us with all the fullness of God. If we would be united as the people of God, it's the 'ark of God' in our homes and the living Lord Jesus taking up his residence in our hearts.

David Gooding, *Mankind's Pathway to the Coming Age of Peace: Six Studies on the Overall Message of 1 Chronicles*, 38, 45–6

7th February

GOD: THE WALLS AROUND US AND THE GLORY IN OUR MIDST

Reading: Acts 5:1–16

'And I will be to her a wall of fire all round,' declares the LORD,
'and I will be the glory in her midst.' (Zechariah 2:5)

Jerusalem was built again with literal walls, with God's approval. But Israel had to learn that literal walls were no ultimate protection against her enemies. Centuries later our Lord stood outside the city and wept over it, saying, 'O Jerusalem, O Jerusalem . . . . How often would I have gathered your children together . . . and you would not! See, your house is left to you desolate' (Matt 23:37–38). The walls and fortifications of a city from which the glory of the Lord has departed will never be adequate protection against the enemy. If we may be allowed to translate the whole thing into our own experience, not merely for us personally but for the churches of which we are members, what ultimately is their protection but the presence of the Lord?

They were sterling days that Luke records in the early beginnings of the church. Yet those who study his book of Acts find themselves wondering why Luke chose to devote large paragraphs in the opening section of his work to their faults. Among other examples, he reminds his readers of Ananias and Sapphira and their hypocrisy, and we think of the severe and summary judgment coming upon them because the living God was there.

Would that we knew something of the reality, the solemnity, the wonder of the living God in our churches. They're not entertainment parlours. The presence of the living God in all his glory brings with it the ever-present possibility of his discipline of his people. I think sometimes we have lost our sense of what a church really should be: the honour, the dignity and the awe of knowing the living God in our midst.

Jerusalem needed walls, but the walls weren't God. 'Not only shall I be the wall of protection around her,' says God, 'I will be the glory in her midst.' What's the good in having walls, if you've nothing much inside worth protecting? The Lord should be the glory in the midst, and may God give us to know it in our day and generation. Does God still want to be the glory in the midst of his people? Listen to our blessed Lord: 'Behold, I stand at the door and knock. If anyone hears my voice and opens the door, I will come in to him and eat with him, and he with me' (Rev 3:20).

David Gooding, *An Offer of Restoration: Four Studies on God's Character in Zechariah*, 17–18

8th February

COMING TOGETHER TO MEET WITH GOD

Reading: John 1:14–18

*'And you shall put the mercy seat on the top of the ark,
and in the ark you shall put the testimony that I shall give you.
There I will meet with you.' (Exodus 25:21–22)*

The centuries rolled on and one day the ark was replaced by a person. The Word, through whom all things were created, by whom all things are made, became flesh and dwelt [tabernacled] among us, and we have seen his glory (see John 1:1–3, 14).

What days they were. God's omnipresence was undiminished, but now there was one place on earth where God's presence was known in its special sense: 'There I will meet with you.' It was magnificent. He lived amongst fallen men and women in their grubby sins. Little innocent children could come and sit on his knee, and all the fullness of the Godhead dwelt bodily in him.

Ah, that age was to see another tremendous thing, wasn't it? At the last, when the soldier took a spear and plunged it into his side, there came out blood and water (John 19:34). That blood alone had solid and eternal value so that we might come and meet with God:

> He entered once for all into the holy places, not by means of the blood of goats and calves but by means of his own blood, thus securing an eternal redemption. (Heb 9:12)

As I talk of that, I know that your minds are racing on. I can't stop you thinking again of Christ and his gracious word: 'For where two or three are gathered in my name, there am I among them' (Matt 18:20). This is the Lord of eternity, Lord of the universe, the blessed incarnate Christ and man of Calvary, who is now risen from the dead. Can't you see clearly the secret of the unification of the church? It is the known presence of the Lord, and our seeking for it. My dear brothers and sisters, isn't it so easy to lose sight of it?

An elder was telling me of the difficulty they had of getting people out to the meetings of the church. He said that some believers say, 'If you can't put on a better show than they put on the TV, we won't come.' There could be the slight suggestion that when the dear folks are coming to meet the Lord, they're coming to a show. May God help us to get, or to regain if we've lost it, the sense that when we come it is to meet the Lord and to wait upon the living God.

David Gooding, *Mankind's Pathway to the Coming Age of Peace: Six Studies on the Overall Message of 1 Chronicles*, 39–40

9th February

ONLY ONE HOUSE

Reading: 1 Kings 12:25–33

But you shall seek the place that the LORD your God will choose out of all your tribes to put his name and make his habitation there. (Deuteronomy 12:5)

The first set of plans for the temple said there had to be only one house—many side chambers for convenience of work and that kind of thing, but one house (see 1 Kgs 6). There came a king over the ten tribes of Israel, his name was Jeroboam. God had given him leadership of the ten tribes, but Jeroboam became afraid in his heart that if the ten tribes continued to go up to Jerusalem, to the temple of the Lord there, they might eventually abandon him and go back to obeying the kings of Judah.

He said, 'I'll tell you what. It's old fashioned, going up to that Jerusalem house; the modern thing down here in Israel is to have two houses.' So he made one 'house of God' in Bethel and another one in Dan. You can see the remains of it to this present day if you go to Dan. Whereas God had made one house and one divine headquarters in Bethel, Jeroboam's sin was that he set up other headquarters and stopped the people going to God direct. That was an affront on the first and basic principle of the house of God, that every believer has direct access to God. It didn't mean that the people were to disobey their king. What it meant was that Israel would obey their king, so long as the people themselves had direct access to God. Jeroboam came between the people and God, inserting himself and his houses. It led to disaster, and the melancholy comment of the historian is that Israel never recovered from the sin of Jeroboam (see 2 Kgs 17:22–23).

What should that teach us? It will teach us that whatever our organization, the first basic thing to hold on to for dear life is the great gospel fact of our direct dependence upon the living God. I confess to you that I have fears in my own heart sometimes. They run like this. Why are the people coming? I hope they're not coming to wait on me—what a broken reed that would be. I hope they come to wait for and on the living God. For if ever we get our eyes off him, and simply put our eyes on men or whatever, we have begun the downward slippery slope into a desert of spiritual poverty.

David Gooding, *God's Programme and Provision: Lessons from History in Chronicles and Kings*, 24–5

10th February

PEACE IN FAMINE AND TROUBLE: JEHOVAH SHALOM

Reading: Judges 6:11–24

Then Gideon built an altar there to the LORD *and called it, The* LORD *Is Peace. (Judges 6:24)*

It was fortunate that Gideon was able to make a bit of broth, wasn't it? Highly embarrassing if you have a guest and you have nothing to put in front of him. If that guest should happen to be the Lord himself, what an embarrassing disaster that would be. One of the tragic results of strife and disobedience is that it withers our souls, so when we come individually or as a church before the Lord our hearts are barren and we have nothing to worship the Lord with.

Of course, it was the enemy's tactics that it should be so. And therefore how wise of this man, and of the God who was informing him, that he should go for the big things first and maintain the food supply. He argued and gained his point with God first, and had enough food to entertain the Lord. In those moments he was given an experience that perhaps above all qualified him to lead Israel to deliverance. When Gideon saw that it was the angel of the Lord, he said,

> 'Alas, O Lord GOD! For now I have seen the angel of the LORD face to face.' But the LORD said to him, 'Peace be to you. Do not fear; you shall not die.' (vv. 22–23)

At that moment he had a vision of God and saw the face of God. At first that was consternation indeed. He was a part of Israel in all her brokenness, failure, disobedience, strife and famine, so he thought he was going to die. He then discovered something about the nature of God that filled his soul with wonder and worship. God made himself known to him as *Jehovah Shalom*, the God of peace.

Blessed is a man or woman, a servant of the Lord, who finds peace of heart when all around is interminable strife, fury, shouting and disagreement, famine and starvation. Where shall they find the strength to endure it without becoming warped in spirit and poverty stricken? It is in that fellowship with God, being led by God's Spirit into the knowledge of Jehovah Shalom, even in the middle of the tornado. The Hebrew word *shalôm* means not only the cessation or absence of hostilities; it means positively peace and plenty, integration and wholeness.

David Gooding, *The Lord Saves His People: Fourteen Seminars on the Book of Judges*, 69–70

11th February

COMFORT AMIDST STRIFE

Reading: 2 Corinthians 1:3–11

Blessed be the God and Father of our Lord Jesus Christ, the Father of mercies and God of all comfort. (2 Corinthians 1:3)

As I read the ancient story of Gideon, one or two things remind me of another servant of God in a much later time. I am thinking of the Apostle Paul and how at one stage he planted a church in Corinth. He gave his heart to it and worked for it, slogging night and day making his tents, so that he shouldn't have to charge them anything for his spiritual ministry. Fathering them, praying with them, tending them, teaching them, he was rewarded at length by a church torn with strife from end to end. There was party strife, brother hauling brother to the law court, social distinction at the Lord's Supper, heresy raising its head and causing division and endless strife in the church.

They had very able tongues at Corinth, so they knew well how to issue withering criticisms of Paul himself. They criticized his bodily form, his imperfect oratory and his temperament; questioned what he was doing with the cash of the freewill offerings and all kinds of things like that; until you would have thought the man's soul would have been withered to a cinder. Certainly, the souls of the believers in Corinth were pretty starved. When they were asked to make a contribution to the poor of Jerusalem, they said they hadn't got money to spare. Whereas their brothers up in Macedonia, as poor as the proverbial church mice, had already taken an enormous collection, until Paul was embarrassed to accept it.

What was the difference? Not the money market, but the state of their hearts. Corinth was a poverty stricken church with strife running through it. How did Paul survive it? Why didn't he get out his apostolic guns and blow them out of the water? Where did he get the grace to put up with it? Listen to him,

> Blessed be the God and Father of our Lord Jesus Christ, the Father of mercies and God of all comfort, who comforts us in all our affliction, so that we may be able to comfort those who are in any affliction, with the comfort with which we ourselves are comforted by God. For as we share abundantly in Christ's sufferings, so through Christ we share abundantly in comfort too. (2 Cor 1:3–5)

When the trouble increases, so does the comfort of God increase. Isn't God magnificent!

David Gooding, *The Lord Saves His People: Fourteen Seminars on the Book of Judges*, 70

Part 4

The Eternal Living and Transcendent Creator

12th February

RESTING IN THE KNOWLEDGE THAT GOD IS OUR CREATOR

Reading: Isaiah 43:1–4

But now thus says the Lord, he who created you,
O Jacob, he who formed you, O Israel. (Isaiah 43:1)

In chapters 40–48 of Isaiah we read how Israel will again discover not just the doctrine that God is Creator, but they shall discover it in their own experience when God recreates Israel. It will not be simply that Israel will tell the nations that God the Creator is the true God; they themselves will be the chief exhibit. The nations shall look at Israel and see the reality of God, for God has recreated his people. Israel is encouraged with these wonderful words that we read from chapter 43, 'But now thus says the Lord, he who created you . . . I have called you by name, you are mine' (v. 1). As God recreates Israel among the nations, their very recreation will be a testimony to the living God.

What will happen to Israel has in some part happened to us, hasn't it? Let me remind you what a lovely thing it is: 'For we are his workmanship, created in Christ Jesus for good works, which God prepared beforehand, that we should walk in them' (Eph 2:10). Sometimes, as we get busy working for the Lord, it's our effort that comes to loom large in our minds. Then there are those lovely occasions when we sit back and remember that it's not merely what I am doing for God, but what God is doing through me and in me, and in every one of us. You, sir, and you, my dear good sister, are a creation of God.

'If anyone is in Christ,' says Paul, 'he is a new creation' (2 Cor 5:17). Nestling underneath the externals of our bodies there is this miracle of divine grace. You have been created in Christ Jesus, and if any person is in Christ, he or she is a new creation. May God help us to lean upon it and discover again the reality of God as our Creator.

'You see,' says God to Israel, 'I chose you' (see Isa 41:8). 'I have called you by name, you are mine . . . I will work, and who can hinder it? . . . that [you] might declare my praise' (Isa 43:1, 13, 21 DWG). And the Lord Jesus said to his disciples, 'You did not choose me, but I chose you and appointed you that you should go and bear fruit' (John 15:16). So as we face each day, let our inner hearts be learning evermore to rest upon God our Creator.

David Gooding, The Restoration of Israel: One Study on Prophetic Lessons from Isaiah 43, 53 and 59, 4

13th February

THE DANGERS OF THE UNIVERSE POINT TO A SUPREME CREATOR

Reading: Exodus 4:1–19

When the earth totters, and all its inhabitants,
it is I who keep steady its pillars. (Psalm 75:3)

It is sometimes the very danger of our world that points to the fact that there is a creator behind it. This was a lesson that God taught to Moses at the burning bush when he commissioned him with his task of confronting Pharaoh. To go in and defy Pharaoh of Egypt was in itself a highly perilous thing. To counter the fear of meeting him, God instilled in Moses' heart a certain remembrance of the fear of this universe in which we live. He said to Moses, 'Throw down the staff that is in your hand.' When he threw it down, that innocent shepherd's staff immediately became a dangerous, poisonous serpent and Moses fled from it in alarm.

Now modern science has shown us how possibly lethal a shepherd's staff could be. Even this pencil that I hold in my fingers, should its atoms be split, who knows what the consequences of the nuclear fission might be! How can it be that these potentially dangerous things hold together and make life possible on our planet?

'Moses,' said God, 'put your hand inside your cloak.' When he took it out, the hand had become leprous, and Moses was again filled with horror and fear. His hand had previously been so healthy. But remember for a moment the fantastically complex machinery that keeps your hand healthy. Should any one of those tiny mechanisms go wrong, it could spell disaster. That is not to be wondered at. What is to be wondered at is how such complicated mechanisms keep together to make life possible on this planet—not just one cell, but multi-billions of cells.

'Moses,' says God, 'take some water from the Nile and pour it on the dry ground', and immediately the water became blood. In our modern world, with all our worries about pollution, it points to the fact that the balance of the forces of nature is actually really critical.

What keeps our earth's forces so balanced that there is enough air to breathe and wholesome water to drink? The wonder is that there is any world at all, when one considers its position and surroundings. The very dangerous way in which it is poised and put together points us to the fact that behind this miracle there lies the infinite power of God.

David Gooding, *King of kings and Lord of lords: Four Studies exploring God's Sovereignty over Various Spheres*, 4–5

14th February

THE LIVING GOD

Reading: 1 Kings 18:18–39

Turn to me and be saved, all the ends of the earth!
For I am God, and there is no other. (Isaiah 45:22)

When the nation was sunk in idolatry, worshipping Baal, Elijah challenged them to a contest on the top of Mount Carmel to decide who the true God was. He said to the priests of Baal, 'build your altar and put your sacrifice on it, and then call upon Baal. I'll build my altar and call upon the name of the Lord, and the God who answers by fire, he is God' (see 1 Kgs 18:23–24).

Well, the priests of Baal built their altar and called upon their god, but the historian notes that 'there was no voice; no one answered' (18:29), which isn't surprising. Who was Baal anyway? Baal was the old pagan deification of the storm god, and sometimes represented as a bull as the deification of the principle of fertility: both impersonal, natural forces. By this time, Israel had sunk into the same idolatry as the other nations. Leaving the living God Creator, they had gone over to the idolatrous interpretation of the universe and the worship of the impersonal forces of nature.

Our modern world has done the same, and atheists refuse to retain the knowledge of the living God. They say they want to be free, but they have to admit that the ultimate powers that control them are not the powers of other humans. If there is no God, the ultimate powers that control us are the blind, impersonal forces of nature. So you live your forty years as an atheist, the sun shines on you and you feel happy that you haven't got any god. But if you get yourself into trouble, and go and stand on the top of your mountain and cry for help, there is nobody there to hear you. You cry to gravity, to electromagnetism, to basic energy, and there is no god. You stand alone in the universe, which one day is going to crush the very breath out of your body, or destroy you by a virus or something. And when it's done it, it won't even know.

Alas for our neighbours and friends who live without God and have no hope in the world. Alas for Christendom that's gone after atheistic evolution. We have cases of theologians who don't even believe in God!

What is the church? It is the house of God, 'the church of the living God' (1 Tim 3:15). We have the message the world needs. How shall we get it to them? We can't content ourselves to stay within our little huddled group. We've got to get out to the masses that are dying without hope and show them the reality of the living God.

David Gooding, *God's Programme and Provision: Lessons from History in Chronicles and Kings*, 25–6

15th February

THE FEAR OF THE LIVING GOD

Reading: 2 Samuel 6:1–7

Our God is a consuming fire. (Hebrews 12:29)

David prepares to bring back the ark of the Lord out of the house of Abinadab. But it wasn't just a question of having the box; it was bowing to the government of the living God. It was important, therefore, that they should seek God 'according to the rule', the ordinance (1 Chr 15:13). That was not legalism; it was God himself. God isn't there for us to use him. God's method of transport for the ark was that he should have a whole series of men who were devoted to him, chosen by him, sacred, sanctified and holy, and they would carry the ark upon their shoulders. If the people wanted God to come to them they didn't go and fetch him themselves; they had to let the Levites bring the ark (15:2). But this time they brought up the ark on a cart, if you please, and we wait now to see what God does.

The result of putting it on a cart was that the cart came upon a piece of uneven ground, the oxen stumbled and the ark began to fall. With very good intentions, the best in the world, Uzzah put out his hand to steady the ark, and in that moment God struck him down (2 Sam 6:7).

You say, 'That's unfair, because he meant well.'

Yes, but if you went outside and made contact with high-power electricity, your good intentions wouldn't matter a lot; they would kill you. Such is the holiness of God.

But behind the severity of the discipline there were two wonderfully positive messages. The oxen stumbled, and it looked as if the throne of God was going to tumble to the ground. Can I give you a little advice? When you get home to glory and see the throne of God, if you get the impression that it is beginning to fall over, whatever you do don't try and hold it up. You should run from it as hard as you can, because if the throne of the God of the universe falls over you'll never keep it up. It will crush you.

And in that lies the whole difference between heaven and hell, salvation and perdition. You see, the idea of idolatry is that you have to hold up your god, but the idea behind the true God is that you don't hold him up, he holds you up.

David Gooding, *Mankind's Pathway to the Coming Age of Peace: Six Studies on the Overall Message of 1 Chronicles*, 10

16th February

THE LIVING GOD WILL CARRY AND HE WILL SAVE

Reading: Isaiah 46:1–7

I have made, and I will bear; I will carry and will save. (Isaiah 46:4)

Let's turn again to the wonderful story of the gospel. Through Isaiah, God is trying to show the people the difference between idolatry and the true God. He pictures an ancient town, and in that town there are big idols. As the enemy comes to storm the city, the inhabitants collect their wares in order to flee, lest they be overwhelmed. So they get all their pots and pans together and put them on the donkeys to carry them. The poor old donkeys are buckling under the weight of all the paraphernalia, and they're about to flee when they turn round, and there are their idols.

You can't leave your idols behind, can you? So, in the last-minute hurry, they take the idols down from their perches and put them on the poor old donkeys' backs. Already overloaded, instead of helping them to escape, the idols bog them down. 'That's idolatry,' says God, 'you have to carry your idols' (see v. 7).

The true God is the other way round. 'I will carry you', he says. What a gospel there is in discovering the reality of the living God. Will you join with me in my old age in thinking for just a moment about this magnificent God?

> Listen to me . . . [you] who have been borne by me from before your birth, carried from the womb; even to your old age I am he, and to grey hairs I will carry you. I have made, and I will bear; I will carry and will save. (Isa 46:3–4)

When we discover that the God who made us is waiting to be God to us, we don't have to carry him. He carries us.

David Gooding, *Mankind's Pathway to the Coming Age of Peace: Six Studies on the Overall Message of 1 Chronicles*, 10–11

17th February

GOD AND NATURE

Reading: Acts 27:13–38

For I am sure that neither death nor life, nor angels nor rulers, nor things present nor things to come, nor powers, nor height nor depth, nor anything else in all creation, will be able to separate us from the love of God in Christ Jesus our Lord. (Romans 8:38–39)

When mindless nature mocks all mankind's accumulated knowledge and expertise, frustrates all our endeavours, and tosses us and our inventions aside like broken straws before the gale, these situations raise life's haunting question. Is human life nothing more than an ultimately insignificant part of nature's closed system, helplessly caught up in her endless, pointless cycles of deceptive calm and mindlessly destructive storm, or is there a purpose for mankind beyond and above nature's cycles?

Are nature and her seasons both the stage and the whole drama that is being played out on it? Or is nature only one temporary stage on which we humans play our part of the drama that is given us to play, before we move on to bring the drama to its glorious and triumphant conclusion on a different stage elsewhere? Thank God for the answer that came loud and confident through the howling gale and the driving rain, when all other hope was gone:

"You were foolish to undertake this voyage against common sense and my advice. But, courage! Last night an angel of the God to whom I belong and whom I serve stood beside me and said, 'Do not be afraid, Paul. You must stand trial before Caesar; and God has graciously given you the lives of all who sail with you.' So keep up your courage, men, for I have faith in God that it will happen just as he told me" (see Acts 27:23–25).

Unarguably Paul's was a special case; but only a particular instance of the general truth that undergirds all God's people. There is a God before, above and beyond nature, and every believer can describe him equally with Paul as 'the God to whom I belong'. We are his property. To him, his invaluable property; purchased, as Paul reminded the church elders at Ephesus, with the blood of his own dear Son (see Acts 20:28). Not all the forces of nature combined shall rob God of his priceless possession. And every believer can add with Paul, 'and the God whom I serve'. Whether the service is large or small, public or private, the mindless forces of created nature shall never frustrate the Creator's purpose in assigning that service to us. God's weather cannot hinder God's work.

David Gooding, *True to the Faith: The Acts of the Apostles—Defining and Defending the Gospel*, 487–8

18th February

THE SON OF GOD AND THE MAINTENANCE OF THE UNIVERSE

Reading: Isaiah 65:17–25

He upholds the universe by the word of his power. (Hebrews 1:3)

This is something that Christ has always done and always will: 'he upholds all things by the word of his power'. He sustains the universe, which he himself made. He not only sustains it as though it were some dead weight that he has to hold up; he bears it in the sense that he is conveying it along to its final goal and destiny.

The scientists talk about the possibility of nuclear fission or fusion, about the possibility of someone blowing up the world in which we live. But you need not be worried, for it is Christ whose powerful word maintains and guards its existence. We are told that the universe is expanding; that stars already millions of light years away are constantly travelling farther away from earth at tremendous speeds. Where is it all going to, and where will it end? The fact is that the Son of God is upholding it all and leading it to its destiny.

There is more. 'He provided purification for sins', says our verse. The King James Version reads, 'when he had by himself purged our sins . . .', but the thought is bigger than that. It is not a question of our sins only, bad and big as they are, but of the whole defiled and disjointed universe. He made it all, he sustains it all; and when sin spoiled everything he himself came to put it right. He is not a mere creature, tinkering with a universe that he himself did not make. The universe's Creator has also become its Redeemer. He has done the work that makes possible the eventual reconciliation of all things to God, whether things on earth or things in heaven, by making peace through his blood shed on the cross (Col 1:20).

David Gooding, *An Unshakeable Kingdom: The Letter to the Hebrews for Today*, 30–1

19th February

BEING INTERESTED IN GOD'S UNIVERSE

Reading: Colossians 1:12–17

All things were created through him and for him. (Colossians 1:16)

This portion of Scripture talks in the first place of God's magnificent creation: the earth with its plants, animals and human beings; and then the heavens, the stars and the galaxies; and the unseen part of the universe inhabited by the angels of God in their serried ranks.

Then it tells us that Christ is the head of it all. Born in a manger though he was, let us grasp again in our hearts who this Jesus Christ is. He is the head of the creation around us. It is his world!

When I was young I was taught that 'this world is a wilderness wide,' and the sooner it is burnt up the better. I know what they were trying to tell me. This world has been marred by sin, and because of sin we groan within ourselves. We long for home, and 'for new heavens and a new earth in which righteousness dwells' (2 Pet 3:13). But we must not let that lead us to think that there was something originally bad with this earth. God made it and it is his world still.

It was made through him. When Christ thought up the universe, he himself made it. Amongst all the millions of things he ever made, he made me. That is a great comfort to my heart. He really meant me to be, and he meant you to be too! Christ made you—he really wanted you to be. What did he make it all for? It was made for him. Ultimately elephants are for him; they were made for him. If you ask what the galaxies are for, they are there for him too.

It is good to be interested in creation. I go into all sorts of people's homes and I find all sorts of things! You meet a lady who has an interest in ceramics. She has an oven in her home, and she paints these plates and things and puts them into this oven. She knows how long to leave them in, and out they come as beautiful pieces of ceramic. She is interested in it. You are her guest, so you have to show an interest in it too. It would be rude not to.

If the universe was made by Christ, through him and for him, common decency would suggest that we ought to be interested in it for his sake.

David Gooding, *Where Does God Dwell Today? Two Studies on the Purpose and Nature of the Church*, 13–14

20th February

NATURE AND THE BELIEVER

Reading: Acts 28:1–10

'Those eighteen on whom the tower of Siloam fell and killed them: do you think they were worse sinners than all the others who lived in Jerusalem? No, I tell you; but unless you repent, you will all likewise perish.' (Luke 13:4–5 DWG)

The islanders on Malta were ready with their interpretation: 'This man must be a murderer; for though he escaped from the sea, Justice has not allowed him to live' (Acts 28:4 DWG). They fell into a cluster of mistakes that superstitious, not to say religious, people can still fall into even today. They supposed that all the natural disasters that befall human beings are because of their sins; and therefore, if a human being suffers some natural disaster, it is safe to conclude that they must have secretly committed some heinous sin, even if there is no other evidence for it.

But to start with, nature and her impersonal workings are not the judge of mankind. Her processes in themselves are amoral. A sore throat is not evidence that the patient must have been telling lies. Sometimes God does use natural disasters to express his disapproval, and the effect is clear for all to see. The effect of the conflagration that destroyed Sodom and Gomorrah put an end to their physically and socially poisonous behaviour. But they had a reputation for it even before the disaster fell; it was not something that had to be deduced from the fact that the disaster happened.

But not all natural disasters are necessarily expressions of God's judgment, though that was the purpose of Sodom's overthrow (2 Pet 2:6; Jude 6–7). A black official limousine could be conveying a drug baron to prison, pending trial. But a black official limousine could also be conveying a national hero to take tea with the King or the Queen. Many a natural disaster has ushered saintly believers into the presence of the Lord. If we are going to take any general lesson from natural disasters, so-called acts of God, and atrocities, it had better be the lesson taught by Christ himself: Don't suppose that the people who suffer them must necessarily have been especially or secretly sinful, while those who escape them are not. All people are sinful. Let natural disasters serve rather as reminders that all need to repent (see Luke 13:1–5).

David Gooding, True to the Faith: The Acts of the Apostles—Defining and Defending the Gospel, 490–1

21st February

WHAT IS MAN?

Reading: Psalm 8

So God created man in his own image, in the image of God he created him; male and female he created them. (Genesis 1:27)

If you ask your atheist or humanist friends what their interpretation of the universe is—what is responsible for bringing us human beings here, and what will be responsible for our end and destiny—they will say that what controls our destiny are the great forces of nature: energy, gravity, and the processes of physiology and biology, all of them mindless, impersonal forces. What hope is there in that, I wonder?

Thank God for the biblical revelation, and in particular for God's protest to the nations through the nation of Israel, witnessing once more that there is a living Lord, the one true God and Creator, and man is made in his image. Man is vastly superior to the physical forces of the universe. It's good to tell that to the scientists these days. When you go home tonight and you want to read, you'll put the electric light on. Now tell me, is the electric light more important than your brain, or your brain more important than the electric light? And which is more important: my brain or the sun? My brain's very tiny and the sun is very big, yet even I can see that my brain is more important than the sun. I know the sun is there; the sun doesn't know I'm here. With the help of scientists I know how the sun works; it doesn't know how I work. Poor thing, it's only a lot of gas and stuff.

We are self-evidently more significant than all the vast impersonal forces of the universe put together. One baby's brain is more important than the whole lot of forces in the universe, and the Bible has been saying so for centuries. Man is not made to be a slave of the impersonal powers. Man is made in the image of God. And though we as a race are fallen, God has made a way of redemption. Mankind can be redeemed; God is going on with his great purpose: for man, made in the image of God, there is hope. It was not the least significant thing in this unique nation of Israel that they not only talked of a God, the Creator, the true God in whose image man is made, but prophet after prophet taught that one day God would send his Messiah to be the Saviour and Redeemer of the world.

David Gooding, *God's Programme and Provision: Lessons from History in Chronicles and Kings*, 6–7

22nd February

MAN'S POSITION IN GOD'S UNIVERSE

Reading: Genesis 1:26–31

Then God said, 'Let us make man in our image, after our likeness. And let them have dominion over the fish of the sea.' (Genesis 1:26)

When God made this universe, he made it in stages. And when we look more closely at those stages we find that there is a progressive order leading to a climax, which is man made in the image of God.

This, of course, is gospel. In the mythologies of the heathen, the gods themselves are the product of the material forces of nature; whereas in the book of Genesis, God is the self-existent Lord, independent of the created universe. Zeus of the Greeks could strike terror into the hearts of subordinate gods, but he himself was bound by fate. The Hebrew revelation challenges all such idolatry and proclaims that God is genuinely the Creator of all.

It proceeds to announce that man is made in the image of God as his viceroy—made to rule. Though we do not now see all things put under man, that programme is very far advanced and one day all shall be put under his feet (Heb 2:7–8). 'But we see him who for a little while was made lower than the angels, namely Jesus, crowned with glory and honour because of the suffering of death' (2:9). Even now, this is our charter; not only for digging our garden, as Adam dug his, but for the development of the deserts that lie outside Eden's garden and for mining its gold. For us, it is our chemistry, our geology, our mathematics, and all the fun of those many disciplines that reverently follow the teaching of God.

I know you advanced spiritual men and women will tell us that the physical universe is only like toys compared with the glorious spiritual blessings with which God has blessed us. I know it. I know that when we get beyond our childhoods and beyond the nursery floor, God will dismiss this present universe and there will be a new heaven and a new earth. But I'm content for a while to be like a child. It's fun understanding our world and its surrounding universe! What a lovely thing it could all have been, had man remained loyal to God.

But, alas, science can find itself sullied by the spirit of some of her practitioners, who go at their work as a means of rebellion against the very idea of God. The Russians told us that they've been out in space and didn't find God there. Who thought they would? Others will tell us that they have searched the human cell and haven't found God there either. Who thought that they would?

David Gooding, King of kings and Lord of lords: Four Studies Exploring God's Sovereignty Over Various Spheres, 7–8

23rd February

THE SOURCE OF LIGHT COMES FROM OUTSIDE OF US

Reading: Job 38:12–21

God called the light Day, and the darkness he called Night. And there was evening and there was morning, the first day. (Genesis 1:5)

Let us remind ourselves that, whereas man was made in the image of God to be God's viceroy, he is viceroy so long as he remains dependent upon God and God's sovereignty. That is written into our very created universe. Take just one example from Genesis 1.

On day one, God created the light. He divided the light from the darkness, and then he proceeded to call the light 'day' and the darkness 'night'. If you ponder the way the lighting system of our planet is arranged, you may be struck with the apparent oddness of it. On this planet we must have light; it is vital to our life and all our activities. Yet the curious thing is that the light upon which we depend as our number one basic necessity is not in our earth; it is around ninety million miles outside of our earth. We are so arranged on this planet that, for roughly twelve hours per day, we are spun round into the light—and that twelve hours of experience of the light is called 'day'. When those twelve hours are done, it spins out again. But light doesn't cease to exist; it's just that we're spun out of it. Whether we are ready or not, whether we agree or not, there's nothing we can do about it. We're spun out into the dark—and there we sit for the next twelve hours of 'night'. The number one basic necessity is not within us: it is not within our power.

This humble lesson of human existence is that man can be lord of his world, so long as he is dependent, not only on the provisions that God has made and deliberately stationed outside, but on the God who put them outside. As our Lord summed it up, 'Are there not twelve hours in the day? If anyone walks in the day, he does not stumble . . . . But if anyone walks in the night, he stumbles, because the light is not in him' (John 11:9–10). Of course it isn't in him, nor in the world; it's ninety million miles outside of it. God has put his thumb print on the organization of our universe, to teach us from the physical facts those deeper lessons of our relationship with him as moral and spiritual beings.

David Gooding, *King of kings and Lord of lords: Four Studies Exploring God's Sovereignty Over Various Spheres*, 8–9

Part 5

The Sovereign Lord's Use of Power

24th February

GOD'S SOVEREIGNTY IS GOOD NEWS

Reading: Isaiah 51:12–16

Do you forget the Lord your Maker, who stretches out the heavens and who lays the foundations of the earth, that you live in constant terror every day because of the wrath of the oppressor? (Isaiah 51:13 DWG)

The Bible maintains that God is and ever remains sovereign in the maintenance of the universe that he has made. Rejoice with me over the gospel that this is! What pessimism we would live in, if we were not persuaded by God's self-revelation that he is sovereign in his created universe! You who have loved life and enjoyed its beauty may now see it beginning to slip away from you. You have turned middle-aged and are perhaps feeling the insidious working of decay and disease in your body and mind. If you didn't believe that God is sovereign, even in the physical things of this universe, you might be facing the future with despair, and indeed with fear.

If you have a compassionate heart, you pity the atheists when you consider what a prison they are in. They can't believe there is a God and are obliged to think that this universe comes of blind matter, produced and worked upon by mindless, purposeless forces. A little virus—visible only with the aid of a powerful electronic microscope—will one day do its dastardly work, and the irony of it is that it won't know it has done it. Even a first-class scientist with his giant of a brain, full of intelligence and purpose, is torn to pieces by a mindless bit of stuff. This poor man is in a prison, whose walls gradually contract upon him. One day they will crush him and mindlessly destroy his brain, and finally destroy him.

Thank God we have discovered through our blessed Lord Jesus that there is a God behind this created universe, who holds it in his hand. We think of that occasion when the Creator incarnate was in a boat with his frightened fishermen apostles. The storm came, and those great physical powers threatened to engulf them. When he commanded the wind it was muzzled, the waves reduced and there was calm. In Jesus Christ, we have met the incarnate God who is ultimately in sovereign charge of the physical powers of the universe. What a comfort it is for us to consider the gospel that this is: not merely when we think of the ultimate destiny of our physical world, but when we think of our present situation.

David Gooding, *King of kings and Lord of lords: Four Studies Exploring God's Sovereignty Over Various Spheres*, 6

25th February

GOD TAKES RESPONSIBILITY FOR HIS UNIVERSE

Reading: John 9:1–12

I will restore to you the years that the swarming locust has eaten. (Joel 2:25)

Some people are born into this world with a major physical disability and sometimes it is hard for them to believe that God is behind this physical universe, and behind their bodies. It's easy for the young and healthy to think about the love of God, and so they should. But there is another side to the physical universe. Nature produces disease, maimed bodies, imperfect minds. Some try to explain nature's imperfections by saying that God is not ultimately to be held responsible. Others view these things as being some accident over which God has no control.

I know I've touched a vast subject that cannot be properly dealt with in just a few moments, but let us hear from the word of God. When Moses protested his inability to go and preach before Pharaoh because he was slow of speech, God replied to him, 'Who has made man's mouth? Who makes him mute, or deaf, or seeing, or blind? Is it not I, the Lord?' (Exod 4:11). Ultimately God holds himself responsible even for those apparent vagaries of our genes, our inherited disabilities, our imperfect bodies.

I am not forgetting all the intermediate steps of the rebellion of God's created universe against God, and all the necessary sufferings that have been brought as a result of that. There are vast wheels within wheels when we come to consider the actual day-to-day workings of God's universe. But it is a tremendous comfort to know that he who set it all going in the first place, and delegated its powers through nature, holds himself ultimately responsible for the outcome. My dear brother or sister, if you have found yourself afflicted in life with some major disability, learn to find comfort in this if you can. God won't try to wriggle out of his ultimate responsibility. He started the whole thing going, and it led to you. You will find that the Lord is kind indeed. Not only will he compensate in the end for what you have suffered in life, but he is the God of your very disability now, and he can use it and turn it into something potentially beautiful.

David Gooding, *King of kings and Lord of lords: Four Studies Exploring God's Sovereignty Over Various Spheres*, 7

26th February

THE LAMB, THE SHEPHERD KING

Reading: Revelation 5:11–14

And in the midst of the throne and the four living creatures and in the midst of the elders I saw a Lamb standing, as though it had been slain. (Revelation 5:6 DWG)

This is not a fairy story. Our hope is based on the fact that the God of the universe gave his Son as the Lamb to die for us, and the Lamb is now in the midst of the throne. We are with John up in heaven, and the vision does not reach its conclusion until here.

The Lamb is described as being 'in the midst of the throne' (v. 6 KJV) and in the midst of the twenty-four elders, which is a Hebraism for saying he is between the throne and the elders. 'In the midst of the throne' is an exceedingly important theological statement. It's not just that it has absolute power, but in the very centre of the throne of God is the principal source of redemption through the Lamb. Who is Jesus Christ, this Lamb? He's not just a superior angel, he is God incarnate. Jesus Christ is God; and the man of Calvary, the Lamb slaughtered, that is what God is like. He tells out the heart of the government of the universe. Almighty? Yes: all authority is given to him now in heaven and on earth (Matt 28:18), yet he remains the Lamb of God. And when his redeeming work is done, he shall lead his redeemed people.

> For the Lamb in the midst of the throne will be their shepherd, and he will guide them to springs of living water, and God will wipe away every tear from their eyes. (Rev 7:17)

He shall fulfil the role of the Shepherd–King and lead them to the source of all the inexhaustible fountains, pure and undefiled, that will quench the thirst of every redeemed person throughout the universe. 'He makes me lie down in green pastures. He leads me beside still waters . . . for his name's sake' (Ps 23:2–3). And 'he will wipe away every tear from their eyes' (Rev 21:4).

David Gooding, *The Past, Present and Future Revealed: Eight Comparative Studies on Daniel and Revelation*, 98

27th February

THE NATURE OF TRUE KINGSHIP

Reading: Mark 10:41–45

Behold, your king is coming to you; righteous and having salvation is he, humble and mounted on a donkey, on a colt, the foal of a donkey. (Zechariah 9:9)

Why couldn't God immediately restore the king? Well, Israel herself had no true idea of what divine kingship should mean. They had to be trained and taught, and it was a long and bitter lesson. They thought that kingship meant somebody like old Nebuchadnezzar with his big moustache and all his power and arrogance. That idea persisted, sometimes in very unexpected quarters.

In his final prophecies, Zechariah points to the day when at last Jerusalem shall cry aloud in her joy, 'Behold, your king is coming to you'. On that breathtaking day when it happened, and the long expected King came, if you had looked to the Mount of Olives you would have seen the unbelievable sight of the blessed man from Nazareth coming down the slopes—the King had come.

But even in sight of the sacred emblems of the body and blood of Christ, the learned apostles were wrangling amongst themselves as to who should be the greatest. In their hearts, their concept of kingship meant that you bossed the most people. What kind of restoration can be built on such a concept? The whole glory of paradise will be that the divine persons shall serve. What a wonderful thing your heaven is going to be!

If you could go home tonight and sit down at your table with your beautiful linen and your silver and gold, and you pressed a button and the waiter came in and washed your feet, and served your food, you would be somebody, wouldn't you? My brother and sister be careful, for when you get home to heaven the Lord will do that for you. He shall gird himself and serve you. That's what will make the millennium the millennium, and make heaven, heaven.

Like Peter, do you say that you couldn't have the blessed Lord serving you? You try to stop him! You'll find out that this is true kingship. It is really the one who serves most who is the biggest; and so it is that the Lord shall forever bear the glory (Zech 6:13).

David Gooding, *An Offer of Restoration: Four Studies on God's Character in Zechariah*, 33–4

28th February

TRUE KINGSHIP AND THE GREAT RESTORATION TO COME

Reading: Zechariah 12:10–13:3

And I will pour out on the house of David and the inhabitants of Jerusalem a spirit of grace and pleas for mercy, so that, when they look on me, on him whom they have pierced, they shall mourn for him, as one mourns for an only child, and weep bitterly over him, as one weeps over a firstborn. (Zechariah 12:10)

But how would he convert these ungodly rebels? How would he establish his kingdom? He wouldn't do it by just sitting on an ivory throne, nor even by parading the streets of Jerusalem on a donkey with all the ceremony attached. How would you do it, and bring a rebel world and a rebel Jerusalem back to God?

I'll tell you the story; you remember it well. The King got off his donkey. It may not be much of a beast in your estimation, but in those days kings came on donkeys. Later he came out from the upper room and went back to the Mount of Olives, not now as a king on a donkey, but coming to a place where the stones were hard, as hard as Israel's rebel hearts, the King knelt and said, 'Not my will, but yours, be done' (Luke 22:42). By that will, and the doing of it by the blessed Saviour, 'we have been sanctified through the offering of the body of Jesus Christ once for all' (Heb 10:10). In no other way can paradise be built, sinners saved, nor Israel restored, other than by the rebel being broken through the love and mercy of God, displayed when the King himself bowed to the will of God and died for us ungodly sinners.

The death of Christ was no disaster, and Zechariah's final visions tell us how God has used Israel's rejection. They despised the King in their day and sold him for thirty pieces of silver (Zech 11:13). They were contemptuous of his attitude, but we who love him, and value him more than silver and gold could ever express, rejoice to hear Zechariah prophesying of the day when the King shall come in all his glory.

Israel shall look on him whom they pierced, and a fountain shall be opened to them for sin and uncleanness (12:10; 13:1). All Israel shall be saved and reconciled to their true Messiah and King (Rom 11:26). The Lord shall be King in that great day, and God will have arrived for the time being at the fulfilment of his purpose. They shall keep the last and final feast in Israel's calendar of redemption, the glorious Feast of Booths or Tabernacles (Zech 14:16). And when it happens, my brother, my sister, you shall be there. You shall see the King in his glory, and what a thing it will be.

David Gooding, *An Offer of Restoration: Four Studies on God's Character in Zechariah*, 34–5

29th February

GOD DOES NOT PLAY GAMES WITH OUR LIVES

Reading: 2 Samuel 2:10–28

'But even the hairs of your head are all numbered.' (Matthew 10:30)

In some countries still, on the coronation of the sovereign, acknowledgement is made that power actually comes from God. Happy are those nations that have some concept of the sacredness of power; that it should not be simply the biggest bully with the biggest bombs who automatically qualifies to be the boss. The world will never be free from strife until it is brought to the acknowledgement that power is a sacred thing that comes from God.

The Israelites went out with some of their troops to a place called the pool of Gibeon. Joab and his men sat down on one side of the pool, and Abner and his men on the other side. 'And Abner said to Joab, "Let the young men now arise, and play before us", and Joab said, "Let them arise"' (2 Sam 2:14 KJV).

Play? What do you mean? Football? No, it was a war game. The Hebrew word 'play' should really be understood in the military sense, as in conducting manoeuvres. In the end, Joab and Abner tell each other very wisely, 'We had better not take this too far; it will end in bitterness' (see 2:26).

I wish you could hear the dying groans of the millions of men who walked behind Alexander the Great, Antiochus Epiphanes, Julius Caesar, Napoleon, and Adolph Hitler. In the days when those leaders made them *play* their little war games and carved up Europe, if it cost them millions of soldiers what were soldiers for anyway? Power games, war games: is that all human life is? Are men's lives merely pawns in the struggle of international power politics?

Thank God for a king who disapproved of it, even in those ancient days. And for a greater king who shed his own blood indeed, rather than we should perish. If you are a Christian, you serve a king who holds your life to be of infinite value, and gave his life for it. He will never play power games with you. What is this life all about? Is it just an afternoon's sport? God will never abandon the whole show and go off to some other galaxy. Indeed, not! In Jesus Christ we have the very heart of God revealed. He'll be loyal to you, my friend; not playing games with your life, not rising to power simply by regarding you as expendable, but one for whom he himself willingly died.

David Gooding, *Governing for God: Four Studies in 2 Samuel on the Major Stages of David's Life*, 17, 19–20

1st March

WHAT THE BLIND BEGGAR SAW

Reading: Luke 18:35–43

*And he cried out, 'Jesus, Son of David,
have mercy on me!' (Luke 18:38)*

Long before he received his physical sight, the blind beggar had seen in Jesus far more than other people discerned. They simply saw the man from Nazareth; he saw the messianic Son of David with all the resources of the kingdom of God at his command. Vigorously he appealed to him for the gift of sight and the king gave him his request. He never had to beg again; his prayer had gained him true independence. Even today, someone who suffers from a disability that makes him totally dependent on others in one sense, can find in prayer a means of conferring on others far greater benefits than they confer on him.

When the beggar first appealed to the Lord, however, the crowd tried to silence him. His persistence in crying out reminds us of the widow who persisted in her pleading with the unjust judge until she too got what she wanted (see 18:1–8). Their tactics were the same, but it will be instructive to consider the difference in what they received. The widow managed to get the judge to give her justice against her adversary, and our Lord used the parable to direct our faith to the time when the Son of Man shall come in all his divine power and majesty to execute God's justice and put right earth's wrongs. That vision of the coming Christ will sustain us in times when we are called upon to bear injustice.

But it was a very different vision that filled the eyes of the blind man when his persistence was rewarded. It was not the Son of Man appearing in the glory of his Father and of the holy angels, not even a figure in royal clothes, with a noble entourage, on his way to his throne. It was simply a dust-stained traveller on his way to Jerusalem, where he would be mocked, insulted, spat on, scourged and killed. Yet the blind man's new sight was not playing tricks with him. This was the Son of David, and this indeed was what he was like, and what being the king must mean for him. The blind man followed him on his road (18:43), grateful to God that the Son of David had ever come his way. When he eventually saw what happened to the king at Jerusalem, perhaps he realized that if the king had not come near enough for men to spit on him, he might not have come near enough to hear a blind man's cry.

David Gooding, *According to Luke: The Third Gospel's Ordered Historical Narrative*, 313–14

2nd March

GETHSEMANE AND THE AUTHORITY WE CAN TRUST

Reading: Matthew 26:47–56

The life I now live in the flesh I live by faith in the Son of God, who loved me and gave himself for me. (Galatians 2:20)

King Herod had decided not to execute John the Baptist, but during his birthday celebrations his wife sent in her daughter to dance. As she danced Herod completely lost his self-control, and to show himself off as a powerful man he promised to give her anything up to half of his kingdom. She consulted her mother, who told her to ask for the head of John the Baptist on a platter (Matt 14:8). The king did not want to do it, for it was a fearful crime to execute any citizen who was innocent. It was worse still to execute a prophet of God who was innocent. Herod knew that John was innocent, but he had so lost control of himself that he gave the order, and John's head was taken from his body.

The priests also were in a position of power. After the trial of our Lord, Judas came and flung down the silver in the treasury and said, 'I have sinned, in that I betrayed innocent blood' (27:4 RV). He was on the brink of hell, with a tormented conscience. He came to the men whose job it was to help him and to show him the way to forgiveness and eternal peace with God, but they said, 'What is that to us? You see to it.' How sad! They were charged with the spiritual care of their flock, but had no interest in their souls. Judas went from them out into eternity, unsaved and uncared for.

Pilate, the governor was there to see that justice was done. When the crowd gathered round and kept shouting, he saw that he could prevail nothing, governor though he was. He lost control completely, washed his hands, and said to the crowd, 'See to it yourselves' (27:24). For a Roman governor to fling an innocent man to that raving mob was a serious dereliction of duty.

Will Christ be trustworthy? Can we trust our lives to him? He too was a king. He too shed blood in order to establish his kingdom. But it was not his citizens' blood; it was his own blood. We should not fear to hand our lives over to him, body, soul and spirit. Did he give his life because he could not help himself nor resist the circumstances? No! Matthew tells us how Christ gave himself for us with sublime and perfect self-control.

David Gooding, *The Battle in Gethsemane: One Study on the Lord Jesus Submitting to His Father's Will*, 4–5

3rd March

GOD'S TACTICS IN WINNING THE JAILER

Reading: Acts 16:16–40

For Christ also suffered once for sins, the righteous for the unrighteous, that he might bring us to God. (1 Peter 3:18)

Almighty God could have done a miracle before the mob and the magistrates that would have had them all grovelling before Paul and Silas instead of beating them and flinging them into prison. Is it credible that God should deliberately lead his messengers into such shame, abuse, injustice and agony simply to bring the jailer to faith? And would he allow them to suffer so much for just one man and his family?

To ask this question is inevitably to ask another and a bigger question; this time about the heart of the gospel itself and its credibility. It claims that the almighty Creator of the two hundred and fifty billion suns in the Andromeda galaxy, and of all other galaxies besides, handed over his incarnate Son by his set purpose and foreknowledge into the hands of sinful men. He suffered an unjust trial, abuse and physical violence, and finally the agonies of crucifixion. All this was on behalf of one tiny planet. Indeed, he did it personally for the jailer at Philippi; and as we, one and all, might say, he did it for me.

This surely is the most difficult thing in all the gospel to believe. And yet it is altogether credible. For the issue at stake between God and the power of darkness has never been, 'Who has the greater power?', or 'Who can do the most impressive miracles?' The answer to that has always been self-evident: the Almighty. Too many human beings are fascinated by power; they suppose that sheer power is the final arbitrator in the universe. But it is not so. The issue at stake has always been—at least since Eden—the validity or otherwise of Satan's slander that put into question not God's power, but his love. That slander has penetrated and poisoned the human race ever since. It is still the mainstay of the power of darkness over people's minds. By definition it could not be settled by any exhibition of miraculous power, however stupendous. Power by itself could have everyone grovelling in terror or open-mouthed with wonder at the Almighty's strength; but that could never convert the human heart from suspicion, disobedience, proud independence and fear, to love, trust, gratitude and obedience to God. Only almighty love could do that. And Calvary was the place where that love was forever demonstrated beyond all question.

David Gooding, *True to the Faith: The Acts of the Apostles—Defining and Defending the Gospel*, 327–8

4th March

COVENANT KINDNESS

Reading: 2 Samuel 9:1–11

And David said, 'Is there still anyone left of the house of Saul, that I may show him kindness for Jonathan's sake?' (2 Samuel 9:1)

When David had his last meeting with Jonathan (1 Sam 20), it dawned on both of them that Israel was going to officially reject their messiah and David would have to go into the desert. He left his hiding place and embraced Jonathan and they both wept.

Then Jonathan said to David, 'In spite of the fact that the nation is now rejecting you, one day you'll be king. Swear to me that when power is in your hand, you will be kind to me and to my offspring for ever.' And David swore, and they made a covenant (see 1 Sam 20:14–17, 41–42).

How delightful it is now to see David honour that covenant. David is in power and Jonathan is long since dead. Would David say, 'It suited me at the time to make that arrangement, but circumstances are different now and I don't have to honour it'? Not David. It was in weakness that he made the covenant with Jonathan. Now that he has come into power, even though Jonathan is gone, he will honour it. In spite of his many faults, perhaps you perceive another reason why David was called 'a man after [God's] own heart' (see 1 Sam 13:14), for you see in him a prototype of the coming Messiah himself.

Israel were sworn enemies of their Messiah, and they would repeatedly reject him. On that very night, when he took bread and a cup filled with wine, and said, 'This cup that is poured out for you is the new covenant in my blood,' he had to tell his disciples. 'For the Son of Man goes as it has been determined' (Luke 22:19–20, 22).

That little band of men went down into the darkness of the garden, and presently Jesus Christ our Lord was dead, crucified on a tree. Now the heaven of heavens isn't big enough to contain him, and all power is in his hands. I bid you, as the writer to the Hebrews bade his readers, 'Therefore, holy brothers, you who share in a heavenly calling, consider Jesus, the apostle and high priest of our confession' (Heb 3:1). He made a new covenant and he will honour its terms to an endless eternity. He doesn't need Martha's dining room now, nor Peter's boat, but he will remember his covenant with his people forever.

David Gooding, *Governing for God: Four Studies in 2 Samuel on the Major Stages of David's Life*, 30–1

5th March

THE RAINBOW ROUND THE THRONE

Reading: Genesis 8:15–22

Around the throne was a rainbow that had the appearance of an emerald. Around the throne were twenty-four thrones, and seated on the thrones were twenty-four elders, clothed in white garments, with golden crowns on their heads. (Revelation 4:3–4)

Round about in full circle of the throne, there went a rainbow, green in colour. I presume the circle went vertically. Then, round about the throne—this time presumably horizontally, there were twenty-four other thrones with elders clothed in linen and golden crowns upon their heads. Can you visualize it? A throne occupied, and two circles: the one going vertically all the way round, and the other going horizontally all the way round. Everything that goes out of that throne—every command that is issued, every act of judgment—must go through and past those two circles.

What are those two circles? The first is a rainbow—*the* rainbow, indeed. With its mention we are back to the story of Noah and the flood. Because of the great wickedness and violence of men, God at one stage drowned our whole world in a flood. After that judgment he promised that he would never destroy the world again with water.

Ponder it, and read something of the heart of God. The transcendent Lord, who didn't need to give account to anybody, puts a limit to his judgment. Tormented, grieved and provoked by man's sin and continuous violence and stupidity, God himself put a limit to his judgment.

We remember how men took God's incarnate Son and pulled the beard from his cheeks, nailed him hand and foot, and mocked him in his misery; yet the transcendent Lord of time and space allowed them to do it. The earth continued and men went on living. Any heart that has begun to know itself will presently forget about other people and wonder, 'How does the Almighty put up with me?' There is a rainbow round his throne, and the one who sits on it 'desires all people to be saved and to come to the knowledge of the truth' (1 Tim 2:4).

Why does this great transcendent Lord of time and space allow an eternal lake of fire? Because his judgment is limited. He could save men and women by removing their free will, but that would be to turn them from people into cabbages. God has given us free will, and he respects our personalities so much that he would never override it. When we've made our final choice, he will honour it to all eternity. That's how much he loves you.

David Gooding, *The Adoration of Christ: Six Studies on the Nature and Practice of Worship*, 13–14

6th March

THE SEA OF GLASS

Reading: Titus 3:1–8

He saved us, not because of works done by us in righteousness, but according to his own mercy, by the washing of regeneration and renewal of the Holy Spirit. (Titus 3:5)

Before his throne not only are there seven lamps of fire, there is also a sea of glass (Rev 4:6). What shall that tell us about God's power, and what you think about that will depend upon how you interpret the symbol. I suppose you could regard it as referring to the *sea*, any sea; and you could further point out the fact that the sea now is like crystal, pure and calm.

And then we should have to say that God has provided it in order that we should contemplate his power, and judge that power by the effect it can produce—he calms the raging of the sea. We measure the power of the throne by its ability to bring calm and peace.

But notice, it's not just a calm sea; it's a sea, as it were, of crystal, in which there is no mire or dirt. How shall God get rid of the mire and dirt? If it's the wind that rouses the Atlantic, then it's the mire and dirt in their human hearts that rouse the politicians. How shall God get rid of it, so that at length there comes true peace? In the court of Solomon's temple there was a laver, so that the priests might be purified as they waited in attendance upon God. That laver was so large that they called it a *sea*, and I suspect that in this figure of the sea the Holy Spirit is conjuring up in our minds a vision of the great laver in Solomon's temple.

Now it is not simply the sea of physical creation; it is the sea as an emblem of God's great spiritual recreation. It is the washing of water, the regeneration of the Holy Spirit, which Paul makes reference to in Titus 3:5.

This is the power of God to renovate, to recreate, to regenerate, and thus to purify. Happy are those who have already experienced the power of God personally in their lives. Peace is brought about by not ignoring the mire and dirt that keeps the tossing sea troubled; it comes through knowing the power of God, as the regenerating Holy Spirit brings us new life.

David Gooding, *The Adoration of Christ: Six Studies on the Nature and Practice of Worship*, 19

7th March

THE POWER OF THE LAMB

Reading: 1 Peter 3:13–21

By your blood you ransomed people for God from every tribe and language and people and nation, and you have made them a kingdom and priests to our God, and they shall reign on the earth. (Revelation 5:9–10)

In the great battle of the universe, can the almighty God win back the loyalty of his creatures? When John looks round to see the Lion of the tribe of Judah who has conquered and can solve the problem, he sees not a lion, but a Lamb (Rev 5:6). Don't mistake the symbol. I say it reverently; it's not a lamb with wobbly knees, bleating out a few pathetic protests to a godless world—'Don't be quite so wicked, please'. It is a Lamb 'with seven horns and with seven eyes, which are the seven spirits of God sent out into all the earth.'

Still in possession of ultimate power and possessed of divine wisdom, see how he solves the problem. How shall he win men and women back to God in redemption, rid nature of her curse and at last fulfil the Creator's purpose? The angels have been watching the progress of our planet, amazed at the courage God had in creating a human race like us, and wondering what answer he would find to salvage it and bring it back. With relief and joy they see the Lamb triumph and go forward to take the book. He has been found worthy to do it. The ground of his worth is this, 'Worthy are you to take the scroll and to open its seals, *for you were slain*' (5:9).

In the cross of Jesus Christ we discover what God is like: he would rather die than we should perish. And in that moment you will see the wisdom of those seven eyes and perceive the power of those seven horns, for here is a power beyond nature's atomic power, beyond the power of the mightiest archangels. This is the power of a God who will be loyal to what he made, a God who is prepared to suffer for mankind's redemption.

This is no fairy story. It has worked millions upon millions of times, and admiring angels have seen it as prodigal after prodigal has come home, thinking the best they could be is hired servants. For not only was he slain, but his worthiness lies in the fact that he has brought men and women back to God. And not only brought them back to God; he has made them into men and women who will love to obey God.

David Gooding, *The Adoration of Christ: Six Studies on the Nature and Practice of Worship*, 26–7

Part 6

The Sovereign Lord's Government and Guidance in our Lives

8th March

THE EASY YOKE

Reading: 2 Chronicles 10:1–11

'For my yoke is easy, and my burden is light.' (Matthew 11:30)

When our Lord says, 'My yoke is easy, and my burden is light', he uses the word that the people used when they came to Rehoboam, saying, 'Your father Solomon made his yoke heavy, now you, his son, please make it lighter' (see 1 Kgs 12:4). What they meant by his yoke was his kingly rule, for we remember, surely, that he was king.

Now there have been some folks who have interpreted the yoke in this fashion. They say, 'A farmer who ploughs with the horse, for instance, will have two horses. One is a youngster, full of pranks and prancing around about the place, difficult to manoeuvre. So the farmer will put an older horse beside the younger one so that they're sharing the same yoke, and the older one will keep the younger one in check and somewhere near the line of the plough.' So they say, 'You know, God in his mercy has given us a Saviour. He is (excuse the term) the counterpart of the older horse. We are the youngsters who have to be trained, and he joins us in the yoke. It is his yoke, really, but he loves us and he helps us to plough a straight furrow in life.'

It's a very nice thought, and the Lord is certainly with us; but as far as I can see that is not what he meant here. When he talks about his yoke, he is using the term in the sense they used it in 1 Kings, of a king's rule. 'Take my yoke upon you', he says (Matt 11:29). Our Lord is king and he tells us, 'All authority has been given to me in heaven and on earth' (Matt 28:18 NASB). He is the sovereign Lord; his yoke is easy, his burden is light, he is there to serve us; but he is king and will insist on ruling us. What should we say to him? He is the Son of David. Shall we say to him, like the crowd said, 'We have no portion in David' (see 1 Kgs 12:16), or shall we not bow our knees and hasten to say, 'Lord, forgive me that I have not taken your yoke so fully as I should have done. Help me to bow my neck and my heart to receive it and live according to your guidance.'

David Gooding, *Apostasy and Revival: Ten Studies on Major Themes in 1–2 Kings*, 21

9th March

NOT THE YOKE OF THE LAW

Reading: Luke 13:10–17

'And ought not this woman, a daughter of Abraham whom Satan bound for eighteen years, be loosed from this bond on the Sabbath day?' (Luke 13:16)

You might think it is instinctive in the human heart to love freedom. That isn't true. And in the spiritual realm it is often very untrue. History has been the witness that freedom is a thing that God's people will often begin by compromising, and then lose altogether.

The ancient people of God turned what God meant for their freedom into a bondage. Luke records an incident, where our Lord was teaching on the Sabbath in the synagogue. There came in a woman bent double, whom Satan had *bound* these eighteen years. In she came, shuffling her difficult way, to listen to Jesus. In his infinite compassion, the Saviour stopped his preaching, delivered the woman and made her stand upright! Whereupon the ruler of the synagogue was filled with dismay and preached a very vigorous sermon that they should not come and be healed on the Sabbath day, but wait and come another day to be healed. And our Lord rebuked him, of course (vv. 15–16).

The poignancy of the situation will come home to our hearts, if we remember that the reason for the celebration of the Sabbath was that Israel had once been slaves under the yoke of Pharaoh, and God in his goodness and power had broken that yoke and brought them freedom (Deut 5:12–15). In the book of Leviticus, God has the most beautiful description of what he did for Israel. This is how it reads:

> I am the LORD your God, who brought you out of the land of Egypt, that you should not be their slaves. And I have broken the bars of your yoke and made you walk erect. (Lev 26:13)

What a glorious philosophy of man the Creator has, giving us the posture of free men and women who have been made in the image of God: to walk upright, to look the world in the face. The marvel of it! Sinners though we are, God's redemption is still geared to this purpose—to break the yoke that sin and Satan have placed upon us and cause us to go upright. We have been freely forgiven by God and begotten as his children. We have access to God, and can look him in the very face and know ourselves accepted. Oh, what a glorious God we have!

David Gooding, *Back to the Gospel: Three Studies on True Progress in Spirituality, Freedom and Church Life*, 14

10th March

DON'T REPLACE ONE YOKE WITH ANOTHER

Reading: Acts 15:1–11

Now, therefore, why are you putting God to the test by placing a yoke on the neck of the disciples that neither our fathers nor we have been able to bear? (Acts 15:10)

In Acts 13, Paul went into the synagogue at Antioch and preached the glorious message of justification by faith (see vv. 38–39). But presently some men came down from Judea and taught that unless they were circumcised they could not be saved (15:1). So Paul and Barnabas were sent up to Jerusalem to ask the apostles and elders about this question. With great honesty, the historian Luke tells us: 'But some believers who belonged to the party of the Pharisees rose up and said, "It is necessary to circumcise them and to order them to keep the law of Moses"' (v. 5). Very roundly and sternly, Peter stood up to rebuke them (vv. 7–11).

Would to God that that had been the end of all attempts in Christendom to restrict and compromise the liberty that we have in Christ, but history tells us otherwise. Some of the early Christians got hold of the Jewish Old Testament, and, finding that Israel had a priesthood separate from the laity, they thought it would be a good idea to bring that into Christianity, thus restricting the priestly liberty of all God's people. Finding also the tabernacle with its layout—its Holy Place and Most Holy Place, and the wall of the veil separating the two—they thought it would be a good idea to build Christian meeting places on that pattern.

In many a church building throughout Europe and Asia to this day, halfway down you will find there is a wall stretching from one side to the other. In the middle there is a door and a veil, and on each end a door. Behind that wall is the holiest of all, deliberately built after the form of the tabernacle. The door leads into what they would call the most holy place, where only the priests may come. The people must always stand outside. Oh, the sorry result in the hearts of millions who are constantly taught that it is not possible for the ordinary person to enter the 'Most Holy Place' and into the presence of God.

If we would fulfil the commission that our gracious Lord has given us, we must prepare ourselves carefully, with the compassion of our Lord Jesus, so that we may be used of God to help these many millions to find the glorious liberty of forgiveness of sins, justification by faith, acceptance with God and certainty of his heaven.

David Gooding, Back to the Gospel: Three Studies on True Progress in Spirituality, Freedom and Church Life, 15–16

11th March

FALSE LIBERTY

Reading: 2 Peter 2:12–16

What shall we say then? Are we to continue in sin that grace may abound? (Romans 6:1)

As we stand for true Christian liberty according to the gospel, we must beware of false liberty. Very early on in the church there arose teachers preaching liberty, but it wasn't true liberty; it was permissiveness. As we read Peter's denunciation of those false teachers: 'Forsaking the right *way*, they have gone astray' (2 Pet 2:15 emphasis added), the term reminds us of our Lord Jesus' description of what the way to life is. It begins with a narrow gate, but it is followed by a *way*. Neither is optional. When you enter the gate justified by faith, you have peace with God and acceptance; but you will then be expected to follow the way (see Matt 7:13–14).

We must carefully emphasize here the difference between the conditions of eternal life, and the evidence that we have eternal life. They are two different things, aren't they?

Apparently in years gone by, when a midwife delivered a new born baby, they delivered a slap upon the appropriate part of the baby's anatomy and the youngster protested with a vociferous yell. The mother and everybody else was delighted to hear the yell. Of course, everybody knows that a baby doesn't get life by yelling (even I know that); but the yelling was very important because it was evidence that the baby had life.

Salvation is a free gift, but God himself will require evidence that the person claiming it is a believer, has repented and does have life. There is a great danger that the doctrine of the grace of God will be turned into licence and permissiveness—so long as you say you believe, you can go on in the permissive ways of the world. That is not so, my Christian friends. That kind of permissiveness is not freedom. It is a lie.

The Lord Jesus said, 'And you will know the truth, and the truth will set you free' (John 8:32). Those ugly rebellious passions that are within us are not our friends; they are our jailers. Listen to the Lord Jesus; he'll tell you the truth about them and make you want to be free. Then he will set you free, and that is true freedom.

David Gooding, *Back to the Gospel: Three Studies on True Progress in Spirituality, Freedom and Church Life*, 21

12th March

HOW SHALL WE ESCAPE THE AUTHORITY OF GOD'S WORD?

Reading: Hebrews 2:1–4

How shall we escape if we neglect such a great salvation? It was declared at first by the Lord, and it was attested to us by those who heard. (Hebrews 2:3)

In our modern world, where everybody's opinion in religion is ranked equal with everybody else's, it is perilously easy to treat God and his word as simply one authority among many, to be consulted if thought desirable, but not necessarily to be followed. And perilously easy, too, to come to feel that God would be unreasonable, if he got upset because people sometimes preferred to follow their own ideas, or some other authority, rather than his word. But if God is God, unbelief, disregard, neglect of his word is the cardinal sin of sins.

When God spoke to Israel, therefore, through the agency of angels, he had to teach people that they could not disregard his word with impunity: 'the message spoken by angels was binding, and every violation and disobedience received its just punishment' (Heb 2:2 DWG). Now God has spoken again, and this time not indirectly through the agency of angels, but directly in the person of his Son. This time he has spoken, not simply to restate his law but to proclaim his gospel. Not to warn innocent people not to break his law; but to offer a salvation, staggering in the dimensions of its mercy and grace, to people who have flouted his word and broken his law times without number.

God has not only given the message: the messenger is God, and God is the message. It tells the almost incredible story that God 'the Incarnate Maker died for man, his creature's sin'. It offers not only reconciliation and pardon, but eternal life through spiritual union with the Son of God, and participation in the joys and glories of his eternal kingdom. How shall we escape if we ignore such a great salvation? Our original sinfulness was bad enough. Compounded by disregard of the offered salvation, it would be a certain recipe for disaster.

David Gooding, *An Unshakeable Kingdom: The Letter to the Hebrews for Today*, 73

13th March

THE HOUSE OF GOD

Reading: Genesis 28:10–22

*'This is none other than the house of God,
and this is the gate of heaven.' (Genesis 28:17)*

As Jacob slept, he saw a ladder erected on earth, and the top of it was going towards heaven. The angels of God were ascending and descending on the ladder. And where was God standing? Some would say that God was standing at the top of the ladder, and the Hebrew will bear that translation. But the Hebrew would also bear the translation that God was standing at the side of the ladder; and perhaps Jacob's own comment when he woke up settles the question for us. For when Jacob woke up from this vision, he said, 'Surely the Lord is *in this place*, and I did not know it' (28:16 emphasis added). What a wonderful thing it would be if we woke up to it. 'God is in this place and I knew it not,' said Jacob, 'surely this is the house of God.' That's what you mean by the house of God—'God is in this place.'

What did he mean by, 'this is the gate of heaven'? In an ancient city, the gate was the place where the elders sat to administer the city. It had just been revealed to Jacob, not only that God was in this place but what he was doing there. At Jacob's very elbow was the centre of the whole administration of heaven. God, as I would take it, was at the bottom of the ladder, with the angelic hosts going out from the divine presence to do his work and his will, and then returning to await further orders. What a spectacular thing that was. If we could be given the same vision, would it not overwhelm us? What kind of civil service do you imagine is necessary to maintain our universe? 'Surely the Lord is in this place,' said Jacob, sensing that he was at the very centre of the administration of heaven and earth (see vv. 16–17).

He took what God had said to him seriously. God had renewed his promise to be with him and to fulfil all his promises given to Abraham through Jacob and his offspring (see vv. 13–15). So he made a vow: 'God, if you're real like that and you're concerned with me, and you will be with me and keep me, and give me bread to eat and clothing to wear, and bring me back, then you'll be my God.' Some people have criticized him for being so mercenary as to be concerned with his wages and his living. I think it might do us all a bit better, if we were concerned to take God to our factory or to our office, and if we wrote above our desk, 'God is in this place.'

David Gooding, *God's Programme and Provision: Lessons from History in Chronicles and Kings*, 17–19

14th March

THE SOURCE OF POWER

Reading: 2 Samuel 1:5–16

*You shall worship the Lord your God and him
only shall you serve. (Matthew 4:10)*

Here comes an Amalekite with the crown of Saul in his hand, and he offers it to David.

'Where did you get that?'

'I was on Mount Gilboa,' said the Amalekite, 'and there was Saul, trying to commit suicide to avoid capture by the Philistines. He asked me to kill him, so I killed him, and here for you is his crown.'

What would you have said? Would you have said, 'Isn't it marvellous how God guides; thank the Lord for taking you to Mount Gilboa that day'?

David said nothing of the sort. He said, 'Where do you come from?'

'I am the son of a sojourner, an Amalekite,' he said.

To understand the significance of that, we had better remember that the Amalekites are consistently represented in the Old Testament as outright, deliberate opponents of God. They had tried to prevent God from bringing his people to the promised land. They were rebels against God.

So, as the Amalekite stood there offering the crown, David said, 'No, thank you. I am very choosey from whose hand I accept royal power.'

The crown may be attractive, but to take power from the hand of a rebel against God will ultimately put you in their camp.

Your mind may be travelling forward many centuries to the desert, when Jesus Christ our Lord was tempted of the devil. He took him up a high mountain and showed him all the kingdoms of the world. 'And he said to him, "All these I will give you, if you will fall down and worship me"' (Matt 4:9). That day Christ could have had universal dominion; but had he taken it from that source, you and I would have perished as slaves in Satan's darkness for ever.

The Source of Power, then. The first thing we must consider is, who is offering it? Many a man in business or in politics has sold his soul for power. Many a preacher has been compromised by doctrinal or moral evil for the sake of power. If it were given to me, and it isn't, to advise elders of churches, I would say that, in your desire to be an elder, if you allow yourself to be swept into position by people who have no intention of obeying holy Scripture, then your true function of an elder, which is to get people to obey God, will be ruined before you start.

David Gooding, *Governing for God: Four Studies in 2 Samuel on the Major Stages of David's Life*, 16–17

15th March

THE USE AND ABUSE OF AUTHORITY

Reading: Luke 12:42–48

Masters, treat your slaves justly and fairly, knowing that you also have a Master in heaven. (Colossians 4:1)

Willingness and courage to face the facts is a sign of maturity. If a schoolboy is under the false impression that the square root of 49 is 24½, the teacher who is afraid to tell him that he is wrong, in case it should upset his ego and induce in him an inferiority complex, is helping the boy to remain in the unreal dream world of an infant, thus arresting the process of his growing up.

Certainly, if the captain of a liner is not allowed to issue peremptory orders to the engineers and the deckhands, but all must be given an equal say in how the ship should be manoeuvred, I pray that I am never aboard his liner during a storm.

There can be no yielding here to sentimental egalitarianism. Life without authority would be chaos, even if it survived. And a Christ who neither possessed nor asserted authority would be no Saviour of the world but altogether bogus. While he was meek and lowly of heart, ever compassionate and merciful, it is in fact a mark of the genuineness of Christ's claim to be the Son of God that he nevertheless claimed absolute authority.

A hostile reaction to authority may spring from bitter experience of some abuse of authority in the home, or the state, or the church. And of all tyrannies, that which is exercised in the name of Christ and the church is of course the worst. I suppose we should not be surprised whenever we come across such a tyranny, for our Lord himself warned us that such abuses would occur in his kingdom. He told us what he would eventually do with them. Listen to this passage:

> But if that servant says to himself, 'My master is delayed in coming,' and begins to beat the male and female servants, and to eat and drink and get drunk, the master of that servant will come on a day when he does not expect him and at an hour he does not know, and will cut him in pieces and put him with the unfaithful. (Luke 12:45–46)

These are very severe words, but designedly so. All three synoptic Gospels make it clear that nothing angered our Lord so much as the sight of people being oppressed by religious leaders abusing their authority. And he took no pains to conceal his anger.

David Gooding, *Windows on Paradise: Scenes of Hope and Salvation in Luke's Gospel*, 97

16th March

POWER FOR THOSE WHO SEE THE TRUE VALUE OF GOD'S PEOPLE

Reading: Ephesians 1:15–23

So with yourselves, since you are eager for manifestations of the Spirit, strive to excel in building up the church. (1 Corinthians 14:12)

We are so impatient to get our hands on the power, aren't we? But power can be dangerous stuff. So, before we allow too much power into our hands we need the eyes of our hearts enlightened, that we may know 'what are the riches of his glorious inheritance in the saints', which means that we need our eyes opened to see what a valuable treasure Mrs Smith down the road is. If you can't see that every redeemed soul represents to God a measureless treasure, perhaps you'd better not be allowed to have any power, because if you don't come to value people you can hurt them.

Power isn't given to me to make me feel good; power is given so that I should help other folks. If I'm going to help them, I shall need to have my eyes open to their real value. It's difficult to see it sometimes, is it not? If you lived with me you'd find it more difficult every day, and I'm not joking. You would need your eyes open to see it, for the mere charm, if I had any, of outward exterior soon wears very thin. You wouldn't need to be with me a week before you'd begin to get a little irritated by my funny mannerisms, and a good deal else that's worse than mannerisms. And then you would need spiritual enlightenment to see that, in spite of all that, I represent to God what he regards (who can tell why?) as the riches of his glorious inheritance—even in such a one as I.

If I have no understanding of the value of dear Christian people to God, I'd be better without the power. But by the help of the Spirit within me, if I do have some concept of the hope of my calling and the tremendous value of God's people to him, then, for my own progress and to fulfil my responsibilities to them, I shall need to know the power that is available to me. It is a power so wonderful that, if you want to know how big it is, it is the power that raised Jesus Christ our Lord from the dead. 'That's what I'm praying for you,' says Paul; and as Christians wouldn't we do well to pray it for our fellow Christians?

David Gooding, Christ Living in You: One Study on the Gift and Gifts of the Holy Spirit, 7–8

17th March

GOD'S SIGNET RING

Reading: Haggai 2:20–23

'On that day . . . I will take you . . . and make you like a signet ring, for I have chosen you', declares the Lord of hosts. (Haggai 2:23)

God says here to Zerubbabel that on that day he will make him like the signet ring on his finger. In those days it was the fashion for a person to have a large ring with a stone set into it on one of his fingers. On the stone was the emblem of the person wearing it—perhaps his initials or something else. When he wanted to sign something he would get wax and squeeze the signet ring down on to it. That was his signature.

Did we realize that God wears signet rings? He does; and we know that the name of one of them is Zerubbabel! God promised to make Zerubbabel as a signet ring, to stamp his own initials on earth. God was going to have his temple built and stamp his impression on this world—and he was going to use Zerubbabel to do it. So, when God signed his documents, he would sign them with his signet ring, expressing his authority. Thus the character and authority of God were impressed on this world through Zerubbabel. Today we know the name of Zerubbabel, and that he built a temple. What did his contemporary Gentile kings do—what were their names? The world has forgotten them, but God used Zerubbabel to stamp his lasting impression on this world.

It was a prophecy, of course, of the one who is greater than Zerubbabel. Our Lord Jesus Christ is the very stamp of God's nature: 'He is the radiance of the glory of God and the exact imprint of his nature' (Heb 1:3). In Jesus Christ God stamped his very character and authority on our world, and he will do it again. What a wonder it will be to see the final thing fulfilled!

What about us? Would we like to be a signet ring on God's finger, so that he could stamp his character and authority on wherever we live? It could happen! Despite all the show that wicked men make, and the powers of politics combined, believers can be signet rings on God's hand. He'll put his mark on men and women on earth, save them and stamp his testimony to Christ upon a district. He does it for his name's sake, as a testimony to what he is doing and shall yet do before and on that final day.

David Gooding, *Rebuke and Encouragement: One Study in Haggai on God's Messages to His People*, 9–10

18th March

THE CHURCH IS CHRIST'S BODY AND FUNCTIONS AS HIS CIVIL SERVICE

Reading: Colossians 1:24–29

And he is the head of the body, the church. (Colossians 1:18)

The Bible says that the church is the body of Christ (Eph 1:22–23). To help us understand that, Paul reminds us of Christ's relationship to the great universe. Christ made it for himself: it exists for him (Col 1:16). But since our Lord was here on earth there has been a new thing: 'he is the head of the body, the church.'

So our universe has seen two stages. First, there was the making of the universe and all physical things and people in it. Christ was the head of that. And to administer that vast universe he made angels, principalities, powers and dominions. Can you imagine what it takes to keep a galaxy in place, and keep it working! God has a lot of angels to do that. Colossal intelligences they are, and enormously powerful. They are God's civil service, serving the Creator who made them to run this gigantic universe.

But there was another stage. This creation went wrong: some angels rebelled, and human beings also rebelled. God sent his Son so that we might be redeemed and restored. The Lord Jesus suffered at Calvary, arose from the dead and ascended into heaven. Instead of just having angels to be his civil service and executives, Christ now has a new scheme. He has a body!

Let's think about our body. It is my head that controls my arms and feet. Your body is the executive civil service of your head. You are not too pleased if some of the fingers don't do exactly what you want them to do!

So Christ has created this new executive division. He has a body; it is different and better than angels. Angels are mere one-off productions: he just said the word and they existed. A body is different, for it is part of him and joined to him. Just like your hand is a part of your body and under the control of your head, so the body of Christ is made up of all those who have trusted the Saviour. He has taken them into himself and made them members of himself, so that his life runs through them. That is why it says we are seated with Christ above the principalities and powers, for they are not members of his body. They are simply his servants, whereas we who trust Christ are members of the Saviour's body.

David Gooding, Where Does God Dwell Today? Two Studies on the Purpose and Nature of the Church, 10

19th March

THE CHURCH AND THE KINGDOM OF GOD

Reading: Matthew 16:13–20

'And I tell you, you are Peter, and on this rock I will build my church, and the gates of hell shall not prevail against it.' (Matthew 16:18)

In the name of the coming Messiah, John had insisted that Herod repent and prepare himself for the rule of the kingdom of God. Herod defied John, defied God and the coming Messiah, and executed John, leaving the early apostles flabbergasted. How could Jesus be the Messiah if he couldn't even protect his own forerunner from execution?

But hear now the tremendous statement of our Lord, consequent upon Peter's confession: 'on this rock I will build my church, and the gates of hell shall not prevail against it'. Some people hold that the 'gates of hell' is a Hebrew metaphor for the power of Satan. They observe that in the ancient world the gate of a city was the place where the elders of the city sat, and therefore it's a metaphor for government. And they suppose that our Lord was assuring his people that the wiles and the government of Satan would not prevail against the church. That is true, of course; but I think that it is not perhaps what Scripture means. Scripture doesn't normally represent Satan as being a king in hell. He will be a prisoner there, not a king.

Hades is the invisible world to which people go when they die, and our Lord was announcing that he was now setting up a church and the gates of death itself would not prevail against that church. Why not? Because his church is an 'institution' that links together the seen and the unseen world, and lets us have concourse between earth and heaven, and heaven and earth. The Messiah himself would one day die at the hands of men; yet, by the determinate counsel of God, he would rise from the dead and ascend to that heavenly realm. Now he is the risen, living head of the church. In his person and by his Spirit the church has concourse and contact with heaven, and heaven has concourse and contact with earth.

The enemies of the church may do their very worst; they may torture, they may kill. But what would it do to execute a servant of Christ here in this world? It remains gloriously true—it would merely transport them to another department in the self-same kingdom! The church exists on the other side of death, and death has no more power over its members because already their citizenship is in heaven.

David Gooding, *King of kings and Lord of lords: Four Studies Exploring God's Sovereignty Over Various Spheres*, 14–15

20th March

BEING TRAINED TO GOVERN

Reading: Luke 19:11–19

*The throne of God and of the Lamb will be in the city, and
his servants will serve him. (Revelation 22:3 NIV)*

The body of Christ is going to hold the central, supreme position in God's restored universe. Let us get hold of this. We are members of this body—see what it means! Christ was head of all the vast powers in the first creation, but the body of Christ is going to replace them and be above them. The body of Christ, in fact, is going to be the vehicle by which Christ administers the eternal heavens and earth.

Not angels then—man is going to be the centre of the whole administration. What man? In the first place, our blessed Lord Jesus, who is now exalted and one day coming again. But in that day it will not just be Jesus himself alone; it will be the Lord Jesus and all his people. In other words, Christ and his body. You are in the body of Christ, and this is what the body of Christ is and what it was designed for. The ultimate purpose is that Christ and his body shall administer the whole of the universe for God.

And that is what we are being trained for. When we go home to glory, the body of Christ won't be scrapped. You say, 'Hold on, don't spoil our ideas of heaven! On earth we are meant to work for the Lord, but we don't have to work when we get home to heaven, do we? We shall all sit on heavenly sofas and put our feet up on heavenly foot rests. Singing hymns will be the nearest we shall ever come to having to work again!'

Yes, we shall sing hymns; but if you are going to enjoy heaven you will have to get used to the idea that God loves working. He doesn't have to work for a living, so why did he make all the stars? He loves making things, and he has schemes galore for the unfolding ages of eternity. As each scheme unfolds before us, the Bible soberly tells us that he will show the exceeding riches of his grace toward us (Eph 2:7). It will take all eternity to do it. Of course we shall be working, as we have never worked before! So it will be good now for us to get used to working as the body of Christ and its many members.

David Gooding, *Where Does God Dwell Today? Two Studies on the Purpose and Nature of the Church*, 14–15

21st March

THE ABSENT CHRIST WHO COMES TO MEET HIS PEOPLE IN THEIR NEED

Reading: Matthew 14:22–36

'Whoever believes in me will also do the works that I do; and greater works than these will he do, because I am going to the Father.' (John 14:12)

Before he left them, Christ began to train his apostles to live in the church age when, in his person and by his spirit, heaven and earth will be in contact. In Matthew 14, for instance, after he had fed the multitudes, our Lord sent the disciples away in a boat while he went up the mountain to pray. It was dark and the apostles were in their boat. They were buffeted by wind and waves and not making much progress. Our Lord was up the mountain, away from them, praying—and doubtless praying for them. In the middle of the night he came to them, walking on the water. As they saw Jesus of Nazareth, whom they knew as a real man who walked on terra firma, now walking on the waves, Peter was inspired for the moment to do what his Lord did, and walk on the water himself.

If you cannot see in that a preparatory experience to prepare the apostles for their life in the church, you're forgiven! Our Lord has now gone up another mountain, and in the world it is night as his people travel, as it were, across the water. And all down the ages, the one who is risen and has ascended so that he might intercede for his people comes to them and empowers them to begin to live as he lived.

You will remember another occasion when he went up a mountain with three of his apostles, and was transfigured (Matt 17:1–8). Travelling back down to the rest of the disciples, a crowd had gathered, and he was presented with a father and his boy. The father said, 'My boy is demon possessed. I brought him to your disciples, and they couldn't cast out the demon.' And our Lord said, 'how long am I to be with you?' Later, the disciples asked him, 'Why couldn't we cast out the demon?' (see vv. 15–19). Had the Lord been with them, they would doubtless have brought the boy to him. But the Lord had gone up the mountain, so what could they do?

'Look how slow you are,' said Christ, for they didn't get the point. 'I am going away one of these days, and this time until my second coming. That's going to make no difference. You ought, while still here on earth, to be able to exercise the Messiah's powers in his absence.'

So it seems to me thus that the church is the place on earth at this moment through which the government of God is and should be known, and recognized and obeyed.

David Gooding, *King of kings and Lord of lords: Four Studies Exploring God's Sovereignty Over Various Spheres*, 15–16

22nd March

GROWING UP TOGETHER IN THE CHURCH

Reading: Ephesians 4:11–16

Therefore let us leave the elementary doctrine of Christ
and go on to maturity. (Hebrews 6:1)

We who trust Christ are members of the Saviour's body. Why have a church? The church is that body! Every believer is in the body of Christ, but the trouble is that some of us haven't yet grown up.

Have you ever watched a little chap about eighteen months old? He is alive, but he hasn't grown yet and he has a lot to learn. He goes to grab something and he can't quite get hold of it. He has not yet learned coordination with the brain, and the brain hasn't quite got control over his hand. The infant will have to grow up, so that his hand will be able to do exactly what his head wants it to do.

We have to grow up and that is why we have a church. It is his body, and in the church God has made provision so that we can grow up as members of Christ. In the church God has put gifts: apostles, prophets, teachers and evangelists. What for? So that they can help the rest of us to grow up and be able to carry out the commands of the Head, so that the whole thing might be beautifully coordinated. That is why we 'come to church'. We need to come so that we might take advantage of the great gifts that God has put in the church, learn from them and grow up.

Satan himself doesn't like God's schemes. Paul warns us that Satan has his 'soldiers' all around us to distract the believer and fill his mind with all sorts of untruths, silly and dangerous doctrines. Satan wants to get believers confused and wandering all over the place, so that the Head cannot control them as he wants to do. To stop that happening, the risen Lord has put gifts in the church. He uses each one of the members of the body to help each other, so that we might grow together as a coordinated body to be Christ's executives within his universe. So it involves a lot more than which hymnbook to have!

It could be that what I have said sounds strange to some of you. If it does, I suggest that you read the Epistle to the Ephesians again and say to the Lord in your prayers that you want to understand it and grow, so that you can function well as part of his church.

David Gooding, *Where Does God Dwell Today? Two Studies on the Purpose and Nature of the Church*, 10–11

23rd March

GOVERNING FOR GOD

Reading: 1 Peter 2:9–12

'And I will raise up for myself a faithful priest, who shall do according to what is in my heart and in my mind. And I will build him a sure house, and he shall go in and out before my anointed forever.' (1 Samuel 2:35)

If a theocracy is going to work—if you are going to have God's people in autonomous groups, responsible directly to the Lord, the *sine qua non* of it all will be a priesthood that leads the people of God into the knowledge of God, makes the people sense the reality of God, expounds to them the wonder of God and the glory of God and the majesty of God, until the people are so inflamed with the love of God and the worship of God that they want to obey God!

But suppose the priesthood fails, and the worship of God becomes a mere routine, as dead and dry as the Sahara desert; suppose the priests lose the sense of the majesty and holiness of God and begin to live selfish lives, according to the standards of the world; then I tell you that the principle of autonomy as direct dependence on and obedience to God will go out of the window.

In the question of the governing of God's people today, the role of his priesthood is still absolutely vital. We shall listen with all our ears to those who exhort us on this topic, because we too are priests. The mere laying down of the law as regulation has, of course, an important part to play—we must know the commandments of God. But if God's people are going to have a heart to obey them and keep them, it is important for you and me to fulfil our function as priests and bring to the people a sense of the overwhelming majesty and wonder and wealth and holiness of God Almighty.

If people's hearts are inflamed with love and worship for him, they won't be too difficult to govern for God. If they should lose that because we as priests fail, then you will hear clamour for other forms of government.

David Gooding, *The Problems of Becoming and Being a King: Fifteen Seminars on Major Themes in 1 & 2 Samuel*, 13–14

24th March

BEING A TRUE PRIEST

Reading: 1 Samuel 2:1–10

And she vowed a vow and said, 'O LORD of hosts, if you will indeed look on the affliction of your servant and remember me . . . but will give to your servant a son, then I will give him to the Lord all the days of his life.' (1 Samuel 1:11)

Hophni and Phinehas didn't *know* the Lord. He never had been a living reality to them. When, therefore, the elders suggested that they bring the ark and it would save them, that suited Hophni and Phinehas very well. To them it was a magical box of works, like your fire extinguisher; so that if the enemy threatened you could bring out this magical box and it would save you. As you can see, that is the essence of paganism. It is nothing but superstition.

How different Hannah was. She wasn't a priestess (there weren't such things in their day), but she knew the Lord in the ordinary, humble affairs of life—in the longings of her heart in her desire to be a mother, in suffering the taunting of Peninnah and that rather silly self-satisfaction of Elkanah (1:6–8).

You might say it was nature and instinct that compelled Hannah to seek a son, and it may well have been at the beginning. But as she took the whole matter of those frustrations to God she got to know the Lord, and he brought her to the point where she saw that just having a child was not life's acme and goal.

Why live? Why have a family? Why have a career? We are hardly priests, if we are in our careers merely for career's sake. Hannah took her natural career of motherhood and was brought to the place where she said, 'God, if you'll give me a son, I'll give him back to you.'

It's what a priest is meant to do, isn't it? It means that in all the affairs of life, our motherhood, fatherhood, business ability and profession shall be laid at the feet of God, which is our reasonable priestly service (Rom 12:1).

Hannah knew God, and though her experience was at the humble level of a home, yet in her song we discover that she had been taught the principle upon which almighty God proposes to govern our earth. She celebrated the fact that he has blessed and visited the barren, and the woman that had borne a number of children he set aside. He sets aside those who are full and perfectly content, and he takes the beggar off the dunghill so that he may sit him with princes.

David Gooding, The Problems of Becoming and Being a King: Fifteen Seminars on Major Themes in 1 & 2 Samuel, 21–2

25th March

OBEDIENCE IS THE PATH TO REIGNING WITH CHRIST

Reading: Hebrews 5:7–10

Son though he was, he learned obedience from what he suffered (Hebrews 5:8 DWG)

When the chronicler comes to describe the tremendous glories of the golden age of peace and plenty that occurred under David and then Solomon, he says that Solomon sat on the throne of the Lord (1 Chr 29:23). Beginning with Adam and following through the long travail of history, he comes to the point when at last a man sits on the throne of the Lord.

We all know that the golden age didn't last. We should perhaps be sitting here in a mood of pessimism did we not know that one day King David's greater son would be born. Jesus Christ the Lord was born in Bethlehem, crucified at Calvary and raised from the dead. We rejoice to think that our blessed Lord Jesus at this very moment sits in the absolute sense on the throne of the Lord. And then we allow ourselves to enjoy the stupendous fact that one day, according to the promise of the New Testament, if we overcome we shall sit down with him on his throne and reign with him for all eternity (see Rev 3:21).

There was a king before David—a king of Israel appointed by God to govern his people—but he never sat on the throne of the Lord. You'd be sorry for Saul, wouldn't you? Poor man, he never wanted to be king in the first place. He tried, but he never sat upon the throne of the Lord, and that was for an obvious reason. As king of Israel, Saul himself turned rebel against God. Given God's word to obey, Saul disobeyed and didn't keep it. How could God possibly put on the throne of the Lord a man who was prepared to disobey God to his very face?

Amidst all the wonderful euphoria of thinking how the church shall reign with Christ, we must remember the terms of salvation. In the days of his flesh, Son of God though he was, our blessed Lord Jesus learned obedience by the things that he suffered. Being made perfect and qualified, he became the author of salvation to those who obey him (see Heb 5:7–9). It is utterly unthinkable that God should ever put upon the throne of the Lord those who are not prepared to take his word seriously and obey it. How can he put on the throne of the Lord men and women who positively trespass against him?

David Gooding, *Mankind's Pathway to the Coming Age of Peace: Six Studies on the Overall Message of 1 Chronicles*, 15–16

26th March

SAUL'S TRAINING IN GOD'S GUIDANCE

Reading: 1 Samuel 9:1–24

*Some trust in chariots and some in horses, but we trust
in the name of the LORD our God. (Psalm 20:7)*

How on earth would Saul rule the people and bring them back to God? It wasn't that God didn't train him; and sometimes simple things get at the root of the matter. Saul's father had some donkeys that went astray. His father asked him to search for them, but wherever he went he couldn't find them. So he said to his servant, 'Let's go home.'

Said his servant, 'Well, sir, we're near to a city where there's a prophet. Shouldn't we consult the prophet, and therefore consult God?'

'Well,' said Saul, 'now we're here, we might as well.'

So they went up to the city and met some young women coming out to draw water.

'Could you tell us where the prophet is?' said Saul.

'Hurry,' they said, 'he's just ahead of you! We've got a feast today; the prophet is coming to bless the sacrifice and the people won't eat until he comes.' I hope Saul was listening, because that was part of his training. 'The people won't eat until he comes,' and they wouldn't sacrifice either.

As they were entering the city they met an elderly gentleman. 'I am the prophet; I was expecting you,' said Samuel. 'God told me last night that you were coming.'

'Really? Is life like that? Is there a living God who knows about me—and even about my stupid donkeys and the mess I'm in trying to find them?'

'God is going to give you the chief post of honour in the whole of Israel,' said Samuel. Did the message get hold of his heart, that the God who was calling him to be king was the God who was prepared to stand behind him? If Saul would learn to trust him, God would order the circumstances and bring back the donkeys. 'Don't worry about your donkeys. God knows where they are,' said Samuel. 'They've been found them and they're coming back.'

It was an extraordinary exhibition of the government and providence of God in this man's life. God was trying to teach him that if he was going to rule for him, he must know the rule of God in his own life. If ever he's going to get people to trust and obey the Lord, he must learn to trust and obey the Lord himself. With the responsibilities that were to be on his shoulders, sometimes it would be a big order to dare to trust the Lord.

David Gooding, *Mankind's Pathway to the Coming Age of Peace: Six Studies on the Overall Message of 1 Chronicles*, 16–18

27th March

SAUL'S FAILURE TO WAIT

Reading: 1 Samuel 13:8–14

To do righteousness and justice is more acceptable to
the LORD than sacrifice. (Proverbs 21:3)

Having been put through his schooling, Saul faced his examinations, and the first one was this:

> Then go down before me to Gilgal. And behold, I am coming to you to offer burnt offerings and to sacrifice peace offerings. Seven days you shall wait, until I come to you and show you what you shall do. (1 Sam 10:8)

Samuel said, 'Do you remember, Saul, when you were looking for me, the people wouldn't start the sacrifice until I came? This time, you are not to start the battle until I come and offer the sacrifice.'

But now here was Saul, and the Philistines were coming out in their battalions with all their armour. When the people of Israel saw them, they got collywobbles in the stomach and began to run away (13:5–7).

Saul said, 'What shall I do? I can't let the people run away from me. I shall be left without any people. I must start—where is this prophet?' But he didn't appear, and he seemed to be late. So Saul offered the burnt offering and was about to commit the people to battle when the prophet appeared. 'What have you done?' said Samuel. 'You have acted foolishly' (13:11–13).

Yes, he was a fool, wasn't he? You see, to start with, the Philistines weren't going to have any battle. They were just on manoeuvres; there never was a battle. And the second thing was that the Philistines were armed to the teeth, whereas the Israelites had very little more than a few, sort of, pea shooter things. If Saul had taken the armies into battle with the Philistines that day, Israel would have been cut to ribbons. How could God entrust the people of God to a man like that, who would jeopardize the lives of thousands of his followers simply because he couldn't trust God's word and do what God said?

If you were going into an operation to have a kidney taken out, and the anaesthetist didn't turn up and the surgeon said 'Well, no matter, I'll go ahead without the anaesthetist', would you appoint him as head of the college of surgeons?

If Saul couldn't keep the word of God, he wasn't to be entrusted with the lives of God's people.

David Gooding, *Mankind's Pathway to the Coming Age of Peace: Six Studies on the Overall Message of 1 Chronicles, 18–19*

28th March

SAUL'S FAILURE TO LISTEN AND OBEY

Reading: 1 Samuel 15:1–23

Behold, to obey is better than sacrifice, and to listen than the fat of rams. (1 Samuel 15:22)

A bigger test came for Saul. There was an outstanding enemy of the people of God and of God himself. When God was bringing Israel out of bondage in Egypt and taking them to their promised inheritance, the Amalekites said, 'No, you don't,' and they lifted up their hand in defiance, not only against Israel but against God's very throne itself. God swore that he would have war with them until Amalek was no more (Exod 17:16).

So the second test of Saul's kingship was this. Said the prophet in the name of God, 'I want you to go with your army and obliterate Amalek. Spare nothing' (see 1 Sam 15:3). It was a positive, clear command, and as the people returned from the battle with Saul at their head, Samuel went to meet him.

'How's it gone?' said Samuel.

'Very well,' said Saul, 'I have performed the commandment of the Lord' (15:13).

'You've done everything! Really? What's all this bleating of sheep and lowing of oxen that I hear?'

'Don't get upset, Samuel, for you know what the people are like. If I were to insist that they obey Scripture they might all forsake me. The people wanted to spare the best of the flocks, and what we propose to do is to offer them in sacrifice to God. Won't that be nice, Samuel?'

And Samuel said, 'Stop! Do you think you can carry on being king when you take an express command of almighty God to destroy the rebel that would overturn God's throne, and you compromise with him? Having disobeyed the command of the Lord and spared the rebel, do you suppose you're going to offer your disobedience as a sacrifice to God? You can no longer be king' (see 15:16–23).

It's true to the logic, isn't it? 'Man shall sit upon the throne of the Lord'; but on whose authority and on what conditions? Could the Lord have me sitting on his throne, only to find that I'm not even prepared to carry out his word?

Our Lord himself once observed the seriousness of those who are in office:

> Therefore whoever relaxes one of the least of these commandments and teaches others to do the same will be called least in the kingdom of heaven, but whoever does them and teaches them will be called great in the kingdom of heaven. (Matt 5:19)

David Gooding, *Mankind's Pathway to the Coming Age of Peace: Six Studies on the Overall Message of 1 Chronicles*, 19–20

29th March

FRUSTRATING GOD'S GOVERNMENT IN OUR LIVES

Reading: 1 Corinthians 11:27–32

*Let a person examine himself, then, and so eat of the
bread and drink of the cup. (1 Corinthians 11:28)*

We can frustrate the government of God by failure to cooperate with him. In his divine sovereignty, God allows us the initiative to examine and judge ourselves. I must surely know that there are many things in my life that are not yet as they should be, and I must pray that God will search me and see if there be any wicked way in me (see Ps 139:23–24).

As I take that holy cup at the Lord's Supper, the cup of the new covenant, and hear him say that he will write his laws on my heart, I must cooperate with him. 'Lord, show me if there is something in my heart that still goes against your laws. Help me to seek your Spirit's power to correct it.'

Suppose I fail to discern it, come idly and take that cup of his covenant which expresses his government, and I myself am not too seriously concerned to see that his kingdom in my life extends as it should. Then I am frustrating his purpose, and in faithfulness to his covenant he will take me in hand and discipline me. For it is he who has made the covenant, and he will write the laws (Heb 10:16). He will do it with my cooperation if he can; but if he can't, he'll still do it.

If I'm not careful I can also frustrate his government in the lives of other people. Some of the early Christians were very good at that. They were forever interfering in other people's lives where they ought to have kept out. There are some things where God's word is abundantly clear, and God has explicitly made clear what should be done. But there are other areas of life where God's word has not declared itself explicitly and in detail. Those areas, it seems to me, have been left deliberately. It is not that God didn't foresee things like television, and therefore forgot to tell us whether we ought to have it or not; whether we ought to eat beef or vegetables, and so on. In these things God's desire is that each individual should be exercised in heart, taking his or her own personal decisions solemnly and responsibly before God, so that, in making up their mind over all these details, each person might have personal, practical experience of the government of God.

David Gooding, *King of kings and Lord of lords: Four Studies Exploring God's Sovereignty Over Various Spheres*, 17

30th March

THE LORD WILL JUDGE

Reading: James 2:8–13

And if you call on him as Father who judges impartially according to each one's deeds, conduct yourselves with fear throughout the time of your exile. (1 Peter 1:17)

This is a very solemn subject and liable to dampen our spirits more than the weather; but it is obviously a topic that we cannot afford to overlook. Indeed, as an incentive, it is a tremendous help for me to remember that one day I must stand before the Lord Jesus as judge. Let us then take as our motto the advice that James gives, 'So speak and so act as those who are to be judged under the law of liberty' (2:12).

It seems to me that we could do with reminding ourselves of this topic now and again. Perhaps by failing to remember it we sometimes have gone astray and brought public disgrace upon the Lord. Sometimes the very way we preach the gospel fosters the idea that we won't have to stand before the Lord Jesus as judge. 'He is our saviour,' we say, and we tell the unconverted, 'Decide tonight, for tonight the Lord Jesus offers himself as your saviour and as your advocate!'

We know what we mean, of course; and as far as we mean it our gospel is true. We are pointing out that, because the Lord Jesus has died for us and borne the penalty of our sin, 'there is therefore now no condemnation for those who are in Christ Jesus' (Rom 8:1). We shall never have to bear the terrible curse and penalty of sin, for Christ bore that penalty for us when he was forsaken of God at Calvary and 'bore our sins in his body on the tree' (1 Pet 2:24).

But we would be wrong to give the unconverted person the idea that once he has trusted Christ he will never have to face him as judge in any sense—that would be untrue. We need to balance our preaching by the other side, 'If you call on him as Father who judges impartially according to each one's deeds, conduct yourselves with fear throughout the time of your exile' (1 Pet 1:17). The Father judges! It doesn't matter who you are, whether you are rich or poor, a young convert or an experienced and mature elder, it makes no difference to God when it comes to judgment. 'The Father judges without respect of persons,' says Peter, 'and he judges every man according to his work.' He has every right to judge, hasn't he?

David Gooding, A Vision of the Perfect Man and Woman: Seven Studies on Major Themes from James, 33–4

31st March

THE PRINCIPLE OF MERCY

Reading: 2 Timothy 1:13–18

For judgment is without mercy to one who has shown no mercy. Mercy triumphs over judgment. (James 2:13)

So we come to this great principle that at the judgment seat of Christ there will be mercy. That could sound very strange to you, because you may have been attracted by that rather shallow definition that is sometimes bandied around when people say 'grace is giving people what they don't deserve'—salvation is by grace, and so you get the gift of salvation although you didn't deserve it. And then, 'mercy is withholding what you did deserve'—you deserve eternal hell, and by God's mercy you have been saved from it. That sounds very nice and neat; but if you hold that definition you will say, 'Why would any believer need mercy at the judgment seat of Christ?'

Mercy does not always mean withholding some terrible thing that you have merited; the word mercy in Scripture is wider than that. It means 'compassion' (see Luke 10, Matt 20). Our blessed Lord will never be less than just. By his very nature he reserves the right to be more than just and to show mercy and be generous.

You will need mercy at the judgment seat of Christ! What Paul says in 2 Timothy should convince us of that fact: 'Onesiphorus . . . often refreshed me and was not ashamed of my chains, but when he arrived in Rome he searched for me earnestly and found me—may the Lord grant him to find mercy from the Lord on that Day!' (2 Tim 1:16–18). Paul is not praying that the Lord would show this man mercy now in this life; he is praying that God will show him mercy 'on that day', the day when the Lord comes. I am glad it is so. When I stand before the judgment seat of Christ, if I get simply what strict justice would give me, how little I would get!

Because the Holy Spirit is available to the youngest convert, would you say that he or she must overcome all sinful tendencies overnight? No, the Lord is gracious in his assessment of what is possible, and he will be merciful. The trouble is that I have been a believer for some fifty-five years and so have less excuse. I pray that the Lord will be merciful when he assesses my reward and place in his kingdom.

But that lays on me an urgent consideration. If I want him to be merciful to me then, I had better start being merciful now. The Lord loves to be merciful in his judgment. When it comes to our judging the behaviour of our fellow-believers, may God save us from an overly censorious and critical spirit.

David Gooding, *A Vision of the Perfect Man and Woman: Seven Studies on Major Themes from James*, 40–2

1st April

THE SPIRIT OF SONSHIP

Reading: Galatians 4:8–11, 28–31

For you did not receive the spirit of slavery to fall back into fear, but you have received the Spirit of adoption as sons, by whom we cry, 'Abba! Father!' (Romans 8:15)

How does a slave go about his work? Well, many slaves went about their work through fear. So they did the minimum of work, and did it resentfully. We have not received the spirit of slavery to fall back into fear (Rom 8:15). We may say in passing, if believers ever find themselves driven by excessive fear, they might know at once that it is not the Holy Spirit. The Holy Spirit will provoke reverential fear of God, but not unhealthy fear and panic. We have received the Spirit of adoption as God's dear sons.

When I was a child, if we ran in from the garden with muddy shoes across the floor that mother had recently hoovered, means were brought to bear to dissuade us from that action. In a way we were no better than slaves, in that we had to be, kind of, driven to it. But when we grew up, it was different. Why? Because we were grown-up sons; we had come to value the home just as our parents valued it, and we didn't want to muddy the carpet.

My brothers and sisters, God isn't going to fill heaven with a lot of slaves: people saying, 'What, another prayer meeting in heaven? Do I have to come? Do I have to listen to God's word?'

There will be no slaves in heaven. God's business is to produce sons who share the nature, attitude and outlook of their father, and do his will. Therefore, they give evidence that they are sons of their Father. Being led by the Spirit (Rom 8:14) is not just a matter of 'What shall I do in life?'—although obviously it comes to that, as well as other things. Being led by the Spirit is to behave as sons and daughters of God are meant to behave. That's how the Spirit leads us.

Notice then what it says: 'but if by the Spirit you put to death the deeds of the body, you will live' (Rom 8:13). We need that healthy balance. As grown-up sons and daughters of God, we are to take responsibility ourselves to deal with the misbehaviour of the various members of our bodies. That's important, isn't it? It's not an irresponsible 'letting go' and seeing what happens next. If we are sons and daughters, the Holy Spirit exhorts us to put to death the [wrong] deeds of the body.

David Gooding, *Obtaining the Goal of Salvation: Three Studies on the Work of the Holy Spirit*, 32–3

2nd April

THE PRINCIPLE OF PRIVATE PROPERTY

Reading: 2 Samuel 12:1–14

Now the full number of those who believed were of one heart and soul, and no one said that any of the things that belonged to him was his own, but they had everything in common. (Acts 4:32)

There are those who would tell us that it is an essential part of Christianity, when you get converted, to give away all your private property. Of course, it's not true. In the early days of the Acts, some of the early Christians voluntarily gave away their property. But not even to Ananias and Sapphira did Peter say, 'Look here, your sin is dreadful; if you are a Christian you ought not to have any private property.'

Of course he didn't. It is a fundamental principle of life. Consider how fearful it would be if a man and his wife were both the common property of anyone who liked to come and take them. How long would the concept of love survive in such a society?

In the ancient world many oriental monarchs, including King David, committed serious offences. But, unlike him, most didn't repent and put it on public record that they'd done wrong. It was an extraordinary thing that, as king, David would confess himself to be a guilty sinner for having stolen the wife of one of his soldiers (2 Sam 12:13; Ps 51). God's concept of power is that, if the man on the throne abuses his power and destroys your right to private property, God will judge him. God himself insists upon the right to private property and he will never deprive you of your basic personal right to it.

You say, 'What do you mean?'

You have a free will, haven't you? God loves you, but he will never overrule your free will and take you without your consent. If you persist in saying no to God's advances, God will respect your choice and your decision forever.

That's God's concept of government. For David to abuse his power and rob a man of his wife, that most sacred element in his private property, and then also rob him of his life—it was such an outrageous slander on the character of God who anointed him as king that God had to deal with him. Where David was not acting as 'a man after [God's] own heart' (1 Sam 13:14), the world must be told.

David Gooding, *Governing for God: Four Studies in 2 Samuel on the Major Stages of David's Life*, 33–4

3rd April

GOD'S PROVIDENCE

Reading: Job 1:6–12

'The words of the holy one, the true one,
who has the key of David, who opens and no one will shut,
who shuts and no one opens.' (Revelation 3:7)

We cannot understand all the mysteries of providence; why God allows certain things in our lives, and why his enemies so often seem to triumph. Yet we comfort our hearts in the thought that it is no accident and God remains in supreme control, even of his enemies. When he says, 'Stop,' they stop. Indeed, they have to get his permission to start.

You will remember what our Lord said to his apostles in the upper room: 'Satan hath desired to have you, that he may sift you as wheat' (Luke 22:31 KJV). 'Desired', is old English for 'asked', from which it appears that Satan cannot just assault the people of God at his whim and pleasure, but must ask permission of almighty God. God normally maintains a hedge about his people.

The same thing is said in the book of Job (1:6–12), as Satan comes accusingly into the presence of God. 'Does Job fear God for no reason? Have you not put a hedge around him and his house and all that he has, on every side? . . . take the hedge away and let me get at him and he will curse you to your face.' God gave permission to Satan, without which he could have done nothing. That surely is a comfort.

Similarly, it is an encouragement, as we read the words of the living Lord addressing his churches about the persecution that was to come upon them: 'Behold, the devil is about to throw some of you into prison, that you may be tested, and for ten days you will have tribulation' (Rev 2:10). Even before it happened, the time was already set.

And then again in the matter of their pioneer evangelism: '[He] has the key of David, the one who opens and no one can shut, and who shuts and no one can open' (Rev 3:7). What a lovely thing it is to hear in our hearts the jangling of the keys on the belt of our blessed Lord. It is not ours to question the strategies of almighty God. There are now vast countries under Muslim sway that seem to have been penetrated so little, with wave after wave of missionary endeavour apparently falling back. We must not loosen our hold on the glorious fact that ultimately our Lord holds the key of David, and when he opens the door no one can shut it.

David Gooding, An Offer of Restoration: Four Studies on God's Character in Zechariah, 14–15

4th April

GOD'S GUIDANCE

Reading: Ezekiel 34:11–16

In all your ways acknowledge him, and he will make straight your paths. (Proverbs 3:6)

Isn't it strange how some people will twist even the loveliest things! In my youth I turned the matter of guidance into a miserable bondage of law; rather than treating it as a delightful gospel.

I heard a sister tell of extraordinary providences that made me as jealous as could be. I said to myself, 'Well of course, you have to be a super-duper saint before that kind of guidance would ever come your way.' So I set out to be that super-duper saint. But the guidance didn't come, and I thought what a desperately difficult thing life is. My silly mistake was to look on guidance as something that you'll only succeed in if you are of special excellence. Whereas God's guidance is not law, but gospel.

Here is a shepherd who has brought a sheep into his field to eat grass. The sheep is going here and there about the field eating the grass, and the shepherd is delighted. So long as the sheep is within what the shepherd intends, he sees no need to give any special guidance. If it started going too dangerously near a precipice, the shepherd might throw a clod of earth at it—as I've seen in the Middle East—warning the sheep not to go in that direction. And if it was given to going through holes, the shepherd might put a barrier across them. But ordinarily the sheep would go about its business, secure in the knowledge that there is a shepherd whose eye never closes, enjoying the security of knowing it is being watched.

My brother and sister, your shepherd doesn't have to be implored before he'll guide you, because his eye is always on you. The shepherd who gave his life's blood for you watches you moment by moment. Wouldn't we be wise to keep in touch with him constantly? His guidance of us is not a burdensome law but a glorious gospel.

David Gooding, *Daring to be Different: Seven Studies from Acts on Defining and Defending Christianity*, 62

5th April

GOD'S LEADING IN LYDIA'S LIFE

Reading: Acts 16:11–15

*You will seek me and find me, when you seek me
with all your heart. (Jeremiah 29:13)*

Lydia was born in Thyatira, a city famous for its production of purple dye. What brought her to Philippi? Trade, apparently. She had to earn a living like anyone else, and naturally enough she had learned the purple trade in her home city. Being a Roman colony, Philippi would have had plenty of people with sufficient money to spend on this expensive textile. Inscriptions tell us that there was in fact a guild of purple merchants in that city. So she went there to set herself up in the import and retail trade. Her business prospered, and when she was converted she had a house big enough to accommodate Paul and all his companions (Acts 16:15).

We may be sure that none of this was mere accident. The God who determines where we live had watched over her birth, her growth, her choice of career, her emigration to Philippi and the prosperity of her business which would eventually play a part in the evangelization of Europe. Even so, she might never have met Paul. We do not know where she had become a worshipper of the true God, whether it was in her home city of Thyatira or after she came to Philippi (16:14). We do know, however, that in Philippi she attended 'a place of prayer' by the riverside (perhaps an embryonic Jewish synagogue). Through the Jews she had discovered that there is only one God, and as we see from her regular attendance at this humble place of prayer, she had personally set her heart to seek the true and living God.

The transcendent Lord, who knows the hearts of all, read her longings and heard her prayers. Unknown to Paul and his companions, God had directed them on their long journey to meet Lydia and satisfy her quest. He did more: he opened her heart to respond to Paul's message. Only when you have had a similar experience will you recognize what this means. The illumination of the Spirit grips the attention and fills the mind with the intuitive awareness and certainty that what you are hearing is the very word of God being spoken directly and personally by the Lord to your heart.

And Lydia responded by believing in the Lord Jesus. She had met the God she sought.

David Gooding, *True to the Faith: The Acts of the Apostles—Defining and Defending the Gospel*, 311–12

6th April

GOD'S GUIDANCE OF ELIEZER'S WAY

Reading: Genesis 24:10–27

The man bowed his head and worshipped the LORD and said, 'Blessed be the LORD, the God of my master Abraham, who has not forsaken his steadfast love and his faithfulness towards my master.' (Genesis 24:26–27)

It was no small task to find a wife for Isaac, so the servant came at length to a place and used his common sense and judgment. When he met these young women, he asked one of them to give him a drink, and she not only gave him a drink but volunteered to draw water for his camels as well!

Presently he enquired who she might be, and found she was none other than a distant relative of the very same family as Abraham. In that moment the servant saw something of the wonder and the faithfulness of God (vv. 26–27). Do you notice what the man is saying? He's not saying, 'O God, how marvellously kind of you to have picked someone so glorious looking!' It wasn't her beauty that the servant was looking at; he had caught a vivid sight of the faithfulness of God and the wonder of his providence that controls our lives behind the scenes.

When the going is difficult and for months on end we see no evidence of the divine hand and our duties almost overwhelm us, yet we see that God has been planning for our good. He has been faithful and merciful to us all along.

Oh the wonder of it, that the God of heaven should descend to such a small detail and guide that man so precisely. Think of the places he could have gone to, the young women who would have been willing to say yes. God is big, yet his providences concern themselves so precisely and he is faithful and true. In that moment it was as though a veil had been drawn aside and he saw into the very heart of God.

I don't know what blessings have come your way this week. I know you have been grateful for them, and from time to time it's not so much for the gift as the insight it gives you into the wonder of God's providence, the precision of his timings and the sense of his faithfulness.

David Gooding, *The Adoration of Christ: Six Studies on the Nature and Practice of Worship*, 7

Part 7

The God of Love and Grace

7th April

GOD COMMENDED HIS LOVE TO US WHILE WE WERE STILL SINNERS

Reading: Romans 5:6–11

But God commends his love toward us, in that, while we were yet sinners, Christ died for us. (Romans 5:8 KJV)

What would you like God to give you? Go on, think of something big. Would you like a whole cluster of stars to look after? It wouldn't impoverish the almighty God to give you ten thousand galaxies; to him that would be a very small thing. The biggest thing that God will ever do for you, he has already done. He gave his Son for you.

Ponder it. Exactly when did he give his Son for us? Did God say, 'I can see those folks are really doing their best, so perhaps it wouldn't be too extravagant of me at this stage to give my Son for them'?

The whole point is that it was while we were still weak, while we were still sinners, while we were enemies that God gave his Son for us. Here is the Holy Spirit arguing with us. He has to do that sometimes, doesn't he? When we prefer to trust our feelings, or anything else, rather than rest in the very unchangeable character of God, the Holy Spirit has to argue against our emotions and against our fear, and point us to this foundational thing: God gave his Son for us *while we were still weak*.

All sin is the same in one sense, but it has these different forms and symptoms. Sometimes it's *weakness*, sometimes it's *ungodliness*—lack of reverence for God or respect for man. Sometimes it's *missing the mark*, sometimes it's positive *enmity against God*. Yes, 'God commends his love toward us.'

What a . . . I nearly said, what a *humiliation* for almighty God! Have you ever had a salesman come to your door, and you didn't want the brooms and the polishes? The poor chap needs to make a little profit and he puts his foot in the door so that you have to listen to what he has to say. He's commending his wares to you.

I find it astonishing that God comes to recommend, to *commend* his love to us. Just imagine it, my dear fellow believer. Almighty God is standing at the door of your heart, commending his love to you: praising its virtues and extolling its details. This is a picture of the Holy Spirit pouring out God's love into our hearts.

David Gooding, *Obtaining the Goal of Salvation: Three Studies on the Work of the Holy Spirit*, 12

8th April

LOVE MADE MANIFEST

Reading: 1 John 4:7–12

In this was manifested the love of God toward us, because that God sent his only begotten Son into the world, that we might live through him. (1 John 4:9 KJV)

It is easier to grasp what love is if we can first see it by an actual example. For instance, here is a nine-year-old boy and he's been plaguing his father to buy him a bicycle for Christmas. But money is scarce, and there are bills for the gas and coal unpaid. So father and mother save what they can, and when Larry comes down on Christmas morning, there is a new bicycle waiting for him. When the boy sees it, he gets the point that they love him because he can actually see something in it.

Give him another twenty years and he's got a child of his own. At Christmas time, when money is a bit short, he'll look back and say, 'Ah, dad and mum hadn't much then, and yet they bought me a bike.' Now he will begin to see the problems involved in loving. But first it had to be in the manifestation, and then behind the scenes to the principle.

And so it is here. 'In this was manifested the love of God.' How was it manifested? *God has sent His only begotten Son*: a gift that God deliberately gave and will never withdraw. He didn't merely sit in heaven and talk to us about love, but he put that love into action and sent his Son. Notice those extra three words, *into the world*. Love always wants to come as near as possible. 'Herein is love' (v. 10): God has sent his Son into the world—as far into the world as he could possibly send him. He'd come a long way by the time he was born in flesh and blood. Who can measure the distance when the Word, who was absolutely God, became flesh and dwelt among us (John 1:14)?

But he went further than that. Not only was he made like his brothers in every respect (Heb 2:17), but he went right into the world until the Pharisees thought he'd gone too far. They said, 'Why does he eat with tax collectors and sinners?' (Mark 2:16). Those Pharisees understood so little of the heart of God. He sent his Son as near to all human beings as he could possibly get: he sent him, not into the church but *into the world*.

David Gooding, *Love is from God: One Study on 1 John 4:7–21*, 5–6

9th April

CHRIST CAME DOWN

Reading: John 6:25–40

*'For I have come down from heaven, not to do my own will
but the will of him who sent me.'* (John 6:38)

Some years ago the mountain guides in Switzerland gave notice that if anybody was so foolish as to try and climb the north face of the Eiger in wintertime, and then got stuck, the guides would not come to rescue them. Two mountaineers decided to brave the challenge and try it, and they got stuck. Watching them from the other side of the valley, the guides said, 'We're not going to risk our lives to rescue fools like that.'

A Frenchman heard of it and got together an international team of mountaineers. They took the train up the side of Eiger, walked the rest to the shoulder, and got to the top. They had a great winch with them and put it as near the edge as they could. They couldn't see the men hundreds of feet below them; they had to be guided by lights from the hotel across the valley. One man volunteered to be tied to the rope and go to reach at least one of the men. He took a mountain cradle and stretcher with him. They let him down, down, down, until he came level with the man, but he was some feet away. With the man nearly mad with terror he had to leave him, and signalled to those aloft to bring him up. Then they took the risk of changing the position of the great winch and the man went down again, right where the man was in all his manic struggles and fears. Putting the man on the stretcher and the stretcher on his back, he signalled to his friends to haul them up. Putting his feet on the face of the mountain and leaning back with that heavy load, he walked up the north face of the Eiger to the top.

What a faint little picture this is of the marvel of God's grace in the gospel. When we were weak, godless and sinful, when we were even enemies of God, the Saviour came exactly where we were, and he still comes to us exactly where we are, pleading for us to repent of our own inabilities and cast ourselves on his mercy. Through faith in Jesus Christ and his substitutionary death, we find forgiveness with God, eternal life, and the power by God's grace to live for the Saviour who loved us and gave himself for us.

David Gooding, *The Heart of the Gospel: Two Studies on Keeping the Cross at the Centre*, 8

10th April

CHRIST ANNOUNCES THE ACCEPTABLE YEAR OF THE LORD

Reading: Matthew 11:1–10

The Spirit of the Lord is upon me, because he has anointed me to proclaim good news to the poor. He has sent me to proclaim liberty to the captives and recovering of sight to the blind, to set at liberty those who are oppressed. (Luke 4:18)

It is almost impossible to exaggerate the importance of the point that Christ was making so dramatically here. He was the Messiah; his coming had instituted the year of the Lord's favour; but it had not begun the day of vengeance. At this stage in history he had no intention of executing the wrath of God upon evil men or evil societies and institutions.

For many people, particularly those who believed in him, this was a shock and a disappointment; especially when they found out what it would mean. John the Baptist had announced that the Christ would do two things: not only would he impart God's Holy Spirit to those who believed, but he would also burn up the chaff with unquenchable fire (Luke 3:16–17). The expectation was true: Christ will one day execute the wrath of God (see 2 Thess 1:7–10). But John's disappointment seems to have arisen from the mistaken idea that Christ would immediately proceed to put down evil and destroy unrepentant men. In the name of the coming Christ, John had denounced Herod's sins, and Herod, unrepentant, had John imprisoned. John therefore apparently expected Christ to come, chastise Herod and release him; and when Christ made no attempt to do so, John was disappointed (see Luke 7:18–23). He had to be reassured that the fulfilment of the prophetic programme had not failed, ceased or gone astray.

It was not that evil was so powerfully entrenched and Christ and his followers so few and weak that it was not prudent just yet to attack Herod and try to break his power. Christ had no intention of overthrowing Herod's political power in order to open John's prison door, nor of executing judgment on Herod or on any other evil men. He had come to institute the year of the Lord's favour, the purpose of which was the proclamation of the gospel and the provision of a way of escape from the wrath to come. Not until that year was over (and God's merciful longsuffering would see to it that it was a very long year) would the comparatively short, sharp day of vengeance come.

David Gooding, *According to Luke: The Third Gospel's Ordered Historical Narrative*, 83–4

11th April

THE TRUE GOD IS KNOWN IN SACRIFICE

Reading: Psalm 94:3–11

If the LORD *is God, follow him. (1 Kings 18:21)*

How can we prove that Jehovah is God, so that we may know it in our very hearts and fearlessly dare to give our lives utterly and solely over to him?

Well, you know how Elijah proved it. He assembled the people on Mount Carmel, told the priests of Baal to build their altar, put their sacrifice on it and call upon Baal. So they called upon Baal, but there was no answer.

There are some folks nowadays who tell us there is no Creator and the universe just happened. You may believe that, but in the day of your need, when you call upon the atoms and the cosmic rays to hear you, no voice will come back. When the human heart asks if there is some real meaning to life and, if there is a God will he speak to me, how shall I know who the true God is? The answer is a sacrifice. In Elijah's day, the sacrifice was laid on the altar, and when he called on the God of heaven, Jehovah sent down fire and consumed the sacrifice. Everyone knew that it was God. In our day, it is still a sacrifice, but how can I know that Jesus is the Son of God?

John the apostle tells us this, to start with: 'This is he who came by water *and blood*' (1 John 5:6 emphasis added). The second half of that phrase means that when Jesus Christ came into our world, it was announced from the very start that he was the Lamb of God who had come to take away the sin of the world (John 1:29). Nobody else ever claimed that. There were prophets galore who exhorted us to be good. But our trouble is that we haven't been good. We have sinned against ourselves and against others, and our hearts are from time to time harried with guilt.

There has been only one in the whole of human history who has ever suggested an answer adequate to the need. 'He came by blood', to tell us that sin matters and must be judged by the fire of God's wrath. Ah, but also to tell us that the true God is the one who sent the fire from heaven; not on those guilty people standing around but on the sacrifice; and Calvary is where I find the true God of heaven.

David Gooding, Keys to Revival: Three Studies from 1–2 Kings on the Leadership of Elijah, Jehoiada and Josiah, 8–9

12th April

PROPITIATION

Reading: Leviticus 16

'There I will meet with you, and from above the mercy seat, from between the two cherubim that are on the ark of the testimony, I will speak with you.' (Exodus 25:22)

Propitiation is perhaps one of the hardest New Testament words to get a hold of. We could best illustrate it to our minds by going back to the Old Testament, to the wonderful ceremonies that clustered around the Day of Atonement.

God said, 'I'm holding the Day of Atonement because all through the year the sins of my people have been defiling my tabernacle. By rights of the law, when I look at their sins I oughtn't to stay among them. I am a holy God who cannot tolerate the presence of sin, and the idea of remaining in their midst and being in contact with people who are constantly sinful is abhorrent to me.' His own holy character was repelled by it.

Then how could God stay among those Israelites? The answer is that year by year blood was shed, brought to the ark, the very throne of God, and sprinkled on *the mercy seat*—the place of propitiation. 'And there, where the blood is shed,' says God, 'I will meet with you, and from above the mercy seat, between the two cherubim that are on the ark of the testimony, I will speak with you.' The blood cleansed the tabernacle so that God might remain among them in all their defilement (see Heb 9:21–22).

Day in and day out, night in and night out, the presence of blood on that mercy seat made it possible for God to stay there. When anyone sinned, but hadn't the slightest notion that what they'd done was sin, and certainly they hadn't repented, God could remain among the people because of the blood on the propitiatory seat.

The Lord Jesus sat with tax collectors and sinners, and now I begin to see how his heart was feeling, when every fibre in his being raged against sin. Through what happened on the cross, God was determined to come near to sinners. Though they beat his Son in the face, clawed the hair from his cheeks and stripped and scourged him, God said, 'I want to come near them'. And the blood that stains the mercy seat today was cudgelled out of God's Son and speared by the hands of sinful men. In this is love, that God so loves sinners that he found a way of being near them, cost what it might.

David Gooding, *Love is from God: One Study on 1 John 4:7–21, 7–9*

13th April

LOVE AND PUNISHMENT

Reading: 2 Samuel 14:12–21

For Christ also suffered once for sins, the righteous for the unrighteous, that he might bring us to God. (1 Peter 3:18)

We find David involved in a very difficult case of discipline. His son Absalom murdered his half-brother, and then ran away to escape punishment. This raised the question of whether David would insist on punishment, or whether with time he would bring Absalom back without any punishment. We often hear the case that punishment in and of itself is offensive and ought to be put aside in the name of love and charity. That raises some very large questions: *what is the relationship of love to punishment, and punishment to love?*

We see David won over by the *permissive* argument on punishment and he brings Absalom home again. But one of the greatest horrors in David's life was when the son whom he had brought back and excused from all punishment, led a revolt against his father, and nearly threw him off the throne. *Unjudged sin has terrible potential.*

David was torn in two, between his responsibility as a king to destroy the rebel, and his concern as a father to save his son. How would you solve the problem?

A similar problem has beset the very throne of God. God Almighty himself has suffered an enormous offence, and not only here on earth but in high places as well. Earth unfortunately has become involved in this rebellion against God and his government. That raises the problem that lies at the very heart of the universe, the question of punishment and law. *Are punishment and law irreconcilable opposites to love?*

God himself has only been able to solve it by by the extreme and drastic measure of giving his own Son to die a rebel death.

The central message of the gospel is that God loved us and did not spare his own Son, but gave him up for us all so that we might be truly reconciled with God. So what is the significance of the cross of Christ? *Is it right to talk of the sufferings of Christ in terms of him being punished by God?*

Liberal thought says no. Liberal thought believes in a God who wouldn't punish anybody. But then, if God wouldn't punish anybody, you can see at once that that changes the whole significance and interpretation of the death of Jesus Christ on Calvary.

David Gooding, *Governing for God: Four Studies in 2 Samuel on the Major Stages of David's Life*, 28

14th April

LOVE ONE ANOTHER

Reading: 1 John 4:7–21

Beloved, let us love one another, for love is from God, and whoever loves has been born of God and knows God. (1 John 4:7)

Love is not some sugary sentiment. It certainly isn't winking at sin or condoning sin, but it is a willingness to accept others when their sinfulness and awkwardness cut and bruise and hurt. Says God, 'Do you not remember how it hurt and cut and wounded me to keep you, and to guarantee that you will never be cast out?' This is what it means to love, accepting the other person as he or she is.

The love of God is such a wonderful thing. Right from the start of our Christian experience we gained some glimmerings of it, and it is a matter that we shall constantly be pursuing and only gradually getting to know. It doesn't mean, of course, that God doesn't already love us perfectly; but it does mean that we don't always see and appreciate God's love, or understand it. There are times when we still doubt his love, when we find it hard to reconcile with our circumstances, and there may come times as believers when we doubt whether God has really accepted us. When we've blotted our copy books more than we had ever expected to, sometimes we wonder whether at last it has taken God by surprise and diminished some of his love for us.

'Then,' says the apostle, 'let us learn to give ourselves to those exercises which day by day will make it easier for us to comprehend God's love.' But how shall we do that? The simple answer is by trying to learn how to love one another.

You say, 'What's that got to do with it?'

Well, in the first place, *all* love is from God. But love is an activity: it isn't merely a state, a nice sort of a feeling. The best way to find out what electricity is and what it does is for the wire to let the electricity come through and make a light at the other end. And because all love is from God, if you will know God's love in its fullness, says John, then be a sort of a wire and let the current of God's love come through you.

David Gooding, *Love is from God: One Study on 1 John 4:7–21*, 9–10

15th April

THE PRINCIPLE OF LOVE

Reading: 1 Corinthians 13

Let brotherly love continue. (Hebrews 13:1)

Do you hope to get a reward and reign with the Lord Jesus in his kingdom when he comes again? Of course you do! Then it will have to be according to the laws of the kingdom. The royal law proceeds according to this ancient scripture, which has not changed, 'You shall love your neighbour as yourself' (Lev 19:18).

James exhorts us to remember that in the law we are called upon to observe, it is not enough to do one part and neglect other parts.

> For whoever keeps the whole law but fails in one point has become accountable for all of it. For he who said, 'Do not commit adultery', also said, 'Do not murder.' If you do not commit adultery but do murder, you have become a transgressor of the law. (Jas 2:10–11)

Many of us have preached it to the unconverted, wanting to bring them to repentance. Now and again it can be quite a healthy thing to preach our gospel sermons to ourselves!

James is talking here to believers about the royal law (v. 8), and it is not a lesser standard than the Old Testament. Our Lord himself declared that there were two great commandments embodied in the principles of Old Testament law: 'You shall love the Lord your God with all your heart and with all your soul and with all your mind. This is the great and first commandment. And a second is like it: You shall love your neighbour as yourself' (Matt 22:37–40). And then he reinterpreted it, 'A new commandment I give to you, that you love one another: just as I have loved you, you also are to love one another' (John 13:34). What heights he has put before us!

Paul would say the same when it comes to using my gift for the Lord. 'If I have knowledge (and know all things), and if I have faith (so I could remove mountains), but have not love, I am nothing' (see 1 Cor 13:2). Not seventy-five percent. Nothing! Do you feel the earth beginning to quake under your feet? *If I have not love, I am nothing.*

How carefully and honestly I must review my work before the Lord, if I want to pass his judgment in a coming day. God is not going to have people occupying thrones and ruling others, if they did not learn on earth to serve according to the basic principles of the kingdom.

David Gooding, *A Vision of the Perfect Man and Woman: Seven Studies on Major Themes from James*, 38–40

16th April

SEEKING SPIRITUAL GIFTS

Reading: 1 Corinthians 12:27–31

Pursue love, and earnestly desire the spiritual gifts, especially that you may prophesy. (1 Corinthians 14:1)

There's no need for us to feel that we must each have all the gifts there are. I have one gift, you have another. I can't say I don't need your gift; any more than my hand can say it doesn't need my foot. That's nonsense. Every single member is needed and every gift is needed.

'But,' you say, 'once we have become Christians and are members of the body of Christ, is there no room for seeking other gifts?' Yes, there is; we are to 'earnestly desire the spiritual gifts,' said the Apostle Paul. Just like my hand has a general gift of grasping things—it can learn to grasp a pen, a paintbrush or the wheel of a car—so it is possible for us to seek gifts, abilities and faculties. And if it so pleases God, he may add them to us.

But let us again be humble enough to listen to God telling us the motive that should be ours when we seek extra gifts. We must see to it that our preeminent motive is love, for the simple reason that the whole purpose of a gift is to help others.

What would you think of me at the breakfast table tomorrow, if I had Kellogg's Cornflakes and I didn't swallow the stuff? My stomach says, 'Pass it on, pass it on.' 'No,' says my mouth, 'I'm going to do it for my own sake.' That would be nonsense. Certainly, the mouth enjoys the Cornflakes; but the whole purpose of the operation is to get the stuff to my stomach and for my stomach to pass it on to all the rest.

In the exercise of your gift you will be edified, but that wasn't the purpose of giving it to you. The purpose of the gift is to help others, and if you seek a gift without the motive of helping others you are sinning against the basic principle of life.

'Earnestly desire the higher gifts . . . especially that you may prophesy' (1 Cor 12:31; 14:1), because prophecy helps others. If you've got a gift that doesn't help others, be very careful how you use it, lest you offend against the basic spiritual principle of love.

David Gooding, Christ Living in You: One Study on the Gift and Gifts of the Holy Spirit, 11–13

17th April

GREATER LOVE HAS NO ONE THAN THIS

Reading: John 15:9–17

*'This is my commandment, that you love one
another as I have loved you.' (John 15:12)*

We must make sure we have understood the point of the statement of basic principle that Christ is teaching when he says: 'Greater love has no one than this, that someone lay down his life for his friends' (15:13). Some have thought that our Lord was pointing out how superior his love was to the very best love that mere men are capable of: greater love has no *one* than this, that someone lay down his life for his *friends*; whereas *Christ* loved and gave his life for his *enemies*. Now it is true that Christ died for us while we were still his enemies (Rom 5:6–10), but that was not the point of our Lord's statement in John 15. For here Christ was talking to those who were already his friends, as verse 14 makes clear; and obviously he was not telling them that while he loved them to some extent, he loved his enemies even more.

No, the context is that our Lord had just commanded his disciples that they must love one another, as he had loved them (v. 12); and therefore he must now explain what the extent of their love for one another would have to be, if they were going to love each other after the pattern of his love for them. Love can go no further than to lay down its life for others; and this, and nothing less than this, was the extent to which their love must be prepared to go.

That being so, we must obviously take care to understand what is implied by the phrase 'to lay down one's life for one's friends'. It can, of course, mean literally 'to die for one's friends'. Christ literally laid down his life for us on the cross; and there may come times when we are called upon to literally lay down our lives for the sake of our fellow-believers. Or, at least, to be prepared to lay down our lives for them.

Normally, however, we are not called to heroic action of that kind but to something that may in fact be far more difficult: to the laying down of our lives. That means our time, our energies, our patience, our care, and attention in the interests of others in the everyday affairs of life in the home, in business and in the church. That may be far less romantic, but it doubtless forms the regular agenda of ordinary Christian life.

David Gooding, *In The School of Christ: Lessons on Holiness in John 13–17*, 158–9

18th April

A TWO—WAY FRIENDSHIP

Reading: 2 John 4–11

'You are my friends if you do what I command you.' (John 15:14)

We are to lay down our lives for our friends, but friendship is not just one way traffic. As members of God's family, if we act as friends to our Christian brothers and sisters, they in their turn are just as responsible to act as friends to us. If those whom we treat as our friends never act like friends to us, how are they worthy of the name of friend?

But once we begin to think like that, our Lord's next saying will bring us up sharp: 'You are my friends if you do what I command you'. The conditional conjunction 'if' is inescapable: '*if* you do my commands'.

Perhaps at this point someone will want to object: 'How can it be said that Christ's love for us is conditional on our keeping his commandments? Did he not love us originally while we were still sinners? And does he not remain our friend even when in our weakness we fail to keep his commandments?'

Certainly he does. He who was described by his critics, malevolently but quite correctly, as a friend of quisling tax collectors and prostitutes, will never cease to be a loyal friend to those who trust him, even when, like Peter, they fail and fall.

But the objection rests on a misunderstanding. Christ does not say, 'I am your friend if, and only if, you do the thing which I command you.' What he says is: 'You are my friends if you do what I command you.' Let us never forget it; true friendship, even between the Lord and us, is a two-way process. It would be a shocking thing if we relied on our Lord always to act as a friend to us, but we made little deliberate attempt to act as friends to him by doing what he commands us to do.

David Gooding, *In The School of Christ: Lessons on Holiness in John 13–17*, 159–60

19th April

DEVOTION TO GOD'S PEOPLE AND TO CHRIST

Reading: Ruth 2

'For where you go I will go, and where you lodge I will lodge.
Your people shall be my people, and your God my God.' (Ruth 1:16)

Boaz began to take Ruth seriously when she started to go gleaning in devotion to her mother-in-law. At lunchtime he called her, and encouraged her to 'Come here and eat', and he gave her some food. Then he told the foreman to let her glean among the sheaves, and also to pull out some from the bundles for her. He didn't say what some romantic gentlemen would have said: 'Now, Ruth, gleaning is heavy work. So after lunch you go back home and I'll send a whole sack full of stuff round.' After lunch he let the woman go back to work hard.

May God give us some young men and women who are prepared to work hard, and save us from the notion that young people can't take to rigorous doctrine. They can take physics and they can take computers; surely they can take God's word and glean at it so as to maintain themselves and the people of God. And not only devoted to the people of God but devoted to the Lord Jesus.

Given all the other attractions of the younger men, Ruth was prepared to say no to them and submit to marry Boaz, old as he was. I know you talk about the lovely Lord Jesus, but it doesn't always appear to some people like that. The world has many attractions for the young. May God raise up younger men and women who will decide that their ambition is to live for Christ, and God will reward them.

Ruth made her decision, when to believe God and be devoted to his people seemed to be a dead end in life; getting nowhere; even remaining single for the rest of her days. But God had other plans and he honoured her faith. She gave herself to be married to elderly Boaz for the sake of God's people and the maintaining of a name. How we could do with that focus again, and the power of Ruth's life experience. To know what it is to 'lie on the threshing floor overnight', and discuss with Christ the wonders of what he will do when the morning dawns and the marriage supper of the Lamb takes place. The wonder of what it is to be part of the bride of Christ; to see his plans for the restoration of Israel and the blessing of the world, and to know that we have a part in it.

David Gooding, *A Story of True Love: Three Studies on Understanding the Book of Ruth*, 22

20th April

LOVING ONE ANOTHER HELPS US TO UNDERSTAND GOD'S LOVE

Reading: 1 John 4:7–17

By this we know that we abide in him and he in us, because he has given us of his Spirit. (1 John 4:13)

How am I going to know that his Spirit is in me? Well, we shall know it first of all because God says so: 'when you heard the word of truth, the gospel of your salvation, and believed in him, [you] were sealed with the promised Holy Spirit' (Eph 1:13). We take it as a fact of history that God gave us his Holy Spirit when we believed.

Another way of knowing is by experiencing the power and impulse of that holy personality who resides within us. The Holy Spirit inside of me will always be activating me to love people. If I clinch tight to the hardness of my heart and relish the spite of my tongue, how shall I know God, and how shall I really come to enjoy and understand what loving is?

There are some people who have the misfortune of being what is technically called *tone deaf*. You could set Tchaikovsky himself down at a piano, get him to play the most heavenly music, and it wouldn't mean a thing, for the person concerned is tone deaf. The poor fellow can't help that; he'll never understand all those raptures that other people go into when they listen to Tchaikovsky, because the music doesn't sort of filter through him.

And if we're going to understand God's love we shall need to see it in action. We shall read about it in the Scriptures, of course. 'But there's another way,' says John, 'and that's by letting the love of that Holy Spirit come through you to somebody else, so that God will be able to perfect his love in us' (see 1 John 4:12).

When people have been a little thoughtless—you've done your best and they haven't acknowledged it, others have stamped on your toes a little bit, sometimes you feel like giving up, or at least giving them a piece of your mind, but you don't and you keep on going to the meetings of the church. It's then that you learn what it meant for Christ to keep on living in our world, and for God to give his Son to the cross. Then you say, 'When I see what it involved for God to love me; and the fact that he loved me in spite of my unloveliness, it makes me understand more of what that love means.

David Gooding, *Love is from God: One Study on 1 John 4:7–21*, 10

21st April

LOVE IS A SOURCE OF CONFIDENCE BEFORE GOD

Reading: 1 John 3:16–24

Little children, let us not love in word or talk but in deed and in truth. By this we shall know that we are of the truth and reassure our heart before him. (1 John 3:18–19)

John knows that in genuine godly believers at times there wells up within them a sense of failure, and doubts creep in. Middle life is a very fertile ground for them to wonder, 'Am I truly a believer? Look what I've gone and done now: have I got eternal life?'

So John now gives us some very practical advice. He tells us that if our hearts condemn us, one of the things that can reassure us before the Lord is if there has been evidence in our lives that we have loved one another. We shall be happy men and women, if there's been evidence of real devoted self-sacrifice for our brothers and sisters for the Lord's sake. That can serve to give us confidence before the Lord, for we must remember that 'whenever our heart condemns us, God is greater than our heart, and he knows everything' (v. 20).

For myself, I read that not as a threat, but as an encouragement, for I too have to take my place with Peter. Should the Lord ask me three times, 'Do you love me?' then I should have to stammer out, 'Well, Lord, I'd like to say I do, but what about all the inconsistencies? But you know all things; you know that I love you.' Love is a source (not the only one, but a source) of confidence in the presence of God when our hearts begin to condemn us. It gives us a certain basis of confidence in prayer; for if our hearts don't condemn us, we have the things that we ask of him (vv. 21–22). But if I come to God, expecting God to give me something, yet when my brother comes to me in his need I refuse to give him anything, it is obvious that I'm going to be in a little trouble with the Father.

And finally, in our talk of loving let's notice the sanity with which John ends. 'This is his commandment, that we should believe in the name of his Son Jesus Christ and love one another' (v. 23). Faith and doctrinal correctness, love and obedience, these are the secrets of our abiding in God, and simultaneously the evidence that he abides in us.

David Gooding, *Unity, Origin and Victory: Fourteen Studies from 1 John on Life in the Family of God*, 57–8

22nd April

GOD ACCEPTS US AS WE ARE

Reading: Romans 5:6–11

For while we were still weak, at the right time Christ died for the ungodly. (Romans 5:6)

Many people are waiting until their lives have improved enough for them to begin to think that they are now Christians, and consequently they live a life of drudgery. They have never seen that God is prepared to take them and receive them now, just as they are, knowing all they have done and will ever do. That is a marvellous thing, and it is the glory of God and his gospel. 'God shows his love for us in that while we were still sinners, Christ died for us' (v. 8).

The marvel of God's salvation is that, if a man or woman will come as a bankrupt sinner, God will not only receive them there and then, he promises never to cast them out (see John 6:37). He will cling to them when they grow tired or weary, however bad they prove to be. He knows them through and through, from the beginning to the end, and he loves them just as they are. He is willing to receive them, quite irrespective of their past behaviour and future progress. When men and women see that and come to the Saviour, the love of God begins to sink down into their hearts.

That's how the Holy Spirit does it. He begins to pervade their hearts with a sense of the eternal love of God that will never let them go. Because they are at ease and secure in God's love, they then have the courage to face their sins and shortcomings. You wouldn't confess your weaknesses to your enemy, would you? Or even to a critical friend? If you had a friend who would love you even when they knew the worst, then you might be bold enough to confess your weaknesses.

That's how God acts. He knows the worst; you can't tell him anything that would shock him or do anything that would surprise him. Yet he offers us his love, and receives us if we'll come just as we are. I repeat, his acceptance does not depend on our progress afterwards. When he has received us and set us at ease in his presence he gives us his Holy Spirit, who will begin to wage a relentless war inside us against sin, and at the same time supply the desire and the power to please God.

David Gooding, *Christian Foundations: Ten Studies on Key Biblical Concepts*, 43

23rd April

ZACHHAEUS AND THE RESULTS OF BEING ACCEPTED

Reading: Luke 19:1–10

And Jesus said to him, 'Today salvation has come to this house, since he also is a son of Abraham.' (Luke 19:9)

Christ had been on the journey a long time, but as he passed through Jericho certain things came swiftly together. Zacchaeus conceived a desire, and who shall say where it came from, to see who Jesus was. He climbed up a tree to get a fuller view. And Jesus, with the precision of an eternal purpose, went up to the tree, stopped, looked up into Zacchaeus' downward peering face, and told him to come down because he had to stay at his house.

In that moment Zacchaeus not only saw who Jesus was, he discovered his own long-lost identity. He was a man loved by God with an eternal love, and longed for so much that God had sent his Son on purpose to find him and rescue him from his lostness by coming personally to his home and bringing the sense of acceptance with God into his very heart.

Zacchaeus presently discovered something else. Acceptance with God had given him what he had sought in vain for years from wealth. The compulsive drive to make money had gone. Indeed, he felt that he no longer needed half his wealth and he gave it away. In addition, the thought of entertaining Christ to a meal paid for by money which he had got by fraud, now seemed repulsive and impossible. He confessed his sinful practice, promised to make full restitution and compensate his victims. It was a programme of social concern more generous by far than the Pharisee himself had announced as he stood in the temple (18:11–12).

It was not the criticisms of the crowd that made Zacchaeus do it; their criticisms had never produced any such result before. And certainly Christ had not made it a condition of his acceptance of him. But through being accepted Zacchaeus had recovered his real identity as a true son of Abraham (19:9): that very rich ancestor of his, who was first justified by his faith (Gen 15:6), and then lived to justify his profession of faith by his works (Gen 22; Jas 2:21).

David Gooding, *According to Luke: The Third Gospel's Ordered Historical Narrative*, 315

24th April

THE FATHER LOVES YOU

Reading: John 16:19–28

'The Father himself loves you, because you have loved me and have believed that I came from God.' (John 16:27)

It is the chief thing that every one of Christ's disciples needs to grasp, be he or she a new convert or an aged saint. For as we wrestle with life's problems, try to shoulder our Christian responsibilities or even work out the doctrinal and theological implications of our faith, it is easy to let fade from our minds the sense of the Father's direct, personal love of each one of us. If we lose that sense of his love, we could turn our very prayer life into a burden, weighed down by doubt and fear.

Our Lord, for instance, had told his disciples that after his resurrection and ascension they would be able to make requests of the Father in his name; and that the Father would honour his name and give them what they asked for. But he foresaw that they might misread even this gracious promise. They might think that the reason why they had to pray in the name of the Lord Jesus was that the Father himself was not really interested in them, and would be unlikely to grant their requests unless cajoled and persuaded to do so by the Lord Jesus.

Of course, that was not so at all. 'When you make your requests of him in my name,' says Christ, 'I shall never need to enquire of him, "Why have you not attended to the requests that my disciples have made?" For the Father himself loves you and can be trusted to grant your requests that are consistent with my name.'

It is true, of course, that Christ now acts as our intercessor before God, and in that capacity he does pray for us. But it's not that he has to intercede for us because, left to himself, God would be against us. His appointment as our intercessor is itself an expression of God's love for us and of his determination to do us good (Heb 5:1–10; 7:20–25).

And finally, let us notice that when Christ assured his apostles that the Father himself loved them, he was not thinking of that general love which God has for all his creatures, but of that special love and affection that the Father has for those who love his Son and have believed that Jesus came forth from the Father.

David Gooding, *In The School of Christ: Lessons on Holiness in John 13–17*, 210–11

25th April

LOVE GIVES US SECURITY TO FACE THE FUTURE

Reading: Luke 10:17–23

Husbands, love your wives, as Christ loved the church and gave himself up for her, that he might sanctify her, having cleansed her by the washing of water with the word, so that he might present the church to himself in splendour, without spot or wrinkle or any such thing, that she might be holy and without blemish. (Ephesians 5:25–27)

The person who has discovered God's love in Christ has discovered a love that is bigger than all their failures, that is prepared to receive them now and guarantee that it will never reject them.

And yet this love will not rest content until that person's character has been perfected. When a person finds Christ like this, and knows they are received by God and will never be cast out, it begins to set them free in God's presence. It gives them the courage to turn around and face themselves. Whatever they discover in their character, whatever emerges from the dark depths of their past, they're no longer afraid of it. For God has loved them in Christ, knowing all about their flaws; he loves them still and has forgiven them freely. Moreover, it is not merely a forgiveness that does away with the gloom of the past, but one that casts its joyous beams on towards the future.

Let me remind you of this occasion when Christ told his disciples that they were to rejoice. The disciples had returned from their first mission when they had gone out to evangelize the district for Christ. They had cast out demons, performed miracles and preached their sermons. They came back with great enthusiasm, telling the Lord about all they had done. He understood their joy and their gladness in his service. But presently he said, 'Gentlemen, don't rejoice so much that the demons are subject to you and that you've had some success in your mission, but rejoice above all in this, that *your names are written in heaven*' (see Luke 10:20).

The phrase is interesting. We might paraphrase it, 'your names are enrolled in the citizen lists of heaven.' In the first place, it spelled out that there is a future. God has his programme for a citizen body of redeemed people with whom he will populate the age to come. So these men were to rejoice because here on earth they had discovered this future and they were utterly certain of participation in the glorious scheme that lay ahead—'your names are written in heaven'.

David Gooding, *The Unexpected Christ: Four Studies on the Person and Character of Jesus*, 37–9

26th April

JESUS HIMSELF DREW NEAR

Reading: Luke 24:13–27

*While they were talking and discussing together,
Jesus himself drew near and went with them. (Luke 24:15)*

Things hadn't turned out as the two on the way to Emmaus expected. They had thought Jesus was the one who should 'deliver' Israel and he just didn't do it.

They said that certain women had been at his grave and had seen angels who said that he was alive. They thought that that was completely irrelevant. A messiah who couldn't stop himself being arrested and crucified, how could he be the Messiah? So they were sorely disappointed with the Lord; but in answer to their problems 'Jesus himself drew near.'

Yes, he went on to expound the holy Scriptures, but it interests me from a practical point of view that, for believers whose minds are troubled and disappointed, the first answer was that 'Jesus himself drew near.' In my little experience I have known times when I have faced so-called evidence in the academic world that, had it been true, would have destroyed my faith. And in times when I couldn't think of what the answers were, it was a great comfort to me that Christ knows anyway and he is responsible for my faith. That is what he meant when he said, 'I have given them your word . . . and they have believed that you have sent me . . . Father, keep them' (see John 17:8, 11). He has provoked our faith, and he is concerned to maintain it. So I have learned in those circumstances to commit it to the Lord in the confidence that Jesus knows—though it might have been quite a long while before I saw the answers.

Our risen Lord will make himself known. He will do it in stages. He referred them to Scripture as a solid ground for what he was saying. But how did they know that it was not mere theological talk? He was made known to them in the breaking of bread; they saw the wounds in his hands. How do I know that Jesus Christ is the Son of God, and that he is concerned for me? Amid all the questions that life throws at us, it remains our anchor-hold on reality: 'the Son of God . . . loved me and gave himself for me' (Gal 2:20).

David Gooding, *Jesus Himself, the Father Himself and the Spirit Himself*, 3–4

27th April

AN ATTITUDE TOWARD GOD THAT IS NOT GOOD ENOUGH

Reading: Revelation 3:14–22

And he said to him, 'You shall love the Lord your God with all your heart and with all your soul and with all your mind. This is the great and first commandment.' (Matthew 22:37–38)

The people whom our Lord was addressing in these letters in Revelation had special difficulties. I suspect because they were members of a church they got it into their heads that they were all right. But things were surely not right, were they? For the Lord has to say to the Laodiceans, 'I know your works: you are neither cold nor hot. Would that you were either cold or hot! So, because you are lukewarm, and neither hot nor cold, I will spit you out of my mouth' (Rev 3:15–16).

The Lord never talks to believers in Christ in those terms. What did he mean, 'you're neither hot nor cold'? Well, in my experience there are lots of folk like that. They are keen on gardening, maybe, or music or something, and that's lovely. If you ask them about Christ and God, and being saved, 'Oh well,' they say, 'I'm not particularly interested in that. I'm not against God; I go to church now and again. On the other hand, I'm not madly keen on God, so to speak.' They're neither hot nor cold. Perhaps you might say, 'It's okay for the preacher to be mad keen on God, but I'm not mad keen on God myself. Of course, I'm not against religion.' Do you suppose that's good enough for God?

What would you say if you met a young gentleman who tells you that he is soon to be married, and you say, 'Yes, I've seen your wife to be, she is a most beautiful, charming young woman. You must love her immensely.'

And he replies, 'I don't know about that. I mean, I've got nothing against the girl; but I'm not that mad keen on her.'

You would probably say, 'And you're going to marry her?'

I wonder how they could ever make it a proper relationship. Yet many people feel it's okay to feel like that about God. But wait a minute; that won't do for God. Our Lord Jesus said that we should love the Lord our God with all our heart, mind, soul and strength. That's the first commandment, and you only have to think about it to see how unsatisfactory any other attitude to God is.

David Gooding, *Life's Struggles and God's Judgment: Two Evangelistic Studies from Revelation*, 7

28th April

PUTTING GOD FIRST

Reading: Judges 6:25–32

'But as for me and my house, we will serve the Lord.' (Joshua 24:15)

I have a secret admiration for Gideon, because in one little particular I am just like him—I am as cowardly as ever he was! It was difficult to go out there and face them; so, because he was afraid to do it by day he did it by night. I have often adopted the same tactics myself. Afraid to face them, I will do it when they aren't there and when they come back they will find it's done!

There's another bit of his tactics I admire as well. He was not negative, but positive. Said the Lord, 'You are to take your father's bull, and the second bull as well, build an altar and publicly offer a sacrifice to the Lord.' But there was a difficulty! The altar of Baal was just on the spot where he was asking Gideon to build the altar. 'That's too bad for the altar of Baal!' says the Lord. 'You must obey me, and if the altar of Baal gets in the way it will have to be knocked down.'

That caught the people on the wrong foot. When they woke up in the morning their precious Baal altar was down, an altar to the Lord in its place and the paraphernalia of Baal had been burnt up in a positive act of worship to the Lord. What could they say? Even Gideon's father, who was not renowned for his strength, argued, 'Are you saying that I mustn't worship the Lord then? Will you plead for Baal instead of the Lord?'

In many a matter that has vexed the church and Christendom down the years, over which there are liable to be all sorts of loud arguments and people getting upset, it seems to me that it is good to follow a positive attitude. I must obey the Lord—that's number one. If that conflicts with hoary old traditions or heretical notions, or things that are not clear and confuse the gospel, I must obey the Lord. I am not being negative, I am being positive. If other things are not consistent with this, they will have to go.

David Gooding, *The Lord Saves his People: Fourteen Studies on Understanding the Major Sections of Judges*, 71

29th April

A SWEET-SMELLING OFFERING TO GOD

Reading: Philippians 4:14–20

*Therefore be imitators of God, as beloved children.
And walk in love, as Christ loved us and gave himself up for us, a
fragrant offering and sacrifice to God. (Ephesians 5:1–2)*

There is more in the work of Jesus Christ our Lord than saving us from the wrath of God. Paul exhorts his fellow Christians to live and serve their fellow men and women as Christ did. How did Christ live? He loved us and gave himself up for us. And in the process he did something else that was indescribably marvellous—he gave himself as a *burnt offering* and a sacrifice wholly acceptable to God for a sweet-smelling savour.

Paul is pointing us to ancient Israelite ritual, for one of their main sacrifices was where the whole of it was burnt upon the altar. In the technical language of their ritual, it ascended to God as a sacrifice of a sweet smell. 'Think of it,' says Paul, 'and you will perceive what was going on when Jesus Christ walked this earth.'

Watch him in his infinite compassion seeking the lost; sitting by a well, tired, hungry and thirsty, but overcoming nationalistic prejudices and religious bigotry to reach out to a Samaritan woman and bring her the thirst-quenching draught of God's Holy Spirit' (John 4).

'It was wonderful for that woman', you say.

Yes, but it was also wonderful for God. As he looked down on that well in the little village of Sychar, he saw his magnificent regal Son going out of his way, sacrificing his time and comfort to put the needs of that one stray, forlorn woman before his own. The whole activity came up to God as an offering of a sweet smell, and God was delighted.

We've made it very difficult for Jesus Christ, God's Son, to serve some of us, what with the kicks and our ingratitude, stubbornness and wilfulness. And yet, as he gave himself for us, it did more than just release us from the wrath of God. It filled God with utter delight. It is within your compass this coming week, my good Christian friend, and mine too, so to sacrifice ourselves for others that we shall not merely do them good, but in the process be offering to God a sacrifice that delights his heart.

David Gooding, *The Adoration of Christ: Six Studies on the Nature and Practice of Worship*, 29–30

30th April

THE SLIPPERY SLOPE

Reading: Malachi 1:6–14

*O priests, who despise my name. But you say, 'How
have we despised your name?' (Malachi 1:6)*

God tells them, 'When it comes to bringing your offering, instead of choosing the best bull in your herd, you choose any old thing that is half riddled with consumption and you say, "That will do for the Lord." You try offering that to your governor. You wouldn't think of that; then why do you offer it to me?'

Well, we all are curious people! When we get home to heaven we feel that nothing but crowns will do and they shall all be at the feet of our Lord; but this week we have more important things to think about! We may hastily spend five minutes for the Lord, and the assembly work can be carried on any old way. When we lose our sense of God's love and mercy for us, we will act as though any old slap-dash thing will do for the Lord.

But there was worse. The priests, who should have guarded knowledge and taught the people (Mal 2:7), said that it did not matter and they shouldn't take these things too seriously. 'Go out and enjoy yourselves and don't think too much about God,' they said.

The details of the text tell us what happened next. With the loss of the sense of God's love for them and his specially privileged position for them as his people, they not only became slip-shod in their offerings and service for God, but their family life broke up.

> This second thing you do. You cover the LORD's altar with tears, with weeping and groaning because he no longer regards the offering or accepts it with favour from your hand. But you say, 'Why does he not?' (Mal 2:13–14)

They filled God's altar with tears, the tears of broken marriages and families, and their sacrifices were then not acceptable. It was no good coming into his presence, singing psalms and hymns, if their families were in ruins as a result of having acted treacherously against their wives in divorce. God wished he had somebody there who would close the doors (Mal 1:10) and stop them offering sacrifices, for he did not want to hear them. When we lose the sense of God's mercy and love for us, instead of disciplining ourselves according to God's word, we shall become self-indulgent and careless in family life and disasters will overtake us.

David Gooding, *Spiritual Dullness: One Study on the Message of the Prophet Malachi*, 5

1st May

WORLDLINESS IS A MATTER OF THE HEART

Reading: Matthew 6:26–34

Do not love not the world or the things in the world. If anyone loves the world, the love of the Father is not in him. (1 John 2:15)

Apparently the love of the world and the love of the Father are diametrically opposed. *Worldliness is primarily a matter of the heart.* It must be evident immediately that it's not enough to be unworldly by just observing a code of rules and regulations: 'If I do this, I'm worldly. If I don't do it, I'm unworldly.' It's first and foremost a matter of the heart and the heart's affections.

But let's address ourselves to another question. Didn't God make the whole world and all that's in it? In what sense is John using the term *world* when he says, 'All that is in the world . . . is not from the Father' (1 John 2:16)? How can that be, if the Father made the world and all that's in it? I suggest that our first way of understanding the matter is to go back to the fall of the human race, and remember what happened to Eve and Adam in the Garden of Eden, as we're told it in the book of Genesis.

You'll remember in Genesis 1, as the inspired writer records the creation of the world he tells us repeatedly, 'And God saw that it was good'. God has given us all things richly to enjoy (1 Tim 6:17). How then does this word, which originally described what God made, come to represent something that is bad and evil? Let's just recall the nature of the temptation that the evil one put before Eve.

Satan concentrated Eve's attention on the tree of the knowledge of good and evil and invited her to consider how beautiful it was. Well, of course it would be: God had made the tree, so how wouldn't it be beautiful? But God had said of this particular tree, 'but of the tree of the knowledge of good and evil you shall not eat, for in the day that you eat of it you shall surely die' (Gen 2:17). 'Nonsense,' said the serpent, 'you'll have to learn to grow up and be mature. That kind of thing is only for children.' Satan was suggesting that Eve should take these good things and enjoy them independently of God, contrary to God's explicit word. They should take God's creation and enjoy it as an end in itself, apart from God and in disobedience to God. 'What about the word of God?' says Eve to the serpent. 'You don't need the word of God to enjoy yourself,' said Satan, and she fell.

David Gooding, *Unity, Origin and Victory: Fourteen Studies from 1 John on Life in the Family of God*, 23–4

2nd May

WORLDLINESS IS A MATTER OF DESIRE

Reading: 1 Corinthians 4:6–13

Let the one who boasts, boast in the Lord.
(2 Corinthians 10:17)

When Eve fell, the world went on. Trees were trees and apples were apples, so what was different? There was a difference as high as between heaven and hell. A creation from God, to be enjoyed in fellowship with God, leading to gratitude to God, had now turned into a world to be enjoyed apart from God, as an end in itself. We're told that the serpent tempted Eve by her desires. Notice that he didn't put in front of her something luridly vicious, the kind of thing that we normally associate with the English word 'lust'. I've never heard of anyone lusting for the fruit of trees.

My brothers and sisters, it's more serious than that. *Worldliness is desiring anything in disobedience to God.* 'For all that is in the world—the desires of the flesh and the desires of the eyes and pride in possessions—is not from the Father but is from the world' (1 John 2:16). In this sense the world stands for looking at anything without God as an end in itself. There's nothing wrong with a nice home, but suppose I make it my goal in life. I might sing the formal hymns in church, yet my heart is totally engaged in getting myself a nice home and God is forgotten days without number. This is worldliness.

Worldliness is also 'the pride of life' (KJV); when this world and my success in it become the standard and the goal by which I rate my value, and other people's value. 'My child goes to the best school.' Well, be thankful to the Lord for that; but are you saying that you're someone special now? We have to be careful how we boast, because the Apostle Paul is liable to come along and say, 'What do you have that you did not receive? . . . why do you boast as if you did not receive it?' (1 Cor 4:7). If the Lord gave it to you, thank him. But be humble enough and realist enough to admit that he gave it to you. None of us has grounds for boasting over somebody else. But sometimes a little worldly spirit creeps in and we judge success and pride ourselves on it apart from the Father.

David Gooding, *Unity, Origin and Victory: Fourteen Studies from 1 John on Life in the Family of God*, 24

3rd May

WORLDLINESS IS A MATTER OF FELLOWSHIP

Reading: Romans 14:5–8

For if we live, we live to the Lord, and if we die, we die to the Lord. So then, whether we live or whether we die, we are the Lord's. (Romans 14:8)

What I'm now saying makes it much more difficult in reaching our decisions in life. It's no longer sufficient just to get out the rule book and ask, is this thing worldly or not? It's more subtle than that. *Worldliness is living out of fellowship with the Lord.* There's a question in my heart: is what I'm doing from the Lord, and am I enjoying it in fellowship with him? Or has the thing got a hold of me apart from the Lord?

When Satan succeeded with Eve, it's no wonder that all down the centuries he's adopted the same successful tactics. He even tried them with our Lord, didn't he? May I remind you of the famous occasion when Satan came along and tempted him? 'If you are the Son of God, command these stones to become loaves of bread' (Matt 4:3). Now, there's nothing wrong with hunger in and of itself, and there's nothing wrong or sinful in satisfying hunger. But on this occasion there would have been a great deal wrong with our Lord satisfying it. The most wonderful thing about a meal is that it comes from God.

Although God has given us all things richly to enjoy, sometimes he calls us to sacrifice for his sake and to wait for his word. There will be times when he'll withhold from us what is a good thing in itself. And then very often Satan comes with his temptation to go ahead and take it apart from God, simply because it's a good thing. Our Lord magnificently exposed the sophistication and cynicism of the tempter, and said, 'Man shall not live by bread alone, but by every word that comes from the mouth of God' (4:4).

However humble the thing is, the whole of life is meant to have that dimension as a basis of fellowship with God. In our early days, when life holds out so much that is good in itself, Satan will come and tempt us to grasp it independently of the Lord, or quite in contradiction to his holy word. If I had more experience I would talk to my younger brethren and sisters in Christ about the modern world's attitude to love and marriage, and how it can become very worldly when seized in independence of the Lord. But I wouldn't dare to do that!

David Gooding, *Unity, Origin and Victory: Fourteen Studies from 1 John on Life in the Family of God*, 25

4th May

REASONS FOR NOT LOVING THE WORLD

Reading: 1 John 2:12–17

I write to you, children, because you know the Father. (1 John 2:13)

When I say, 'do not love the world', I have good grounds for saying it. Here's a child playing with a knife; how will you get it out of his hand? If you try to pull it, he will grasp it and cut himself. So you come along with some beautiful toy and give it to the child; the child drops the harmful thing and takes the new thing. Similarly, if you know the Father you will love the Father and automatically your love of the world will recede. Do be careful not to hurt his love: if you love the world, you can't at the same time be loving the Father.

'I write to you, fathers, because you know him who is from the beginning' (v. 14). He is the great eternal being, who is now and ever shall be. How will that help me not to love the world? As John points out, 'the world is passing away' (v. 17). Why lose fellowship with the eternal for the sake of something that's merely temporary? 'You know him who is from the beginning.' Let the glory and grandeur and eternity of it save you from loving a passing world.

'I write to you, young men, because you are strong, and the word of God abides in you, and you have overcome the evil one' (v. 14). The secret of overcoming the evil one is knowing the word of God.

We have the example of our Lord. How did he overcome the evil one? In response to each temptation he cited the word of God.

If I may be forgiven so for speaking of him, here's a boy in the home of Mary and Joseph. And Mary and Joseph read him the holy Scriptures. They read it as they rose up, and as they sat down, as they came in, as they went out (see Deut 6:7)—until the word of God was part of his very fibre. When the days of testing came, he could answer the devil and overcome him saying, 'But it stands written.' If our blessed Lord needed the armour of the word of God, how much more do we need it to save us from the sophisticated temptations of the devil?

David Gooding, *Unity, Origin and Victory: Fourteen Studies from 1 John on Life in the Family of God*, 35

5th May

THE SUPREME JOY OF PAUL'S LIFE IN THIS WORLD

Reading: Acts 20:17–27

And now, behold, I am going to Jerusalem, constrained by the Spirit, not knowing what will happen to me there, except that the Holy Spirit testifies to me in every city that imprisonment and afflictions await me. (Acts 20:22–23)

Why then is he going? Paul takes no credit for the compulsion that impels him, for that has been produced in him by the gracious urgings and persuading of the Holy Spirit. At the same time, he is not driven onwards in blind ignorance of the outcome. The same Spirit who constrains him onwards warns him explicitly of the sufferings ahead.

Why go on? It is, Paul explains, a sense of comparative values. The Lord Jesus has given him a course to run and a task to fulfil. No matter what the course or the task might be, in his eyes that by itself was the supreme honour anyone could be given. To complete the course and finish the task to the satisfaction of the Lord Jesus was his supreme joy. But then consider the task. It was to testify to, and proclaim, the gospel of God's grace (20:24). The majestic magnificence of that grace was a perpetual dynamo of motivation and energy for Paul. It changed his set of values. Life ceased to have any worth to him independent of living and working for Christ. If to complete the task Christ had given him he must surrender life itself, it was a nothing: he would gladly let it go.

Then there was another value that urged Paul to his task: the value of people. Not in terms of their bank balances, nor profitability forecasts for industry. Demetrius' trinket factory has long been left behind. We are thinking of what the old preachers used to call *the value of a soul*. What will it mean for a human being, originally made in the image of God, to perish, to be in torment (Luke 16:23); to suffer eternal punishing, as the Saviour phrased it (Matt 25:46)? To allow fellow human beings to die physically by doing nothing to save them when they could be saved, would be criminal. What then must be said of preachers who refrain from preaching the gospel by which alone people can be saved?

David Gooding, *True to the Faith: The Acts of the Apostles—Defining and Defending the Gospel*, 424–5

Part 8

The God who is Loyal and Humble

6th May

WHO IS LIKE JEHOVAH?

Reading: Micah 6:1–8

You will show faithfulness to Jacob and steadfast love to Abraham, as you have sworn to our fathers from the days of old. (Micah 7:20)

God reminds them of the way he had brought his people out of slavery in Egypt and recalls the later incident when Balak king of Moab incited Balaam to curse Israel. But God gave Balaam the command to bless, and so they were blessed (see Num 22–24).

So, does God's mercy predominate over all things? God had not grown weary of them. Even after their repeated rebellions in the wilderness, it remained his desire to put his name upon them and to bless them (see Num 6:22–27). He would not now give up on his people and allow them to be cursed. For that is not what God is like, as Balak had to learn to his cost:

> God is not man, that he should lie, or a son of man, that he should change his mind. Has he said, and will he not do it? Or has he spoken, and will he not fulfil it? (Num 23:19)

He gave the command to bless, and so it happened—'Has he said, and will he not do it?' And just as assuredly, there will one day come the fulfilment of God's promised future reign of peace (Mic 4:1–5).

Not only was Israel's God different from pagan gods in his desire to bless them, but in the extent to which he would go to in order to bring blessing.

> But you, O Bethlehem Ephrathah, who are too little to be among the clans of Judah, from you shall come forth for me one who is to be ruler in Israel, whose coming forth is from of old, from ancient days. (Mic 5:2)

Even Micah expressed surprise that this ruler should come from Bethlehem. If Messiah had been born in Jerusalem, we may have concluded that he came for others; but he came in humility to this little village, so we see that he came for us. He came near for us. Who is like Jehovah? The man Jesus is; he is Jehovah incarnate! And he came so near that they could hit him in the face. A slap across the cheek is the final insult to a person. By doing that you would 'deface' him. Who is a God like Jehovah? When the Lord Jesus came they took a rod and slashed it across his face. So near he came.

David Gooding, Who Is Like Jehovah? One Meditative Study on the Prophecy of Micah, 4–5

7th May

THE HUMILITY OF GOD

Reading: Philippians 2:5–12

He poured out his soul to death. (Isaiah 53:12)

When some men become dictators of their country, they regard it as the opportunity to grasp everything for themselves. Christ Jesus, being equal with God, didn't count equality with God as a reason for grasping everything for himself, but the very reverse. Instead of grasping for himself, he poured himself out.

The first step of humility was to become a servant. Notice that, won't you? It was not being a man; the first step was *becoming* a servant, 'taking the form of a servant' (Phil 2:7). He had the right to command, but he obeyed as a servant and served. You may think of it this way. It was certainly a vast stoop for God to become a servant; but then angels are servants, aren't they? And angels are higher than men. Gabriel and Michael would be right to think you are somewhat lower than they are. As the Psalm says, 'What is man . . . ? Yet you have made him a little lower than the angels' (Ps 8:4–5). And yet those vast numbers of angels, who are mighty and excel in power, are servants. When our Lord humbled himself and poured himself out, he was not content simply to be a servant, but he took on himself the form of a man—and men are lower than angels, aren't they? He was 'born in the likeness of men. And being found in human form, he humbled himself by becoming obedient . . .' (Phil 2:7–8).

Not all men obey, do they? Augustus Caesar, emperor of the Roman world wasn't given to obeying anybody. Though he was a man, he regarded it as his right to command. And yet our Lord, being a man, humbled himself and became obedient to the point of death; and even then it wasn't a hero's death. Your Lord didn't die surrounded by admiring onlookers, marvelling at the courage of his heroic death. No, indeed not. The death he died was the death of the cross with all its shame, the curse of God's law and the mockery of his creatures.

He poured himself out, but the glory of it is in who he was. Who was it, I ask, who poured himself out like that? And the Bible's answer is that he was God, the eternal God, who never ceased to be God—it was God who thus gave himself. What a story it is!

David Gooding, *Understanding the Trinity: Six Studies on God's Revelation of Himself*, 17

8th May

GOD WAS CONTENT TO DWELL IN A TENT

Reading: 2 Samuel 7:1–16

'I have not lived in a house since the day I brought up the people of Israel from Egypt to this day, but I have been moving about in a tent for my dwelling.' (2 Samuel 7:6)

The substance of what God now began to say was this: 'How very nice of you to come up with the suggestion, David. But wait a minute; whose plan is all this? Did I ask you to build me a house? I don't remember asking you at any time to build me a permanent house. Did I?'

'No, Lord, you didn't actually ask for it. I thought it would be a good idea.'

'Oh,' said God. 'Do you know, David, I've been on the move for centuries, ever since I brought your fathers out of the land of Egypt. For hundreds of years I have been in a tent—in the tabernacle. All these days and in all these places I have walked with the children of Israel, and never once did I ask anybody, commander or prophet, to build me a house. I've been content to dwell in a tent.'

What magnificent imagery this is. Almighty God, who dwells above all heavens, let alone the palaces of the heavens he has created, came to redeem his people. Did he send a few of his footmen to get them out of Egypt? No, he didn't. He came down himself: the transcendent Lord of space and time came down and was content with a tent. In the days when Israel foot-slogged it over the desert, God says, 'I walked with them so that my people might at last attain the final purpose I had in mind for them. Through all their circumstances I walked every step with them all the way until now' (see Lev 26:11–13).

Oh the magnificent grace, just ponder it! To get you from the slaveries of sin and Satan, and home at last to the palaces of heaven, almighty God has come down. As you walked, so has he walked, and will walk with you every step of the way until he gets you home to glory.

David Gooding, *The Problems of Becoming and Being a King: Fifteen Seminars on Major Themes in 1 & 2 Samuel*, 161

9th May

HOW THE LORD RESPONDED TO REJECTION BY JERUSALEM

Reading: Luke 13:31–35

'O Jerusalem, Jerusalem, the city that kills the prophets and stones those who are sent to it! How often would I have gathered your children together as a hen gathers her brood under her wings, and you were not willing!' (Luke 13:34 DWG)

When they set their will to reject him, he respected their will and accepted their rejection. Jerusalem was Messiah's own capital city; the very house of God was there. Christ did not raise an army, nor use his miraculous powers to drive out his enemies from Jerusalem and throw Israel's rebellious priesthood out of his Father's house. Instead he let them throw him out of both the temple and the city, and what had been his Father's and his, he left in their hands. 'Your house', he said, 'is left to you' (v. 35 DWG).

It is an awesome thing to contemplate: if men use the free will God has given them to reject the Saviour, neither God nor Christ will overrule that free will or remove it. That does not mean, of course, that puny humans have the power to defeat the will of the Almighty. It was always God's purpose that mankind's will should be genuinely free, and they should be able to say no to God if they chose to. But when they arrive unrepentant at that house of which he is the indisputable master, he will not be obliged to let them in.

Above all, let us notice in what way Christ accepted Jerusalem's rejection. When the last of his many pleas met with their determined rejection, we imagine that he could have abandoned his final journey to Jerusalem, consigning his nation to the hopeless and endless suffering of the consequences of their fatal decision. But he did the opposite; he continued on his foreordained path to Jerusalem, determined to die at their hands.

One day, however long it would take, that death would be the means of bringing Israel to repentance (Isa 53:3–5), the means of their cleansing; so that when at his second coming they look on him whom they pierced (Zech 12:10–13:1) they might be able to say through their tears of repentance, 'Blessed is the one who comes in the name of the Lord!' (Luke 13:35 DWG).

David Gooding, *According to Luke: The Third Gospel's Ordered Historical Narrative*, 275–6

10th May

GOD'S LOYALTY TO THE END

Reading: Revelation 4

To him who loves us and has freed us from our sins by his blood and made us a kingdom, priests to his God and Father, to him be glory and dominion forever and ever. (Revelation 1:5–6)

Explain to me, if you can, the death that God's perfect, sinless Son was asked to die for a world full of wretched rebels, the likes of you and me. In Gethsemane, faced with such a task, he showed the anguish of his spirit, but said, 'Nevertheless, not my will, but yours, be done' (Luke 22:42). 'Therefore God has highly exalted him and bestowed on him the name that is above every name, so that at the name of Jesus every knee should bow' (Phil 2:9–10). Ah, but I can tell you more about his successes. You will remember the glorious vision recorded by John in Revelation 4–5. He was given to see the throne of God and all the hosts of heaven bowing in their worship to the worthiness of the Creator who sits upon the throne. The logic is very simple: 'Worthy are you, our Lord and God, to receive glory and honour and power, for you created all things, and by your will they existed and were created' (4:11).

He is worthy because of his creatorial rights. Not a thing that moves, not a grain of sand in all the vast universe, has any other reason for existence than it should serve the pleasure of God. Anybody hearing that announcement must perceive its logic.

If that is the *raison d'être* of the universe's existence, it's gone astray, hasn't it? 'We have turned—every one—to his own way' (Isa 53:6). But God has his plans for the redevelopment of the universe, and he isn't going to wait for ever. He is determined that the new heavens and new earth are not to be ruined again by that self-same rebellion on the part of his creatures.

And so the scroll is delivered, that has pronounced the judgments of God upon a godless world, that God might clear the world of its sinners and start again. And the cry is heard, 'Who is worthy to open the scroll and break its seals?' (Rev 5:2)

You say, 'Why doesn't he start at once the judgments that shall clear the world of rebels? God has the right to do it.' Ah, but God is not merely concerned with his rights; he's a God of power and of justice. Having created his creatures, God will be loyal to them to the last. Hear the name announced of the great sovereign king who is worthy to take the book, and hear again the terms of his worthiness. The king himself, slain by rebel hands, is offering the rebels pardon from God, obtained by that very slaughter.

David Gooding, *Mankind's Pathway to the Coming Age of Peace: Six Studies on the Overall Message of 1 Chronicles*, 21–2

11th May

CHRIST STANDS BETWEEN US AND THE FOE

Reading: Exodus 14:10–28

The pillar of cloud moved from before them and stood behind them, coming between the host of Egypt and the host of Israel. (Exodus 14:19–20)

We have not been baptized in a cloud as Israel was when the cloud of glory stood between them and Pharoah's armies (1 Cor 10:1–2). But in a deeper and more profound sense, far more than anything Israel ever knew, we have our blessed Lord between us and our foe. We have been baptized into him and we stand *in Christ*. O the glory of it! 'If anyone is in Christ, he is a new creation' (2 Cor 5:17). 'There is therefore now no condemnation for those who are in Christ Jesus' (Rom 8:1).

Once we were walking according to the course of this world, under the thumb of the prince of the power of the air, the spirit that now works in the sons of disobedience; but God has raised us, given us life and seated us in the heavenly places in Christ Jesus (see Eph 2:1–6). It is a position that not even death shall break—'Once in Christ, in Him forever; Thus the eternal covenant stands'.[1] When at last the apostle comes to describe the believers who have physically departed this life, he adds this glorious fact and distinction about them—they are not just the dead, they are 'the dead *in Christ*' (1 Thess 4:16 emphasis added). Says Christ, 'I give [my sheep] eternal life, and they will never perish, and no one will snatch them out of my hand. My Father, who has given them to me, is greater than all, and no one is able to snatch them out of the Father's hand' (John 10:28–29). Come wolf, come bear, come lion—nothing will pluck them out of his hand.

Pharaoh, you'll have to drive hard! You'll need to sharpen your sword and inspire your soldiers with enormous courage. If you propose to drag these unfortunate Israelites back to Egypt, first you must fight and overcome Israel's God. He stands between you and them, and as far as you're concerned they're 'in him'—they are his!

It is good that from time to time we go back to Calvary and gaze upon the glory of God in the face of Jesus Christ, as we see him bearing the curse of the law to set us free from the wrath of God. It is a wonderful thing as well, to wake up in the dark night of our trouble and temptation and to see the glory of God in Christ—living now, victorious and risen again—and to know that we are in him.

---

[1] John Kent (1766–1843), 'Sovereign grace o'er sin abounding!'

David Gooding, *No Longer Bondmen: Thirteen Studies from Exodus on the True Meaning of Freedom*, 76–7

12th May

THE VICTORIOUS KING IS ONE OF US

Reading: Colossians 2:13–19

In times past, even when Saul was king, it was you who led out and brought in Israel. And the Lord *your God said to you, 'You shall be shepherd of my people Israel.' (1 Chronicles 11:2)*

The first ground for the unifying of Israel was Israel's appreciation of David as being one of them. Notice how they say that in time past, even when Saul was king, it was David who led them out and brought them in. The term is of course to do with leadership in warfare. He led them into battle, he was the secret of their victories and never more so than when he met the giant Goliath. When Saul and Jonathan were skulking in their tents, yellow with fear and panic at the sight of Goliath, it was David who conquered the giant and led Israel's armies out to victory.

It speaks at once to our hearts. What hope would we have in this world, or in this universe; what victory could we ever claim over the powers of nature, let alone the powers of hell, were it not for him who came to lead us and fight our battles for us? We celebrate the one who could say, 'In the world you will have tribulation. But take heart; I have overcome the world' (John 16:33).

I think of a colourful metaphor used by Paul in Colossians 2:13–15. The very hosts of hell surrounded our Lord's cross to defy God in pardoning us sinners. You know, Satan is more interested in morality and in the topic of justice and righteousness than we think he is. If God, as the governor of the universe, had chosen arbitrarily to forgive us just by an act of power, Satan would have gone down to the abyss shouting that God had been defeated because he had been unjust. But the answer was in that man on the cross who, knowing we were sinners, took the long record of debt that was written out against us. It was signed in our handwriting, so to speak, by our conscience, which agreed with God that we were sinners. He took it, wiped it out, and nailed it to his cross. He fought and has won our battles, and therefore we love him. We have no other leader to hide behind. It is Christ who compels the love of his people and in this way draws them together.

David Gooding, *Visions of Eternity: Five Studies on Major Themes in 1–2 Chronicles*, 23

13th May

THE RISEN AND ASCENDED MAN

Reading: Acts 1:1–11

'See my hands and my feet, that it is I myself. Touch me, and see.' (Luke 24:39)

In resurrection (what a lovely story it is), on the other side of the grave our Lord is still a man. But when he appeared to the apostles in the upper room, at first they were frightened; they thought they had seen a spirit. 'Why are you troubled?' he said, 'It is I myself' (Luke 24:36–39).

I love those words, 'It is I myself'. How do we recognize him? How can we see it's him and not just a spirit? 'Touch me, and see,' he says. To be himself, he had to have a body. He became man and he's not ceased to be man. 'A spirit has not flesh and bones as you see that I have.' In resurrection he remains human, and one day we are going to have a body 'like his glorious body' (Phil 3:21). It will be a human body—changed, glorified, with different powers, but a human body like his.

And so it was at his ascension. Who shall explain the wonder of it? He's gone into heaven as a man! In a sense it's nothing to be wondered at that the Son of God should return to heaven and sit on his Father's throne. But what new thing is this: the man, Jesus of Nazareth, has risen into heaven, above the angels, above all principality, and power, and might, and dominion, and has sat down at the very right hand of God? I think Michael and Gabriel the archangels haven't got over it yet! How astonished they were when they saw the man, Jesus, the Son of God, put himself lower than the angels for the suffering of death; and now that same Jesus of Nazareth has been raised above them, and a man is seated on the throne of God.

Whether we can explain it or not, the fact is that Christ has carried manhood into the very heart of the Trinity. That was a *new* thing: he was really human with a human body. And when he comes again he shall be 'this same Jesus'. As they saw him go into heaven the angels said, 'Why are you gazing up into heaven? This same Jesus shall so come in like manner as you have seen him go into heaven.'

David Gooding, *Understanding the Trinity: Six Studies on God's Revelation of Himself*, 32–3

14th May

TAKING HUMANITY INTO THE VERY PRESENCE OF GOD

Reading: Acts 7:40–56

*And he said, 'Behold, I see the heavens opened, and the Son
of Man standing at the right hand of God.' (Acts 7:56)*

Stephen knew instinctively that the risen Christ who was blessing his apostles at the very moment of his ascension would not cease to bless his people. He had neither disowned nor forgotten them. He had entered the presence of God as their Saviour and representative, just as Israel's high priest had entered the Most Holy Place in the temple as Israel's representative. Christ's acceptance with God as his people's representative was obviously complete and permanent, and so was theirs! Through Christ they now had unimpeded 'access to the Father by one Spirit', as Paul was later to express it (Eph 2:18 DWG).

Similarly, when after the provision of the tabernacle of Moses and the even more glorious temple of Solomon God announced through Isaiah that no earthly building could adequately serve the transcendent Creator as a dwelling place, God was not abandoning his idea of his dwelling with men and women, or of their dwelling with him. In the tabernacle and temple, not only did God dwell among them in some sense, but once a year one man at least was allowed to enter the presence of God on earth.

In announcing that Jesus Christ had now made the temple obsolete, Stephen was saying that God had moved on to the fulfilment of that same purpose and desire, but at an infinitely higher level. 'Look,' said Stephen, 'I see the heavens opened, and the Son of Man standing at the right hand of God' (Acts 7:56). No wonder the Sanhedrin saw his face looking like the face of an angel (6:15)!

The Son of Man he saw was none other than Jesus, the real, human Jesus who had so recently walked this earth. Now that same Jesus, risen bodily from the dead and ascended bodily into heaven, was standing at the very right hand of God. And not only for himself. As the Son of Man, the ideal man, he incorporated with and in himself all his people. If he could enter and be welcomed in that exalted heaven, so could they. This was staggeringly, gloriously new. But it was not a denial or repudiation of the idea behind the high priest's yearly entry into the Most Holy place on earth: it was its fulfilment, and therefore its replacement, at an infinitely higher level.

David Gooding, True to the Faith: The Acts of the Apostles—Defining and Defending the Gospel, 143, 148–9

15th May

DOING THINGS GOD'S WAY

Reading: 2 Samuel 6:13–23

'And I will be even more undignified than this, and will be humble in my own sight. But as for the maidservants of whom you have spoken, by them I will be held in honour.' (2 Samuel 6:22 NKJV)

When David brought up the ark the second time it was carried on the shoulders of God's own Levites according to the law of Moses (1 Chr 15:2, 15). They were God's chosen phalanx, and they walked into the city with the ark. It must have been a spectacular moment because Israel believed that the transcendent Lord of heaven and earth sat upon the cherubim above the ark! As the crowds lined the streets and saw the Levites coming with the ark upon their shoulders, they would have believed it was the Lord coming to Jerusalem.

What should the appropriate attitude be? The people gave vent to their praise and homage with shouts and the sound of trumpets in ecstatic worship (2 Sam 6:15). And what about David? Did he line up in front of the ark, crown on his head, sceptre in his hand, conducting the Lord in, and saying, 'Lord, this is the way'?

No, he didn't. He took off all his regalia, and, wearing a linen ephod, he danced before the Lord 'with all his might', just like one of the common people.

Michal, David's wife, hadn't been at the ceremony. She was looking out of the window, and when she saw David 'she despised him in her heart'. When David returned home, she came out to meet him. 'Oh,' she said, 'the king is like one of the vulgar fellows, humbling himself like one of the common people.' And David said, 'I shall be more humble than ever, then, but in the eyes of the people I shall be held in honour.'

When it came to the question of the Lord coming to the city, then King David would take his place among the ranks of the ordinary people, for who was David compared with the Lord? Oh, how important this is. The difference between those who rule amongst God's people and the people themselves is as nothing compared with the vast chasm that separates the highest king from the Lord himself. When the ark returned to Jerusalem, did it lose David any authority over the people when he joined them like an ordinary citizen and danced before the Lord? Of course it didn't. Nor will it lose us authority in whatever sphere we are called upon to rule, if we show those whom we are supposed to be ruling that we stand with them under the power and authority of God.

David Gooding, *The Problems of Becoming and Being a King: Fifteen Seminars on Major Themes in 1 & 2 Samuel*, 160

16th May

TRUE LOVE AND LOYALTY IN THE LIFE OF RAHAB

Reading: Joshua 2:12–21

*'Now then, please swear to me by the L*ORD *that, as I have dealt kindly with you, you also will deal kindly with my father's house, and give me a sure sign.' (Joshua 2:12)*

'Please swear to me by the Lord; give me a sure sign,' said Rahab. So they gave her their word. What a lovely thing it is: a soul being converted, getting saved by finding the true God, discovering that God is love and love means loyalty. She staked her everything on that and proved God true to his oath.

And now what? As the spies disappeared into the darkness, the anxious period began. They had suggested that she should take a scarlet cord and put it in the window through which she had let them down so that the advancing armies could see which was Rahab's house. I don't know how long she waited. If I had been Rahab, I wouldn't have bothered to lock the door before I put that cord in the window! I would want Joshua, at least, to see whose side I was on. The unspoken pledge of loyalty, 'I was loyal to your spies; now you be loyal to me.'

When the army came she was delivered; but not to go back to her old ways. Scripture gives us indications that it was not so. She was not only incorporated into the people of God, she became the wife of a certain Salmon and therefore mother of that steady citizen Boaz, who with Ruth became the great-grand-parents of David the illustrious king. As such, Rahab was an ancestress of our blessed Lord (Ruth 4:18–22; Matt 1:5–6).

As we wait until the Lord shall come, God grant that he may see the unobscured token of truth in the window of our lives and behaviour. By God's grace we are the Lord's and will be loyal to him.

If we see Rahab one day in heaven, we shall not despise her or her doubtful beginnings. What are we, had the grace of God not saved us? We should be all the more careful, so that when we get there we are found uncompromised in our loyalty to the Lord Jesus—'betrothed to him, to be presented as a pure virgin to Christ' (see 2 Cor 11:2). Let not Satan compromise our intellectual, spiritual or moral loyalty to the Saviour.

David Gooding, *God's Great Salvation: Four Old Testament Character Studies*, 8–9

17th May

THE GIBEONITES AND EVIDENCE OF GENUINE CONVERSION

Reading: Joshua 9:3–27

Do not use your freedom as an opportunity for the flesh, but through love serve one another. (Galatians 5:13)

But they told a lie! Yes, but we should notice this about these Gibeonites: they were genuine men. The Israelites were to offer peace to a city that was far off, on certain conditions. Did you notice what the conditions were? If the people wanted peace they had to hand over their city and undertake to be servants of God's people for the rest of their days.

When the Gibeonites came in their funny get-up, they asked the Israelites to make a covenant with them so that they should be allowed to live. The Israelites said, 'We can't do that—perhaps you come from around the corner.' They didn't argue, but notice what they said, 'We are your servants' (Josh 9:11). They heard what Moses said: the condition of being spared was that they should be willing to become servants (Deut 20:11).

> So [Joshua] did this to them and delivered them out of the hand of the people of Israel, and they did not kill them. But Joshua made them that day cutters of wood and drawers of water for the congregation and for the altar of the Lord, to this day, in the place that he should choose. (Josh 9:26–27)

For centuries the Gibeonites and their descendants were known as servants of the people of God and servants to the altar. They were genuine men; they didn't just say this in order to save their skin.

Did you get converted in order to save your skin; to escape the wrath of God? That's a very good reason, but how would I know that you are genuine? Well, I should know it if you've given up your right to your 'city', and handed it over to the Lord. You have become a servant to the people of God and serve them without murmuring and without reserve. And, above all, you have become a servant to the altar.

What do I mean? The gospel is this, 'that one has died for all, therefore all have died; . . . that those who live might no longer live for themselves but for him who for their sake died and was raised' (2 Cor 5:14–15). This is the mark of whether we are true, or whether our confession of faith is a mere say-so to save our skin.

David Gooding, *God's Great Salvation: Four Old Testament Character Studies*, 12

18th May

WHO IS ON THE LORD'S SIDE?

Reading: Exodus 32

Then Moses stood in the gate of the camp and said, 'Who is on the Lord's side? Come to me.' And all the sons of Levi gathered round him. (Exodus 32:26)

It does not merely say 'who is on God's side?' Moses asks who is on the Lord's side, who is on Jehovah's side; for Jehovah is a God with a name. He has declared himself: he has told us what he is like, he has intervened in history. Who is on Jehovah's side?

The sad story that we have read tells us that this question was posed to none other than Israel, the supposed people of God. When Moses came down the mountain from speaking with God, he found these people at their worship. There they were around their altar with their golden image upon it. They were not playing cards, getting drunk, or in some den of vice; they were at their religious exercises. They were praising God and in their fervour they were dancing around the altar. The singing doubtless was vigorous and enchanting and alluring, and no one could possibly question their devotion. Yet when Moses saw it, he took the tablets of God's holy law and smashed them on the ground. What a disaster the people had fallen into.

He cried from his heart, 'Who is on the Lord's side?' He needed to, for this other was not the Lord's side. We have to distinguish between religion that stands on the Lord's side, and religion that stands on the other side. Moses wasn't upset because he was a hard old fellow or narrow minded of heart. These were his people, fervent in their religion; but the god they worshipped was a god of gold that could no more save them than the man in the moon could save them. Here they were in the wilderness, surrounded by enemies galore. There was drought and famine, and hostile tribes on all sides. It was a waste howling wilderness, and they didn't know the way to their desired haven.

They needed a God who could save them. They needed the living God: Jehovah, the God of mercy and redemption and forgiveness; the God of power and light and guidance. But Aaron had diverted their attention and their faith from him, and had got them all occupied with their singing and their dancing around a golden calf that could never save them.

David Gooding, *Standing on the Other Side: One Evangelistic Study on Making a Decision About Christ*, 5

19th May

BEING ON THE RIGHT SIDE WHEN THE KING RETURNS

Reading: 2 Samuel 19:9–24

I have fought the good fight, I have finished the race, I have kept the faith. (2 Timothy 4:7)

I suspect that in middle life King David grew somewhat self-indulgent—it is the danger of the middle-aged. The people became discontented with David, and there arose a son of his called Absalom. Absalom was—what's the word?—cool. I think he was cool; you should have seen the hairstyle! Moreover, he was really down to earth and practical, and he stood for justice.

Mark that: he stood for justice. He pointed out that the king was getting old and didn't care for all the wrong things that were being done in the kingdom. 'If I were king,' he said, 'I'd see that justice was done.' He used to go up to the people by the court door, when they were waiting for the judge to come, and say, 'What is your case?' And whatever the person said, Absalom would reply, 'That's a very good case!' You can't say that to everybody, but he did. And then he would take the people by the hand and kiss them. (I don't know what you'd think if you went to the court and the judge kissed all the defendants.) Hundreds of them fell for him, and he led a rebellion against the king.

Then the king came back. When David appeared again, Absalom was slain and there were a lot of red faces. Why did David's own countrymen and relatives up in Hebron take sides with the rebel? There were some difficult moments when David came back out of exile to be their manifest king again.

And the Lord is going to appear. 'Timothy,' said Paul, 'in view of the coming lie that shall prevail, I charge you to preach without compromise. See that all in the church are rigorously taught the faith! I have fought the good fight and finished the race, and kept the faith.'

In the final battle it will be truth that is at stake. We must fight the good fight of faith without compromise, so that when the Lord appears as the righteous judge we will be able to say, 'I've finished my course. I have kept and propagated the faith in loyalty to the Lord.' And then the righteous Judge shall give us the crown of righteousness because we have been straight down the line for him and his truth.

David Gooding, *Loving his Appearing: One Study on How the Truth Triumphs Against the Lie*, 13–14

20th May

THOSE WHO WILL HAVE STATUS IN THE KINGDOM OF GOD

Reading: Luke 18:15–17

But Jesus called them to him, saying, 'Let the children come to me, and do not hinder them, for to such belongs the kingdom of God.' (Luke 18:16)

The Pharisees, intent on looking for the glory and power of the coming kingdom, failed to recognize the king himself standing in front of them (Luke 17:20–21). Apparently he was not grand enough for them. Now the disciples make the opposite mistake. Some mothers bring their infants for Christ's blessing, and the disciples rebuke them. Obviously they thought that children were not important or grand enough for Christ to spend time and effort on them; and our Lord had to correct them. 'To such,' he said 'belongs the kingdom of heaven.' Little children take their food and their parents' love and protection without beginning to think if they deserve it, or whether they are important enough to merit such attention. That is how we must all receive God's kingdom and enter into it (see 18:17).

Most Christians would have no difficulty in adopting the child's attitude themselves in this context. It is when, like the apostles, we start engaging in 'Christian work' that we are liable to fall into the temptation of thinking that it is more important to attract leaders and magnates to Christ rather than the 'Mrs Mopps' of this world. According to James that is to break the whole law (see Jas 2:1–13). The fact is that when it comes to entry into the kingdom of God no one is more important than any other.

David Gooding, *According to Luke: The Third Gospel's Ordered Historical Narrative*, 310

21st May

STATUS IN THE KINGDOM FOR THOSE CHRIST CALLS HIS FRIENDS

Reading: 2 Thessalonians 2:13–17

To this he called you through our gospel, so that you may obtain the glory of our Lord Jesus Christ. (2 Thessalonians 2:14)

Consider how magnificently God treats us. He has every right to treat us as slaves, simply commanding us to do things without giving any reasons or taking us into his confidence. But he has not done so. Although it is an honour for us to be allowed along with the apostles to call ourselves 'slaves of Jesus Christ' (cf. Phil 1:1), that is not what he calls us, nor how he treats us. 'No longer do I call you bondservants, for the servant does not know what his master is doing; but I have called you friends, for all that I have heard from my Father I have made known to you' (John 15:15).

He does not seek to get his desired results by acting the slave master and driving us to carry out his commands in blind, uninformed, unthinking obedience. He is the Vine, we are the branches, and without him we can do nothing (15:5). Yet, by God's grace—let it be said with bated breath—we are an integral and necessary part of God's process of making himself known, and Christ recognizes and treats us as such. With the perfect self-giving of the true Vine that he is, he has shared with us, the branches, all that the Father has told him.

It would be a shameful thing, then, if we did not joyfully respond to his friendship by being a friend to him, and laying down our very lives for him by doing what he commands us to do. Indeed, if we had any true sense of the relationship which Christ has set up between himself and us, or any realistic conception of its potential, we should constantly be pestering Christ to choose us to do this or that task for him. But without being asked, he has long since taken the initiative himself and chosen us, both for salvation (2 Thess 2:13), and for his service (1 Pet 2:9). We need only to ask him what particular task he has chosen for us.

David Gooding, *In The School of Christ: Lessons on Holiness in John 13–17*, 160–1

22nd May

THE STATUS OF LEADERS IN THE KINGDOM IS THAT OF SERVANTS

Reading: Mark 10:35–45

'Rather, let the greatest among you become as the youngest, and the leader as one who serves.' (Luke 22:26)

When an argument broke out among the apostles at the Last Supper, our Lord took the occasion to teach them the true nature of rule and office and service in his kingdom. The argument on that solemn and most sacred occasion had been about which of them was to be regarded as greatest. That one apostle should desire to be regarded as greater than another apostle would surely strike us as incredible, did we not know our own hearts and recognize that, for all the importance of their office, the apostles were human like ourselves. But so it was, and our Lord had to point out to them how thoroughly unregenerate an idea of power and ruling they had imbibed. 'The kings of the Gentiles exercise lordship over them, and those in authority over them are called benefactors' (Luke 22:25).

And still today all too often greatness is felt to lie not in actually serving other people, but in the personal aggrandisement that accompanies high office, and in the sense of power and ability to control other people's lives that it brings. By some curious twist in logic, the title of *benefactor* doesn't go to the people who actually do the work and serve, but to those who sit aloft and are served by others.

'But not so among you', said our Lord to his apostles. They might be destined to hold high office in the church, so high that none could be higher save Christ himself; but they were not to get it into their heads that office in the church was like office in the great pagan empires. 'Not so with you,' said Christ. 'Rather, let the greatest among you become as the youngest, and the leader as one who serves.'

David Gooding, *Windows on Paradise: Scenes of Hope and Salvation in the Gospel of Luke*, 98–9

23rd May

STATUS IN THE KINGDOM DOES NOT ALLOW FOR PARTIALITY

Reading: James 2:1–4

My brothers, show no partiality as you hold the faith in our Lord Jesus Christ, the Lord of glory. (James 2:1)

We could get our values very wrong if we made a fuss in the church of one believer because he or she happened to be rich and well turned out and undervalued and despised poor believers because they were poor, when our very gospel tells us that the Lord of glory died for both poor and rich alike.

James has the modesty not to tell us, but actually the Lord Jesus Christ, the Lord of glory, was his brother. Why didn't James tell us that he was a brother of the Lord? Because he is a remarkable example of what he preaches. If he had told us, we would have given him a prominent place simply on that ground. But the wonderful fact is that in a far more important sense, every believer is a brother or sister of the Lord Jesus. The epistle to the Hebrews says that the Lord of glory is not ashamed to call us his brothers (Heb 2:11).

When we have our off-days and when we are bad tempered, imagine the Lord amidst the angelic intelligentsia of the universe being called upon to own us as his brothers. Why isn't he ashamed of us and all our wrong ways, small-mindedness and nasty habits?

Notice the real reason why he is not ashamed to call us brothers and sisters. 'For he [the Lord Jesus] who sanctifies and those who are sanctified all have one source.' They have indeed! By his grace he not only died for us at Calvary, but in order to die he took our humanity and became truly human. 'Since therefore the children share in flesh and blood, he himself likewise partook of the same things, that through death he might destroy the one who has the power of death' (2:14).

There is more to it; for now in resurrection he takes all those who trust him and makes them one with himself (Rom 6:5). So don't shun that brother or sister because they are poor, or because they may not be as educated and gifted as you. Don't ask that poor brother to sit down on the floor; you might as well ask the Lord Jesus to sit on the floor because he is one with him and is not ashamed to call him 'brother'.

David Gooding, *A Vision of the Perfect Man and Woman: Seven Studies on Major Themes from James*, 27–8

24th May

STATUS IN THE KINGDOM AND THE DIGNITY OF BEARING CHRIST'S NAME

Reading: James 2:5–9

Your words became to me a joy and the delight of my heart, for I am called by your name, O Lord, God of hosts. (Jeremiah 15:16)

James pleads with his fellow-believers not to become absurd.

> Are not the rich the ones who oppress you, and the ones who drag you into court? Are they not the ones who blaspheme the honourable name by which you were called? (2:6–7)

Not all rich people do this, of course; many have been benefactors. But over the centuries it has often been the rich who have exploited the poor and made their fortunes on sweated labour. They know all about the law of the courts and can wangle their way out of their duties to the detriment of the poor. 'Do they not blaspheme the honourable name by which you are called?' Not all rich people do; some have a great respect for it. But in James's day there were a lot of rich people who did blaspheme the honourable name by which believers were called.

What sense does it make to fawn over such a rich man if he comes into your church, when he is the very man who denies the dignity God has conferred upon you? It would hurt you to hear the name of the Lord Jesus blasphemed, but remember also your own dignity. We are called upon to be humble, but we are not called upon to be worms. My brother, my sister, you can be as poor as poor, but think of the dignity of your position and the name that is called upon you, which is nothing other than the name 'Christian'—the name associated with the Lord of glory.

When I was a youngster, going about doing this and that, my father had no great claim to high social position. But he used to waggle his finger under my nose and say, 'Remember, if you misbehave it is not your name you are bringing into disrepute; it is my name, William Gooding, that you are bringing into disrepute.' The lesson has lasted to this day! Royal offspring have to be careful how they behave; they can't even do what the likes of us do. Why? Because of the name they carry. Don't be proud, but don't be ashamed of your dignity. You are a veritable princess or prince. You carry the royal name itself, and one day you shall appear in glory with him.

David Gooding, *A Vision of the Perfect Man and Woman: Seven Studies on Major Themes from James*, 31

25th May

STATUS IN THE KINGDOM AND THOSE GOD USES TO REVEAL HIMSELF

Reading: 1 Corinthians 3:1–9

*Not by might, nor by power, but by my Spirit,
says the LORD of hosts. (Zechariah 4:6)*

Listen to Paul talking to his fellow believers in Corinth, discussing the matter of building the temple of God. Paul as a wise master builder had laid the foundation (3:10). Other people were building on it, but they were in danger of exalting themselves from being channels to being the centre of the temple. They were dividing up the believers under their various personalities, and getting them to put their confidence in men. That would be a disastrous thing to do and something that inevitably destroys its own objective.

My brother and sister, I am a feeble channel of the Lord's grace as I speak the words of God to you; and unless God Almighty chooses by his Spirit to reveal himself to you, nothing really happens. God is not a thing like an atom. Atoms can easily be understood—all you need is to be a genius! Then you need a cyclotron or something, and a scientist to put the atom through the machine and the poor atom hasn't a chance. It has to yield up its secrets and let you pry into its very heart, because it's only a thing. I rejoice to tell you that I'm not a thing, and even I am superior to an atom. You could put me through your machine and find out all about my chemistry, but unless I choose to open myself up to you, you'll never know me.

You can know God's holy word from A to Z like the Pharisees did, but unless God pleases to reveal himself to you, you'll know nothing. How does he reveal himself? In his mercy and grace and condescension, he uses us as channels. And the vital thing is that it is not by might, nor power or intelligence, but by God's Holy Spirit that God makes himself known. God often uses the foolish things in the world to shame the wise, and the things that are weak to shame the strong (1 Cor 1:27). In this materialistic world, the issue at stake in our day is not whether I'm clever or not. It is whether it is true that there is a supernatural transcendent God. We need to listen because only the voice of his Holy Spirit can demonstrate that it is true.

David Gooding, *An Offer of Restoration: Four Studies in Zechariah on God's Character*, 28–9

26th May

CARRYING LIGHT IN JARS OF CLAY

Reading: Judges 7:15–25

But we have this treasure in jars of clay, to show that the surpassing power belongs to God and not to us. (2 Corinthians 4:7)

Each man was equipped with a clay jar in one hand and a trumpet in the other. Inside every jar was a torch. As they crept up in the dark they would have been invisible until the moment came when Gideon blew the trumpet. 'Look at me, and do as I do', he said (Judges 7:17). So they all blew the trumpets, smashed the jars, held the torches aloft, and cried out, 'A sword for the Lord and for Gideon!' (v. 20).

Woken up with a start in the middle of the night, these poor Midianites looked out to the blaze of lights and they couldn't see whether there were many or few men behind them, so they were thrown into confusion and turned their swords on each other (v. 22). Thus the Lord achieved his victory over the Midianites through Gideon.

Here is light shining in broken vessels. Paul may well be using an allusion to this very battle and this particular tactic, when he says, 'We have this treasure in jars of clay, to show that the surpassing power belongs to God and not to us' (2 Cor 4:7).—'What does it matter if the old earthen vessel is broken and smashed,' says Paul, 'that the excellency of the power of God might be manifest? You've rightly been saying that my body and personal presence are weak. Yes, the old earthen vessel is being broken in the service of the Lord. We carry about in our body the dying of Jesus, "For we who live are always being given over to death for Jesus' sake"' (see vv. 10–11). I take it he is referring to the physical destruction of his person.

Just like his Lord was put to death upon a tree; and from that sorry sight there shone out the splendour of the majesty and the power of God unto salvation; so in his servant. As the earthen vessel was broken, it became evident that the enormous power that came through him was not Paul's but God's. He 'has shone in our hearts to give the light of the knowledge of the glory of God in the face of Jesus Christ' (v. 6). What a glorious privilege! What an expensive ministry, if our earthen vessels must be prepared to be broken up so that all might see that the power is not in oratory, speaker's tricks, or massive theology (though it all may help, who knows?), but in the power of God.

David Gooding, *The Lord Saves His People: Fourteen Seminars on the Book of Judges*, 74

27th May

DAVID'S PRIDE AND THE DANGER OF SERVING FOR OUR OWN GLORY

Reading: 1 Chronicles 21:1–17

Humble yourselves before the Lord, and he will exalt you. (James 4:10)

At this very late stage Satan incited an attitude of pride into the heart of David the king, that he should take glory to himself. David commanded Joab to go and number the people. Why did he do this? In wanting to know how many people he had in all his kingdom, David had fallen to the gratification of pride.

It's no accident that this example concerns the king himself. There are some sins so sophisticated that the drunkard doesn't do them—the drunkard is very rarely given to pride, you know. It's people in high office in the church who are in greater danger of yielding to pride. It's a lovely thing to serve the Lord and it's wonderful to find the joy that comes from the genuine appreciation of God's people; but how easily we topple over that narrow band into doing it for our own glory.

David's was an insidious sin indeed, for it would have ruined the whole age of peace and glory. This was the very sin of the devil, the 'anointed guardian cherub' (Ezek 28:14). Standing in the very presence of God, he sought to deflect the glory of God for himself. That is cardinal sin number one: the proud servant displaces God. 'Man shall sit upon the throne of the Lord'—for whose glory?

My brothers and sisters, we have to learn this lesson before we get home, don't we? Fancy having a whole ten cities or a galaxy or two given to you to rule in the age to come! You run it at first for God's glory; then you do it because you enjoy it (no harm in that); and then, slipping a bit more, you puff out your chest and take the glory to yourself. I know that we all have that tendency to live and work for our own glory; it's been innate in the human heart ever since the fall. We shall have to guard against it all the way home to glory.

You see, when David yielded to pride the people were affected, and that can happen. When preachers get undue fame and are idolized, it harms the people of God who go after them and treat them like their idols. God's discipline fell upon the nation, but David, thank God, recovered.

David Gooding, *Mankind's Pathway to the Coming Age of Peace: Six Studies on the Overall Message of 1 Chronicles*, 65–6

28th May

THE ANSWER TO PRIDE

Reading: 1 Chronicles 21:15–22:1

*'I will not take for the LORD what is yours, nor offer burnt
offerings that cost me nothing.' (1 Chronicles 21:24)*

God was displeased with David, and he struck Israel. As the discipline happened and the pestilence came, David's eyes were opened to see the angel with a drawn sword stretched out over Jerusalem (21:16). His conscience was touched and his heart smote him. Going out into 'no man's land', he said to God, 'Was it not I who gave command to number the people . . . what have these sheep done? It's not their fault; it's my fault. Let your discipline fall on me, but do not let the plague be on your people' (see 21:17).

In response God spared the people, but instructed David what he should do. He was to raise an altar to the Lord on the threshing floor of Ornan the Jebusite and offer a sacrifice upon the altar. When it was over, and he had bought the threshing ground, David said, 'This is the ground where the temple shall be built' (22:1).

And, of course, we can see the parable. The great eternal temple will be built on what ground? It will be built on the ground of Calvary, and all its praise and all its activity shall arise from that spectacular Saviour who, for our sake, took our sin and bore its shame, and gave the glory to God.

When David went to offer a sacrifice, as he was told, Ornan said to him, 'Take it! I'll give you the ground, the animals, the wooden implements—I'll give everything as a gift to my lord the king' (see 21:23).

Ornan didn't know any theology, or at that stage he might have preached to David, 'Don't worry about that sin of yours and that pride of yours; salvation is a gift by faith!' That wasn't the medicine David needed to cure him of his proud attitude and taking the glory to himself. David had learned his lesson. He said to Ornan: 'No, but I will buy them for the full price. I will not take for the Lord what is yours, nor offer burnt offerings that cost me nothing. (21:24)

The answer to the temptation of pride is to yield the sacrifice that costs you the last penny you've got. The Christian pathway to glory is the pathway of sacrifice and self-giving, so that the glory might be God's.

David Gooding, *Mankind's Pathway to the Coming Age of Peace: Six Studies on the Overall Message of 1 Chronicles*, 66–7

PART 9

The Only Wise God

29th May

REDEMPTION DISPLAYS GOD'S WISDOM TO THE ANGELS

Reading: Ephesians 3:7–13

So that through the church the manifold wisdom of God might now be made known to the rulers and authorities in the heavenly places. (Ephesians 3:10)

God has been educating the angels all down the vast centuries. I would like to have been there when God set about the work of creation. He spoke the word and here comes our planet! 'It's nothing like heaven,' says Michael to Gabriel. Then God began inventing the giraffes and the buffaloes and the monkeys, and then human beings! Imagine the variety of creation. That was lesson number one, perhaps, for the great principalities and powers.

But I wonder what Gabriel and Michael said when they saw the blessed Son of God, the second person of the Trinity, take that tremendous step down and be born of the virgin Mary. Did Michael nudge Gabriel and say, 'How can this be? How can the Son lower himself to become lower than us angels?' That was an amazing lesson for the principalities and powers to learn.

What did they say when they saw that same Son of God taken by brutal men, scourged, crowned with thorns, languishing, nailed on a cross? Did Michael say to Gabriel, 'Surely God has gone too far now. Isn't this bordering on folly?'

What would Michael have said if the answer had been told him, 'God has done this to save a sinner called Gooding'? Through that, the angels have learned a staggering lesson.

It was a novel thing when on the fortieth day after the resurrection the blessed Lord Jesus ascended and entered into the very presence of God. 'Whatever next?' says Gabriel—as the angels parted to allow the blessed Son of God come through the portals of heaven and sit at the right hand of God—'a human being, elevated above us!'

God sat him down at his right hand, far above all principalities and powers—a man! God's wonders have not finished. The angels discovered that not only is the man, Jesus Christ, seated above all principalities and powers, might and dominions, but you are as well. If you have got over the wonder of it, the angels have not!

Can you imagine Gabriel whispering to Michael, 'Are we meant to serve them? We knew some of them when they were on earth!' And Michael says, 'They have been bought by the blood of Christ: they are so valuable to God that we shall willingly serve them!' To this present day the angels are watching this marvellous thing.

David Gooding, *Where Does God Dwell Today? Two Studies on the Purpose and Nature of the Church*, 8–9

30th May

GOD'S STRATEGY IN WINNING HEARTS

Reading: Revelation 13:1–17

You are not your own, for you were bought with a price. (1 Corinthians 6:19–20)

Satan is about to launch on earth his last attempt to foster man's absolute insanity. He has put it into the heads of the masses that *man* can be as God. A man will sit upon the throne. Satan will give him his supernatural power, and they shall cry, 'Who is like God.' Will they? No, they won't. They'll cry 'Who is like the beast?' (Rev 13:4). They'll bow down to the beast and deify man, and Satan will give him his throne.

'You will be like God'—isn't that what Satan said to Eve? (see Gen 3:5). Satan holds out all his glittering prizes for people who will follow him, but he says, 'If you don't follow me and take my mark on your right hand or your forehead, you won't be able to buy or sell anything. If you will fall down and worship me, I'll reward you with every material thing you like, but if you don't you won't be able to eat.'

Said God, 'Before that happens, I shall enter the market: I shall become man, and buy them.' How will he buy them? As John is shown a great company following the Lamb, he says that they were singing a new song: 'Worthy are you . . . for you were slain, and by your blood you ransomed people for God from every tribe and language and people and nation' (Rev 5:9). The apostle uses the straight Greek word for 'buying'; not even *redemption*, but *bought*.

In the marketplace God has outbid Satan. I don't know whether you like that idea, but I have to point out to you that God has bought you. He had to capture your heart somehow, and when Satan was offering his great bribe, 'You will be like God', God had to offer a bigger price to get your heart's allegiance. He didn't promise you riches; he didn't promise you gold or silver, or a brilliant career. The price he paid to buy you was the blood of his Son.

> *Jesus, Thou hast bought us, not with gold or gem,*
> *But with thine own life-blood, for Thy diadem.*[1]

Why do you follow the Lamb wherever he goes? What is the secret, and why do you do it? 'Well, I've been bought,' you say. Yes, and at what a price.

---

[1] Frances R. Havergal (1836–79), 'Who is on the Lord's side?' (1877).

David Gooding, *The Past, Present and Future Revealed: Eight Comparative Studies on Daniel and Revelation*, 101–2

31st May

THE WISDOM OF GOD

Reading: Judges 5

And Deborah said to Barak, 'Up! For this is the day in which the LORD has given Sisera into your hand. Does not the LORD go out before you?' So Barak went down from Mount Tabor with 10,000 men following him. (Judges 4:14)

In the battle led by Deborah and Barak against the forces of the Canaanites we notice the apparent folly of their tactics. Having ordered Barak to take his ten thousand men up Mount Tabor, in an inspired moment Deborah commanded him in the name of the Lord to bring them down to the plain. The tactic seemed suicidal, when down in the plain nine hundred chariots of iron were waiting under the skilful generalship of Sisera.

Because she was inspired of God, Deborah knew what Sisera didn't. At that moment it was not merely Barak but the Lord himself who came down to fight with the nobles. 'The stars in their courses fought against Sisera,' says the inspired prophetess (5:20 KJV). God simply put his finger upon the elements and there came a colossal cloudburst, the wadi became a raging torrent and flooded the plain. The quagmire bogged down the chariots and made the Canaanites an easy prey; but it did also depend on a woman who was in touch with God and with his revelation in these matters. What at first sight seemed utter folly and weakness proved to be the wisdom and the strength of God.

As we consider that, let us allow ourselves to jump the centuries and think again of the tactics of the cross, when the Son of God himself came down and was opposed by kings and rulers with Satan at their head. It seemed utter weakness and folly as he hung on Calvary's cross, but the weakness of God proved stronger than men and the folly of God (if one may dare to so call it) wiser than men.

> Yet among the mature we do impart wisdom, although it is not a wisdom of this age or of the rulers of this age, who are doomed to pass away. But we impart a secret and hidden wisdom of God, which God decreed before the ages for our glory. None of the rulers of this age understood this, for if they had, they would not have crucified the Lord of glory. (1 Cor 2:6–8)

The best that their concerted wisdom could do proved to be real and utter folly. What bankruptcy, both of Jewish and Gentile minds, apart from the revelation of God through Jesus Christ our Lord.

David Gooding, *The Lord Saves His People: Fourteen Seminars on the Book of Judges*, 56–7

1st June

GOD'S TACTICS IN DESTROYING FAITH IN MAN

Reading: Revelation 12

For the foolishness of God is wiser than men, and the weakness of God is stronger than men. (1 Corinthians 1:25)

Revelation 13 prophesies that there will come a time when the dragon will bring up his big, big man. He's so big that he will defy the living God and proclaim that he himself is God.

But you will remember how God prefaces that with another vision, of a woman who is clothed with the sun, and the moon is beneath her feet. She is pregnant and about to give birth, and her child is destined to rule the nations (Rev 12:1–5). Who is the child? The child is the one who always had been promised since the devil, the old serpent, was in the garden tempting Eve (Gen 3:15). It is our Lord Jesus.

See the relevance of the situation. Here on earth is the sum total and harvest of Satan's efforts: a man is trying to be God and shut God out of his universe. What was God's plan to deal with him? 'I will become man,' said God. 'He who was in the form of God did not count equality with God a thing to be grasped, but took the form of a servant and humbled himself by becoming obedient to the point of death, even death on a cross' (see Phil 2:6–8).

I refer you to Paul's great exposition of the tactics of the cross. When our Lord died for our sins, why did he have to die on a cross? Why couldn't he somehow or other have laid down his life in a more genteel way? Why the brutality of the cross? Paul explains the deliberate tactics of God.

> Has not God made foolish the wisdom of the world? For since, in the wisdom of God, the world did not know God through wisdom, it pleased God through the folly of what we preach to save those who believe. For Jews demand signs and Greeks seek wisdom, but we preach Christ crucified, a stumbling block to Jews and folly to Gentiles, but to those who are called, both Jews and Greeks, Christ the power of God and the wisdom of God. (1 Cor 1:20–24)

God is choosing tactics that, to the world, are weak and the extreme of folly. And why is he doing it? It is to break our trust in man.

David Gooding, *The Problems of Becoming and Being a King: Fifteen Seminars on Major Themes in 1 & 2 Samuel*, 96–7

2nd June

THE CROSS EXPOSES THE FOLLY OF TRUSTING IN MAN

Reading: 1 Corinthians 1:10–20

My speech and my message were not in plausible words of wisdom, but in demonstration of the Spirit and of power, that your faith might not rest in the wisdom of men but in the power of God. (1 Corinthians 2:4–5)

Paul says to the believers in Corinth: 'What are you doing putting your trust in man: organizing yourself around men, making parties around men? Have you not observed that the very tactics of God in your salvation were designed to break your confidence in man?'

We watch the Saviour on the cross and realize that the only way God can save us is through a crucified Christ. When we see the wisdom of the Greek, the power of the Roman and the religion of the Jew that put the Saviour on the cross, we come to the right conclusion as to the wisdom, the power and the religion of this world. All are exposed for what they are apart from God, in that they crucified the Saviour.

'You are in Christ Jesus,' said Paul (1:30). That's a point I'd like to ask you. How did you get into Christ?

You say, 'Well I was a sinner of the deepest dye.' (I don't know what dyeing has to do with it, but it seems that most people who give their testimonies are 'deep-dyed sinners'.) 'There came a preacher to our place, and oh how he could preach! He could hold your attention, and what a master he was of telling a story. He put me in Christ.'

Well, you poor thing. Be careful that another day you're not somewhere else where another preacher comes and takes you out of Christ, because he happens to be more eloquent than the first one. How would any of us be safe if it were some man who put us in Christ?

'No,' says Paul, 'it is by God's own action that you are in Christ Jesus, who became to us wisdom from God, righteousness and sanctification and redemption, so that, as it is written, "Let the one who boasts, boast in the Lord". See that your confidence is solely in the Lord ' (see 1:30–31).

What God had to do was to overcome what Satan had effected, and bring back our confidence solely to himself. Thank God, he has already done it with millions, and has done it with you. Your confidence for all eternity lies solely in God and not in any man. That is where you are safe.

David Gooding, *The Problems of Becoming and Being a King: Fifteen Seminars on Major Themes in 1 & 2 Samuel*, 97

3rd June

GOD'S STRATEGY OF DESTROYING FALSE CONFIDENCE IN THE FLESH

Reading: 1 Corinthians 4:1–7

Let not the wise man boast in his wisdom, let not the mighty man boast in his might, let not the rich man boast in his riches, but let him who boasts boast in this, that he understands and knows me, that I am the LORD. *(Jeremiah 9:23–24)*

God's strategy of the cross was aimed at dealing with a certain fundamental sinful attitude. It relates to the basic confidence of the human heart. In what should we put our confidence for survival and for doing well? God's answer is, 'The basic confidence of the human personality ought to be in God.'

When the Scripture talks of *boasting*, it's talking of our basic *confidence*. In what is my confidence placed? Our confidence must be in the living God himself, and to transfer that basic confidence from God to anything or anyone else is fundamental idolatry.

All humanity has had its confidence perverted by Satan, and it was God's strategy to undermine that false confidence and bring back confidence in God. Hence the strategy of the cross. Man's falsely placed confidence has taken him away from God. The only way of bringing back that confidence is to present mankind with a man crucified on a cross, and for us to preach through him a way of repentance and a way back to God.

The Corinthian believers had professed to believe that gospel message. But Paul asked them, 'Why then are you calling yourselves after the names of other men?' (see 1 Cor 1:12).

It is understandable that people naturally prefer certain preachers to others. Some liked Apollos. 'Oh, he is such a good preacher.' They felt very stirred by his preaching. Others said, 'We like Cephas. He's not so intellectual as Paul, but he is practical.'

We value all the different gifts in the church and praise God for them. We need them all. To start dividing the church and calling your particular group after one preacher or after one set of doctrines, is to fall foul of God's strategy of the cross. 'We're Pauline Christians', they said. Listen to Paul: 'What are you doing calling yourselves after me? Was Paul crucified for you?' (see 1 Cor 1:13).

Well, indeed not. Between our blessed Lord and Paul there was an infinite division. Paul stands with us as a sinner before God, needing to be saved. Christ and Christ only was crucified for us.

David Gooding, *The Heart of the Gospel: Two Studies on Keeping the Cross at the Centre*, 10–11

4th June

EXPOSING OUR NEED AND COMMANDING US TO REPENT

Reading: Colossians 1:21–23

And you . . . once were alienated and hostile in mind, doing evil deeds. (Colossians 1:21)

The problem is that in the heart of every person there is a basic rebellion against God. When faced with God's own Son and his claim to be our rightful Lord and King, we refuse to submit. This basic rebelliousness can often remain undetected beneath genuine political concern for others and sincere religious endeavour. But it is there nonetheless. It is direct encounter with the claims of the Son of God incarnate that removes the upper layers of political and religious respectability and exposes our basic inherent rebellion against God. 'The mind that is set on the flesh,' says Scripture, 'is hostile to God, for it does not submit to God's law; indeed it cannot' (Rom 8:7).

The first step, therefore, in the salvation of the individual or of society, is the exposure of the real trouble. That is what the cross of Christ does. The second step is the provision of an effective incentive to repentance, which the resurrection of Jesus and his vindication as God's Son provides. In the language of the Old Testament:

> 'You [the risen and ascended Son of God] shall break them with a rod of and dash them in pieces like a potter's vessel.' Now therefore, O kings, be wise; be warned, O rulers of the earth. . . . Kiss the Son, lest he be angry and you perish in the way. (Ps 2:9–12)

Or, if you prefer, in the language of the New Testament:

> God . . . now . . . commands all people everywhere to repent, because he has fixed a day on which he will judge the world in righteousness by a man whom he has appointed; and of this he has given assurance of this to all by raising him from the dead. (Acts 17:30–31)

But hear also the comfort offered by the psalm to all who repent and believe: 'Blessed are all who take refuge in him' (Ps 2:12).

David Gooding, An Unshakeable Kingdom: The Letter to the Hebrews for Today, 43

5th June

HOW FAR THE LORD'S ANOINTED MUST GO TO OVERCOME REBEL HEARTS

Reading: 1 Samuel 20:5–23

'The Son of Man goes as it is written of him, but woe to that man by whom the Son of Man is betrayed!' (Matthew 26:24)

Jonathan lets the arrows fly, and they deliberately go beyond the boy. As agreed, he shouts so that David can hear, 'Look, the arrows are beyond you' (1 Sam 20:22). And in that moment the speeding arrows tell God's anointed that he must go!

How could you read those words without thinking of another scene? In the early days of his ministry the Lord was popular with the people. They came in their multitudes, and would still have come, but officialdom turned against him. Then came our blessed Lord's statement: 'The Son of Man goes as it is written of him, but woe to that man by whom the Son of Man is betrayed!'

Tell me, how far must the Lord's anointed go? He had done amazing miracles, so that the crowd wondered at the tremendous power of God. Yet he told his disciples, 'The Son of Man must be handed over into the hands of men', as though he were some helpless victim. How far did he have to go? Is this the Son of the omnipotent Lord of heaven taken by the hands of lawless man and tied to a tree?

I wonder what Michael the archangel thought of it as he saw the darling of Jehovah, the anointed of the Lord, rejected by Caiaphas and the establishment in Israel, forsaken at last by his disciples, handed over to the Gentiles and nailed to a tree. I wonder what he thought of God for allowing it. Did he think—if it's not blasphemous to use the word—'What *folly* on God's part'? I don't know if Michael would have been much relieved to hear God say, 'Well, I have allowed my Son to be abandoned at Calvary because he has to die for such a sinner as Gooding.' Rather than I should perish, the anointed of the Lord himself would suffer.

Tell me how far he had to go and I will tell you what is the secret of the devotion of your heart to God's dear Son, which has bound you in loyalty to him for all time and eternity. Not only is the weakness of God stronger than men; in the strategies of Calvary the sheer folly of God (as the world counts it) is wiser than men. For these were God's tactics for overcoming rebel mankind and making his Son the crown King of the world.

David Gooding, *The Problems of Becoming and Being a King: Fifteen Seminars on Major Themes in 1 and 2 Samuel*, 103–5

6th June

THE KIND OF WISDOM THAT LEADS MAN TO REFUSE A SAVIOUR

Reading: 1 Samuel 17:4–24

When pride comes, then comes disgrace, but with the humble is wisdom. (Proverbs 11:2)

Saul had to be deposed. Even then, God loved him. He couldn't be king any more, but God sent him a saviour. Saul was a very big man, as you know, and that's where his confidence was.

But one day there came out of the camp of the Philistines a colossal great chap. He had come to threaten the people of God, and to denounce the God of Israel as a mere nothing. When Saul saw how much bigger Goliath was, he skulked away into his tent absolutely scared stiff.

Then young David came from looking after the sheep, and said, 'I'll go out and kill him.'

Saul said, 'You can't do that. He's a big man—look at him.'

'Yes, I can,' says David. 'I'll tell you the secret. One day there came a lion to kill the sheep, and another day a bear. I couldn't possibly have mastered those enemies of the flock myself, but I know God and I dared to trust him. I went out and God gave me victory over those evil beasts and I delivered the sheep. I know these are only the small things of life, but it's in the small things where you learn to obey God and trust him. I have proved God, and now that the big crisis has come I will find that he is real.'

> Then David said to the Philistine, 'You come to me with a sword and with a spear and with a javelin, but I come to you in the name of the LORD of hosts, the God of the armies of Israel, whom you have defied.' (1 Sam 17:45)

'The foolishness of God is wiser than men, and the weakness of God is stronger than men' (1 Cor 1:25)—that was how the battle was won, and God saved Saul and the nation.

Then what did Saul do? He showed a very curious but easily credible reaction of the human heart; he wouldn't have his saviour. Proud, trusting his own self, his own wisdom and power, rather than David's God, he so persecuted David until David was forced to run away to the Gentiles, and the nation of Israel was left without their messiah (1 Sam 27:1–4).

David Gooding, *Mankind's Pathway to the Coming Age of Peace: Six Studies on the Overall Message of 1 Chronicles*, 20–1

7th June

THE WISDOM OF THE CROSS AND THE HOUSE GOD IS BUILDING

Reading: Ephesians 2:19–22; 1 Corinthians 1:18–31

The house that is to be built for the Lord must be exceedingly magnificent, of fame and glory throughout all lands. (1 Chronicles 22:5)

'The house of God has to be exceedingly magnificent,' said David. Of course, it had to be. If God was going to dwell in the house, the house couldn't be some poor broken down thing. And I remind you that, if you are part of God's house, you've got to be exceedingly magnificent too. Not with flashy outward adornment, but as sons and daughters of the Most High, built into the temple of God with the name of God on us and the Lord Jesus living within us, our behaviour and reactions have to be magnificent. Our personalities have so to be refined by the grace of the Holy Spirit that we are magnificent. That is God's intent.

Look at the cost of this magnificent house; see the precious stones, the gold and the silver. When we get home to heaven, I'm looking forward to the Lord giving me a conducted tour around the glorious city, our dwelling place for all eternity. When I come to one bit, and it's you, my dear sister, I'll say, 'Lord, why did you incorporate this woman into your scheme? What's so special about her?' And the Lord might reply, 'Perhaps you don't know how expensive she has been? Have you any idea what it cost me to redeem her as a proud independent woman; the grace it took to refine her through life and bring her home to glory at last?'

I'll say, 'Lord, this is a marvellous house that you've got; how did you get all these redeemed people?'

And he will say, 'Well, think of how Solomon, through his superb wisdom, managed to build that house for me; it was through my Son, who is wiser than Solomon, that I've built this house. These were rebel hearts; my problem was how to break their rebellion and make them my loyal servants. Philosophy couldn't do it and miracles couldn't do it. I solved the problem by my divine wisdom—the wisdom of the cross. My dear Son was crucified for them, and when they saw that I loved them so much as to give my Son for them, they found it was impossible to rebel against me any more and gave in. They said to themselves, "If this is what God is like, I want to serve him and be like him for ever."' Here is the wisdom of the cross.

David Gooding, *Visions of Eternity: Five Studies on Major Themes in 1–2 Chronicles*, 44–5

8th June

SUFFERING IS NOT MEANINGLESS

Reading: James 5:7–11

For to this you have been called, because Christ also suffered for you, leaving you an example, so that you might follow in his steps. (1 Peter 2:21)

What grounds do we have for thinking that pain is not absolutely meaningless? As I watch my fellow men and women, I find that we don't think all pain is bad. There are hefty folks who get together and play rugby. They know they're going to get bruised, beaten, banged and come out with sore knees and joints, but they do it nonetheless in spite of the pain. And if you ask them, 'Whatever do you do that for?', they'll say, 'For the fun of it!' Curious, isn't it? As long as the pain isn't too bad, they enjoy doing it.

Then we notice that when nurses and doctors give their lives to tending those with pain and suffering, it produces in them a certain quality of character, which we admire. Whereas people who are out just to enjoy themselves become selfish in the extreme, and we come near to despising them. We seem to hold the view that if tremendous benefits come from it, the suffering has been worthwhile in spite of the pain that it involves.

If we ask God why he has built this universe and put us in it, the answer he will give us is that he made it with an exceedingly glorious future in mind for those who repent and trust him. The Bible talks about the possibility of human beings becoming children of God by being born again of God's Spirit (see John 1:12; 3:6–7). That is the proposition that God our Creator is putting to each one of us. 'And if children, then heirs—heirs of God and fellow heirs with Christ' (Rom 8:17)—inheritors of all that God has and is.

When Christ comes to reign, we are to reign with him; and when there comes a new heaven and earth, we shall be part of his administration. I nearly said, what fun it will be—what glory it will be, to be with Christ when he comes to reign! In God's estimation the glorious provision that he offers us is worth all the pain that life on earth might involve for any one of us.

David Gooding, *Understanding the Trinity: Six Studies on God's Revelation of Himself*, 60

9th June

THE SUFFERING WILL BE WORTH IT

Reading: 2 Corinthians 4:13–18

For this light momentary affliction is preparing for us an eternal weight of glory beyond all comparison. (2 Corinthians 4:17)

This world has been out of joint ever since Adam rebelled against God. By God's own providence, this world doesn't run as it should. In one sense that's a good thing too, for if men and women could live in a paradise without God in this world, perhaps they would never seek the Saviour. That would be disastrous, for we'd end up in perdition.

This is a broken world. Let it remind us that life is only temporary and that here, in this life, we must decide what our eternal destiny shall be. Those who trust the Saviour don't necessarily get freedom from pain, but what happens is that there comes a new slant, a new attitude to it, even when that pain becomes almost unendurable. In their hearts they know that it is not meaningless. God says he can take the pains of this natural life and turn them for our eternal benefit, so that we may be purified and our faith in the end strengthened so that we may be able to appreciate the joys of heaven even more.

And if you want another opinion, ask some senior believer. My mind goes to an elderly man in my home assembly. Occasionally he would pass on a word of encouragement and exhortation. I remember him in his later days, struggling to get to his feet because of arthritis—he had it very severely, the poor man. It was a kind of torture. He would end his remarks by saying, 'But, brethren and sisters, in spite of my pain, it will be worth it all when we see Jesus.'

Yes, that's the view believers take. They know the pain is real, and the suffering is real, but they've caught a glimpse of God's eternal purpose. They're children of God, heirs of God and joint heirs with Christ. They are heirs to the glories of eternity. When we see that, when we discover what God has done and prepared for those who love him, the sufferings of this present time seem a small thing in comparison.

David Gooding, *Understanding the Trinity: Six Studies on God's Revelation of Himself*, 66–7

10th June

THE OFFERING OF COOKED FOOD

Reading: Leviticus 2:4–13

You have been grieved by various trials, so that the tested genuineness of your faith—more precious than gold that perishes though it is tested by fire—may be found to result in praise and glory and honour at the revelation of Jesus Christ. (1 Peter 1:6–7)

The flour might be the very best, the currants and sultanas and the oil of the highest quality, but who would want to eat them in their raw state? Good as they are, before they can become completely palatable they must somehow be cooked. When at last the cake comes out, all nicely risen and looking very tempting, you will observe two things. It's the same stuff as went in the oven that comes out; and yet, though it is the same, it is very different. Most of the time it comes out so much more wonderful. Sometimes it comes out differently, and it is discreetly given to the dog, which is sad. It is sadder still when it happens with a human life.

What is a human personality? Well, its constituent parts are body and spirit; but that's not all a human personality is. At birth another process begins that is designed to complete and perfect that human personality. It is life's *experience*, which tests and 'cooks' it, and does something to the personality every day and every year of one's life.

You point me to a young girl. How beautiful she is, in the flower of her life, delightful. Then you point me to her mother. The sun has done its work and there's a wrinkle or two, but why is it that sometimes Mother is easier to get on with than her daughter? Why does Mother remain calm in a difficult situation and prove to be a tower of strength to her family, whereas the daughter couldn't possibly? The key is in what life has done to Mother. It has ripened and matured her until there is something in her personality now that wasn't there at the beginning.

That's what life is meant to do, and it's a delightful thing when it goes well. It is a disaster when it goes wrong. My dear fellow Christian, how is life *cooking* you? Are you daily enlarging with a greater breadth of mind and kindliness of spirit and sympathy and strength; or is life on the way to making you silly, proud, arrogant, jealous, embittered? Don't look at my cooking too closely. Give the great Cook another hour, please; for there are days when I don't taste very nice.

David Gooding, *The Adoration of Christ: Six Studies on the Nature and Practice of Worship*, 37–8

11th June

PAUL'S WISE ATTITUDE TO SUFFERING

Reading: Acts 21:10–14

'I am ready not only to be imprisoned but even to die in Jerusalem for the name of the Lord Jesus.' (Acts 21:13)

In spite of the explicit statement that imprisonment and afflictions awaited him, Paul was determined to go on to Jerusalem, cost what it may. How do you regard a man who behaves like that? There are some people in this world who are quite ready to suffer and, instead of admiring them, you'd have to pity them—people who like making martyrs of themselves. Too great a readiness to suffer is not always a commendable thing: wanting to be a martyr is psychologically unhealthy.

Was Paul a fanatic of that order? Well, if you read the whole section, you will find that he is exceedingly balanced when it comes to this very matter of his attitude to suffering. If defending the gospel at Jerusalem and Rome means suffering, imprisonment and death, and the Lord has told him to go, then he'll face the suffering. But he isn't going to suffer any more than he has to.

When the captain in the Roman army rescues Paul from the mob and orders that he is to be bound and examined by flogging, it was one of the procedures that the Roman magistrates were allowed to do on people who were not Roman citizens. What does Paul say? 'Yes, flog me. I love being flogged for the sake of the Lord Jesus.' I should think not. He isn't going to take a flogging when he doesn't have to, so he has a word with one of the centurions: 'Is it lawful for you to flog a man who is a Roman citizen and uncondemned?' (Acts 22:25).

When the centurion related that to the captain, he was afraid, for even binding Paul when he was a Roman citizen was highly illegal, and Paul could have made it very awkward for him. Of course, the captain had Paul released immediately. Paul was willing to suffer for the Lord Jesus, but not to suffer more than he had to, and so you will perceive then an exceedingly balanced character. He would suffer for the sake of the gospel, but not if suffering would act against the gospel.

David Gooding, *Daring to be Different: Seven Studies from Acts on Defining and Defending Christianity*, 79–80

12th June

LEADING US IN HIS TRIUMPH

Reading: 2 Corinthians 2:12–17

But thanks be to God, who in Christ always leads us in triumphal procession, and through us spreads the fragrance of the knowledge of him everywhere. (2 Corinthians 2:14)

Paul is accustomed to using military metaphors to explain himself. He uses one here in 2 Corinthians 2, where we read how harassed he was by the conflicting responsibilities that came upon him. He didn't know whether to stay in Troas, where a great door had been opened up to him in the gospel. First he was troubled because of the news that had come from Corinth of the disturbances there; then more recently because no news had come. So he left the gospel campaign and went to meet his colleague, hoping to get some information.

I suspect he was wondering whether he had done right or wrong. How difficult it can be sometimes, in the midst of conflicting duties, to know whether you are doing right or if it would be better to do some other thing. Eventually Paul comes round to comforting his heart, for he perceives that in the end the great skill and wisdom are not his but his general's.

He is using a military metaphor based on Roman practice. If a Roman general had come to Britain, for instance, and won an unusually great victory, if they considered his victory big enough they would grant him a *triumph* back in Rome. They would get him in his chariot with all his other chariots and troops, and then certain Britons would be chained to his chariot and be obliged to walk before, beside and after him as he wended his triumphal way to the capital to give thanks to the gods.

The greatest privilege God ever conferred on any man was to defeat him and chain him to the triumphal chariot of Jesus Christ, so that it is not my cleverness and wisdom which is exhibited but the wisdom and power of the great Commander himself. He has converted and subdued me by the love and mercy and grace of his heart, so that through me, even me, he is pleased to make known the fragrance of the knowledge of God everywhere. And through you, even you; not merely by what you are doing for him, but even more by what he has done for you.

David Gooding, *The Lord Saves his People: Fourteen Studies on Understanding the Major Sections of Judges*, 59

13th June

THE DEEP THINGS OF GOD

Reading: 1 Corinthians 2:9–16

But we impart a secret and hidden wisdom of God, which God decreed before the ages for our glory. (1 Corinthians 2:7)

When he came among them in Corinth, Paul's words were not in man's wisdom, 'but in demonstration of the Spirit and of power, that [their] faith might not rest in the wisdom of men but in the power of God' (vv. 4–5). When people were converted and on their way to becoming mature, he could say, 'Yet among the mature we do impart wisdom' (v. 6). Then he would go on to talk to them of the further riches of God.

So there is a wisdom beyond what you may call 'the ABC of the gospel'. How would you describe it?

> But, as it is written, 'What no eye has seen, nor ear heard, nor the heart of man imagined, what God has prepared for those who love him.' (v. 9)

'Lovely,' you say, 'and when we get home to heaven we shall enjoy it all! We're looking forward to it, for we can't know it now, of course.'

But you've got it the wrong way round; of course you can know it now. That's what Paul is saying: 'These things God has revealed to us through the Spirit. For the Spirit searches everything, even the depths of God' (v. 10). Things that haven't entered into the hearts of unconverted men and women—they don't know, but you can know. Oh, start getting excited! Things that no eye has seen, nor ear heard, God wants to pour into our hearts and minds by his Spirit that he gives us. Lovely things that 'God has prepared for those who love him'.

Someone will say, 'These are deep things, and I'm not a scholar.' Scholarship is helpful if you've got it, but sometimes it's a hindrance. With our new birth, we have received the Spirit of God so that we might know the things that are freely given us of God.

So, if we have God's Holy Spirit—genius that he is in communicating the lovely things of God—he will make known to us these things, such as eyes never saw nor ears heard nor entered into the heart of man, the wonderful things that God has prepared for those who love him.

David Gooding, *Obtaining the Goal of Salvation: Three Studies on the Work of the Holy Spirit*, 18

14th June

UNWISE KINDNESS

Reading: 2 Samuel 10:1–6

Then said David, 'I will show kindness unto Hanun the son of Nahash, as his father showed kindness unto me.' (2 Samuel 10:2 KJV)

You might perhaps wonder whether it was a wise thing for the monarch of Israel to try and show kindness to the monarch of Ammon. Throughout the Old Testament Ammon was constantly attempting to steal Israel's inheritance.

In the time of Jephthah, Ammon said to Israel, 'Look here, you have no right to this territory that you occupy; it belongs to us, and if you don't give it up we shall come and take it' (see Judges 11:13). So Jephthah gave the man a lesson in history. 'I'll have you know,' he said, 'that this is how we came by this land. We're sticking by our God-given inheritance.' Ammon persisted with his claims and Jephthah was obliged to use the sword on them.

Centuries later, when Nehemiah came back to Jerusalem to complete the restoration of the city and get the temple in good working order, he was opposed by many of the nations around him, and not least by Tobiah the Ammonite. Presently, Nehemiah had to go back to the court in Persia, and when he returned to Jerusalem, he found a very curious thing. There was Tobiah, if you please—the very man who had been amongst the foremost opponents of Nehemiah and the rebuilding of Jerusalem and the reuse of its temple—personally occupying one of the rooms in the sacred precincts of the temple. Not only would he steal Israel's inheritance, but God's inheritance as well if he could (see Neh 13:1–9).

We're meant to love our enemies, but we cannot compromise with their objectives. You might as well try to show kindness to the devil himself, who is relentlessly behind every effort that denies God's people their inheritance. Many times he's done it. Denying people the right to read the Bible—'These uneducated people can't make sense of it; it ought not to be given to the ordinary person.' Is it not part of their God-given inheritance?

You cannot make friends with the policy that would deprive people of their God-given inheritance. Who ordained that every believer has the right to know they have eternal life? You cannot make friends with the doctrine that would deny the right of believers to know that they have eternal life. Such compromise, at the very best, is misguided kindness.

David Gooding, Governing for God: Four Studies in 2 Samuel on the Major Stages of David's Life, 30–2

PART 10

The God of Truth

15th June

TRUTH OR POWER AND THE CHARACTER OF THE MESSIAH

Reading: Psalm 45:1–9

In your majesty ride out victoriously for the cause of truth and meekness and righteousness. (Psalm 45:4)

People generally are obsessed with power rather than with moral integrity and truth. When the Lord Jesus told Pilate, 'You are right in saying I am a king. In fact, for this reason I was born, and for this purpose I have come into the world—to testify to the truth.' Pilate replied, 'What is truth?' And then he tried to bring the conversation down to what he thought was a more realistic level. 'Don't you realize', he said, 'I have power either to free you or to crucify you?' (see John 18:37–38; 19:10).

All of us can remember examples of world leaders, and not merely from the remote past, who worshipped power and sought to build their world empires on its basis. But Jesus was different. His passionate concern for truth, his love of righteousness, his hatred of wickedness—these are matters of historical fact, not of pious fantasy. The records of his life have been open to scrutiny for centuries, and still issue the challenge: 'Can any of you prove me guilty of sin?' (see John 8:46). If to love God with the whole heart, mind, soul and strength is the first and greatest commandment of God's law, and to love one's neighbour as oneself is the second, the Lord Jesus fulfilled both in his life and superabundantly in his death.

The records show that in his life on earth he possessed supernatural power, and used it on occasions. But the records also show that he saw more clearly than any that this world cannot be turned into a paradise of justice and peace simply by the exercise of power, even of divine power. The problem of human sin and guilt must be faced and dealt with. What future of justice and peace could be achieved by acting as if the world's past and present sin did not matter, and brushing it under the carpet? Christ certainly would attempt no such thing. He loved righteousness. Divine justice must be upheld. But to use divine power to insist on divine justice, as Christ will do at his second coming—that would mean the execution of sinners. In that case, how many human beings would survive and enter the paradise of peace? Christ loved sinners, and had come to save them and bring them to repentance and make them, like the dying thief, fit subjects for paradise.

David Gooding, *An Unshakeable Kingdom: The Epistle to the Hebrews for Today*, 54–5

16th June

GOD CANNOT LIE

Reading: Joshua 6:15–25

*in hope of eternal life, which God, who never lies,
promised before the ages began. (Titus 1:2)*

The discovery of a God who cannot and will not lie is the beginning not only of security in heaven for us, it's the beginning of the changing of our character. If you promise not to tell them that I said so, there were believers in Crete at one stage who were a little bit difficult.

As one of their own said, 'Cretans are always liars. You can't begin to believe them. They'll promise you they'll be at the prayer meeting then they won't turn up.' How on earth did they get changed into reliable, loyal Christian people whom you could trust? They became people whose profession of love was not mere sentiment, the whim of the emotion blowing hot today and cold tomorrow; but a love of God that expressed itself in constant loyalty to God, to his truth and his people. That's conversion, isn't it?

When Rahab was eventually delivered, she was among Israel 'even unto this day', which is interesting. Apparently she hadn't even taken a tourist ticket back to her former haunts. No, she stood with the people of God. What is it that changes people? What is it that changed the Cretans? Says Paul, 'It's happened through the word of the gospel. The promise that God made of eternal life. A promise made by a God who cannot lie.' We need to discover him. When he talks about judgment on sin, he means what he says. He's not like some soft indulgent parent who says to the difficult child, 'I'll punish you if you do that again.' And the child manages to do it again fifty times before it goes to bed and still doesn't get punished.

But you see what that is doing to people's character. We need to live not only in a stable physical universe, we need to live in a stable moral society where truth is truth. How will you build a paradise or an inheritance on any other principle? You need to come to know a God who will judge when he says he'll judge: he does not lie. And thank God, we need to come to know a God who, when he says he will pardon and save, and give us an inheritance incorruptible and undefiled that fades not away, he cannot lie and means every word he says. That is salvation.

David Gooding, Entering the Inheritance: Studies in Joshua 1–12, 19–20

17th June

GOD'S COVENANT PROMISES ARE SURE

Reading: Hebrews 8:7–13

Behold, the days are coming, declares the LORD, when I will make a new covenant with the house of Israel and the house of Judah. (Jeremiah 31:31)

God himself has scrapped the old covenant and all attempts to build a relationship with human beings on its basis. This is not some new-fangled idea thought up by Christians; God announced his intention of doing so centuries ago through the Jewish prophet Jeremiah. He announced that one day he would make a new covenant with his people. And the very fact that he had to make a new covenant shows that there was something faulty with the first one (Heb 8:7). It was not that its standards were too high. It was that it was a two-party covenant: God had his part to keep and so had Israel.

Israel could not keep theirs but constantly broke it, with disastrous results. So the new covenant had to be different from the old. 'It will *not* be like the covenant I made with their forefathers when I took them by the hand to lead them out of Egypt', said God (8:9)—that is, the law given at Sinai. Do let us notice that 'not', for sometimes we hear it suggested that the new covenant is not that much different from the old. But according to God it is radically and fundamentally different.

In what respects? First, that the new covenant is not a two-party covenant. That was precisely the trouble with the old, for the whole covenant was ruined when Israel could not keep their part and they lost its blessings and suffered its curses. So the new covenant is not going to be like that. It is a one-party, not a two-party covenant. Look at its terms listed in Hebrews 8:10–12 and you will see that there is not one thing that God's people are required to do; not one condition that they are called upon to fulfil. The terms of the covenant—one and all of them—simply announce what God will do. He does it all! And since God will fulfil all the terms he has promised to fulfil, the covenant will never be broken and God's people will never be abandoned or rejected.

David Gooding, *An Unshakeable Kingdom: The Epistle to the Hebrews for Today*, 160–1

18th June

THE TRUTH ABOUT THE FATHER

Reading: Psalm 103:13–22

The Lord passed before [Moses] and proclaimed, 'The Lord, the Lord, a God merciful and gracious, slow to anger, and abounding in steadfast love and faithfulness.' (Exodus 34:6)

A friend of mine was once asked to conduct Christian education classes in a children's home. One day when he walked in, he found a nurse with a little boy of seven or eight years. As soon as he saw my friend, the little boy started to scream, so that the nurse had to ask my friend to go out while she pacified the child. That done, she called my friend in again and, taking off the little boy's clothes, she showed him his body scarred all over with burn marks. The little boy explained: 'My father always burns me.' The fact was that his father used to come home drunk, put a poker in the fire until it was red hot and then beat the child with it. Suppose my friend had tried to tell that little boy that God wanted to be his Father. What difficulties my friend would have had to get across to the child what God was really like, and what he means when he calls himself our Father.

By his dastardly work in the garden of Eden, Satan has to a lesser or greater degree perverted all our concepts of what God is actually like. That is one reason why unconverted people do not come lining up to accept the gospel. Their concept of God is that, if they were to believe him and accept his heaven, it would make their lives miserable and boring.

And then of course there are further problems. By inducing mankind to sin, Satan has filled their minds with guilt, so they fear God's justice and try to convince themselves that he does not exist. And if he does exist, they fear that he must be against them, which makes them feel that God must be a horrible ogre. The believer has discovered that that is not true. God's justice must be against the sinner's sin, but God loves the sinner and Christ died for sinners while they were still sinners. The cross of Christ declares that God's love has found a way to pardon and accept everyone who sincerely repents and is prepared to be reconciled to God through his Son, Jesus Christ. So far as his acceptance with God is concerned then, the believer has perfect peace with God both now and forever.

David Gooding, *In The School of Christ: Lessons on Holiness in John 13–17*, 94–5

19th June

THE OBJECTIVE HISTORICAL TRUTH OF THE GOSPEL

Reading: Acts 7:44–53

And there is salvation in no one else, for there is no other name under heaven given among men by which we must be saved. (Acts 4:12)

There is only one Saviour of the world and only one salvation. In a world full of a thousand and one voices advocating the claims of innumerable religions, it is of the utmost importance that we should have clear, objective, historical evidence to establish who that one and only Saviour is.

God has devoted centuries to providing that evidence: by calling Abraham; by the development of a special nation; by establishing patterns of law, of redemption, and of worship through Moses. And finally and supremely through the raising up of David, King of Judah at Jerusalem, ancestor and prototype of Messiah, with numerous prophecies spread over several centuries foretelling Messiah's birth, birthplace, ministry, death, resurrection, and ascension.

The Christian gospel is not a philosophy that anyone, no matter who and of what country, could think up and develop out of universal general principles—provided only that they had a touch of genius. It is the gospel that God promised beforehand through his prophets in the Holy Scriptures. As Paul would later put it, it is 'the gospel of God . . . concerning his Son, who as to his human nature was a descendant of David' (see Rom 1:1, 3). It is the product of a long, objective, historical and geographical process, controlled at every juncture by the God whose gospel it is.

Historically it is inseparable from Jerusalem. According to Luke, when between his resurrection and ascension Christ briefed his apostles for their worldwide mission, he did so in these words: 'This is what is written: The Christ will suffer and rise from the dead on the third day, and repentance and forgiveness of sins will be preached in his name to all nations, beginning at Jerusalem' (Luke 24:46–47 DWG). Forever and forever the gospel is inseparably linked with certain historical events that happened at Jerusalem.

David Gooding, *True to the Faith: The Acts of the Apostles—Defining and Defending the Gospel*, 168–9

20th June

THE SECOND COMING AND OUR LORD'S STAND FOR THE TRUTH

Reading: Revelation 19:11–16

'For this purpose I was born and for this purpose I have come into the world—to bear witness to the truth. Everyone who is of the truth listens to my voice.' (John 18:37)

What a wonderful thing it will be when the God of heaven vindicates the Lord Jesus, and the stand he took for truth. When Pilate enquired if Christ was a king, his answer was, 'Yes, but not in the sense that you understand it, for my kingdom is not of this world.' He was testifying that this world is not a closed shop; there is another world and another kingdom. God incarnate came into our world to bear witness that there is another world—this is the truth of the matter.

It raises a very fundamental question of our existence. What is our planet, and what is the significance of human life upon it? This world is obsessed by power, is it not? The soldiers scourged Jesus, and with his back bleeding he tells Pilate, 'You would have no power at all against me except it were given you from above.' And we pause to think: is it true that Pilate had been given power by God? Yes, it is true; and in those next few hours God was going to show Pilate a demonstration of the truth about our world—had he the eyes to see it.

Pilate is allowed to use his God given, delegated power to put Jesus Christ upon the tree, so let's look for a moment and see what the truth is. The truth is, there is a God who made us, and when rulers with God given power take that power to crucify the very Son of God, God still loves them. At that moment, why was Michael not sent with his thunderbolts to obliterate our planet? Because the truth is that the God who made us is loyal to his creatures. In biblical language, truth is not merely accurate fact; truth is loyalty.

When the patriarch Jacob was reviewing his life, he made this earnest prayer to God: 'O God, I'm not worthy of all the mercies, and of all the *truth* that you have shown me' (see Gen 32:10). What did he mean? It wasn't just the doctrine that God had shown him; he meant that in all the promises God had made to Jacob, God had been loyal to him. That is truth. Yes, it means factual accuracy and speaking truthfully: those things are not only truth but also loyal behaviour. But the day of the appearing is coming, and what shall that do? Why, the first thing is that it shall vindicate the Lord Jesus, and the stand he took for the truth.

David Gooding, *Loving his Appearing: One Study on How the Truth Triumphs Against the Lie*, 6–7

21st June

HE WILL DESTROY THE LIE

Reading: 2 Thessalonians 2:1–4

And then the lawless one will be revealed, whom the Lord Jesus will kill with the breath of his mouth and bring to nothing by the appearance of his coming. (2 Thessalonians 2:8)

What shall the Lord Jesus do by the appearance of his coming? There are many things that he shall do. He shall take his church home to glory, and you could think of many other things, couldn't you? But what will his appearing be for? Well, he stood for the truth in front of Pontius Pilate, and at his appearing he will nail the lie. That is what he will do.

And what shall 'the lawless one' be doing? Well, he will have been spreading *the lie*; exalting himself above all that is worshipped, sitting in the temple of God, proclaiming himself to be God (see 2:3–4). That may sound grotesque to you, but it is the full flowering of the original lie spoken to our human forebears in the garden of Eden. It wasn't that Satan tempted Adam and Eve to some grotesque evil vice. What was it, then? It was the notion that you can live a beautiful, enjoyable, self-contained and satisfying life, ignore God and still enjoy it to the full. That is *the* lie.

Multitudes have swallowed that lie, and never more than now. It will eventually come to its harvest. The end of this age will arrive at the point of the deification of man. He won't be a grotesque monster. Anybody who objects to him will seem like the oldest dinosaur of a survivor from the pre-scientific age, and positively anti-social now that mankind has solved their problems. But as Daniel prophesied, 'he shall cast down truth to the ground' (see Dan 8:12). He will not tolerate anybody who dares to say that there is a power beyond him—that there is a God in heaven.

Don't just say it is grotesque. We have had enough totalitarian dictators in this last century to know how real this is, and to see where the age is moving to. Oh, what a lovely thing it will be when the Lord Jesus appears, and by that very act of his appearing he will expose the falsity of it and destroy the man of sin.

David Gooding, *Loving his Appearing: One Study on How the Truth Triumphs Against the Lie*, 9–11

22nd June

STANDING FOR THE TRUTH

Reading: 2 Kings 18:9–16, 32–35

'O Lord, the God of Israel, enthroned above the cherubim, you are the God, you alone, of all the kingdoms of the earth; you have made heaven and earth.' (2 Kings 19:15)

In the days when Assyria came up with all their massed battalions and military might, they mocked Israel's faith in the living God. That great world power mocked what they thought were stupid and primitive beliefs on the part of this tiny little market town in the hills of Judea. The great truths of redemption, the election of Israel, the purposes of God to bring in Messiah through Israel, and Jerusalem with the house of the Lord there. They told Hezekiah and all the people to abandon these old-fashioned biblical myths in favour of the political theories and ideologies of the Gentile empire of Assyria.

Shaking in his knees, as anybody would when they first had a look at the Assyrians and their armies, Hezekiah thought he could do a kind of a compromise, by hacking off a bit of the gold out of the house of the Lord here, trimming down a little bit there, and giving it to the Assyrians in the hope that, if you trimmed down your faith just a little bit, they might find it more acceptable and let you go on. But he soon found that it was a terrible mistake.

Christendom hasn't found that out yet. Alas for those theologians who, one by one, abandon this fundamental and that fundamental of the Christian faith under the plea that, if you still stand for the fundamentals and for supernaturalism in all its glory, the modern man and woman can't believe it. So, to get them inside your church, you'll have to carve off a bit of the faith here, or trim down supernaturalism there, and hope somehow to convince them. Of course, the people will only conclude that you don't really believe what you say you believe, scorn both you and your faith, and go further from your church than ever.

Hezekiah and his people had to face the issue: *were they going to stand for God's truth?* When were they going to stop whittling down their faith and learn to stand for the objective truth of God's revelation? Through their trust in God they stood rooted and grounded in the faith, like those marvellous pillars in the house of the Lord, Jachin and Boaz (1 Kgs 7:21).

David Gooding, *Keys to Revival: Three Studies from 1–2 Kings on the Leadership of Elijah, Jehoida and Josiah*, 22–3

23rd June

LOVING HIS APPEARING MEANS STANDING FOR THE TRUTH

Reading: 2 Timothy 4:1–5

Preach the word; be ready in season and out of season. (2 Timothy 4:2)

'Timothy, you must preach,' says Paul. Why? Because the thing at issue is *the* truth, that's why. That, in this context, is *the* interest of the whole universe. We witness to him who stood before Pontius Pilate, witnessing for the truth, and died on Calvary's cross in consequence. My dear brothers and sisters it will mean preaching, and you don't have to do it all from a pulpit.

Bear the words of a curmudgeonly old man, and preach the word! You love his appearing, don't you? Then you are looking for the vindication of him who witnessed before Pilate the good confession about the truth. And if you love him, you will be standing for the truth and disseminating the truth. 'For the time is coming when people will not endure sound teaching, but having itching ears they will accumulate for themselves teachers to suit their own passions, and will turn away from listening to the truth and wander off into myths' (see 4:3–4).

The time has come already. Do you believe in creation; in the resurrection; in the second coming? Nowadays many of the leading theologians will reply, 'Well, not literally. The virgin birth is merely a story which makes the point that Jesus is somehow special. The resurrection of Jesus didn't literally happen, it's a story made up by the church. It tells you that the truth will somehow prevail in the end, but we wouldn't like to say that Christians have *the* truth.'

We used to unashamedly announce him who said, 'I am . . . the truth . . . . No one comes to the Father except through me' (John 14:6). But not now; that could soon become an offence against the State in order to keep people from fighting each other.

How clever the devil is. He gets Christians so to depart from the commands of Christ that they fight out their disputes by the sword and the bomb. And then Satan says, 'It's doctrine that has caused all this fighting, so get rid of the doctrine and you'll have peace.' What a cunning tactic of the enemy it is.

We are called upon to stand for the truth.

David Gooding, *Loving his Appearing: One Study on How the Truth Triumphs Against the Lie*, 11–12

24th June

THE SPIRIT OF ANTICHRIST

Reading: 1 John 2:18–21

They went out from us, but they were not of us; for if they had been of us, they would have continued with us. (1 John 2:19)

John says, 'they went out from us'; that is, 'they went out from us *apostles*.' I suggest that we ought to notice this very carefully. When John talks about 'we' and 'us' he is talking primarily about the apostles. Their authority isn't something that we can possibly exaggerate. The Lord Jesus said of them, 'whoever receives the one I send receives me' (John 13:20), and conversely, to reject an apostle, to refuse to believe what he says, is to reject our blessed Lord himself (Luke 10:16).

In recent years we've been treated to ecclesiastics telling our nation at large that the virgin birth is not, in that sense, historical, and the bodily resurrection of Jesus Christ isn't to be understood literally either. They still claim to believe in the truth of these things, but in themselves they're myths, so they say.

'But then,' says the Apostle Paul, 'it isn't a myth. This happened. And if it didn't happen we apostles would be false witnesses. And what's more, the whole Christian gospel is futile and we are still in our sins' (see 1 Cor 15:12–17).

It's a curious phenomenon in modern times that certain clever scholars seem to think they can take what they've now told us isn't true, and somehow reinterpret Christianity to make it true.

If the apostles say, 'You believe this, for this is the gospel and it happened—and if it didn't happen it's a lie', how will you come along now and say, 'It didn't happen. In that sense, it's not true, but we can rescue the Christian gospel from it and somehow make truth of it.' The thing is intellectual nonsense.

John then points out something that is very serious. He says that they never were true believers at all. I would not have dared to say it, but John says it: 'They went out from us, for they were not of us' (1 John 2:19). They never were. It's possible to advance to great lengths in theology and yet never to have been born again. 'They were not of us and they went out. If they had been of us, they would have continued.'

Isn't that an interesting note about apostates? Apostates aren't believers who have lost their faith. 'They never were of us', says John. They went out, and their going out makes it evident and manifest.

David Gooding, *Unity, Origin and Victory: Fourteen Studies from 1 John on Life in the Family of God*, 40–2

25th June

TEST THE SPIRITS

Reading: 1 John 4:1–6

By this you know the Spirit of God: every spirit that confesses that Jesus Christ has come in the flesh is from God. (1 John 4:2)

Faith is one of the cardinal things about Christianity. We are called upon to believe. And yet there is another sense in which the child of God will not be too quick to believe: 'Believe not every spirit', says John. Just to believe everything that you're told, simply because it is accompanied by a miracle, is not a mark of spiritual maturity, or even wisdom. The gracious Holy Spirit himself calls upon us to test the spirits whether they are from God or not (4:1).

With tremendous and remarkable condescension he invites us to test him: 'By this you know the Spirit of God'. He doesn't mind being tested. If the Spirit has moved somebody to say this, to announce the other and it is genuinely the Holy Spirit behind this gift, then he will be delighted if you in all due humility test him. He has nothing to fear. If I may put it this way, he'll pass all his examinations with flying colours.

Sometimes people have wrongly said that even to question somebody who claims to be speaking in the name of the Holy Spirit is to be in danger of committing the sin against the Holy Spirit, which is the unpardonable sin. So you'd better believe at once. 'No,' says the Holy Spirit, 'you'd better not. It's better that you test the spirit to see if it is indeed the Holy Spirit who is speaking through this gift.' John says that the test you should apply is a doctrinal test, because we are testing a message that a preacher has preached.

Here I must give you a little lesson in Greek. You could translate this Greek sentence as 'every spirit that confesses not that Jesus Christ has come in the flesh'; or you could translate it as 'every spirit that confesses not that Jesus is the Christ come in flesh'. In other words, the true answer to the question, 'Who is Jesus?' is 'Jesus is the Christ come in flesh.' He is the incarnate Christ, and what is more he is truly human at the same time. It is a mark of seriously false doctrine that it will deny one or other of those two things. Jesus come in the flesh—his true humanity; the Christ—his true deity.

David Gooding, Unity, Origin and Victory: Fourteen Studies from 1 John on Life in the Family of God, 60–1

26th June

AN EXAMPLE OF HERESY

Reading: 1 John 2:22–27

Who is the liar but he who denies that Jesus is the Christ? (1 John 2:22)

Years ago I met a gentleman who had read deeply in all kinds of Indian philosophy, with the practical yoga that goes as part of the courses towards the Hindu religion. A Christian work colleague began to talk to him.

In the end the man felt a longing in his heart to trust the Saviour. He didn't know how to do it. He said to me, 'Where do I get peace of mind?'

I cannot tell you the long story of the tremendous psychological and physical convulsions that man went through as he considered the Word of God with me. As we read together, I found prayer was useless; he only went off into his yoga. It was the Word of God that calmed him down physically, and he eventually expressed faith in the Lord.

He wanted to take back some books that he had long ago borrowed from theosophists in town. However, he was afraid to go back among them. I asked him, 'What did they teach you about Jesus in those theosophical circles? Did they teach you that Jesus is the Christ?'

'No,' he said, 'they said that Jesus isn't the Christ; the Christ is the great world spirit. Jesus lent himself to the Christ and the Christ used him, and now Jesus is in the seventh heaven somewhere. But the great Christ is the infinite world spirit, and you couldn't get the infinite world spirit into the limited body and personality of a man.'

I explained to him what God's word says: 'Who is a liar but he who denies that Jesus is the Christ?'

So some friends and I went with the good gentleman to the theosophists. The leaders among them were a man and his wife who had once been members of the Salvation Army—how dreadfully possible it is for folks to get deceived. They gave me some of their theosophical literature, which said that all holy books—Christian, Jewish and Hindu—tell us that the Christ is coming. Then they add, 'but Jesus isn't the Christ'. You can see the way the thing is being prepared in the minds of people for the coming of the Christ, but it won't be Jesus. It will of course be the one whose coming is 'after the working of Satan' (2 Thess 2:9 KJV). As you might understand, I never forgot that experience.

David Gooding, *Unity, Origin and Victory: Fourteen Studies from 1 John on Life in the Family of God*, 61–2

27th June

THE AUDIENCE FOR FALSE TEACHERS

Reading: 2 Peter 2:1–10

*They are from the world; therefore they speak from the
world, and the world listens to them. (1 John 4:5)*

Very often false doctrine seems right to the worldly and unregenerate person. Hence, the doctrines of modernism seem right to many an unregenerate theologian. It seems to them that those who stand fundamentally by the inspired record of holy Scripture are perverse and wrong-headed. But notice John's explanation. The false teachers are of the world; they speak from the world and the world hears them. The contrary is true of genuine believers because the Holy Spirit is within them and doctrinally and intellectually they overcome the world.

In my home town there was a delightful believer. He was somewhat eccentric, but a gracious gentleman who tried to serve the Lord as best he knew how. There came some preachers who took public buildings and held forth their particularly lurid brand of heresy. At their final meeting the leader got up and said, 'Ladies and gentlemen, we've had a marvellous response here and it is our intention to set up a church.' As quick as lightning, this elderly gentleman stood up and said, 'Sir, and if I may add, the devil won't hinder you.' He may have spoken crudely, but he spoke the truth. There is that sense of frustration we all feel sometimes, when people strongly resist the truth, and then fall so easily for what to us are such obvious perversions of Christianity. Preaching our gospel is a battle, and every generation will find they will have to fight the battles over and over again.

Finally John says of himself and his fellow apostles, 'We are from God. Whoever knows God listens to us; whoever is not from God does not listen to us' (1 John 4:6). I remind you, this is being said by a holy apostle. If we were to say, 'Anyone who is of God hears us, and anybody who doesn't agree with us is not of God', that would be arrogance beyond description. But what we can't say as individual believers, the apostles had every right and authority to say. When our Lord was here on earth, he said, 'Everyone who has heard and learned from the Father comes to me' (John 6:45). It was he who commissioned the apostles: 'He that receives you, receives me. He that rejects you, rejects me' (see John 13:20; Luke 10:16). We do well in our day to emphasize the importance of these historic apostles on whose foundation the church is built.

David Gooding, *Unity, Origin and Victory: Fourteen Studies from 1 John on Life in the Family of God*, 63

28th June

THE CHRISTIAN'S RESPONSE TO IDOLATRY

Reading: Acts 19:23–37

For you have brought these men here who are neither sacrilegious nor blasphemers of our goddess. (Acts 19:37)

Nature is a wonderful servant-guardian of mankind, to be treated with great respect, as the modern Green movements rightly stress. But she was never meant to be a goddess; nor was our care of her meant to turn itself into a religion. Whenever human beings have turned nature into a goddess, she has invariably degraded man from being king of the earth into a slave of natural instincts, with ultimately less significance than the material world and the forces of the universe which control him.

It is interesting to notice the city clerk's assessment of the Christians' behaviour. Here he was on delicate ground, for undeniably Paul would have preached many times that man-made gods are no gods at all, and he would have called on people to turn from their idolatry to the true God. The silversmith's bank balance had not fallen for no reason at all: the implications of what Paul preached for their trade in silver shrines of Artemis were fatal. On the other hand, the first part of the city clerk's statement was altogether true: 'these men are not robbers of temples' (v. 37 DWG).

In this Paul and his friends set us a permanent example. The Christian abhorrence of idols does not justify showing anything but courtesy and respect to pagan temples. On becoming a Christian, if a person destroys their own personal idols that is good and proper. But a Christian has no business treating other religions' temples and idols disrespectfully. So the second part of the city clerk's statement was also true in a sense: 'they have not blasphemed your goddess'. Paul would have regularly preached against idolatry in general, but he would not have publicly denounced Artemis or any other pagan deity in offensive, abusive language. Nor should we.

And finally, the clerk's reference to the law courts and the political assembly remind us that truly civilized human life becomes impossible where raw human-animal instinct is allowed to trample over reason, morality and the law. Religion appeals to deep-seated human emotions. But a religion that encourages its followers to disregard civilized law and hunt down those who may have offended it, like animals hunt down their attackers—call it what you will, it is nothing but old pagan Artemis dressed up in other clothes. Its own defence of itself does away with its credibility, for it destroys what distinguishes mankind from the animal.

David Gooding, *True to the Faith: The Acts of the Apostles—Defining and Defending the Gospel*, 418–19

29th June

TRUE AND FALSE DISCIPLES

Reading: John 13:16–20

'Truly, truly, I say to you, whoever receives the one I send receives me, and whoever receives me receives the one who sent me.' (John 13:20)

The fact that Jesus knew in advance that Judas was a pseudo-apostle is a comfort to us. The New Testament epistles show us that the early Christian churches were troubled from time to time by false apostles and by preachers and office-bearers who were not even regenerate men (see 2 Cor 11:13, 26; Gal 2:4; 2 Pet 2:1; 3 John 9–10). The church at large has been plagued with such people ever since. Christ himself warned that it would be so (Luke 12:45–46). It didn't happen because he failed to foresee and prevent it.

But at the same time Christ has indicated to us where true spiritual authority lies, and what our attitude to it must be. 'Truly, truly, I say to you, whoever receives the one I send receives me, and whoever receives me receives the one who sent me.' Let's start at the top of this pyramid of authority. If we receive the Lord Jesus, we thereby receive God who sent him. But how do we know that God sent him? Jesus himself tells us. Speaking to the Father about his disciples, he says: 'Now they know that everything that you have given me is from you. For I have given them the words that you gave me, and they have received them and have come to know in truth that I came from you; and they have believed that you sent me' (John 17:7–8). We know that Jesus was sent by God then, because the words he speaks to us are self-evidently the words of God.

In that same way, if anyone claims today to have been sent or appointed by the Lord Jesus, we can know whether the claim is true by a similar test. Are the words that this claimant speaks and preaches self-evidently in tune with the words of the Lord Jesus and his apostles in the New Testament? The corollary of this is true as well. The mark of true believers is this: when they read the words of Christ's apostles in the New Testament, they will accept and obey them. For to reject the words of Christ's apostles in the New Testament is to reject Christ; and to reject Christ is to reject the Father who sent him.

David Gooding, *In The School of Christ: Lessons on Holiness in John 13–17*, 46

30th June

SAUL DISCOVERS THE TRUTH ABOUT GOD

Reading: Acts 26:12–23

And he said, 'Who are you, Lord?' And he said, 'I am Jesus, whom you are persecuting.' (Acts 9:5)

When Moses discovered why the burning bush was not consumed, and stood asking the Lord within it 'What is your name?', he also discovered to his immense encouragement that the God of his forefathers was not simply a remote figure in past history. Nor was he only the exalted Lord in the heavens; he had 'come down' to earth to deliver his people and stood identified with them in their suffering (Exod 3:8). Not all the persecution that Pharaoh could fling against them would ever destroy them.

But it was with fearful consternation that Saul saw the inextinguishable glory of the risen Lord and heard him say, 'I am Jesus, whom you are persecuting.' The vision blinded him physically, as well it might, for spiritually it turned all his former boasted knowledge of God into virtual darkness.

God had come down to earth as a missionary 'to seek and to save what was lost' (Luke 19:10 DWG), and Saul had not recognized him. In the person of Jesus he had lived here, and 'burned' in the fires of Calvary. Saul had seen nothing in this great sight. Now returned to his heaven, the Lord Jesus still stood inseparable from his persecuted believers, disciples and saints. And here was Saul, the supposed champion of orthodoxy, playing the impossible role of a modern day pharaoh!

The Ethiopian's heart had been captivated by the message of the lowly Servant of the Lord who was led as a lamb to the slaughter, dumb before his shearers, wounded for our transgressions and bruised for our iniquities (Acts 8:26–39). But this lowly Servant was the exalted Lord; the Nazarene was God incarnate. A sight of his glory had now brought his enemy Saul to the ground; his mercy spared him, and his divine authority ordered him to proceed to Damascus and await further instructions. Saul of Tarsus had discovered God as he really is.

David Gooding, *True to the Faith: The Acts of the Apostles—Defining and Defending the Gospel*, 183

1st July

EVIDENCE OF TRUE REPENTANCE AND BELIEF

Reading: Acts 9:10–22

For some days he was with the disciples at Damascus. (Acts 9:19b)

Saul had addressed the exalted Jesus as '*Lord*'. Did he mean what he said? Was it the genuine expression of a repentant heart, or merely a superficial, temporary response from him against his will by the overpowering effect of the vision? How would you tell? Very simply! If Saul had genuinely accepted Jesus as Lord, he would be prepared to acknowledge the people he had despised and had been persecuting as the Lord's people. He would recognize them as his brothers; and not only recognize them but accept them and be identified with them both in private and in public.

Ananias, whom the Lord used as his agent on this occasion, was not one of the apostles. As far as we know he held no high office in the church. He was an 'ordinary' believer; there was no sacerdotal magic in his fingers. But when he laid his hands on the erstwhile persecutor of the despised Nazarene, the gesture expressed the reality of his words, 'Brother Saul' (9:17)! And what he said next indicated how this new relationship had been brought about and what was its vital force. 'The Lord Jesus who appeared to you on the road by which you came, has sent me so that you may regain your sight and be filled with the Holy Spirit' (9:17).

Here then is a basic principle of true conversion. You can come to saving faith in Christ all by yourself, as Saul did, through personal acceptance of Jesus as Lord. But if that faith is genuine it will lead to acceptance of the Lord's people. I can be interested in birds without going anywhere near the local birdwatchers' society. Indeed, I can refuse to have anything to do with its members and still be a very good birdwatcher myself. But I cannot genuinely accept Christ and refuse to have anything to do with his people. They are his disciples, his saints, they call on his name; and in giving the Holy Spirit to each one of them he unites them all in one body (cf. 1 Cor 1:2, 12:13). I cannot receive the Holy Spirit and refuse to be a member of that body. I cannot claim to love the Lord Jesus and refuse to love his saints. I cannot claim to be identified with him and refuse to be identified with his people.

David Gooding, *True to the Faith: The Acts of the Apostles—Defining and Defending the Gospel*, 184–5

2nd July

KNOWING THAT WE ARE TRUE BELIEVERS

Reading: 1 John 2:1–6

*And by this we know that we have come to know him,
if we keep his commandments. (1 John 2:3)*

How can I know that I am a true believer? If I could know that, then I could face life's trials with joy. The Apostle John is a great help to us here: 'And by this we know that we have come to know him'. Notice exactly what it says, '*We know that we know!*' Why the repetition?

Here is a person and she says, 'I know the Lord.' How can that person be sure she knows the Lord? How can she know that it is a true faith that she has? Can you know that you know the Lord? Of course you can! What is John's way of doing it? 'And by this we know that we have come to know him, if we keep his commandments.' That is one way of knowing. We don't have to trust moods and fancies; we have to ask ourselves, 'Is there a desire in my heart to keep the Lord's commandments?'

There are many things in which we fall short, but if we are true believers that will grieve us. The set of our heart is that we will want to do the Lord's commandments. A person who says, 'I know the Lord,' but doesn't want to do the Lord's commandments, obviously doesn't know the Lord.

Let me illustrate the whole point. Suppose you say to me, 'Which country in the world do you like the best?'

I say, 'Switzerland is the country for me!'

'That's very interesting. Are there any features in the landscape of any country that you don't like?'

'I don't like mountains and lakes and snow-capped glaciers and cows with tinkling bells around their necks. I wouldn't go anywhere near them.'

'And you like Switzerland!'

I think you would conclude that I am talking nonsense and I do not know Switzerland.

If we say, 'Yes, I know the Lord,' and we don't have any intention of keeping his commandments, we show that we just don't know the Lord. If we knew him, we should know that the Lord is exceedingly beautiful; we should love his word and want to do it and be the first to admit with sorrow that we fail to do it. Yes, we can know that we know.

David Gooding, *A Vision of the Perfect Man and Woman: Seven Studies on Major Themes from James*, 8–9

3rd July

TRUE FAITH AS OPPOSED TO SUPERSTITION

Reading: Acts 19:13–20

*But the evil spirit answered them, 'Jesus I know,
and Paul I recognize, but who are you?' (Acts 19:15)*

When the incident of the sons of Sceva became known, says Luke, fear came upon all, and the name of the Lord Jesus was magnified (19:17). Indeed, Luke's own studied use of 'the Lord Jesus' (vv. 5, 13, 17) contrasts markedly with the way Sceva's seven sons and the evil spirit itself refer simply to 'Jesus' (vv. 13, 15), and surely sets us a pattern of due reverence.

The effect on those who were already believers was particularly healthy. The fear of spiritism sometimes dies hard in converts from paganism, reinforced as it is by the practice of their families and by social pressures. But liberated by this demonstration of the authority of the Lord Jesus, and shocked into seeing the true nature of spiritism, they came and confessed that they had been secretly continuing some of these evil practices. Many also brought their books on occult arts and made a public and very expensive bonfire of them.

'So the word of the Lord spread mightily and prevailed' (v. 20 DWG); and though this comment is one of Luke's formal summaries that marks the end of this section and the beginning of the next, it is not otherwise without its function. The bulwark against superstition is faith; and true faith comes through the word of God, its reading and its preaching (Rom 10:17). It was with the detailed and authoritative statements of the word of God, understood with the mind, believed in the heart and applied to the life, that the Lord Jesus himself met the temptations of the devil in the desert (Luke 4:4, 8, 12).

Weaken or destroy faith in the word of God, and what you get is not always unbelief, pure and simple; but the opening of the floodgates to the invasion of Christianity by the hoary superstitions and occult practices of both ancient and modern paganism, as for instance in the New Age Movement. All Christians need to be on their guard. The desire for instant spiritual experience can make both individuals and congregations impatient of serious Bible study and Bible based preaching, and lead to the temptation of downplaying Scripture in favour of more exciting programmes and procedures. But it is a temptation to be resisted at all costs if the real spiritual battle is to be won.

David Gooding, *True to the Faith: The Acts of the Apostles—Defining and Defending the Gospel*, 390–1

4th July

CARNALITY MASQUERADING AS SPIRITUALITY

Reading: John 16:1–4

'Indeed, the hour is coming when whoever kills you will think he is offering service to God.' (John 16:2)

Our hearts are indeed deceitful. Our base passions—pride, jealousy, narrow-mindedness, the desire to dominate—these things sometimes have a way of disguising themselves by dressing up in the clothing of godly spirituality. We let ourselves be deceived by them and imagine that we stand for the truth of God. Yet all the while it is not a godly loyalty to the Lord Jesus, it is our own ugly bad tempers, our desire to dominate other people, our revenge or whatever that is masquerading as godliness. Being deceived, instead of humbly and shamefacedly repenting of these dastardly attitudes, we glory in them as though they were exhibitions of godliness.

In our Lord's time he warned his apostles that the time would come when anyone who should murder them would think that he does it in God's service. The history of the great Reformation days shows that Christendom was guilty of this very thing. Religious authorities murdered and executed, tortured and burnt alive thousands of our dear brothers and sisters in Christ, imagining that they were doing God a service. We should remember it was not only Roman Catholics who executed Protestants; some of the magisterial reformers themselves burnt, tortured and drowned their fellow believers who demanded the right to observe believer's baptism according to the New Testament. They had those dear believers trussed up and thrown into rivers, their tongues cut out or their bodies burned, imagining that they did it in the service of God.

And who could read the history of even recent centuries and not be struck silent and shamefaced by the story of endless divisions amongst God's people? To think with sorrow of men who stood up and split the Lord's people from stem to stern and made their endless little parties. Had you asked them what they were doing, they would have told you they were standing for God's truth. As we watch and read of the cruelty, the narrowmindedness, the tyranny with which they pursued their little causes, it becomes apparent it wasn't just concern for God's truth that moved them; mixed in with it was a good deal of self-seeking, envy one of another and pride in one's little interpretation of some matter. 'My dear brothers,' says James with tears in his voice, 'don't let yourself be deceived by carnality masquerading in the clothes of supposed godliness and spirituality.'

David Gooding, *A Vision of the Perfect Man and Woman: Seven Studies on Major Themes from James*, 13–14

5th July

DON'T BE DOUBLE-MINDED

Reading: James 1:5–8

*If any of you lacks wisdom, let him ask God, who gives generously
to all without reproach, and it will be given him. (James 1:5)*

We come to God and wish for wisdom: wisdom to face the unexpected event, wisdom to know how to handle my prosperity and joy. Wisdom to know how to face my unexpected success, wisdom to know how to face sorrow. I shall constantly need to come and ask for wisdom and I must, therefore, not be double minded.

Suppose you are a famous teacher of the piano, and I think to myself, 'I would like to play like that person does.'

So you say you will give me a chance: 'OK, be here once a week then!'

I come for the next four weeks and then I don't turn up for the next four; and when I finally do turn up, you say, 'Oh, you are the man who wants to play the piano?'

'Yes, I am indeed!'

'Where were you this last four weeks?'

'Four weeks! I didn't realise the gap had been so big. The first week there was a marvellous film on TV and I couldn't miss it; the second week my friends asked if I would come out for a game of golf; the third week Aunt Jemima invited us all to Maud's Ice Cream Parlour!'

'Do you really want to play the piano?'

'Yes, of course I do! You are not going to tell me there's anything wrong with ice cream, are you?'

'No,' she says, 'but if you want to play the piano you will have to make your choice. Do you want to play the piano, or do you want to eat ice cream?'

If we would know the crown of life in the coming days, then we have to make up our minds. Do we really want it, or is it just a feeling that comes over us now and again? A double-minded person, who wants to go on with the Lord today and forgets it for the next month, is unstable. 'For that person must not suppose that he will receive anything from the Lord' (v. 7).

So may God use his word to help us show our divine master, our teacher, that we are not double minded and we want to go on. By his grace we are prepared to make progress as Christians in the school of Christ the number one activity in life that must take precedence above all else. And so we shall be blessed.

David Gooding, *A Vision of the Perfect Man and Woman: Seven Studies on Major Themes from James*, 10–11

6th July

FACING THE TRUTH ABOUT OURSELVES

Reading: James 4:1–4

But each person is tempted when he is lured and enticed by his own desire. (James 1:14)

We mustn't blame the devil too much; he is a common scapegoat. He certainly does enough damage, but sometimes we are inclined to blame him when we should be blaming ourselves. 'That wasn't me,' says somebody, 'it was the devil.' Somebody says, 'I've got a demon of pride.' No, you haven't! That's just you, not a demon. Be careful! If I say, 'I've got an old demon of jealousy,' that kind of excuses me—it's a bug that has got hold of me and I need it exorcised or something. No, it isn't—it's me.

Part of our growing up into maturity is to *face the reality of ourselves*; not to keep blaming our faults on other things and other forces, but to face the fact that it is me. I am the one who is guilty of the pride and the jealousy and I must repent and seek deliverance. I must learn to stand against it and put to death the things of the flesh.

Another area where James indicates that it is possible to delude ourselves is by simply hearing the word of God, and not doing it (1:22). This comes immediately to my heart, for this is one of my many weak points. I find the word of God so interesting, so intellectually stimulating, such marvellous literature that I get carried away. My danger is that when I come out of the study I forget about it and forget to do it. It's not enough to read about holiness; we won't become holy by reading about it—we will become holy by being holy. We don't become courageous by reading about courage—we become courageous by facing life's circumstances and daring to stand for God in them and making decisions according to his word, whatever the price may be. We don't become truthful by reading about it in the Bible—we become truthful in our school examinations, in our courses, in our trade, or whatever it is by learning in practice not to cut corners, not to cheat, but to do a proper job.

How easy it would be to deceive ourselves. After a lovely meeting, studying God's word and savouring its delights, to go out and think we have become holy, whereas holiness waits for our doing what we have heard.

David Gooding, *A Vision of the Perfect Man and Woman: Seven Studies on Major Themes from James*, 15–17

Part 11

The God of Revival and Restoration

7th July

GOD IS A GOD OF RESTORATION

Reading: Zechariah 8:11–13

The God of all grace, who has called you to his eternal glory in Christ, will himself restore, confirm, strengthen, and establish you. (1 Peter 5:10)

I propose that we should listen to God speaking to and through his ancient prophet, so that we might see again what kind of a God our God is. As we see him reacting to the behaviour of his ancient people and discover something of his heart, something of the personality that is God, we shall find it speaking its own words of encouragement to us in our very different circumstances.

The first great lesson that we shall learn is that God, our God, is the God of restoration. He was then and he is now. Granted that in this prophecy God will be concerned chiefly with the restoration of the city of Jerusalem, yet even that is a remarkable thing and speaks volumes to our hearts about the nature of God. Remember how uniquely privileged Jerusalem city had been of all the cities upon the face of the earth, throughout the length and breadth of history. It was favoured uniquely above all by God dwelling there in his temple. Yet, in spite of that incalculable grace, Jerusalem city had grown ungrateful and obstinate in her sin and perversity, until at length the infinite patience of God could do no other than bring grievous discipline upon her at the hands of the ancient Babylonians.

Why didn't God take the easy route and destroy Jerusalem city completely? What need has almighty God of a few bricks there, in a tiny little postage stamp size country? Could he not start again afresh? But no, not God. What a marvellous God we have. God is a God of restoration and he will have patience with his people still and restore even that city.

The fact that God is a God of restoration is made clear to us on the first page of our New Testament. As it opens up the new vistas that come with the birth of Jesus Christ our Lord, it pauses to survey the story up to that point. Matthew divides the history from Abraham to our Lord's coming into three parts, ingeniously arranging the genealogies so that we might see the point. Three equal parts, as Matthew counts them, of the ways of God with his people, leading up to the birth of the Lord Jesus.

David Gooding, *An Offer of Restoration: Four Studies on God's Character in Zechariah*, 4

8th July

RESTORATION IN ISRAEL'S HISTORY

Reading: Zechariah 7:8–14

*I will strengthen the house of Judah, and I will save the house of Joseph.
I will bring them back because I have compassion on them. (Zechariah 10:6)*

The nation became middle-aged, and when Israel should have gone forward they went backward; instead of uphill they went downhill. They tottered from one disaster to another and from one apostasy to the next. It is a danger that besets the middle aged, but let me not point the lesson further. Yes, there came times of great revival and encouragement. Names like Elijah and Elisha come from this period, with godly men like Jehoshaphat leading revivals amongst God's people. But there is no denying that the overriding trend was down, until it ended in nothing short of disaster. Israel was carried away to Assyria and Judah to Babylon, there to hang their harps upon the willow trees, mourning for what might have been and all that was now lost (see Ps 137:2).

If God's people must be such a desperate crew: so ungrateful, so short-sighted, so disobedient, so apostate, we ask ourselves, 'Why, with all that evidence in front of him, and in spite of his patient work these many centuries, didn't God finally abandon them to their fate and start again with something new?' But if you think like that, you haven't read the heart of God: 'How can I give you up, O Ephraim?' (Hos 11:8). God is the God of restoration. He patiently restores broken things and restores his people when they go astray. So Jerusalem was restored.

And God is not only a God who restores his favoured people. Let me turn you aside for a moment to the story of Daniel 4. God is so much a God of restoration that he will bother to restore even an ungodly monarch like Nebuchadnezzar, that great beautifier of Babylon, the developer of Babylonian culture with its glorious splendour and riot of aesthetics. But Nebuchadnezzar got puffed up in his pride and his culture, and he went astray and became corrupt. Instead of bringing his judgments upon him and upon the city, God disciplined the king, intending to restore even a Nebuchadnezzar; and that he did.

As we think of these things, our hearts surely begin to burn within us. We may feel ourselves better than Nebuchadnezzar; we might even feel ourselves better than Israel and Jerusalem city. But which one of us will lay our hand upon our heart and say, 'I don't need restoration'? Where would any of us be at this very moment in our spiritual pilgrimage were it not for this glorious thing about God? We share David's sentiment in his twenty-third psalm: 'He restores my soul.'

David Gooding, *An Offer of Restoration: Four Studies on God's Character in Zechariah*, 5–6

9th July

FUTURE RESTORATION

Reading: Zechariah 14:5–11

And on that day there shall be inscribed on the bells of the horses, 'Holy to the LORD'. And the pots in the house of the LORD shall be as the bowls before the altar. (Zechariah 14:20)

We should not despise what Israel were able to perform in that long-distant day when they came back from Babylon. Sure, they didn't accomplish what we've accomplished, but there were many good and faithful souls who worked their fingers to the bone as they scrabbled amongst the rubble of broken Jerusalem and its destroyed temple. In faith in God and his promises they built it again and toiled at their particular part of the restoration. Granted, the glorious promises were not all fulfilled for them; some of them still wait to be fulfilled. But God was not mocking them when he held before their eyes visions of a world so wonderful, so cleansed, so beautiful; of a nation restored and so filled with God's Spirit that the very saucepans in Jerusalem would be holy to the Lord (Zech 14:21). As they thought of those visions by day and dreamt of them by night, it gave them courage to start again; to build again broken things, and know the restoration of God in national life and in their own personal lives, as far as they could be known in that distant age.

Shall we not take courage too? It is not ours to rebuild a literal Jerusalem, nor a literal temple in that city, but anybody's restoration is an encouragement to me. We serve the same God and we fight the same war. Granted we fight different battles on different battlefields, and often with vastly different weapons to what Israel used, but it is ultimately part of the same great battle. As we read of God's way of restoration with them, it is surely legitimate that we take encouragement in our hearts.

God is a God of restoration, and he who restored Jerusalem city in power in bygone centuries will not leave off until the whole war is won. He will restore Jerusalem city yet again and make it the wonder of the world. According to Peter in his sermon, one day God will restore all those things that any prophet has ever talked about from the foundation of the world (see Acts 3:21). And he will restore our sad and suffering planet until 'creation itself is set free from its bondage to corruption' (Rom 8:21). That is the God who today thinks on you and me. He is the God who restores my soul.

David Gooding, *An Offer of Restoration: Four Studies on God's Character in Zechariah*, 6–7

10th July

KEEPING ON GOING IN TIMES OF UNCERTAINTY

Reading: Isaiah 6:1–8

In the year that King Uzziah died I saw the Lord sitting upon a throne, high and lifted up; and the train of his robe filled the temple. (Isaiah 6:1)

It was against a background of tremendous uncertainty that the prophet Isaiah was called to his famous ministry. He tells us that in the year King Uzziah died the fortunes of the royal house of David had sunk to the lowest they had ever been.

Isaiah drew tremendous comfort from that vision, as did the people to whom he ministered. Even though Judah's kings were tottering, the purpose of God was going on. His earthly representatives might fail and fall, the thrones of earth seem insecure, but the great King who one day would come of David's line was already in reserve—the blessed Son of God Almighty.

In that there is a reference to revival: revival for continuance in times that are difficult. Have you ever felt you have preached your heart out and got very little result? Have you ever preached to congregations that dwindled away to nothing? You say, 'Yes I have, but that is because I am a very bad preacher.' I understand your feeling!

When God commissioned Isaiah to preach, he told him bluntly that when he had done his preaching over long years there would be fewer believers than there were before. 'I want you to go and preach,' God said to Isaiah, 'until the land is emptied of its people' (see 6:9–12). Scarcely anything would be left! Now, if I were going to choose to be a preacher, I would choose to be a great evangelist—anybody with any sense would—with great crowds coming and vast success. You wouldn't want to be an Isaiah, preaching to dwindling, diminishing congregations, would you?

But that same faithful prophet wrote a gospel tract that has led millions to Christ. Through Isaiah 53 myriads have been brought to faith in God. Through Isaiah 40 countless thousands of believers, wearied with the journey, have been lifted to the very skies by the lovely words that he wrote. Here, then, is the secret of keeping going when times are difficult: the vision Isaiah had, looking behind the scenes to the great purposes of God that shall be fulfilled, and no power on earth or hell shall prevent them.

David Gooding, *Keys to Revival: Three Studies from 1–2 Kings on the Leadership of Elijah, Jehoiada and Josiah*, 13–14

11th July

WORSHIP RESTORED

Reading: Zechariah 3:1–4

Now Joshua was standing before the angel, clothed with filthy garments. (Zechariah 3:3)

Consider Israel's high priest at this juncture. Judge the abysmal state of the man as he stands in that holy place and before such holy personage, when now it is perceived that his garments are filthy. Not only the garments that symbolize his own personal state, but the garments that indicate his holy office.

Let us think for a moment then of his office. In order that the people of God might worship him acceptably and with godly fear, God had provided them with a high priest. And the New Testament comments that every high priest must be able to 'have compassion on the ignorant, and on them that are out of the way' (Heb 5:2 KJV). If God's people were to worship him, they would need a priest to come out in all his glorious garments and represent God to them, and help the people in their appreciation of God.

Worship is not a question of working up wonderful bursts of emotion and enjoying them. True worship is my response to the reality of almighty God, to the wonder and the beauty of his holiness. So in those early days, as they came out from God, Israel's high priests were provided with garments of glory and beauty. You will say, 'What are mere garments and a bit of gold thread and a bit of blue, purple and scarlet and fine-twined linen?' As Christians we see it only as a picture and a type, but in those early days of mankind's spiritual childhood it did convey something.

No scruffy old high priest this, in jeans or something, but a high priest in his robes of glory and splendour. Even those humble symbols mediated something of the glory of God and the people felt that they must prostrate themselves before such an exhibition of glory. And as they learnt about the glory of God, there was their glorious, but kindly and compassionate, high priest, who had mercy on those that were ignorant and out of the way.

See now a disaster. As Israel's high priest stands there, his garments are filthy. We shall judge the seriousness of it by the measure with which we have apprehended the majesty and the glory of God to the extent that we have apprehended that the chief function of our worship is not so that I shall have a good time, or you either, but that we shall minister to God's pleasure.

David Gooding, *An Offer of Restoration: Four Studies on God's Character in Zechariah*, 22–3

12th July

THE HIGH PRIEST RESTORED

Reading: Zechariah 3:5–10

The LORD who has chosen Jerusalem rebuke you!
Is not this a brand plucked from the fire? (Zechariah 3:2)

Not only did the priest stand before the Lord in his filthy garments, but there was Satan at his right hand to accuse him (Zech 3:1). That relentless accuser of the brethren (Rev 12:10), calling God's attention to the failure of his official and of the people the priest represented, pointing out to God that anything this priest could do must prove unacceptable to the standards of almighty God. The fire of God's judgment had almost consumed Joshua, when the voice of God's grace is heard breaking the silence and rebuking the accuser. The arm of divine mercy snatches him as a brand from the burning. A dirty, smoking, filthy, sooty brand from a fire, with all its horrible stench in the nostrils of almighty God.

And he gives to the adversary, Satan, the reason. It was because he had chosen him. 'The Lord who has chosen Jerusalem rebuke you!' says God. As we stand by, what a revelation it gives us of the grace of almighty God: that God should choose such a stinking, oily, sooty firebrand to have the privilege of ministering in the thrice holy presence. Normally in Israel's temple it was the smell of incense that greeted the nostrils of almighty God. Now it was the stench of the sooty burning firebrand that God had chosen.

As we read it, our minds irresistibly go to ourselves and try to account for the enormous grace of God towards us who were almost being burnt in the refuse dump of eternity. I tell you what it's done for your ministry, my brother and sister, and what it will do for all eternity. It will be the end of you parading your virtues and excellence in the courts of God. But it will infinitely increase the wonder of your appreciation of a God like that, who could rescue burning firebrands and choose them for the high office of priestly ministry.

And then the angel of the Lord took up his gracious work:

> And the angel said to those who were standing before him, 'Remove the filthy garments from him.' And to him he said, 'Behold, I have taken your iniquity away from you, and I will clothe you with pure vestments.' (Zech. 3:4)

These are fit accompaniments for the presence of God, given to the high priest as the representative of God's people.

David Gooding, *An Offer of Restoration: Four Studies on God's Character in Zechariah*, 23–4

13th July

OUR GREAT HIGH PRIEST

Reading: Hebrews 7:11–18

And I said, 'Let them put a clean turban on his head.' (Zechariah 3:5)

It's nice when God's people get enthusiastic and begin making suggestions to God, and Zechariah got caught up in the excitement here. I think at that point the angel of the Lord may have smiled a bit, for here was Zechariah entering into the glory and the wonder of God's grace.

When they were making Aaron's priestly garments, at the front of the 'mitre' they fastened a plate of pure gold, with the engraving, 'Holy to the Lord'. It was on Aaron's forehead, and Aaron was to bear any guilt from the holy things, so that the people may be accepted before the Lord (see Exod 28:36–38).

If each of us knew our own inherent unsuitability to be a priest before God, I think that we too would cry out 'Let them put a mitre on his head that he might bear the responsibility of ministering on our behalf in those courts above, to bear the iniquity of the holy things'? For, with my childish prattle, how shall I bear the responsibility of my high calling to minister before almighty God?

And so they put the mitre on Joshua's head and clothed him with garments. But then the angel of the Lord protested to him:

> 'If you will walk in my ways and keep my charge, then you shall rule my house and have charge of my courts, and I will give you the right of access among those who are standing here.' (Zech 3:7)

Joshua was to represent the people before God and represent God before the people, and train his people in the responsibilities of holiness.

We read here that 'the angel of the LORD was standing by' (3:5). I wonder what he was thinking, for he was none other than the Son of God. Even in those moments, he must have been looking down the centuries to the time when he would come to take up the robes as our great high priest and bear our iniquity of the holy things. When he would express the Father to us and make the name of God known in the midst of the congregation (see Ps 22:22), until our hearts are aflame with life for God and admiration of his glory and holiness; and then in turn lead back the praise of his people to God.

David Gooding, *An Offer of Restoration: Four Studies on God's Character in Zechariah*, 24

14th July

THE RESTORATION OF OUR WALK

Reading: 1 Samuel 2:22–25

If you will walk in my ways and keep my charge, then you shall rule my house and have charge of my courts, and I will give you the right of access among those who are standing here. (Zechariah 3:7)

Restored to his office, and beautified with forgiveness and reinstatement by God, Joshua was not to engage in self-indulgence. You will remember the disgraceful episode of Eli and his high priesthood, taking advantage of the grace of God. He had been chosen to lead the people, discipline them and make them aware of the glories of God, yet he allowed his sons to grow up as self-indulgent hideously sinful men. They saw the priesthood merely as a way of indulging their own satisfaction; they forgot God and his glory and descended to the most shameful iniquity.

Restoration by the grace of God will never mean that. Joshua is called upon to be a judge in his courts, to train and discipline the people so that their behaviour may be well pleasing to God.

At this juncture we do well to remember the challenging words of Hebrews 12:18–29: We are not come to Sinai, all on smoke at the presence of the glory of God, so that Moses himself said, 'I tremble with fear.' Have we come to something less majestic or less awe inspiring? Of course not. We are come to Mount Zion, and to the city of the living God, the heavenly Jerusalem, and to all that august assembly of the ministers of God and the redeemed. We come to serve him whose voice once shook the earth, and he promised that when he speaks again his voice will shake not the earth only, but the heaven also, so that all those things that can be removed are removed. What is left will be abiding and eternal. Seeing then we have received a kingdom that cannot be removed, let us seek grace that we may serve him with godly fear, for our God is a consuming fire.

We shall not increase our joy if we lose sight of the awe inspiring majesty of the God whose priests we are called to be. In that far off day Joshua was a foreshadowing of the coming of our great high priest who 'by one offering' has 'perfected forever them that are sanctified' (Heb 10:14 KJV), and now stands 'in the presence of God for us' (9:24 KJV), his junior priests.

David Gooding, *An Offer of Restoration: Four Studies on God's Character in Zechariah*, 27–8

15th July

RESTORATION BY THE HOLY SPIRIT

Reading: Zechariah 4:1–10

The hands of Zerubbabel have laid the foundation of [the house of the Lord]; his hands shall also complete it. (Zechariah 4:9)

Still today the Lord faithfully keeps his charge. What shall restoration mean? Our minds go to those sacred scenes in the visions of John in Revelation 1–3, of the seven golden candlesticks. In their midst is one like the Son of Man. He is clothed in his priestly garment down to the foot, moving in the courts of the Lord, investigating his junior priests, praising their good works, seeing with his penetrating eye their shortcomings and sins and calling on them to repent, so that they might join in their priestly office of being bright and burning lampstands for God in this ungodly world.

And then we think of the ministry of Zerubbabel, the civic leader of the people, who was charged with the task of rebuilding the temple. He faced opposition from all the little nations constantly snapping at Israel's heels, and the mighty imperialist power of the time. The glorious gospel message from God through the vision given to Zechariah was: 'Not by might, nor by power, but by my Spirit, says the Lord of hosts' (v. 6). As we read it, we hear it not merely as gospel, but once again as exhortation.

Zerubbabel was to be both encouraged and exhorted by that famous statement. There in the vision he and Joshua stood as those olive trees that poured the oil into the vessel of testimony. They were privileged by God to be the channels of God's Holy Spirit to the people of Israel. And we in our little way rejoice in the marvellous privilege that God has given us, my sister, my brother, to be the vessels of God's Holy Spirit to that testimony where God has given us responsibility. The message is gospel that says it is God's Holy Spirit who maintains the testimony against all the opposition. What confidence we may have in the Lord.

I repeat the promise with which Paul comforted his own heart as he sat in jail, thinking of his work in Philippi and having seen evidence in the lives of the believers:

> He who began a good work in you will bring it to completion at the day of Jesus Christ. (Phil 1:6)

David Gooding, *An Offer of Restoration: Four Studies on God's Character in Zechariah*, 28

16th July

THE BALANCE OF REBUKE AND ENCOURAGEMENT

Reading: Haggai 1:1–15

You looked for much, and behold, it came to little. And when you brought it home, I blew it away. Why? declares the LORD of hosts. Because of my house that lies in ruins, while each of you busies himself with his own house. (Haggai 1:9)

Haggai has left us only four messages, all delivered within a very short space of time. The first one came in the second year of Darius the king, in the sixth month, on the first day of the month (1:1); and the last one of them came that same year, on the twenty-fourth day of the ninth month (2:10, 20). The third one also came on that day, so they all came within four months. In that period Haggai had ministered so effectively by the Spirit of God that the work of the building of the temple, which had completely stopped when he began his ministry, was revived and carried on until it was finished.

Of the four messages, it is very interesting to see that the first one is a rebuke for having left the work of restoration unfinished and settling down in ease. It went home to the hearts of God's people, so that within a matter of a week or two they had got back to the work, rolling up their sleeves once more, bending their backs and carrying on God's work. It was a very effective rebuke. The other three messages were words of encouragement. No one knew better than Haggai that when the people came back the going would be hard. Stung in their consciences and beginning to get on again with the work of rebuilding life, it was encouragement above all else that they would need.

Let us remember this too. It is very easy to give words of criticism that may well be deserved—we all deserve such rebukes at times. But if we are rebuked too much we shall lose heart altogether and go home with our legs weakened and our faces dropped, saying that we were never much good anyway. We have done our best but it has all gone wrong. So why bother again? Let us rebuke one another if we have to; and we do have to, you may be sure. But let us remember to give three messages of encouragement for every one of rebuke. That is what we shall need to go on again, if we are not to become totally discouraged. That is how to promote God's work of restoration—give one faithful word of rebuke and then three of encouragement! In this we shall be following Haggai's example.

David Gooding, *Rebuke and Encouragement: One Study in Haggai on God's Messages to His People*, 3–4

17th July

PETER'S RESTORATION

Reading: John 13:36–14:3

And we know that for those who love God all things work together for good, for those who are called according to his purpose. (Romans 8:28)

Serious as Peter's fall was, two or three good things, at least, would come out of it. In the end God works all things together for good, even the mistakes, for those who love him and repent of their failures. For instance, it would destroy Peter's misplaced trust in his own strength and induce in him a sober realistic awareness of his weaknesses.

Next, it would convince him of Christ's realism. Christ had not been misled by Peter's fervent protestations of devotion. Nor in one sense had Christ been disappointed by his fall, for he had foreseen it happening and loved him still.

Thirdly, Peter would now be ready to listen to Christ in a way he was not before he fell, and learn to assimilate the provision that Christ was going to make for maintaining, developing and eventually perfecting his devotion to himself and to the Father.

And finally, in the light of all this Peter would be especially able to strengthen his fellow believers (Luke 22:32).

'Let not your hearts be troubled,' said Christ (John 14:1); and we do well to listen to his advice. For there are two equal and opposite mistakes that believers can make in regard to their failures. The one is to treat them lightly as if they did not matter at all—to fail to repent of them; to refuse to let the Lord Jesus 'wash their feet' and cleanse them from their defilement (John 13:6–11). That way leads to increasing failure and fruitlessness.

The other mistake, however, lies at the opposite extreme. It is to allow ourselves to become engrossed with self, our failures and inadequacies. The mind then becomes absorbed with a sense of defeat; the spirit becomes weak, and Satan himself takes advantage of the situation and induces despair, joylessness and further defeat. This is not true holiness! True holiness leads us to confess and repent of our sins, and then to rest on God's assurance of forgiveness (1 John 1:9); to agree with God that 'in [us] (that is, in [our] flesh,) dwelleth no good thing' (Rom 7:18 KJV). We look away from ourselves to Christ and to the glorious provision he has made, and is making, for overcoming our weaknesses and eventually perfecting our devotion. So with divine wisdom Christ now turned his disciples' attention away from their inadequacies and Peter's failure to the glorious future before them.

David Gooding, *In The School of Christ: Lessons on Holiness in John 13–17*, 77–8

18th July

THE WAY BACK

Reading: James 4:6–10

Draw near to God, and he will draw near to you. (James 4:8)

It remains true of God that 'he gives more grace' (v. 6)—grace to repent and grace to come back. And James now exhorts us to come back. If we have got away in heart and our loyalties have been divided there is a way back. 'Submit yourselves to God; but resist the devil.' Learn to say, 'No, I am not going further down that road. I am going to close the gap that has opened up and come back to the Lord.' Come near to the Lord to hear his very heartbeat and taste his love again.

'Cleanse your hands, you sinners, and purify your hearts, you double-minded' (v. 8). Therein lies the trouble: double-mindedness, meaning one minute living for the Lord and the next minute living for the world. If we are going to make spiritual maturity, that double-mindedness and double-heartedness must come to an end and be a single heart beating for the Lord.

'Be wretched and mourn and weep. Let your laughter be turned to mourning and your joy to gloom' (v. 9). This isn't the recipe for every day of the Christian life. God has put desires into our personalities, which he fulfils with lovely gifts and beautiful pleasures. But if those things have taken us away from the Lord, then rather than the laughter of enjoyment and the cackle of fun we would be better off breaking our hearts in floods of tears and coming back to the Lord in genuine repentance, saying 'Sorry, what fools we have been to have wasted so much of life.'

When you come back, 'he will exalt you' (v. 10); and after the rain of the tears will come the lovely sunshine of the joy of his presence. He is not wanting to be a killjoy. The one who gives us desires and pleasures assures us that at his right hand there are 'pleasures forevermore' (Ps 16:11); but you can't ultimately have the pleasures if you have no time for the Lord. Those who permanently and finally reject the Lord must come where desires will never be satisfied, and will haunt them like writhing worms in their very insides for all eternity. Ultimately there is no satisfied desire, no thirst quenched, no hunger met, no joy, no real music apart from the God who made us and longs to redeem us.

David Gooding, *A Vision of the Perfect Man and Woman: Seven Studies on Major Themes from James*, 66–7

19th July

RESTORATION CAN BE TOUGH

Reading: Ezra 3:11–4:4

The latter glory of this house shall be greater than the former, says the LORD of hosts. (Haggai 2:9)

For all the golden promises that we shall read in prophets like Zechariah and Haggai, there's no disguising the fact that this restoration was a difficult business. It had started some years earlier with great enthusiasm on the part of people like Ezra and Nehemiah, and those keen souls who dared to leave the comfort of their well paid jobs in Babylon and come to rebuild Jerusalem. But that early enthusiasm had waned; the work was so very difficult. It's easier sometimes to build a house from scratch than to repair one that's gone wrong. Easier when you don't have to cope with the past and its mistakes, you have a clean sheet and can build afresh. It's more difficult when first of all you have to take away the rubble of past failures.

And it's frustrating work—knowing how to discern between what's broken beyond repair, and what's good material but fallen just a little bit and must be valued and reused. There were many sore fingers in those days from sorting out amongst the rubble and retrieving things. But the God who sent them for that task is a God of restoration. He loves you now, my brother and sister, and should you ever get broken like Peter was broken—all of a sudden and to his great consternation, God will not write you off. God values you. He will want to restore you and use you again, if it is at all possible.

It wasn't only the frustrating work of beginning again and restoring the broken that was difficult. It was the opposition that came upon them; so heavy, so altogether out of proportion. Soon the initial enthusiasm had departed and they were in the doldrums. Some of us might have a fellow-feeling in our hearts. Some of our great grandfathers tried to do a job of restoration in Christendom. It would be very easy, my brothers and sisters, now in our generation to give up and say it's unworkable and the complications of Christendom are so intricate and such a vast weight, that trying to restore things to a New Testament situation is more than can be hoped for. Then perhaps we too need to pause and take encouragement from what it was that God said would accompany the work of restoration, in spite of all the difficulties.

David Gooding, *An Offer of Restoration: Four Studies on God's Character in Zechariah*, 7–8

20th July

PERSEVERANCE IN RESTORATION

Reading: Nehemiah 2:17–20

Let us also lay aside every weight, and sin which clings so closely, and let us run with endurance the race that is set before us. (Hebrews 12:1)

As they came to Jerusalem and saw its desolations, it wasn't that Ezra got out some magic wand and, lo and behold, a newly built temple and a delightful Jerusalem began to spring out of the ground. It didn't happen like that. We who know the realities of life could scarcely believe a Bible if it said that's what happened. There is miracle with God, but there's no magic. The work of restoring Jerusalem city and its temple from the ruins that Israel's sin had brought upon them was a work to which God called his people in perseverance. They were patiently and persistently to work with him, and he with them, through the difficulties of repairing the damage.

That of course is a thing that will not surprise us in this day and age. God forgives the sins of the repentant sinner, but he doesn't always immediately remove the consequences of their sin. If you've given yourself to drinking methylated spirits every morning and getting involved in drunken brawls and you lose one of your legs in consequence, when you turn in repentance to the Lord he will forgive your sin and fill your heart with his joy but he won't restore the leg you've lost. He'll do it one day, at the resurrection. He will leave you with one leg to hobble your way through the rest of life, and you will have to learn the patience of living with the past and its consequences.

When we observe the lives of believers who have gone on with the Lord consistently since their conversion without grievous lapses, we can see that the work of their sanctification is no lightning procedure, but a long drawn out path of progress. As Paul reminds us in his classic words, 'Not that I have already obtained this or am already perfect . . . but . . . I press on toward the goal' (Phil 3:12–14). And Peter tells us likewise that if we would qualify not merely for entrance into the eternal kingdom, but for an abundant entrance into that kingdom, then it calls for patient continuance and perseverance with the Lord. We are to make every effort to add to our faith, moral goodness, knowledge, self-control, endurance and brotherly love, if that's the kind of entrance we want to have into that kingdom (see 2 Pet 1:5–7, 11).

David Gooding, *An Offer of Restoration: Four Studies on God's Character in Zechariah*, 12

21st July

REMEMBERING PAST FAILURES

Reading: Zechariah 1:1–6

Your fathers, where are they? And the prophets,
do they live forever? (Zechariah 1: 5)

Even though they have returned from Babylon, in the early verses of the prophecy God reminds his people of the sins of their fathers in past days. There is a sense in which we are called upon to forget those things which are behind, for unnecessary regret can be depressing and debilitating. Yet God does not always remove the past and causes us to remember it.

I remember my good father in the days of my infancy, when I broke his command and played ball near the drawing room window and cracked the whole thing from top to bottom. I was duly forgiven, but my father in his wisdom left the old cracked pane of glass for a long time. Why? Because it taught me not to play ball so near again to the lounge window. For, if in five minutes the thing had been repaired, I would not have learnt the seriousness of sin.

Peter was forgiven and he knew it, and revelled in the joy of the forgiveness with which Christ had restored him. But as you read his letters you will observe that the memory of his past comes peering through his writing. He teaches his fellow believers that same lesson that he had learnt so painfully: it wasn't the sorrow of the world, but 'godly sorrow' that helped Peter, and through him has helped us. As he writes, 'Since Christ has suffered, arm yourselves to suffer' (see 1 Pet 4:1), what memories would have flooded through Peter's heart. Oh, that he had never done it! He was forgiven, yet the memory would never perish this side of glory.

As these people in Zechariah's day stand in the ruins, God calls on them to remember the past—'Remember your fathers: where are they now?' It wasn't to discourage his people, but at that moment the path of restoration was so difficult the danger was that they would give up and rest content. They had returned in the sense that they had returned geographically to the land. But with the opposition growing so great and the difficulties so large, they had for the time being lapsed once more into complacency, which is a dangerous state for anyone to lapse into. Like a well-run business, the Christian life either goes forward or it tends to go back.

David Gooding, *An Offer of Restoration: Four Studies on God's Character in Zechariah*, 13

22nd July

SETTING OUR OWN HOUSES RIGHT

Reading: Zechariah 5:1–4

For the word of God is alive and active . . . it judges the thoughts and attitudes of the heart. (Hebrews 4:12 NIV)

If God is going to use Zerubbabel and Joshua the high priest to revive the testimony and rebuild the temple, then these next visions remind the people that if they would build the house of the Lord it has implications for their own houses. So Zechariah is given a vision of a flying scroll that enters into the houses of iniquitous sinners and destroys them. Should we read the vision as a threat, warning Israel to close and bolt their doors in case the scroll comes flying in through their windows? Well surely not, for it's not a threat, it's a promise. Oh for the day when it will finally be fulfilled, and evil is eliminated from among the people of God. By the grace of God we shall be made channels of his Holy Spirit and join in the work of building the house of the Lord.

At this moment do you not pray silently in your heart to the Lord, 'I wish you'd send a scroll like that my way', so that the Bible, God's holy word, would cease to be merely a book? 'Lord, let it enter into the floor and the rafters of my home and into every fibre of my being. Lord, use it to eliminate all that is not well.'

In that day how would they build the house of the Lord and be a testimony among the nations, if unworthy things still prevailed in their own homes and houses? When the people had built the temple to the glory of God amongst the nations, there was an occasion when Nehemiah came back from his business duties to find that in his absence Tobiah had moved in with his household stuff. He was related to one of the prominent Israelites and you couldn't make a fuss, could you? Well, Nehemiah made a fuss. 'We've not rebuilt this temple to have this kind of thing going on. Get out,' he said, and booted the man out along with all his stuff.

How shall I in my day build the house of the Lord and be a testimony for God amongst the people, if my own home is not governed by God's word, and his gracious disciplines are not releasing me daily from the power of sin?

David Gooding, *An Offer of Restoration: Four Studies on God's Character in Zechariah*, 30

23rd July

MOTHERS LEAD THE REVIVAL

Reading: 1 Samuel 1:21–28

*'For this child I prayed, and the L*ORD *has granted me my petition that I made to him. Therefore I have lent him to the L*ORD*. As long as he lives, he is lent to the L*ORD*.'* (1 Samuel 1:27–28)

The Philistines got distressed at God's judgments on them for having the ark among them (1 Sam 5). When the ark was brought into the temple of the Philistine god, Dagon, he fell over. What do you do if your god falls over? You heave him up and put him back in his place! But then the next day he fell over again, and his head and hands were cut off. What was this ark? And was it the God of Israel now who was doing this thing to their idol?

So they said that they would have an experiment. They got two cows that had calves, so their udders were full of milk. They shut their calves in the barns, attached the cows to a cart and put the ark on the cart. Now they would see if Israel's God was real, for it would be a tremendous force that would overcome the instinct of nature to make those cows leave their calves. The Hebrew, with sublime simplicity, calls them 'their sons' (1 Sam 6:10). Is there a God whose power exceeds the power of natural instinct? The cows went straight down the road. It wasn't that they didn't feel it—they lowed as they went (6:12). They took the ark of God back and left their sons behind.

When they got to the other end the Levites took down the ark and the people of Beth-shemesh split up the wood of the cart and offered the two animals as a burnt offering to God. You say, 'Poor old cows!' Yes, they left their sons by a power that was beyond human instinct and ended up on an altar in sacrifice to God.

I'm not to be inhuman; it's not a bad thing when my heart is full of natural instinct. However, God might call me to go beyond my selfish interest and give myself to him. Indeed, the injunction for us all is: 'I appeal to you therefore, brothers, by the mercies of God, to present your bodies as a living sacrifice, holy and acceptable to God, which is your spiritual worship' (Rom 12:1).

The wife of Phinehas, Eli's son, cared more about the glory of God than even the birth of her own son (1 Sam 4:21). Hannah before her gave her son to God's service. So here, even these cows, as they left their sons, show us that the glory of God is greater and more essential than even natural instinct. It was the beginning of the way of revival from the horrible moral tangle and spiritual disaster that Eli had allowed his sons to produce in Israel, when these mothers took their sons, and in their way, put God first.

David Gooding, *Priesthood, Sin and Atonement: Three Studies on Select Themes in 1–2 Samuel*, 7–8

Part 12

The Eternal God whose Purposes are Fulfilled in History

24th July

CHRIST THE LORD OF TIME

Reading: Isaiah 46:5–13

And he is before all things, and in him all things hold together. (Colossians 1:17)

This is a vast universe in which we live. This year we and our little planet have been travelling millions of miles on our annual journey round the sun. Travelling with the sun in the rotating arm of the galaxy that we're in; and then travelling in another direction with the whole of the galaxy in the direction that our galaxy is moving.

And of course that raises the practical question, where are we travelling to? And also the bigger question of life and life's travel, for in another metaphorical sense life is a journey, isn't it? Even within the confines of our little seventy years, the matter of the past and the future often looms up in front of us, sometimes with worrying concerns. Here's a good mother and wife, preparing her husband's dinner. 'He is coming home from work,' she says, but she doesn't know that already there's been an accident and the man is lying dead on the roadside. It will take some time for the news to catch up with her because, generally speaking, we are behind things. They happen and then later we discover them; and what has already happened we don't necessarily know. That future, which is now past, is still future to us and we shan't learn of it until sometime later.

That could be a worrying thing, couldn't it? How happy are those who have discovered Jesus to be the Christ, the Son of God. Not only were all things made by him and through him and for him, but 'he is before all things'. Not, he *was* before them, he *is* before them. And seeing he belongs to God's eternity all things in our space and time do not come before him; he is before them. Nothing will happen to you, my brother and sister, that he has to learn about six or seven days later.

'He is before all things, and in him all things hold together,' and we go forward into the future calm and confident, knowing that whatever happens nothing will be a surprise to him. If we receive a shock, a grief and a calamity, then let us comfort our hearts that he is before all things, in him all things consist and he knew it was going to happen. It didn't happen because he was asleep in a boat or something.

David Gooding, The Lord of Space, Time and History: One Study on the Person and Character of Jesus, 4–5

25th July

GOD'S ORIGINAL PLAN FOR MANKIND

Reading: Hebrews 2:5–9

You have made him a little lower than the heavenly beings and crowned him with glory and honour. (Psalm 8:5)

'For what is man?' That is a question which has often been asked, but it has never received a more noble answer than that given in the Hebrew Old Testament. The psalmist is reaffirming the Creator's own declared purpose in Genesis 1:26–30. Human beings are not pure spirit as angels are; they are part spirit and part animal. As originally created therefore, they are lower than angels. But they were not made, as so many ancient mythologies and religions taught, to be the menial slaves or playthings of capricious gods, who were themselves the mere products of the conflicting masses and forces of primeval chaos.

Nor is man a mere particle of the rational but utterly impersonal material that the universe is made of, as so many modern theories teach. Our human love and reason, our aesthetic sense and our ability to look forward, to hope and to plan, are not illusions doomed to be shattered by mindless matter and impersonal forces, which one day (however distant) will inevitably destroy all human life, along with the earth. And the crowning irony of it all is that they won't even know they've done it!

No. Men and women were made in God's image; made to be God's viceroys, to subdue the earth and progressively to take over control of it in fellowship with the Creator, to rule it and all its various levels of life and to make of it something glorious for God and for themselves. To grow up from their original moral infancy, to learn to 'think God's thoughts after him', as Kepler would put it, and in partnership with God, as sons with a father, to be masters and not prisoners of the matter and forces of the universe.

That at least was God's original plan. But we do not need to be told that the plan seems to have gone wrong somewhere. 'At present, we do not yet see everything in subjection to [man]' (Heb 2:8). We find ourselves in a world that is hard and cruel, and in spite of our great advances in science it seems to be too much for us. How little is left of the glory that God once gave us!

David Gooding, An Unshakeable Kingdom: The Letter to the Hebrews for Today, 77–8

26th July

PROTOTYPE AND FULFILMENT

Reading: Hebrews 9:23–10:7

Thus it was necessary for the copies of the heavenly things to be purified with these rites, but the heavenly things themselves with better sacrifices than these. (Hebrews 9:23)

When I was a boy, aeroplanes were funny contraptions generally made of brown paper and wood, some elastic bands and string! The reason they were able to fly at all is that they did embody, even at that crude level, some basic principles of aeronautics. The big jumbo jet at thirty-five thousand feet looks very different from those first few biplanes. But the same principles of aeronautics that were embodied in those prototype aeroplanes are now embodied at the vastly higher level of the jumbo jet.

And that's how history has been. When God set his heart upon the redemption of our human race, he began with Israel and went through the basic principles of redemption; from the time he redeemed them from the tyranny of Egypt with the blood of a Passover lamb and brought them into the promised land, and then to the age of peace and glory under Solomon. That was only a prototype and of course it didn't last. But have you noticed how the historian describes it in the last chapter of 1 Chronicles? 'Then Solomon sat on the throne of the Lord' (1 Chr 29:23). That's some doing, isn't it? At that level, it means he sat on the throne that God himself had set up. Wonderful as it was, it was only a prototype of something bigger.

Now, if in some lowly sense Solomon of Israel sat on the throne of the Lord, vast things have happened since then. There has come of the seed of David according to the flesh this Jesus Christ, Messiah, redeemer of the world. He was crucified and on the third day he rose again, and on the fortieth day he ascended into heaven. Literally at this very moment, this man, Jesus, who once worked in a carpenter's shop in Nazareth, sits on the throne of the Lord. Did you ever hear such a story? And it's true. If you start with Adam, now that we've got this far along it's not bad going that a descendant of Adam is seated on the throne of the Lord. And the New Testament gospel is that in some sense all who trust in him are seated with Christ in the heavenly places, and one day shall be transported bodily to sit with him on his throne.

This is the message of history.

David Gooding, *God's Programme and Provision: Lessons from History in Chronicles and Kings*, 7–8

27th July

ABRAHAM AND THE ROYAL ROAD OF REDEMPTION

Reading: Genesis 12:1–9

*Now the L*ORD *said to Abram, 'Go from your country and your kindred and your father's house to the land that I will show you.' (Genesis 12:1)*

There is a battle that lies at the very foundation of human existence, on whose outcome our eternal success and the destiny of our souls depend. It is waged a thousand times a day—it is the battle for the faith of a human heart. There are but two contestants. On the one side there is God; on the other side, the world and everything that is in it. Sometimes the battle seems to be between God on the one hand, and vice or sin on the other; but it is unlikely that it shall be vice of some sort that will damn our souls. If I may speak frankly, it is much more likely that the thing that shall damn your soul and mine is in allowing some bit of this beautiful world to claim from us the faith that should be God's alone.

Our story takes us way back into the dim past. The world has been cleansed by the flood and Noah's descendants are busily repopulating it. They built some magnificent cities in those far off days; we must not think of them as semi-savages running around in their loincloths. As the archaeologists uncover the remains of some of these cities we can see what magnificent civilizations they were. Their art remains unsurpassed; their architecture is still one of the wonders of the world. It is even more marvellous than our skyscrapers because they lacked the technology that we now have. In the course of later centuries these cities were the first to develop the great arts of astronomy and mathematics. The damning thing that must be written over them all is that each one of them became idolatrous, and Abraham was just as much an idolater as any.

> And Joshua said to all the people, 'Thus says the LORD, the God of Israel, "Long ago, your fathers lived beyond the Euphrates, Terah, the father of Abraham and of Nahor; and they served other gods."' (Josh 24:2)

God had to call Abraham out from that idolatry. He broke its grip on that one man's life and set him free to put his faith in God and in a glorious future. This was the start of the great royal road of redemption.

David Gooding, *The God of New Beginnings: Eighteen Seminars on the Book of Genesis*, 80

28th July

ISAAC: THE CHILD OF PROMISE

Reading: Romans 4:4–25

For we are the circumcision, who worship by the Spirit of God and glory in Christ Jesus and put no confidence in the flesh. (Philippians 3:3)

Have you grown discouraged as a Christian? You thought that by now you would have made tremendous strides. You say, 'It's not as though I'm not keen. There was a period in my life when I was just about saved and couldn't care less, but now I want to please the Lord. What an up and down thing it has been. Here I am today, and all I seem to know is how strong the flesh is.'

But that's progress! It would be extraordinary if you got home to heaven without knowing that the flesh is bad. It is a negative but necessary part of the lesson to discover that 'the arm of flesh will fail you, | ye dare not trust your own'.[1]

God took a long time to demonstrate it in Abraham's life. It wasn't until Isaac was born that Ishmael was cast out. Eventually it happened, the promised seed was born and the bondwoman and her son were cast out.

What God had taught Abraham, for many long centuries he had to teach to the nation that came from Abraham. He brought them out of Egypt, redeemed by the blood of the Passover lamb; he met them at Sinai and offered them a covenant relationship on the basis of the law: If you do this I will bless you; if you do not do it I will curse you (Deut 11:26–28). They said that they would do it. They had to learn that there was nothing wrong with the Law, it was holy, just and good. They had to learn its function; and through Israel the world would see that it is impossible for the flesh to fulfil the law of God.

They were long and bitter lessons, but one day the promised seed came and the old covenant was made obsolete. He was born in Bethlehem and died at Calvary. A new era had begun; the era of the new covenant and a new method of making people holy. But it means abandoning all trust in the flesh—both evil flesh and religious flesh—and learning to rely directly on the power of God's Holy Spirit.

---

[1] George Duffield (1818–88), 'Stand up, stand up for Jesus' (1858).

David Gooding, *The God of New Beginnings: Eighteen Seminars on the Book of Genesis*, 111

29th July

OUR DEBT TO JUDAISM

Reading: Isaiah 45:20–25

For what great nation is there that has a god so near to it as the Lord our God is to us, whenever we call upon him? (Deuteronomy 4:7)

There were three distinctive elements in Judaism as it stood amongst pagan idolatry. Firstly, it testified to the true and only true, invisible God; transcendent above all time and space. In all the pagan nations, God was not the creator of the whole universe: he was a part of it. Many pagan cultures debased the likeness of God into the likeness of a man, or even creepy crawly things. They had deified the forces of nature as though they were the ultimate forces of the universe. Israel stood against the folly of idolatry to witness to the true God, saying in the words of Isaiah,

> Turn to me and be saved, all the ends of the earth! For I am God, and there is no other. (Isa 45:22)

For if there is no creator, then mankind has no saviour other than their own wits. And you will not need me to tell you how feeble they are against the material and physical forces of the universe.

Secondly, Israel stood as a witness to morality. The God whom they worshipped in that temple was also the God whose divine authority lay behind morality. In the pagan world, perhaps the last place on earth you looked for morality was in their temples; many of them were full of sexual immorality. If you wanted to concern yourself with morality then you went to the philosophers, who tried to fathom what man's duty is. Israel stood head and shoulders above all other nations in that it said that the creator was concerned with morality, and all his divine power lay behind the sanctions of his holy and moral law.

Thirdly, Israel and its temple stood for the glorious assertion that there was point and purpose in history. They maintained that the world was not just going round in circles getting nowhere. There was a purpose in history inasmuch as Israel was God's chosen people and one day through Israel God would introduce his Messiah. He would come and God would restore all things and bring creation to its glorious fruition, the purpose for which it was ultimately made. Israel stood as a gospel of hope in a world that was without God and therefore without any hope. Israel was God's testimony to the nations.

David Gooding, *Daring to be Different: Seven Studies from Acts on Defining and Defending Christianity*, 27–8

30th July

THE SIGNIFICANCE OF JERUSALEM

Reading: Daniel 11:28–35

In the third year of Cyrus king of Persia, a revelation was given to Daniel. . . .
Its message was true and it concerned a great war. (Daniel 10:1 NIV)

The veil was gently pulled aside a little and Daniel was given to understand the battles in the heavenlies as the rulers of darkness strive against the angelic powers that are loyal to God. The centre of the great field of their campaign is the city of Jerusalem. Why is that? Because it is the city where in time past almighty God was pleased to put his name (see 2 Chr 6:6). It was the capital city of that nation whom God chose; whose King David was to be the ancestor and prototype of the Messiah himself. That city holds a fascination for the great powers of darkness in their determination to blot it from the face of the earth.

Here comes an exceedingly dark thing. Daniel was told that one day there would arise a wilful king. Not content to ban religion, he would put himself in the very place of God and set up in the temple of God 'the abomination that makes desolate' (Dan 11:31). Satan's counterfeit beast imitating God; for this is the battle of the ages and at its heart lies the struggle between almighty God and his inveterate rebel foe. The battle is for the hearts of men and for the dominion of planet earth.

When eventually the Messiah came, such was the hold of the power of darkness upon the minds of people that Israel rejected their Messiah—not all of them, but officially as a nation. The Son of David was cast out of his own capital city.

My friend, don't think that was the end of it. When Christ rose from the dead and went back to glory he didn't slink out of this world. In resurrection life he came to Jerusalem city and took his departure to heaven from the Mount of Olives. He commanded his apostles that they were to preach the gospel worldwide—beginning at Jerusalem (Luke 24:47). Our Christian gospel is based on that great movement which God began centuries before the Lord Jesus came. Amongst his purposes was the establishment of David's city, the city of Jerusalem. And forever and forever, to the remotest times of eternity, salvation and the gospel will be concerned with and based on the events that took place just outside Jerusalem (John 19:20). Hence the venom of the enemy towards it.

David Gooding, *Days Yet to Come: One Study from Daniel 10–12 on Israel's Future and Ours*, 8

31st July

THE INCARNATION AND THE FULFILMENT OF GOD'S PLAN FOR MANKIND

Reading: Psalm 110

But we see him who for a little while was made lower than the angels, namely Jesus, crowned with glory and honour because of the suffering of death. (Hebrews 2:9)

At present we do not see everything subject to man. But that does not mean that God has abandoned his original purpose. Sin has spoiled everything, and man by his folly and disobedience has thrown away much of his dominion. But God has not admitted defeat. Far from it. In his original plan man was deliberately designed to be a little lower than the angels. Perhaps that was because the creation of man was God's tactical answer to rebellion that had broken out in the spirit realm to which angels naturally belong. Who knows? But when Satan very early on successfully corrupted God's viceroy, man, and set him on a course of disloyalty and rebellion against the very God in whose image he was made, the wisdom of God's strategy in making man a little lower than the angels eventually became apparent.

Angels in their proper state do not marry or produce offspring. Mankind can do both. And that made God's long planned strategic move possible, by which he had himself born into our world as a man, so that as man he could defeat the enemy and bring to victorious fulfilment God's original purpose for mankind. And already, says Hebrews, we see the first stage of that purpose fulfilled. 'We see Jesus.' Note his name: it is his human name, a Hebrew name given to him by human parents under the direction of an angel.

We see Jesus, who for a little while was made lower than the angels, just as the first man Adam was. He has taken on flesh and blood and has become what angels never were or will be: human. See him, then, lying as a baby in a crude manger, apparently helpless, in an obscure village called Bethlehem. But don't suppose it is anything to be ashamed of! This is a tremendous leap forward for mankind. It is the first step on the way to mankind's redemption and triumphant glorification.

David Gooding, *An Unshakeable Kingdom: The Letter to the Hebrews for Today*, 79

1st August

GREATER THINGS FORESHADOWED IN THE HEALING OF JAIRUS' DAUGHTER

Reading: Luke 8:40–56

For since we believe that Jesus died and rose again, even so, through Jesus, God will bring with him those who have fallen asleep. (1 Thessalonians 4:14)

Why did Christ not relieve Jairus of his agony of suspense by using his well-advertised power of saving at a distance and by delivering his daughter from dying without waiting to come to his house? We may surmise that one reason might have been to test and so to strengthen Jairus' faith. When the centurion said to Christ, 'Lord, do not trouble yourself' (Gk. *mē skyllou*), it was an expression of faith (Luke 7:6). When someone from Jairus' house told him not to trouble the Teacher any more (Gk. *mēketi skylle*, 8:49), it was a temptation to give up faith in Christ on the grounds that it was now too late: the situation had gone beyond Christ's ability to do anything about it. Christ countered that temptation and saved Jairus from hopeless sorrow by challenging him to persistence in faith: 'only believe, and she will be well' (8:50).

Then, of course, there is the simple and obvious fact that if Christ had saved the girl at a distance it would have been a case of salvation from dying. As it is, it is appropriately enough a case of salvation from death itself. The centre point is that while all the people knew that the girl was dead—and she was really dead—Christ insisted that death for her was only sleep (8:52). Taught by Christ, believers ever since have regarded the death of the body as a sleep, and through the apostle Paul they have been further taught to believe that the final phase of their salvation will occur when the Lord comes and awakens their dead bodies from the sleep of death (1 Thess 4:13–17).

In light of this, one would have to be impervious to every drop of imagination not to treat the story of the raising of Jairus' daughter as the Fourth Gospel treats the raising of Lazarus (see John 11). In that case also, Christ refused to heal Lazarus at a distance or to go to Bethany in time to save Lazarus from dying. He first stayed away until Lazarus 'fell asleep' and then came to Bethany to wake him out of sleep (11:11), and finally made his raising from the dead a foreshadowing of the great resurrection of the dead at the second coming (11:24–27).

David Gooding, *According to Luke: The Third Gospel's Ordered Historical Narrative*, 154–5

2nd August

GREATER THINGS FORESHADOWED IN THE FEEDING OF THE FIVE THOUSAND

Reading: Luke 9:10–17

And the angel said to me, 'Write this: Blessed are those who are invited to the marriage supper of the Lamb.' (Revelation 19:9)

When the apostles returned from their mission and reported what they had accomplished, Christ withdrew with them to Bethsaida; but the crowds found out where they had gone and followed them. Understandably so: the preaching and ministry of the apostles all around the nation would have raised in them expectations and wistful hopes that the ancient prophecies of a coming age of universal peace and sorrowless paradise might after all be true and on the point of fulfilment. Knowing the hunger of the human heart for release from the frustrations and disappointments and pain of life in this present age, Christ did not rebuke the crowd for intruding on his privacy. He welcomed them and spoke to them of the kingdom of God and healed those who had need of healing (Luke 9:11), which would have fed their hopes still further.

But presently the apostles intervened to point out to Christ (as if he had not realized it) that the hour was getting late, there were no shops or lodging houses in the remote area where they were, and he had better send the crowd away to find food and lodging in the surrounding villages. Perhaps this unintended impertinence in taking the initiative and telling Christ what to do was the result of a sense of power and authority induced in them by the success of their recent mission. But what happened next shows how inadequate their ideas were even yet about the person and powers of Christ, and the nature of the coming kingdom which they had been heralding round the country.

Christ had no intention of sending the people away. He was going to give them a foreshadowing of what the kingdom of God, fully come, would mean. Isaiah in his poetic way had promised that one day God would spread a banquet for all the nations of the world: a feast of rich food, vintage wines, succulent satisfying dishes and the finest of beverages. One element in that divinely satisfying banquet would be the banishing of death for ever and the wiping away of every tear (see Isa 25:6–9). The time for the spreading of that actual banquet had not yet come, of course, but Christ was going to give the crowds and the apostles a vivid foretaste of it and a demonstration of the powers that would eventually bring it about.

David Gooding, *According to Luke: The Third Gospel's Ordered Historical Narrative*, 165–6

3rd August

THE SACRIFICE OF CHRIST WAS PLANNED AS THE TURNING POINT IN HISTORY

Reading: Luke 9:28–36

He was foreknown before the foundation of the world but was made manifest in the last times for the sake of you. (1 Peter 1:20)

Their conversation up on the mountain was about Christ's exodus. In this world Moses had superintended the offering of the Passover sacrifice to save Israel from the wrath of God, as the first step towards their liberation from bondage and their exodus from Egypt. In that other world, if not before, he would long since have discovered that his Passover sacrifice and exodus had another dimension. They were a prototype and prophecy of the sacrifice of Messiah, a pledge which one day would have to be 'fulfilled in the kingdom of God' (Luke 22:16). Moses would further have learned that his own Passover in Egypt was not simply a useful analogy, which fortunately happened to lie to hand when God decided that Messiah must die. The sacrifice of Messiah to save Israel, and all who will, from the wrath of God and the domination of Satan had been decided upon ages before Moses' Passover.

Elijah, too, when in this world, had offered a sacrifice (see 1 Kgs 18). Its purpose had been to win back Israel from her vain idolatries to serve the true and living God. Its method was simple: the God who could show, by fire from heaven, his acceptance of the sacrifice offered on Israel's behalf was to be acknowledged as the true God. In that world, Elijah too would have learned that his sacrifice was also a prototype of the way by which God had already purposed to bring back Israel and all mankind from their false gods: the sacrifice of Messiah was offered on behalf of all men, and its acceptance was demonstrated by the resurrection of Christ and the coming of the Holy Spirit from heaven.

A few days before, news of the coming death of Christ had appeared to the apostles as a sudden unexpected shock; an obstacle in the way of their hopes put there by the perversity of the religious leaders of their nation. Now on the mount of transfiguration they were beginning to discover that the death of Christ was a sacrifice, foreknown before the foundation of the world, spoken of and foretold by both the law and the prophets, and now about to be as deliberately fulfilled as it had been deliberately planned.

David Gooding, *According to Luke: The Third Gospel's Ordered Historical Narrative*, 172–3

4th August

THE ONCE-FOR-ALL PASSOVER

Reading: Hebrews 9:11–14

For Christ, our Passover lamb, has been sacrificed.
(1 Corinthians 5:7)

Israel were now setting off through the desert towards their great inheritance. Along their road many discoveries would be made, many blessings entered into and there would come many enemies and many battles. But however far they progressed, however resplendent their blessings, however tough the battles they would be called upon to face—never again would they need to be redeemed by the blood of a Passover lamb from the wrath of God against sin. The Passover was not only important—the Passover was unique.

Generations of Israel would grow up in centuries to come living in the luxuries of the land of Palestine, munching their grapes and enjoying their honeycombs. Every generation that ate its food in the land of Canaan and enjoyed that inheritance would have to look back to that one single event—the Passover that took place in Egypt—and attribute to it the basis of all their subsequent enjoyment. There was never a blessing in Israel that could not be traced basically to that once and for all Passover celebrated on that night in Egypt.

I have only to describe the Passover thus and you will at once see it has immediate parallels with another night, likewise unique in history. That night in which our blessed Lord was betrayed. That fearful night, shrouded from the eye of man in three hours of darkness, when the sword of Jehovah woke against the victim that was his Son and the blood of Christ was shed for sin, so that through him we might be redeemed from the wrath of God. That sacrifice of Jesus Christ our Lord is unique in all history; it shall never be repeated. There were types of it before it happened, but it itself had never happened before. There is a memorial supper to that event still constantly repeated, but never again is that sacrifice to be repeated. It was a once-for-all act—a thing never to be enacted again—when Jesus Christ our Lord, God's Son, bowed beneath the wrath of God on Calvary and cried at length, 'It is finished!' (John 19:30).

However great and marvellous the blessings that we now enjoy; however far beyond our present imaginings those great kindnesses that God shall show to us in a coming eternity; every one of those blessings can be attributed to this unique event of the sacrifice of Jesus Christ our Lord.

David Gooding, *No Longer Bondmen: Thirteen Studies from Exodus on the True Meaning of Freedom*, 60–1

5th August

THE RISEN CHRIST BRINGS US TO GOD

Reading: John 20:10–18

I am ascending to my Father and your Father,
to my God and your God. (John 20:17)

I was in Italy the other month and went to the great treasury in one of the big cathedrals of the Medici dynasty. There was a glass cabinet in the middle to show relics, and in it were bones of saints or something. How the heart does cling to these things.

Christ had meant so much to Mary Magdalene, and she had come with her spices to the tomb. Had nothing happened, she and the other women would have built a shrine there, and they would have come frequently to pray, because they felt it was holy. But we know that not just Mary but all the women abandoned the place; they never did turn it into a shrine nor did they make pilgrimages to it. Why not?

When she got there the body was gone, and it was very distressing. She turned and saw what looked like a gardener. And she said, 'Sir, if you've taken him away, tell me where you've laid him, and I will come and fetch him and take him away.' She would have embalmed him and made a shrine of the tomb. But the stranger said, 'Mary', and in that moment she recognized the voice! For the Lord himself had said that his sheep know his voice. She realized it was the Lord and started to cling and take hold of him, so as to never lose him again.

Gently he said, 'Mary, stop holding me for the moment. I'm not yet ascended to my Father. But go and tell my brethren, "I am ascending to my Father and your Father, to my God and your God."' He not only spoke it, but as she listened to him saying those words it formed in her heart a personal, living relationship with the living Lord Jesus.

They didn't make a shrine to him. You don't make a shrine to somebody who's alive, do you? Oh, what a wonderful thing that is—it's called eternal life, you know! It is to know God in that personal sense. Have you heard the voice of Christ say, 'My Father is your Father; my God is your God. I am the living Lord, and you have me as a living Saviour'? That's what it meant to Mary.

David Gooding, *Understanding the Trinity: Six Studies on God's Revelation of Himself*, 10–11

6th August

HOW THE RISEN LORD JESUS MAINTAINS OUR FAITH

Reading: Luke 22:28–34

He is able to save to the uttermost those who draw near to God through him, since he always lives to make intercession for them. (Hebrews 7:25)

Let's ask the apostle Peter, 'What did the resurrection of Christ mean for you?'

I think Peter would say, 'Well, I was a believer in Christ before he died, and I thought I was so strong. I loved the Lord, and I gave up my job. I preached for him and I served him. And I really thought I would have given my life for him. But I messed it all up. When Jesus Christ was arrested and was in court, I went to see it, and the people standing around began to question me. I lost my nerve and I denied the Lord.'

'So it must have been embarrassing for you to have to meet the Lord after he rose from the dead. What was he like when you met him?'

'Well,' says Peter, 'even before he died, he warned me. He said, "Peter, you're going to deny me three times." And I wouldn't believe him, but it happened. That night when I denied him for the third time the cockerel crowed, and Jesus turned and looked me in the face. Now I believed him; I had no choice for it had come true. Then I remembered something else he'd said on that occasion. "Peter, Satan has desired to have you—all twelve of you—to sift you like wheat, but I've prayed for you, Peter, that your faith may not fail. And when you're restored, Peter, strengthen your brethren."

'In all the confusion of my emotions, I remembered that he'd said, "Peter, *when* you are restored," not, "*if* ever you are restored." I'd made a mess of everything else. My testimony was spoilt; my courage had gone. Thank God for a Saviour who interceded and prayed for me; my faith was not destroyed and he brought me through. And when I saw him in resurrection he talked privately to me, but later on he said, "Peter, do you really love me?" and I said, "Lord, you know." He said, "Feed my sheep, Peter."

'Oh, the marvel of the Saviour,' says Peter, 'he rose again from the dead and ever lives to make intercession for me that my faith shall not fail!'

David Gooding, *Understanding the Trinity: Six Studies on God's Revelation of Himself*, 8–9

7th August

OUR PERFECT HIGH PRIEST'S OATH OF APPOINTMENT

Reading: Hebrews 7:20–28

This one was made a priest with an oath by the one who said to him: 'The Lord has sworn and will not change his mind, "You are a priest forever."' (Hebrews 7: 21)

The oath has appointed one as our high priest who is not only perfectly qualified, but also perfectly equipped and therefore perfectly efficient and effective. The priests appointed by the law were hardly this. Suppose you came with your pressing needs and got one of them to deal with God on your behalf. First of all, he might well have to put himself right with God and offer a sacrifice for his own sins. And in the meantime he might suffer some accidental physical or ceremonial pollution, which would oblige him to call in a deputy.

And not even the best of them could offer a sacrifice that was sufficient for you for all time. They offered a sacrifice one day, but they had to offer another one the next day, and next week, and next year. And when you came to die, and they had performed for you all the rites and ceremonies they knew, they still could not guarantee that God would immediately accept you into his heaven. They could not accompany you on your passage from this world to the next—you were on your own then!

How different Christ is! See how well qualified he is. Never at any time did he know the weakness of sin or have to offer a sin offering for himself. He was always holy, blameless and pure, and is now set apart from sinners (7:26). During the days of his life on earth he knew the weakness that is inherent in being a man with a natural (though sinless) body. But now that he is exalted above the heavens, his body is a spiritual body and he knows no weakness or frailty. He never grows weary in his praying; he always persists energetically in his ministry.

And see how well equipped he is. The sacrifice of himself at Calvary once and for all is sufficient to cover every sin of every believer until 'all the ransomed church of God | be saved, to sin no more.'[1] As the almighty Son of God, he has been fully equipped to be perfectly effective for evermore. And when, or if, we come to die we shall not be on our own. For us, to be 'absent from the body' will mean to be instantaneously 'present with the Lord' (2 Cor 5:8), where he 'is seated at the right hand of the throne of the Majesty in heaven' (Heb 8:1).

---

1 William Cowper (1731–1800), 'There is a fountain filled with blood.'

David Gooding, *An Unshakeable Kingdom: The Letter to the Hebrews for Today*, 154–5

8th August

BAPTISM IN THE HOLY SPIRIT AT PENTECOST

Reading: Acts 2:1–13

'For John baptized with water, but in a few days you will be baptized with the Holy Spirit.' (Acts 1:5 NIV)

A new and distinct epoch in God's operations on earth was about to dawn. And understandably so. The incarnation had been an event unprecedented in all the annals of creation. Calvary too was unique. Never before had earth witnessed its Creator spiked to a cross. The resurrection that followed was a first in all the history of the race since Adam. And never had heaven's eternity experienced before what it was about to experience with the ascension of the man Jesus Christ into the very presence of God.

What this at last made possible, therefore, was a happening unparalleled and hitherto impossible, the coming of the Holy Spirit to take up permanent residence in the individual believer (1 Cor 6:19) and in the church (3:16–17). In the third place, Christ further underlined the newness of the approaching epoch by emphasizing the unique distinction of the operation that was to inaugurate it. 'John baptized you with water,' he reminded them, 'but you will be baptized with the Holy Spirit not many days from now' (ESV).

John, we remember, had electrified the whole nation when he first appeared in public. His voice had broken the centuries-long silence since Israel's last recognized prophet had spoken. His was the predicted 'voice in the wilderness', announcing the arrival of the long-promised Messiah, whose forerunner he was (Isa 40:3; Luke 3:1–6). According to our Lord, John was the greatest of all mankind (Luke 7:28). Even so, there was on John's own confession an immeasurable difference between him and Jesus.

John could point to the Lamb of God: Jesus was that Lamb. John could announce the impending sacrifice for the sin of the world: Jesus offered it. John could preach about forgiveness: Jesus had the authority personally to grant it. John could demand repentance and baptize people in water in token of it. However, by his own admission he could not baptize repentant and forgiven sinners in the Holy Spirit and thus unite men with God. But the Lord Jesus could, and was now about to. And when at Pentecost he did so, he would do what no other man, however holy, however exalted, had done ever since the world was formed. At Pentecost a new epoch would begin: God's redemptive work would move on to an altogether higher plane.

David Gooding, *True To The Faith: The Acts of the Apostles—Defining and Defending the Gospel*, 39

9th August

ABRAHAM AND PAUL CHOSEN IN GOD'S REDEMPTIVE PLAN

Reading: Acts 9:1–19

But the Lord said to him, 'Go, for he is a chosen instrument of mine to carry my name before the Gentiles and kings and the children of Israel.' (Acts 9:15)

At the beginning of his story Stephen remarks, 'The God of glory appeared to our father Abraham' (Acts 7:2). In chapter 9 Luke records that 'suddenly a light from heaven flashed around [Saul of Tarsus]' (9:3). The similarity in word and idea is obvious; but consider its significance.

The appearance of the God of glory to Abraham was the fundamental spiritual experience behind the birth of the Hebrew nation. It would be impossible to exaggerate its importance. Its effects are with us still. But notice the direction of the movement it initiated. It brought Abraham out of the Gentiles to found a nation that would thereafter be distinct from all others: unique in its testimony to the one true God and in its protest against Gentile polytheism. 'Leave your country and your people,' God said, 'and go to the land I will show you' (7:3 NIV).

When the light from heaven shone round about Saul, it began another phase in Israel's history, no less important or significant. It took Saul, however, in exactly the opposite direction from Abraham. 'A Hebrew of the Hebrews' (Phil 3:5), he was sent out of the bosom of the Hebrew nation and back among the Gentiles, 'to carry [God's] name before the Gentiles and kings' (Acts 9:15).

At first sight it might seem that the second movement contradicted the first. But that is not so. The second movement fulfilled and completed the first. When God called Abraham out of the Gentiles, it was with the purpose that in him all the families of the earth should eventually be blessed (Gen 12:3). With the coming of the Messiah and the conversion and commissioning of Saul of Tarsus, God's original purpose in calling Abraham out of the Gentiles was going to find fulfilment in hitherto unmatched worldwide blessing to the Gentiles. Through Saul of Tarsus, his preaching and his writings, uncountable millions of Gentiles over the course of the centuries would come to faith in the God of Abraham.

David Gooding, *True to the Faith: The Acts of the Apostles—Defining and Defending the Gospel*, 129

10th August

THE SIGNIFICANCE OF PETER'S DELIVERANCE FROM PRISON

Reading: Acts 12:1–18

But our citizenship is in heaven, and from it we await a Saviour, the Lord Jesus Christ. (Philippians 3:20)

Now the credibility of miracles depends in the first place on the character and reliability of the witness and of the record. But it depends also on a certain sense of proportion. If we were told that God intervened by sending an angel to help Peter find a button that had dropped off his shirt, the means used would appear to be so out of proportion with the importance of the situation that the story would be difficult to believe.

The credibility of the story of Peter's miraculous deliverance out of prison depends in the first place on our estimate of the reliability of the inspired historian, Luke. But it will also depend on our estimate of the importance of the issue at stake. Some commentators have suggested that the story of the angel is only a heightened poetic way of saying that in God's good providence somebody in the prison authority, sympathetic to Peter, let him out. But that explanation will not do. First, because Luke says it was an angel (Acts 12:7–10). But in addition, only a direct miraculous intervention of God would have been adequate to settle the issue at stake.

Just as God himself had given Israel the food laws, so God himself had set up the state of Israel as a sacralist state with the civil power necessary to enforce religious belief and practice. When God cancelled the food laws, therefore, he had to be seen to do it himself. It would have been no good for Peter to suggest to his colleagues in Jerusalem that he thought the food laws could now be ignored. God had to settle the matter, by taking things out of Peter's hands and himself pouring out the Holy Spirit on the Gentiles.

Similarly, if God wanted people to see that all **divine authority** had been removed from the sacralism of the state of **Judaea, the only way he** could do it was by direct divine intervention. **The mere opinion of Peter**, or of all the apostles combined, would have been **inadequate. And as to** proportions: the release of the faith and the **preaching and practice of** the gospel from the control of the Jewish state—**and from all other** sacral states—was, next to the gospel message itself, **a matter of fundame**ntal importance to the evangelization of the world.

David Gooding, *True to the Faith: The Acts of the Apostles—Defining and Defending the Gospel*, 231–2

11th August

THE ARK COMES TO JERUSALEM

Reading: 1 Chronicles 15:16–28

'And if I go and prepare a place for you, I will come again and will take you to myself, that where I am you may be also.' (John 14:3)

First of all David founded the great city Jerusalem, then he brought the ark up to Jerusalem. The first time he did it, he made a mistake—we'll pass by that for the moment and come to the second occasion when he did it properly. Things were in great disorder in those days, so he didn't bring up the tabernacle to Jerusalem, but he did bring up the ark.

We have to ponder that for a moment. We must go back into history to ask what it would have meant to David, and to the crowds that lined the road towards Jerusalem and the city streets for this tremendous spectacle. To the devout Israelites it wasn't just a golden box with cherubim on the top that was now coming to Jerusalem. Israel fervently believed that on that box, that wooden box overlaid with gold, between the outstretched wings of the cherubim, was the divine presence. The Lord of heaven and earth sat enthroned between the cherubim. That's what they believed anyway, even if you don't! They believed that when they saw the ark, it was the Lord coming to Jerusalem. Hence the exceeding fervour of King David as he humbled himself in his devotion before the ark. It was the transcendent Lord, enthroned invisibly upon the ark of his covenant, now coming to Jerusalem to be installed in the city.

You'd love to have been there, wouldn't you? But my brother, my sister, one day we shall really see him; not in prototype nor in mere symbol. What a wonder that will be. We'll see him coming in his glory and his feet will stand on the Mount of Olives. This is our hope. The angels said:

> 'This Jesus, who was taken up from you into heaven, will come in the same way as you saw him go into heaven.' (Acts 1:11)

> *Jesus is coming! O sing the glad word;*
> *Coming for those he redeemed by his blood.*
> *Coming to reign as the glorified Lord;*
> *Jesus is coming again.*[1]

---

1 Daniel W. Whittle (1840–1901), 'Jesus is coming!'
   David Gooding, *God's Programme and Provision: Lessons from History in Chronicles and Kings*, 11

12th August

THE LORD'S RETURN

Reading: Hebrews 10:19–25

So Christ, having been offered once to bear the sins of many, will appear a second time, not to deal with sin but to save those who are eagerly waiting for him. (Hebrews 9:28)

We are to draw near in spirit into the Most Holy Place where Christ is now (10:22). But we are also constantly to remember that Christ is coming again. As the end of chapter 9 told us, he will appear the second time (v. 28). He will come bodily and visibly (Acts 1:11); and he will come soon, the day is approaching (Heb 10:25). 'In just a little while, he who is coming will come and will not delay' (v. 37 NIV). Only true believers will be ready for him. Only true believers will rise to meet him and be taken to the Father's house to be for ever with the Lord (John 14:1–3; 1 Thess 4:14–18). If we are true believers, we must show that we are and act as true believers. We must live by faith, as all God's righteous ones do (Heb 10:38).

What will that involve? It will mean holding unswervingly to the hope we profess. Christ promised to come again; he is faithful and he will assuredly keep his promise. We must not allow liberalism to empty that promise of its meaning. It is not a myth—our Lord's promise means literally what it says. We must give equal weight to the prophetic side of our faith and to the doctrine of the second coming, as we do to our other Christian doctrines. It is not irrelevant to practical Christian living.

The thought of his coming is in fact a very necessary spur to holiness and loyal diligent service; and the nearer we can see the day approaching, the more we need to meet together with our fellow-believers to encourage one another (10:24–25). We need to get and to give all the help we can. To imagine we don't is an ominous sign.

David Gooding, *An Unshakeable Kingdom: The Letter to the Hebrews for Today*, 196–7

13th August

THE COMING OF ELIJAH

Reading: James 5:13–20

Elijah was a man with a nature like ours, and he prayed fervently that it might not rain, and for three years and six months it did not rain on the earth. (James 5:17)

Before the day of the Lord comes, in his supreme mercy God will send Elijah to prepare for the restoration of all things (Mal 4:5). Just as John the Baptist came in the spirit of Elijah to prepare the way for the Lord at his first coming, so Malachi's prophecy, as interpreted by our Lord, says that one day Elijah shall come: 'Elijah does come first to restore all things' (Mark 9:12).

Elijah shall come with powers to shut up the heaven, as he did in ancient time, and do his spectacular miracles. But he'll do more than that. Shall he not preach to the nation of Israel, scattered around the world, that their true Messiah is the one who died at Calvary? He shall prepare them for his coming by way of repentance, and when they see him there shall be great lamentation, mourning as for an only child, as they look on him whom they have pierced (see Zech 12:10). The nation shall be saved, according to God's gracious prophetic programme.

So the Jewish nation will be converted as a whole. Not every person, many shall perish in the judgments; but at his appearing the nation as a whole shall repent and believe. What a marvellous God, marvellous in his mercies.

You say, 'Yes, but that's all theoretic. What has it to do with us? We're not Elijahs.' No, I think not, but we could imitate him. Says James, 'Elijah was a man with a nature like ours, and he prayed, and God heard his prayers.'

> If anyone among you wanders from the truth and someone brings him back, let him know that whoever brings back a sinner from his wandering will save his soul from death and will cover a multitude of sins. (Jas 5:19–20)

Wouldn't you like to be doing that work? But you're doing it already, aren't you? How soon the Lord will come, who can tell? We're moving on, aren't we? And some of the men and women who rub shoulders with you may one day stand under the reign of the terrible beast, the man of sin, and say that there's no God. In God's hands, wouldn't you like to be someone who would prepare them for that terrible day, by showing them how they could find the true God, hear his voice, know him, and be at peace with him? That's the work of someone like Elijah, to convert a sinner from the error of his way and save a soul from death.

David Gooding, *Restoration and Repentance: One Study on the Past and Future Ministry of Elijah*, 16–17

14th August

BUILDING THE ETERNAL TABERNACLE

Reading: 1 Chronicles 29:1–9

In [Christ Jesus] the whole structure, being joined together, grows into a holy temple in the Lord. In him you also are being built together into a dwelling place for God by the Spirit. (Ephesians 2:21–22)

'Solomon my son', said David, 'is young and tender' (1 Chr 22:5 KJV). Thank God for that; he hadn't learned to be cynical and he wasn't old enough yet to be vain. 'And God has told me that he shall build God a house' (see v. 10).

What is the eternal temple going to be built of? Here's the wonderful news. When we leave this world, we shan't say, 'Thank God that's over. Let's leave it all and go up to heaven and find a temple that's been built out of materials we've never seen before.' It isn't going to be that.

David says, 'I've prepared the materials, Solomon. All I want you to do is put them together and erect what I've already prepared. They came from many a battle and many a sacrifice. They came from raw life; from the things of this world, the family, the business.'

And such are the materials out of which God is going to build the eternal tabernacle. The eternal tabernacle is not some fairy castle. It's real, and the marvel is that when God planned to build a temple for eternity, he didn't start with the best material he could possibly get hold of; he started with old factory rejects. Sorry if I insult you, but I think the whole lot of us are factory rejects! We don't carry the labels, 'sleeves the wrong length', or anything like that; but all of us are marred, substandard, and some of us are broken. The magnificence of the grace of God is that, instead of doing something completely new, he takes us as we are, redeems us, and by his grace and through his Spirit and the gifts he has given in the church, he seeks to remould us. He's going to finish it one day, when every single one of us will be conformed to the image of his Son. Magnificent, isn't it?

But the building of the temple is not committed merely to the likes of you and me. God had appointed his man to build the temple. Delightful, young, tender, son of man, son of David, son of God, that Solomon was, we bypass Solomon and we think of our Lord. 'Consider him: none other than the Son of God,' says the writer to the Hebrews (see 12:3; 1:2). How wonderful he is.

David Gooding, *Mankind's Pathway to the Coming Age of Peace: Six Studies on the Overall Message of 1 Chronicles*, 68

15th August

ANTICHRISTS NOW AND THE ANTICHRIST TO COME

Reading: Jude 11–23

Children, it is the last hour, and as you have heard that antichrist is coming, so now many antichrists have come. (1 John 2:18)

Ever since Messiah came, the world has been now in the last epoch. Hebrews puts it doctrinally:

> God, who has spoken in diverse manners and different proportions to the fathers by the prophets in previous ages, hath in this last age spoken unto us in his Son. (Heb 1:1–2 DWG)

Jesus Christ is God's last word. We are not to expect further revelation. Our blessed Lord is the Word of God.

We are told explicitly in the epistles and by our Lord himself that at the end of this age there shall come a dark figure known under one of his names as the antichrist, the great opposer of Christ. In calling him antichrist, people have wondered whether the original writers meant to imply that he opposed the Christ by straight out frontal attack and opposition; or whether he's called antichrist in the other possible meaning of the preposition *anti*—to imply that he opposes Christ by imitating Christ. By being a false Christ, is he trying to take the place of the true Christ? He will be the antichrist who is to come.

'But already', says John, 'there have gone out many antichrists.' He uses the plural: that is, the coming of the antichrist won't be one sudden unexpected or unprepared for event. The great mastermind of his satanic majesty that lies behind the coming of the antichrist is already at work, and has been at work ever since the Lord Jesus came. The devil himself, who attacked our Lord and tempted him in the wilderness, has been at his foul task to oppose the Lord Jesus all down the ages, particularly by corrupting the truth of the gospel.

We therefore need to be wise, because we may be sure that those movements of thought that will lead up to the coming of the antichrist are already with us. The point of being told about prophecy and what will happen at the end of the age is not merely to satisfy our curiosity about the divine timetable of things to come; it is so that we might be wise even now, and recognize that what's going on around us will contribute to the coming of the great antichrist. People's minds are being softened up, ready to accept that terrible deception.

David Gooding, *Unity, Origin and Victory: Fourteen Studies from 1 John on Life in the Family of God*, 39–40

16th August

SATAN'S BIG MAN

Reading: Revelation 13:1–18

And they worshipped the dragon, for he had given his authority to the beast, and they worshipped the beast, saying, 'Who is like the beast?' (Revelation 13:4)

How is this age to end up? When Satan first tempted mankind to seize independence of God, he broke their confidence in God's word. 'Don't take any notice of that old-fashioned stuff,' he said. 'Anybody knows it's nonsense anyway; you shall not surely die. Take the fruit, woman, and you shall be as God. You won't have to be dependent on God anymore for knowing good and evil' (see Gen 3:4–5).

Where will his tactics end up? By God's permission a mere man, under the influence of satanic impulse and guidance, will stalk on to the stage of the world. He will do such fantastic wonders by the power of Satan and by his deceit, that vast portions of the world will go after him with mad excitement, saying, 'Who is like the beast?'

This phrase is used in the Old Testament to express the fact of God's uniqueness. The prophet Micah's name in Hebrew, *Micayahu*, means, 'Who is like unto Jehovah?' It is a rhetorical question, and of course the answer is presupposed in the question. God says, 'I don't know any other god who is like me. There is none like unto Jehovah!'

'Who is like unto Jehovah?' is a powerful statement of the uniqueness of God. But at the end of this age a figure shall arise, inspired by Satan with all his panoply of publicity and spectacular demonic miracles. The world shall be induced to say, 'What a man! In facet, this man is God. Who is like the beast?' He shall oppose all that is called God and exalt himself above all that is called God (see 2 Thess 2:4). Here is *big man*. And John, the prophet of the Apocalypse, is then given a clue as to this character. He says the mark of the beast is 666. And what is that? It is the mark of a mere man (see Rev 13:17–18). That is the enemy that God has finally to displace in order to bring in the millennial reign of Jesus Christ our Lord. *Man*, therefore, is the great enemy.

David Gooding, *The Problems of Becoming and Being a King: Fifteen Seminars on Major Themes in 1 and 2 Samuel*, 89–90

17th August

THE END RESULT OF MANKIND'S REBELLION

Reading: 2 Thessalonians 2:5–12

[They] exchanged the glory of the immortal God for images resembling mortal man and birds and animals and creeping things. (Romans 1:23)

Man grasps at independence of God, thinking that this will somehow bring him freedom. It never has and it never will. See the misery that it plunged the ancient world into. If the moon went into an eclipse they banged the bin lids to try and chase away the demon who had got hold of the moon. They sacrificed their children to this god and deified the forces of nature, until they became slaves to the elements of a physical universe. In modern society they're not liable to erect statues to Zeus and Aphrodite, but without God they are every bit as much in danger of falling into the slavery of idolatry.

Controlling the forces of nature without God, they are headed for the biggest slavery our planet has yet seen. The man of sin is coming. Because demons are superhuman in their genius, he will have spectacular control of the physical forces. He will make fire come down from heaven, as it did in Elijah's day (see Rev 13:13). Whereas in Elijah's day it was an evidence of the true God, when the man of sin performs these things it will not be evidence of the true God. God will allow man to go to extreme lengths in unlocking the secrets of the physical universe. His lieutenants will be able to give a voice to the statue that they've made, so that it will speak (Rev 13:14–15); and through that final dictator, man will make his bold grasp for complete independence of the very idea of God.

'He takes his seat in the temple of God, proclaiming himself to be God' (2 Thess 2:4). Will mankind be free then? No, they will worship this man, and it will reduce mankind to the most grovelling slavery that humanity has ever seen.

When the man of sin is at the height of his powers, the gospel shall go out in the terms that have always been implicit in any gospel. But they shall have to be spelled out explicitly, calling upon men and women to worship the creator of the earth and the sea. For it is only by trusting him and depending upon him that they can be free from fear of the universe and free of slavery to deified man or the deified forces of nature, let alone be reconciled to God.

David Gooding, *King of kings and Lord of lords: Four Studies Exploring God's Sovereignty Over Various Spheres*, 9–10

18th August

THE NEW JERUSALEM

Reading: Revelation 21:1–4, 15–20

And I saw the holy city, new Jerusalem, coming down out of heaven from God, prepared as a bride adorned for her husband. (Revelation 21:2)

If we want to know what the purposes of God have been, let us stand with John in his vision at the edge of time where eternity was about to begin. He said, 'From his presence earth and sky fled away, and no place was found for them' (20:11). Then what? What has God salvaged? What, if anything, has God got out of time for eternity? When the scaffolding of earth disappears, God is left with what his heart has been set on to produce for eternity. Says John, 'I saw a new heaven and a new earth . . . and I saw the holy city, new Jerusalem, coming down out of heaven from God, prepared as a bride adorned for her husband' (21:1–2).

So what has God got out of it? A city, a holy city—the new Jerusalem. If it's called the new Jerusalem, what was the old Jerusalem? Well, Jerusalem was founded by the great David as the centre that unified the nation. It formed for them a capital city that bound the whole nation together, the centre and heart of the nation. But it was also the administrative centre of the nation and of the empire that God had given them.

As we watch with John as it comes down out of heaven, we see that it's a city, a Jerusalem—only it's a new Jerusalem, and it has twelve gates (21:12). Now in the ancient city, gates were the place where the elders of the city sat to conduct the business of the city and its external relationships, and to organize all the life that took place inside and outside the city. And as the angel pointed out to John, this great new Jerusalem with its twelve gates will be the administrative centre of the eternal universe that God is planning (21:25–26).

According to many of the parables that our Lord Jesus told, God is going to use his redeemed people as the administrators of his eternal kingdom. That has implications for this life. What is life for? Get hold of this. Whatever career God leads you into, all your secular and spiritual exercises should be geared to the purpose of God for the task he has for you in the eternity to come.

David Gooding, *Visions of Eternity: Five Studies on Major Themes in 1–2 Chronicles*, 38–9

19th August

THE DEATH OF THE UNSAVED

Reading: Ephesians 2:1–5

'Besides all this, between us and you a great chasm has been set in place, so that those who want to go from here to you cannot, nor can anyone cross over from there to us.' (Luke 16:26 NIV)

What happens to those who die unforgiven, without ever having been born again and reconciled to God? Let me point out that when physical death comes along in such a case, it only makes permanent a kind of death that those people have already been living (see Eph 2:1). The Bible declares that a man or a woman is spiritually dead until they have personally come to know God; until they have personally been saved through Jesus Christ.

You say, 'In what sense dead?'

They are separated from God. When Adam and Eve sinned and God then came down, they ran off. And to run away from God is death. God is all there is of life: he has given us physical life in order that we might come to the possession of spiritual life. But if we run away because of our sins, we are already spiritually dead.

When physical death overtakes a person who has always been running away from God, it makes that state of spiritual death permanent. And in describing it our Lord said that between them and the presence of God there is eternally a great gulf fixed.

Perhaps you say, 'Well that's very hard. Why doesn't God give them another chance in the life to come?'

My friend, if it were possible to give them another chance, you may rest assured that the God who loves us so much that he gave his Son to die for us would give us every chance it were possible to give.

God offers us his salvation in Christ freely. It cost him the death of his own Son. But it is a one-to-one relationship he is offering. If we want that relationship, we may have it; we may receive Christ personally through an act of our will and faith. But God will never force us to receive Christ and overwhelm our own decision, or crush our own personality. For if he took away our free choice, then we should cease to be humans and become simply machines; and God loves every man and woman too much to turn them into mere machines.

Christ indicates that time is the period when we have the opportunity to change. If I decide to say no to Christ and I die like that, there is no magic. As a man or woman dies, so shall he or she be eternally.

David Gooding, *Can We Be Certain About Life after Death? One Study on the Biblical Doctrine of Resurrection*, 13–14

20th August

PART OF AN ETERNAL PLAN

Reading: Haggai 2:1–9

Who is left among you who saw this house in its former glory? How do you see it now? Is it not as nothing in your eyes? Yet now be strong . . . (Haggai 2:3–4)

There were only a few old grey heads of ninety years or so who remembered the magnificent temple before it was destroyed. It had been built by Solomon and maintained for centuries by the Jewish kings, with all the wealth of the royal house at their disposal. When these people began to work on the ruins, patching up and making amends here and there, they felt that it would never be anything like what it used to be in the former days. Would it be worth it? When they had done their best it would still not be very wonderful.

God told them that he knew it was not what Solomon's temple was. He was realistic enough to see that. He knew these were different times. But he also told them that if they would work with him and be strong then (feeble and small though it was) he would be with them:

> Yet now be strong, O Zerubbabel, declares the LORD. Be strong, O Joshua, son of Jehozadak, the high priest. Be strong, all you people of the land, declares the LORD. Work, for I am with you, declares the LORD of hosts. (2:4)

God would soon get the cash out of the pockets of a few millionaires to help on the work: 'the treasures of all nations shall come in, and I will fill this house with glory . . . The latter glory of this house shall be greater than the former,' says the Lord (2:7–9). How was that possible? God was not just looking at that little house, which was a very poor thing. He was seeing the results of it down through the centuries. It would be replaced by Herod's temple, and to that temple God incarnate would come. It too would be destroyed; and looking on to the future it would finally be rebuilt again before the Lord would come the second time. So, what they were doing was part of the process that would lead to the final glory, which was what God told them through Haggai.

Whatever we are doing for the Lord with an honest heart as best we can, even though it is much less than what used to be done, it is still part of the great and eternal thing, the glory of which will outshine everything there has ever been.

David Gooding, *Rebuke and Encouragement: One Study in Haggai on God's Messages to His People*, 6–7

PART 13

The God who Makes our Lives Part of his Grand Story

21st August

AN ENLARGED CONCEPT OF HISTORY

Reading: Matthew 16:24–17:9

'For whoever wants to save their life will lose it, but whoever loses their life for me will find it.' (Matthew 16:25 NIV)

When our Lord first told Peter that he must go to Jerusalem, be rejected and crucified, Peter rebuked him. Peter thought that there was just this one age, and he was hoping that Christ would be successful in it. If Christ were to be rejected, he would lose everything he had invested in him.

It was in that context that our Lord Jesus took Peter, James and John up the Mountain of Transfiguration and gave them a vision of the Son of Man. Six days before this he had told them, 'The Son of Man is going to come in his Father's glory with his angels' (16:27 NIV). It revolutionised Peter's concept of history when he learned that there was not just this age, there was another age to come.

For Peter it had raised another conundrum. Our Lord said, 'Whoever would save his life[1] will lose it, but whoever loses his life for my sake will find it' (16:25 DWG). That sounded very strange to Peter. But now the conundrum was solved. There's not just one age. There are two ages—the present age and the age to come—and you have to make up your mind which age you are going to live for. If you live for this age you will lose everything that you invest in it. If you live for that age you will keep everything that you invest in it.

What is your soul? It isn't something you can put in a box. A soul is a life; it's got a time element to it and energy. It's got love and ambition and abilities of all kinds. Souls are things that you have to spend. What are you going to spend yours on?

Our Lord shall one day come again, 'and then he will repay each person according to what he has done' (16:27 DWG). If I believe that, what difference will it make? It will give me a new motivation and an enlarged concept of history. It will constantly alert me as to how I should spend my soul—my life, my love, my time, my energy, my everything; lest I should become like Demas, who loved this present age and invested his life in it, only to find at length that he had lost it all (2 Tim 4:10).

---

1 Greek, *psychē* = soul, or life.

David Gooding, *The Son of the Living God: One Study on the Implications of the Deity of Christ*, 13–14

22nd August

OUR PERSONAL SIGNIFICANCE IN HISTORY

Reading: 1 Chronicles 6:31–50

Then David said to all the assembly, 'Bless the Lord your God.' And all the assembly blessed the Lord, the God of their fathers, and bowed their heads and paid homage to the Lord and to the king. (1 Chronicles 29:20)

You couldn't possibly escape the emphasis and proportions of the early chapters of 1 Chronicles, could you? It is clear, judging by the genealogy, that the chronicler is interested in Judah and his sons, and David and his son. They all are important; but of supreme importance is Judah (ch. 2); and in particular the house of David (ch. 3). Chapter 6 is a very long chapter all about the Levites. Why the significance? What is it we're given in these long genealogies? For us, they are just names on a bit of paper: the generations of humanity that have been washed up on the shores of this planet. Each name represents a life—a baby who would grow up with all its hopes and fears and ambitions and career, but now is nothing much more than a name on a bit of paper.

And what will you be to anybody in a thousand years—another name on a bit of paper perhaps? What is the significance of humanity in the history of our world? You are one amongst the trillions who have inhabited it; just seventy years or so and gone forever. Who will make sense of human life and history? Is history going anywhere?

Ah, here we have the story of a man, whose name is given from the tribe of Judah. He's not merely going to subdue the enemies, he's going to make preparations for the great temple of God. He will organize the Levites and the service around that temple: the choirs and harpists and incense makers and showbread cooks, and porters and gatekeepers. David thought it was worth semi-retiring from politics to do that. What would you do if you retired? Is there one thing more than another that you would like to do, and will it be significant for eternity?

David's life-crowning thing was to prepare the material for the temple and to train the Levites; write the songs for the Levites to sing, teach them how to sing properly and praise the Lord properly. Because there's a temple that's going to be built and all things should be one great orchestra for God's praise and delight. God in the midst of Israel in the temple, expressing himself through his people and all their varied gifts; and all the gifts and activities of his people coming back in praise to God.

David Gooding, *Visions of Eternity: Five Studies on Major Themes in 1–2 Chronicles*, 15–16

23rd August

THE SIGNIFICANCE IN HISTORY OF OUR PRESENT ACTIVITIES

Reading: Revelation 5:1–10

And I saw a strong angel proclaiming with a loud voice, 'Who is worthy to open the scroll and break its seals?' (Revelation 5:2)

So the focus is on Judah and the king of Judah, and on the Levites. You will not find it difficult to understand the relevance of this to our New Testament gospel, will you? Who shall take the book; who is ready to open the seals of God's judgment on this earth and bring it back to God? And when no one was found worthy or able to take the book, John began to weep—as any intelligent man might, if there's no answer to earth's problems.

Well, the name was found (v. 5). It was the Lion of the tribe of Judah, the Lamb as though it had been slain; and he's ready to take the book and unleash the judgments that should break the opposition and bring back the universe to God. Why is he worthy?

> Worthy are you to take the scroll and to open its seals, for you were slain, and by your blood you ransomed people for God from every tribe and language and people and nation, and you have made them a kingdom and priests to our God, and they shall reign on the earth. (Rev 5:9–10)

Not only has he redeemed us but he has made us a kingdom and priests. This is genius. Mankind is lost and broken; disordered in activity, thought and ambition, producing the cacophony that we hear around us still. To take it and not just redeem men and women so that they escape final perdition, but to make something of them, organize their lives, take their abilities and purge them and mature them, and unite the whole—that's some job, I tell you. To unite the whole in the great orchestra of God's eternal praise, not just in word but in heart. And not just in word and heart, but in activity; so that the activity of all the redeemed shall be one vast delightful orchestra of praise to almighty God.

David Gooding, *Visions of Eternity: Five Studies on Major Themes in 1–2 Chronicles*, 16

24th August

THE HOPE AND PURPOSE OF OUR CALLING IS TO BRING GOD SATISFACTION

Reading: Ephesians 1:3–10

having the eyes of your hearts enlightened, that you may know what is the hope to which he has called you, what are the riches of his glorious inheritance in the saints. (Ephesians 1:18)

The first thing that we need to know—and know it with our very hearts—is the hope to which he has called us. That is to say, the reason and purpose for which God has saved us and called us.

May I ask you something? You who claim to have trusted in Christ, you have been saved, you have been called? Thank God, but what are you saved for?

You say, 'That's easy. I'm saved to serve. Why, evangelists galore have told me that I am saved to serve—to help to bring others to Christ.'

And may God help you to do it. But half a minute! With everybody saved that's going to be saved, then what are we going to do? What is the point in getting them saved? What is the hope of our calling? Where are we going to?

I know it's lovely to have a lot of power at your disposal, isn't it? Suppose you had one of these mighty great Mercedes-Benz cars and you put the pedal down, and whoomph off it goes! Yes, but before you put the pedal down it might be wise to know where you're going. Power just for the sake of power isn't any good. So, first we need our hearts enlightened to know the hope to which he has called us.

The first answer Paul gives us is that we should satisfy God: 'That we should be holy and blameless before him. In love he predestined us . . .' (Eph 1:4–5). To be able to meet all the interests and demands of God our Creator, he made us for himself, for his own enjoyment. And the first great purpose of salvation is that we should meet all his desires, all his pleasures, all his interests and satisfy his heart.

We have failed miserably, haven't we? Even since I came to know Christ, how easy it has been for me to turn inward upon myself. I am grateful for forgiveness because it makes me feel good, and I seek experience of the Holy Spirit because it makes me feel good. But we have to be careful lest in our spiritual experience we become self-centred, merely seeking our own satisfaction. Whereas the purpose of our being saved is that we should satisfy God.

David Gooding, *Christ Living in You: One Study on the Gift and Gifts of the Holy Spirit*, 4–5

25th August

THE HOPE AND PURPOSE OF OUR CALLING IS TO BE PREPARED FOR THE WORLD TO COME

Reading: Romans 8:18–22

as a plan for the fullness of time, to unite all things in him, things in heaven and things on earth. (Ephesians 1:10)

We remember that when God made this world, he planted a garden in Eden, which shows that the rest of it wasn't a garden, doesn't it? 'Now, Adam,' he said, 'you get on and develop it. I want you to have dominion and fill the earth—I want you to run the place and administer the earth for my pleasure.'

What fun it would have been to have been presented with a brand new earth and have the responsibility of developing the whole show! Where would you start? God gave Adam 'a helper fit for him' (Gen 2:18). Her name was Eve and she helped Adam as God's viceroy to develop this planet. They very soon found that developing this planet isn't altogether child's play. You don't get very far down the road before suddenly very large moral problems come up. Whose world is it, and who's to have the say how it should be run? As we know, they disobeyed God and fell miserably, and introduced into our world the chaos that we now see around us.

You say, 'What's God going to do with it? Ditch it?'

Oh, no, not ditch it. God isn't going to be defeated like that. We see a groaning creation, travailing in sorrow, blasted with disease and blight, and torn with war, greed and jealousy. We do not yet see all things put under man, but—and here's the wonderful bit—God hasn't given up. We do see one man who for a little while was made a little lower than the angels, a genuine man, and he's named Jesus. It was because of the suffering of death that we see him already crowned with glory and honour (Heb 2:8–9).

One day all things shall be put under his feet, and in that glorious day it is God's purpose to sum up all things in Christ. In heaven, yes—but on earth as well. It isn't God's purpose to ditch this world, and we all go floating up to heaven and say, 'Thank God that nightmare is over. No more earth, please.'

God shall unite all things in Christ, both in heaven and earth, and in that day our blessed Lord shall have a helper fit for him, as Adam did.

David Gooding, *Christ Living in You: One Study on the Gift and Gifts of the Holy Spirit*, 5–7

26th August

BELIEVING THAT THERE IS A WORLD TO COME

Reading: Luke 16:19–31

So we fix our eyes not on what is seen, but on what is unseen, since what is seen is temporary, but what is unseen is eternal. (2 Corinthians 4:18 NIV)

It is very important to see that the rich man was not sent to hell because he was rich but because of his unbelief; as the end of the story makes abundantly clear. That unbelief was seen in the way he treated his poor neighbour. The Bible told him that he was to love his neighbour as himself and he didn't make the slightest attempt to do so. But behind his failure to love his neighbour was a deeper unbelief. While perhaps outwardly professing to believe the Bible to be the word of God, he did not take it seriously to mean what it said. The Bible laid down its moral demands and warned that they were absolute, but evidently the man thought he could live all his life paying them no serious attention, and yet after death things would somehow turn out all right. Listen to him pleading with Abraham. He asks that Lazarus should be sent from the dead to warn his brothers who were still on earth, so that they would not come to 'this place of torment' (Luke 16:28).

Abraham replies that there is no need to send Lazarus, because his brothers have Moses and the Prophets. 'Yes, I know they have,' says the rich man, 'but . . .' The 'but' is very revealing. In life he too had Moses and the Prophets, and probably professed to believe them. But he hadn't really believed them at all, and he knew his brothers didn't really believe them either. 'If someone goes to them from the dead, they will repent' (16:30). But it is more likely that they would have dismissed the apparition as a bad dream, or as imagination or something that science could, or would soon be able to, explain away.

No, said Abraham, the brothers will get no ghostly visitations, for if they do not believe the Bible, neither will they be persuaded if someone should rise from the dead. There are no gimmicks in God's message to mankind. He appeals to our moral judgment, not to our ghoulish curiosity. If our moral judgment is so perverse that it can neglect and disregard the plain moral warnings of God's word as being irrelevant and not worthy of serious attention, our sickness is worse than the seeing of any number of ghosts would cure.

David Gooding, *Windows on Paradise: Scenes of Hope and Salvation in the Gospel of Luke*, 72–3

27th August

THE ROAD TO FRUITFULNESS

Reading: Genesis 37:1–11

'Unless a grain of wheat falls into the earth and dies, it remains alone; but if it dies, it bears much fruit.' (John 12:24)

As a lad Joseph had dreams, and he told his brothers that he dreamed that they were all in the harvest field and the other eleven sheaves bowed down before Joseph's sheaf. And then he had another dream. He told his brothers, 'The sun, the moon and eleven stars all fell down and worshipped my star.' Well that didn't just upset his brothers, it upset his father too. His brothers hated him for it, though his father stored it up in his memory. Suppose God was behind Joseph's dreams? So his father kept the matter in his mind.

When Jacob sent Joseph to see how his brothers were getting on, the eleven brothers said to themselves, 'Ha, look who's coming. If it isn't this dreamer.' They decided to cast him into one of the pits, 'then we shall see what will become of his dreams' (see Gen 37:12–20).

Joseph eventually became the man who was to interpret Pharaoh's dreams. Being advised by God about the coming famine, he saved Egypt economically, and its citizens from death by starvation. And not only Egypt, but a lot of the little countries around and even his father and brothers in Canaan. No wonder, when his second child was born, he called him Ephraim: 'God has made me fruitful', he said, 'in the land of my affliction' (41:52).

But how did he get from his initial dreams to their fulfilment in Egypt? He was thrown into the pit and then sold to some Gentile merchants who were passing. He prospered in the house of one of the leading Egyptian politicians, until he was falsely accused by the Egyptian's wife and put in prison.

After some years, two of his fellow prisoners had dreams as well. Joseph interpreted their dreams, and as he said goodbye to the one who was going to be promoted he said, 'You will remember me, won't you, when it is well with you?' But the man completely forgot about Joseph for the time being, and the prison door shut on him again (see 40:14, 23). I wonder how many times he asked himself, 'What about those dreams? Will they ever come true?'

Yes, they came true; but we notice what he had to go through first. It was by the way of suffering, down into the pit, and long years in the dungeon before he became fruitful.

David Gooding, The Christian's Right Perspective: One Study on Living in Light of Present and Future Realities, 5–6

28th August

GROWING IN SPIRITUALITY

Reading: Philippians 3:12–21

I press on towards the goal for the prize of the upward call of God in Christ Jesus. (Philippians 3:14 DWG)

Our spirituality is deepened by the Saviour himself making known to us the name of God and what God is really like in his character. He did it publicly at Calvary, and through his burial and resurrection. He does his work by his Spirit in the depths of our minds and hearts. Cutting through the tangles of misunderstandings, he heals wounds that cause us to doubt the love of God when life's trials and tribulations come until we might be tempted to think that God himself is unfair and has forgotten us. It is by the declaring of the name of God that the Saviour fills our hearts with love that learns to trust, and brings us ever nearer to the consummation of that unity with God.

Why do we need constantly to get back to this glorious gospel? We need to for its own sake; this is life's chief business. Oh, if you have caught the faintest glimpse of this potential glory, you will not rest with humdrum pedestrian spiritual experience. You will say with Paul, 'I press on to make it my own, because Christ Jesus has made me his own' (Phil 3:12). It will become life's chief business for you. It maybe won't be your chief work; that could be looking after the children and cooking the vegetables and writing with the old pen. But your chief business will be that by his grace Christ should use every detail of life to reveal the Father's name. It is a tough course. God is love; but I tell you now, God can be tough. You serve no sentimental, weak, indecisive God. There are scarcely any sorrows that God is not prepared to take us through, if only they will serve to make us more like Christ and ultimately to enjoy God better.

This is life's chief business, but then we have to face our modern world. For us, as it was for the Colossians, there lurk dangers associated with the quest for spirituality, strange as that may sound (see Col 2:18–23). There are other spiritualities in this world, and we need to be wise to discern between what is good and healthy and of God, and what is not of God and not good and not healthy. And how shall we do that, except we come back to the gospel?

David Gooding, *Back to the Gospel: Three Studies on True Progress in Spirituality, Freedom, and Church Life*, 7–8

29th August

A PERMANENT HOME

Reading: 2 Chronicles 6:1–11

*I have indeed built you an exalted house, a place
for you to dwell in forever. (1 Kings 8:13)*

God didn't always live amongst Israel in a permanent house. He lived in a tabernacle or tent. And when King David said to God one day, 'I would like to build you a permanent house,' God said, 'I've never asked yet for a permanent house. Ever since I redeemed my people out of Egypt and brought them through the wilderness, I have lived with them in a tent. Indeed, as they journeyed through the wilderness, I journeyed with them, and every step they took I took. To ensure they arrived I came down and dwelt among them. I was prepared to be on the move and went through the wilderness with them step by step in a tabernacle that eventually grew old and had to be replaced and repaired. And I'm not finished yet, David. I'm still on the move. There's still a journey to be done, but when your son is born he shall build me a permanent house' (see 2 Sam 7).

So at last Solomon built the temple. When that happened, Solomon assembled the people at the dedication of the house, and he said to God, 'Now, Lord, arise and enter into your rest' (see 2 Chr 6:41). A cloud descended and God entered his rest—goal achieved, journey finished, a permanent house. Of course, it was only a prototype, but we shall see the reality one day. We have been redeemed by the precious blood of Christ, and God has walked with us through our wilderness. Every step of the way walking with us, helping us in our progress, bringing us back when we stray, gradually bringing us nearer and nearer the great eternity.

Then the Son of the Father shall gather all the materials that have been in preparation through all the long years of history. He shall put it all together and make God a permanent dwelling place for his eternal residence. What a time it will be; and you'll see it, my friend. One of these days you will see in reality what John saw in a vision. You'll see the great eternal dwelling place of God descend and hear the voice from the throne saying, 'It is done, finished.' God himself will enter into his rest, and his people with him. Wonderful, isn't it?

David Gooding, *Visions of Eternity: Five Studies on Major Themes in 1–2 Chronicles*, 45–7

30th August

BUILDING WORK IN PROGRESS

Reading: Philippians 2:12–18

And now arise, O LORD God, and go to your resting place . . .
Let your priests . . . be clothed with salvation . . . do not turn
away the face of your anointed one! (2 Chronicles 6:41–42)

We are still in the pilgrim stage; still in the tabernacle stage. God help us to rise up and build, to prepare the materials that we may reach the lost and see them brought to the Saviour. God help us to build character into the people of God, to help them to make progress, to lead them on to ever greater conformity to the image of God's Son. Let's rise up and build, for we are building the eternal dwelling place for the name of God. Who is sufficient for it?

My brothers and sisters, if we are being prepared for the eternal dwelling place of God, then this is sure: we shall need to lay hold of our salvation. 'Take hold of the eternal life to which you were called' (1 Tim 6:12). Listen to Paul as he writes to the Philippians, 'Work out your own salvation' (Phil 2:12). Say to yourself daily, 'If I'm being prepared for that eternal dwelling place of God, what must I do today? How can I lay hold of and be clothed with salvation, so that God's great plan might work in my life and I am nearer to his final goal?'

And we may take comfort in this. Picture Solomon, kneeling on his platform with his arms outstretched to heaven, pleading for the people that God would keep them loyal to himself (2 Chr 6:12–42). 'Do not turn away the face of your anointed one! Hear my prayer and bless your dear people and conform them to your way.' And here too it is but a prototype; for through every hour of every day of life until eternity dawns, there stands one in the presence of God with his arms outstretched, pleading for us (Heb 7:25). The very anointed of God is praying on our behalf that we might be conformed to his image, and one day taken home to see God's glory. And we may be sure that God will never turn away the face of his anointed.

May God so inspire our hearts that the visions of eternity will become so real that they will grip our hearts and motivate us to say, 'I've not much time left in life. May God help me to make it count so that every moment I'm here in time might count as preparation for the great eternity to come.'

David Gooding, *Visions of Eternity: Five Studies on Major Themes in 1–2 Chronicles*, 46–7

31st August

THAT WE MAY NOT BE ASHAMED

Reading: 1 Kings 1:38–53

And now, dear children, continue in him, so that when he appears we may be confident and unashamed before him at his coming. (1 John 2:28 NIV)

Let's think briefly of three groups that will be horribly ashamed.

False professors: There are those who profess to be believers and aren't believers at all. Like Adonijah, Solomon's son, who when David was dying seized the kingship, though he hadn't been appointed king (1 Kgs 1:1–10). He was being celebrated as the new king, when King David officially appointed Solomon to be king. And at the king's command, they came down the streets of Jerusalem with Solomon riding on the royal donkey, singing 'Long live King Solomon!' (1:33–34). And when the true king was manifested, the false king and all who followed him were horribly ashamed.

'The Lord Jesus is going to be manifest,' says Paul, 'the great and only potentate' (see 1 Tim 6:15). God the Father is one day going to stage the glorious appearing of our Lord Jesus Christ. Then people shall see who the true king is. And those who have followed false things will be horribly ashamed.

True believers: Wouldn't it be nice if in that day we could walk up to him and say, 'Yes, Lord, in my college, in my street, alas sometimes in my church, men came and preached doctrines that were disloyal to you. But I never compromised.' The Apostle Paul said, 'I betrothed you to one husband, to present you as a pure virgin to Christ. But I am afraid that, as the serpent deceived Eve, he will get at your thoughts, and you will become intellectually disloyal to the Lord Jesus' (see 2 Cor 11:2–3). When the Lord Jesus comes and we have to stand before him, how should we explain it if he has to say, 'But in your essay as a young gentleman in college, you compromised my deity, didn't you? In your church, you permitted doctrines that were disloyal to me.' What shall we say then, my brothers and sisters?

Apostles: Talking as an apostle, John says, 'that we might not be ashamed'. For he is in charge of the flock of God, and when the Lord comes, he wants to be able to say, 'Lord, you appointed me as shepherd over these sheep and I have guarded them.'

God grant to all of us whom he has put into positions of responsibility as elders and shepherds and teachers of his people, that we may do our task faithfully, so that when he comes we may render our account with joy and not with sorrow.

David Gooding, *Unity, Origin and Victory: Fourteen Studies from 1 John on Life in the Family of God*, 44–5

1st September

WHAT SHALL WE SPEND OUR SOULS ON?

Reading: Matthew 6:19–24

For you were straying like sheep, but have now returned to the Shepherd and Overseer of your souls. (1 Peter 2:25)

Peter says, 'You surely realize, don't you, my fellow believers, what was involved in conversion? You became the Lord's sheep.' Now we all know that sheep have no sense in their little heads how to develop their potential to the full. They get lost and they get ill, and their fleeces get all muddled up with thorns and thistles and get bedraggled. You're like that! Your soul—its loves, its hopes, its energies—goes astray. 'For you were straying like sheep, but have now returned to the Shepherd and Overseer of your souls.' That's what conversion is. He died to save us; he's given us eternal security. We're justified by faith, but he stands beside us because, by their very nature, we have to keep *spending* our souls.

What shall I spend my soul on? The wonderful thing is that our blessed Lord stands by our side and watches how we spend our souls. We have to do the deciding but he's there to direct. He'll say, 'Yes, that's a good thing to spend your soul on, but this wouldn't be good—you'd waste your soul if you spent it on that. Don't do that.'

It's like a mother with her young son in a toy shop, and these shrewd manufacturers have put a brightly coloured motor in front of him to get his attention. 'I must have that, Mum,' he says. 'I want to spend my birthday money on this one!' The mother can see that the thing is flimsy old plastic stuff, and the child only has to sit on it too hard one day and the whole thing will break and be gone. So she says, 'I wouldn't spend it on that if I were you, darling. That one over there is more sturdily built and will last you for many years.' The child isn't quite so sure. He hasn't yet understood what is going to last and what is worth spending his £50 on.

So does the Lord stand by us in all life's decisions. As we spend our lives, our souls—our energies, time, love, hopes, ambitions and emotions—the Lord is there to say, 'Now, my dear, don't spend it on that, it's not going to last. You'll lose everything if you invest in that; spend it on this and it will last for all eternity.' May the Lord help us to understand these things and their practical implications so that we may live for him and his coming kingdom.

David Gooding, *The Saving and Losing of a Soul: One Study on Major Themes in 1 Peter*, 10–11

2nd September

REWARDS

Reading: Matthew 19:27–30

And everyone who has left houses or brothers or sisters or father or mother or children or lands, for my name's sake, will receive a hundredfold and will inherit eternal life. (Matthew 19:29)

At my school there was a prize-giving at the end of the year and each form received three prizes. Many of the boys didn't even try to get a prize. They said, 'Who would waste a summer evening studying very hard when you could be out playing cricket, and all for a prize that you mightn't get anyway?' So they didn't bother and enjoyed the cricket.

Believers could take that attitude. 'Some of the keen Christians will get a reward, but I am not in that league. Even if I tried to get a reward I mightn't get it, so I won't try.' But that would be a shallow view. We shall be rewarded for our work for the Lord and for any sacrifice for him. The going rate is marvellous—'Everyone who has left houses or brothers or sisters or father or mother or children or lands, for my name's same, will receive a hundredfold.' On the Stock Exchange one hundredfold is ten thousand percent. And it is not merely the man who has gone out and left his wife at home who will get a reward, but the wife at home who has let her husband go to the elders' meetings and forfeited what, as a wife, she had a right to have.

There will be wonderful rewards, but not merely for spiritual work. In Colossians 3, Paul reminds the slaves that they can work for the Lord even under their grim taskmasters and from the Lord they will get the reward for their daily work (Col 3:22–25).

Then it won't be simply our work, but our behaviour. Take the matter James discusses in his second chapter: the way we treat our brothers and sisters in Christ and value them. It is easy to lay down the law as a preacher and to bask in the undeserved 'thank you' of the congregation, then in daily life to spurn believers because they don't have our knowledge. Do you suppose that, just because I have taught the theory and in practice have not valued my Christian brothers and sisters as I should, when it comes to the judgment seat of Christ he is going to give me a position of authority in his kingdom?

Well, if we want to reign then, we had better start valuing them now.

David Gooding, *A Vision of the Perfect Man and Woman: Seven Studies on Major Themes from James*, 36–7

3rd September

ASSESSING A HUMAN BEING FROM A SPIRITUAL PERSPECTIVE

Reading: Exodus 2:1–10

*When she saw that he was a fine child,
she hid him for three months. (Exodus 2:2 NIV)*

When Moses was born we are told that his mother saw that he was 'a fine child'. Perhaps you might think there is nothing remarkable in the statement, and we can't find fault with the mother who thinks all children are lovely but there never was a child like her child! When we've done with natural affection and some of the sentiments that come with it, it remains a perfectly natural reaction on the part of a mother.

Take any new born child and it is literally true there never was a child like that child. That little personality is unique. The God who never created two blades of grass alike or two snowflakes alike creates with every child a unique personality, a something whose value is infinite and incomparable, whose potential beggars description. Made in the image of God, here is a personality that, if redeemed, shall one day be a prince or princess and adorn the heavenly court of their Creator eternally. The instinct that Moses' mother had over her infant child is not a mockery; it is not exaggerated. This is the beginning of a process that, please God, will grow into something even bigger; an ordinary mother's maternal instinct and love for her child that one day will develop into a care for his soul and spirit. The mother of someone who one day shall be conformed to the image of Christ and made all glorious eternally.

Moses' mother wasn't giving up that value. She would risk her life; she would risk her everything for the child that God had given her and his potential. She goes down in the New Testament as one of the heroines of faith because she saw in nature not something merely to be pleased and proud of, but she saw in that child a potential for God and dared to believe and stake her faith in God for the future of that child. And as it turned out, for the future of her whole nation, for the coming of the Redeemer, for the solution of the problems of the world and in the introduction of the millennium itself.

David Gooding, *No Longer Bondmen: Thirteen Studies from Exodus on the True Meaning of Freedom*, 19

4th September

LIFE'S THORN BUSHES

Reading: Exodus 3:1–6

*Moses saw that though the bush was on fire
it did not burn up. (Exodus 3:2b NIV)*

Moses was about to turn aside and go on when he noticed that the bush was on fire but it was not burning up, so he went near to find the secret of why this scratchy old thorn bush, cursed of God, continued to burn. God had come down and was in the bush.

What a marvellous thing! Man's sin had indeed made a desert and a thorn bush of what God had planted as a garden and ruined it all; why then didn't God scrap it? Why didn't he burn up the thorn bush, the desert and the planet and have done with this sorry phenomenon of humankind? But the God who made it is not to be so easily defeated as to give up now, and God came down to meet with Moses. He isn't standing outside the thorn bush, criticizing it for not being an oak tree or an apple tree—God is in the bush and that's why it is not consumed. And that day Moses had a vision of God that started him on his spiritual pilgrimage.

He had to wait to see this glory. First, he had to see what a tangled disillusioning thing life can be; then he turned to see God in the burning bush, guaranteeing a future for Israel forever. Later Moses was to have more exalted visions of God. Visions of the glory of God in the splendour of Mount Sinai and in the tabernacle; but this was where it started—this was the thing that began Moses on his pilgrimage. And it is a similar sight that will start us on our pilgrimage—a pilgrimage that will give us hope even in this world, fallen and corrupt as it is. It will give us hope for a future for this world and for a future long after this world is done.

Do I speak to somebody who has discovered the thorn bushes of life? You had your ideas of what life could be. Is it now the unreasonableness of your children, the spitefulness of some you have loved dearly, the cruelty and perversity of leaders in industry? Be it what it will, it has disillusioned you. Well, perhaps that's the place where God will meet with you in your disillusionment, to begin for you a pilgrimage to a fairer world and a glorious inheritance that shall never fade.

David Gooding, *No Longer Bondmen: Thirteen Studies from Exodus on the True Meaning of Freedom*, 22

5th September

THE SIGNIFICANCE OF OUR LIVES

Reading: Ruth 4:13–22

Then the women said to Naomi, 'Blessed be the LORD, who has not left you this day without a redeemer.' (Ruth 4:14)

Orpah went back, and in the Bible you never hear of her again. Ruth clung to her mother-in-law and returned with Naomi, because she had come to believe in the God of Israel to start with; and she went back in loyalty to her mother-in-law and to her mother-in-law's God. Naomi herself told Ruth that there was no hope for a husband. 'Never mind,' she said. This is what she wanted to live for. Well, you know the story, and it's subsequent love story, how Ruth got married to this mighty man of wealth.

But it isn't just a love story; God took that love story and made it a part of his centuries-long purpose. Look at the codicil: 'Now these are the generations of Perez: Perez fathered Hezron, Hezron fathered Ram, Ram fathered Amminadab, Amminadab fathered Nahshon, Nahshon fathered Salmon, Salmon fathered Boaz, Boaz fathered Obed, Obed fathered Jesse, and Jesse fathered David' (4:18–22).

Scholars argue as to whether this genealogy is an original part of the story or whether somebody added it on afterwards, but we needn't stop to discuss it. It is a stroke of genius, for it takes in this love story, pulsating with life and human interest and the ambitions of the two girls. One of them said, 'There's no hope this way; I'll go back and make the best I can of life in Moab.' And the other one dared to trust God and follow her mother-in-law in loyalty to God and his people. When you come to the end, it is not only that Ruth had a marvellous marriage and Naomi was restored, but look at it in the grand scope of history.

It takes us right back to Genesis to the time of Judah, the original patriarch of the tribe of Judah, and God's purposes for him: 'The sceptre shall not depart from Judah' (Gen 49:10). Then it takes you far beyond Ruth—a decade or two and a generation or two—to King David of the tribe of Judah, and ultimately to the Lion of the tribe of Judah (Rev 5:5). It shows you how God took this girl and her ambitions, her objectives, plans and decisions, and the love story and all the rest of it, and put it into his age-long purposes.

David Gooding, *A Story of True Love: Three Studies on Understanding the Book of Ruth*, 17

6th September

FIVE ENEMIES THAT MUST BE DESTROYED

Reading: Joshua 10:16–28

Put to death therefore what is earthly in you: sexual immorality, impurity, passion, evil desire, and covetousness, which is idolatry. (Colossians 3:5)

When the battle was over, Joshua came back and commanded his captains that the kings should be destroyed. Can you believe that was of God? Were the Israelites just a bloodthirsty lot, who loved slitting people's throats?

Actually, most of the time the Israelites didn't want to slit anybody's throat; they preferred to settle down and marry their enemies! That was why God had commanded that they destroy every city that was near at hand, lest they should choose wives from them. There was no danger with the Gibeonites; they were genuinely converted. But there would have been danger if Israel had not slain these kings who were quite unrepentant. If his people would enjoy their inheritance, then God made them execute the enemy. Of course, they would never have caught those five kings if God's stones had not come down from heaven and obliged them to take shelter in the cave (Josh 10:11, 16). But when they were brought out of the cave, it was Joshua who put them to death (10:26).

With the great victory of Christ through his cross and resurrection, God has put our enemies into our hand, so to speak, and God guarantees us eternal security. But we do have to fight: 'Put to death therefore what is earthly in you.' And here is our danger. In our security we say we have the oath of God that we shall never perish; and sometimes we would spare the old enemy. But by God's grace we must get after the enemy (and mostly it is inside us) and put to death the sins of the body.

So Joshua put those kings to death and hung them on five trees and made an exhibition of them. God has done the very same thing at the cross (see Col 2:13–15). As we sit at the Lord's Supper, God portrays what our sins did to Jesus. And now he wants us to deal with those sins—we have to put them to death (3:5).

The battle is hard, and it will not be finally won until we get home to glory. But, be of good cheer, one day the victory will be complete! For the Lord says to us, like Joshua said to his captains, 'Do not be afraid or dismayed; be strong and courageous. For thus the LORD will do to all your enemies against whom you fight' (Josh 10:25).

David Gooding, *God's Great Salvation: Four Old Testament Character Studies*, 14–15

7th September

ENCOURAGEMENT TO PERSEVERE

Reading: Daniel 12:5–13

As for you, go your way till the end. You will rest, and then at the end of the days you will rise to receive your allotted inheritance. (Daniel 12: 13 NIV)

The vision has gone long since. It was given specially for the people of Daniel (i.e. the Jews), in a coming age. But we can't go without applying it to ourselves. In the battle of the Lord, may the man above the river (12:6) come to you and comfort you. You are destined for eternity and, as time passes you by, the very eternal and unchanging Christ is with you and in you. Though he may allow you to suffer, be assured of this:

> God is faithful, and he will not let you be tempted beyond your ability, but with the temptation he will also provide the way of escape, that you may be able to endure it. (1 Cor 10:13)

Why would he let you suffer? To give you glory when Christ comes! He has in mind by our very sufferings (though Satan doesn't mean it so) to purify us and increase our holiness so that we might be more like him when he comes.

Carry on, Sunday School teacher. It's a battle sometimes when the children are fractious; it doesn't seem they are listening and nobody takes any notice of what you do. You just carry on! If you turn one to righteousness, what will it mean? One of these days, as you walk through the courts of heaven, you will come round a pillar in the celestial city and there is somebody from your town. They will say, 'It was you that first pointed me to Christ'—and they will tell it to you every time they meet you. Then you shall shine as the very stars for ever and ever (Dan 12:3).

Are you really a believer? Well then start rejoicing, for your name is written in the book. It is enlisted in the citizens list in heaven already and never will be blotted out. If you are a blood-bought child of God there is a 'lot' marked out for you. It is yours, with your unique name on it. You shall stand in your allotted place at the end of the days and throughout eternity.

David Gooding, *Daniel: Civil Servant and Saint—Eight Studies on the Life and Character of Daniel*, 99

8th September

A LIVING SACRIFICE

Reading: Daniel 3:16–30

They trusted in [God] and defied the king's command and were willing to give up their lives rather than serve or worship any god except their own God. (Daniel 3:28 NIV)

When the young men were finally thrown into the fire their decision had been made. The trial and examination passed with flying colours, God chose on that occasion to deliver them from death. They found, as they entered the flame, not merely that the flames did not hurt them; in the flame they found one who is imperishable. Here in this life those young men had discovered the living and eternal God, and they found they had 'the better part of the bargain'. The fire loosed their bonds and set them free to walk. Even at our lowly level so shall we, as we journey through life and are called upon to make our decisions. As we learn to let things go for Christ's sake, we shall find the eternal and the imperishable. Having found him we have lost nothing, we have all.

Nebuchadnezzar had them brought out. Then he began to commend their God to everybody else, and to commend them as sincere and genuine men. How could he tell they were genuine men? They yielded their bodies! The exhortation and command comes to us from holy Scripture through the pen of Paul.

> I appeal to you therefore, brothers, by the mercies of God, to present your bodies as a living sacrifice, holy and acceptable to God, which is your spiritual worship. (Rom 12:1)

Who knows, but one day we may be called upon to yield our bodies in the full and final sense. It is good if we have learned to practise it in the little affairs of our lives. We don't grow courageous all of a sudden; courage is built up by many decisions constantly taken in the smaller affairs of life to prepare us for the big occasion. We have been showered with God's uncountable blessings. I call upon my heart and yours, in the name of him who for our sakes surrendered everything (heaven itself and his Father's presence), to present our bodies a living sacrifice, which is but our reasonable service.

David Gooding, *Daniel: Civil Servant and Saint—Eight Studies on the Life and Character of Daniel*, 107

9th September

REIGNING WITH CHRIST: THE PARABLE OF THE MINAS

Reading: Luke 19:11–19

Now if we are children, then we are heirs—heirs of God and co-heirs with Christ, if indeed we share in his sufferings in order that we may also share in his glory. (Romans 8:17 NIV)

This parable clearly teaches that when the Lord returns to reign, his people will reign with him (see 2 Tim 2:12; Rev 2:26–27).

What then will reigning mean? It will mean sharing the glory of the reigning house (see Rom 8:17; Heb 2:5–10). For some, for most perhaps, it will mean active participation in the government (see Matt 19:28; 25:31; 1 Cor 6:2–3). But here the parable teaches us a number of exceedingly important principles.

First, the amount of practical responsibility that will actually be given to each individual believer in the coming kingdom will in part depend on that believer's faithful use and development of the resources committed to his or her trust by the Lord during his absence. In this connection we might well remember the Apostle Peter's observation in 2 Peter 1:10–11. It is one thing to enter into the eternal kingdom, and all believers will do that; it is another thing to be given an abundant entrance into that kingdom. That will be for those who in the power of their faith have availed themselves of God's resources and added to their character the necessary graces and qualities (1:3–8).

Second, the Lord has entrusted some of his resources to every one of his servants: the number ten in the parable is presumably a representative number.

Third, at his return, he will call all his servants to account for what they have done with their trust. The faithful will be rewarded; and the reward will be in terms of further responsibility and added trust and increased work, as well as the enjoyment of joining with Messiah in his unimaginably vast new enterprises.

David Gooding, *According to Luke: The Third Gospel's Ordered Historical Narrative*, 316–17

10th September

THE UNFAITHFUL SERVANT

Reading: Luke 19:20–27

'I tell you that to everyone who has, more will be given, but from the one who has not, even what he has will be taken away.' (Luke 19:26)

There is one such person in our parable, and he presents us with a problem. He has his pound taken away, but he is not said to be thrown out into the outer darkness as described by Matthew (25:30). And he seems to be distinguished from 'my enemies', who are brought before the king and slain (Luke 19:27).

What is it, then, that still makes it difficult to think that the unfaithful servant in our parable represents a true believer? It is his whole concept of the king. Asked to account for his failure to work for his lord, he replies that it is his lord's fault for being a person who always expected to get something for nothing, to get something out where he had put nothing in. Fear of him, fear of doing wrong, he says, has paralysed him (see 19:21).

Our question, then, resolves itself into this: could anyone who truly believes that Christ gave his life for him ever turn round and tell the Lord that, in asking him to work for him, the Lord was asking for something for nothing? People can be ungrateful; witness the nine lepers. But would a believer ever be so ungrateful? And would anyone who believes that Christ's death has secured him forgiveness for all his sins ever tell Christ that he was afraid to work for him in case he made a mistake? Perhaps our question is too theoretical or too literary. Perhaps we had better ask ourselves what we imagine our own behaviour is even now telling the Lord about ourselves and about what we think of him, if we likewise are not faithfully engaged on the business he has entrusted to our care.

Let us end, however, on a happier note. The servant in our parable who worked faithfully for the Lord found his faithfulness had a snowball effect. The one pound[1] gained ten; the ten pounds brought him authority over ten cities; and over and above all that he was given the unfaithful servant's pound as well. Given his way with pounds, this additional pound would soon turn itself into an additional city. It is a law of the kingdom, apparently, that to the one who already has, more shall be given.

---

1 The King James Version uses 'pounds', but most modern English versions use 'minas' for the coins in the parable.

David Gooding, *According to Luke: The Third Gospel's Ordered Historical Narrative*, 317–18

11th September

THE END OF LIFE: THE UNJUST STEWARD

Reading: Luke 16:1–13

In this way they will lay up treasure for themselves as a firm foundation for the coming age. (1 Timothy 6:19 NIV)

In Luke's day, as in ours, there were many people who refused to think of death, or to prepare for it. Ostrich-like, they put their heads in the sand of business or family life, and tried to forget that death was coming. In so doing they emptied life itself of a good deal of its significance. Life is meant to be a journey to a goal. To neglect that goal, to try to banish from one's mind all thoughts of life's destination, may seem to the shallow-minded a good recipe for making the most of life while it lasts; but actually it debases life's journey into a meaningless and pointless wandering, and it fills the consequent eternity with disaster.

But it is not only unbelievers who need to be reminded of the reality of the world to come. Even those who have believed in Christ—for whom to depart this life is to be present with the Lord (2 Cor 5:8)—even these need to be helped to assess the life to come as a reality and to live their life here in such a way that the carry-over from this life to the next shall be as great as possible. As Paul would put it, they need to learn to be 'storing up treasure for themselves as a good foundation for the future, so that they may take hold of that which is truly life' (see 1 Tim 6:17–19 ESV).

So Luke inserts yet another parable of Christ's, the parable of the Unjust Steward (Luke 16:1–13). It exhorts the believer to use his temporal assets, money, time, talents and the like for the future. He should not of course use them in order to obtain salvation—for that is a gift and cannot be purchased with any assets of ours. He should use them, however, that when these temporal assets come to their end and life here is done, he may find on the other side many people he helped in their spiritual progress by his wise use of his assets in this life, and whose consequent gratitude he shall enjoy forever.

David Gooding, *Windows on Paradise: Scenes of Hope and Salvation in Luke's Gospel*, 48–9

12th September

MEASURING JERUSALEM

Reading: Zechariah 2:1–13

What no eye has seen, what no ear has heard, and what no human mind has conceived—the things God has prepared for those who love him. (1 Corinthians 2:9 NIV)

Now this young man with his measuring line, like the woman in the gospels who suffered from haemorrhage, has suffered many things at the hands of the commentators! They have said what a narrow minded man he must have been, going out to measure Jerusalem city, whereas God had far bigger things for him than just rebuilding Jerusalem.

Yet, if I am reading it right, the young man was merely carrying out in faith the promise that God had given earlier, 'and the measuring line shall be stretched out over Jerusalem' (Zech 1:16). Surely God was going to do more than rebuild it; but he was at least going to rebuild it. In my book there's nothing wrong with a young man going out to measure it all up. Take the young couple who have got their first home. The man is thinking of what he could do here to the floorboards, and the woman is thinking what curtains would look nice and what bit of furniture would go there. It's not merely the fun of the completed thing, but the fun of measuring it up and imagining what it's going to be, and then working at it and seeing at last the thing come into place.

My brother, my sister, we're not in glory yet, but there's a great deal of fun in measuring up what God is yet going to do for us. Get out your measuring tape right now, and under God's Holy Spirit let your imagination enrich your faith. What you're going to be like one of these days, for I'm not thinking now of ancient Jerusalem. Nor do I think of the Jerusalem city above, 'which is the mother of us all' (Gal 4:26 KJV)—that was never in ruins, thank God, and never shall be. I'm thinking of my little life and yours, that God Almighty has graciously undertaken to use as a temple of his presence.

I know you'll tell me that it will go beyond all that we could ask or think, as by his grace he grants us to be strengthened in our hearts by his Spirit, and Christ takes up his residence ever increasingly in our personalities. It would defy your powers to measure what is the length and breadth and height and depth of this great mystery. And for all that, there's no harm in imagining some of it, is there?

David Gooding, *An Offer of Restoration: Four Studies on God's Character in Zechariah*, 15–16

13th September

FUTURE GLORY

Reading: Numbers 14:39–15:2

*[He] will transform our lowly bodies so that they will be
like his glorious body. (Philippians 3:21 NIV)*

If you should see an angel, your reaction would be to grovel in the dust at the sight of such excellence. But that brother or sister who is sitting next to you—when the Lord has come, when God's work in their heart is finished and they are totally conformed to the image of his Son—they will be princes and princesses in the royal family of God. If you could see the glory that they shall be, you'd do more than grovel at their feet.

The trouble is that we look too much at the limitations of what they are now and eat our souls with criticism, instead of feeding our hope with God's glorious promises. It's the hope in my heart of what I shall be, by God's grace, that keeps me going now. Or else I'd have given up long ago.

When Israel came at last to the promised land they decided they didn't want to go in. God said he must discipline them and they must wait for forty years before the nation would go in. In their arrogance they went up without God to storm the promised land, and of course the kings chased them away. And as Numbers 14 comes to its end, it paints that gloomy picture of Israel with their backs turned to the promised land, running as hard as their little legs will take them away from it.

But then chapter 15 opens calmly with the words of the Lord, 'Moses, speak unto the children of Israel and say, "When you come into the land and reap its harvest . . ."' Oh, the magnificent grace of God; though long years of discipline would still intervene for the nation. When Moses spoke that command to them, it went home to the heart of many an Israelite. As they went to sleep that night they began to dream of barley ripening in the sun, and thought of the days when they would gather the harvest. When they woke up the next day, they were still in the wilderness, of course. But the vision they had seen of the purposes of God made the next few miles of the desert a bit easier to tramp. So it is with us. The vision of what we shall be will be our hope, our saving hope, in long days of difficult restoration.

David Gooding, *An Offer of Restoration: Four Studies on God's Character in Zechariah*, 16–17

14th September

CROWN HIM

Reading: Zechariah 6:9–14

*You shall be a crown of beauty in the hand of the Lord,
and a royal diadem in the hand of your God. (Isaiah 62:3)*

Certain men had come from Babylon bringing silver and gold. They are told to take this silver and gold and make crowns. Not several different crowns, but one glorious majestic crown made out of a whole series of little crowns, one piled on top of another. I wonder what they were expecting. Was this the moment when God would fulfil his gracious promise and restore the kingdom to Israel and to the prince of the line of David? Would they be allowed to come with their silver and gold and put it on the head of a restored king? What a thing that would be.

In Zechariah's day they were allowed to take the crown and put it on the head of Joshua. Not to make him political ruler in Israel, but in a symbolic ceremony that he might become a stand-in and a foreshadowing of the coming one who should be both priest and king upon his throne—the Branch, our blessed Lord (Zech 3:8). We have lived to see him risen from the dead and appointed by God as king and priest: 'a priest forever, after the order of Melchizedek' (Heb 7:17). But even yet he sits not on the throne of his glory. He sits upon his Father's throne; and we too wait for the great time when the Son of Man shall sit upon the throne of his glory.

When I see him sitting there, shall I be allowed to come with my little bit of silver and gold that I have beaten and welded into a crown in the furnace of life's experience? It will be lovely to see you coming to him in all his glory and bringing the crown that you have made from your silver and gold of sacrifice and living for Christ, and saying, 'Lord, in your absence I was making a crown. Please let me now put it on your head.' Oh, that would be glory, and glory that we shall be allowed to share.

As we build a temple of the Lord in our day and at our level, may the Lord encourage us to build, not with wood, hay and stubble, but with gold and silver and precious stones, in light of the day when the whole thing shall be complete and he shall enter into his glory.

David Gooding, *An Offer of Restoration: Four Studies on God's Character in Zechariah*, 32–5

15th September

PREPARING FOR THE FUTURE

Reading: 2 Timothy 2:8–13

For the creation waits with eager longing for the revealing of the sons of God. (Romans 8:19)

Why do you need to have your eyes opened to see the power of God available to you?

Because you have a colossal responsibility awaiting you, away there in the future, to reign with Christ, to administer this world with him and for him. You need to be taking the steps to prepare yourself—or to let God prepare you—for the tasks that lie ahead.

Be assured, my dear Christian, that the old hymns that talk of us going home to heaven, taking our shoes off, putting our feet up and resting at last for ever, are a little bit oversentimental. When you get home to heaven you won't want to rest anyway; there's work to be done. We shall reign with Christ.

And oh how creation shall sing then to the praise of its Creator. But it waits. Why not yet? Why not already? It waits for the manifestation of the sons of God. Note the term, not the baby children, but the *sons*: the full grown sons that have achieved spiritual maturity and have been made exactly like Christ. One day those sons will be ready, conformed to the image of God's own personal Son, and God shall hand over creation to them.

When I think of it, sometimes I suddenly have cold feet. I say to myself, 'You're getting long in the tooth, you know. You're getting old at an alarming rate; you haven't got much more time.' Oh, that God would open the eyes of my heart to see what is the hope of my calling (see Eph 1:18), and that I don't waste away my time here on little nothings, when I ought to be getting ready to take over the government of earth with Christ.

David Gooding, *Christ Living in You: One Study on the Gift and Gifts of the Holy Spirit*, 7

Part 14

The God who Saves

16th September

OUR MORAL SENSE DEMANDS JUDGMENT

Reading: Psalm 96

Let [all creation] rejoice before the LORD, *for he comes, he comes to judge the earth. He will judge the world in righteousness and the peoples in his faithfulness. (Psalm 96:11–13)*

A colleague of mine said to me once, 'You can have a morality without God; it is a matter of a *social contract*. If you put your finger in my eye, I shall reply by putting my finger in your eye and you will learn that it doesn't pay. You don't need God to support that.'

What will the atheist say to a row of people who are going to be gassed? They are pleading with him, 'We want justice!' What the atheist will have to say is this, 'I am sorry, but there is no point in your crying out like that. You are not going to get justice, you are going to be gassed and there is nothing that anybody can do about it. You won't get justice in this life, and because there is no God you won't get justice in any life to come either.'

If there is no God, our moral sense is in the end a mirage. But of course there is a God and there is a judgment. When the ancient Israelites heard there was going to be a judgment, they clapped their hands together and asked the mountains to join in: 'Clap your hands, for the Lord is coming to judge' (see Ps 98:8–9). Don't you clap your hands at the very thought that in heaven there is a God of judgment and one day he will arise to judge the world?

And don't you rejoice at the fact that evil men, like the terrible industrialists James speaks of (see Jas 5:1–6), who have trodden on the poor so wickedly, shall be dealt with?

We shouldn't always preach the coming judgment as though it were a gloomy thing. We should preach it as a subject over which you should clap your hands for joy. Why don't we clap our hands?

If God came along and cut off the heads of all the unrighteous and left the good, where would our heads be? That is why our gospel is so marvellous. It has the answer to the predicament of human beings with a conscience, a moral judgment—a capacity to understand right and wrong that comes from God himself. We are conscious that not only has the world sinned, but we have sinned too; and we have the answer in the gospel, from which we can find forgiveness and peace with God.

David Gooding, A Vision of the Perfect Man and Woman: Seven Studies on Major Themes from James, 70–1

17th September

THE DILEMMA OF A JUST FORGIVENESS

Reading: Romans 3:21–31

It was to show his righteousness at the present time, so that he might be just and the justifier of the one who has faith in Jesus. (Romans 3:26)

If sin matters and matters absolutely, on what grounds can anyone be forgiven? Forgiveness that sets aside the sanctions of the moral law and agrees simply and conveniently to forget the sin, denies in effect the moral law and admits that sin does not matter much after all. On the other hand, to insist on the absolute sanctions of the law is to consign us all to disaster, for we have all broken that law. To this fundamental dilemma mere morality has no solution, even if the morality in question is the law of Moses or the Sermon on the Mount.

Christ's death solves our dilemma, but at the same time it proclaims Christ as unique. No other religious leader or philosopher in the course of the whole of known human history has ever entered our world heralded by prophets like Moses and Elijah and the rest of the Jewish seers. No other has ever entered announcing that he had come primarily to give himself to God as a ransom for the sins of the world. On this point of fundamental importance and paramount significance there is no question of judging between the claim of Christ and anybody else, because only Christ has ever made the claim. And we may know that it is true, as a person knows bread is true for it satisfies hunger, and water true because it satisfies thirst. So we may know that the claim of Christ is true: the death of God's Son as the God-given sacrifice for the sins of the world satisfies the fundamental problem of the human situation as nothing else does or can.

The central topic of conversation on the mountain of transfiguration was the death of Christ (Luke 9:31). But there was nothing gloomy about the occasion. Quite the opposite; all was radiantly glorious. The aspect of Christ's face was changed, we are told, and his clothing became brilliant as lightning. Moses and Elijah too appeared in glory. This was no occasion for grief or mourning. Some days earlier, Christ had promised his disciples that they would not see death before they saw the kingdom of God (9:27); and now on the Mount of Transfiguration they were evidently being given the promised foreview of that coming kingdom.

David Gooding, *Windows on Paradise: Scenes of Hope and Salvation in Luke's Gospel*, 55–6

18th September

THE BASIS OF SALVATION

Reading: Galatians 3:10–14

It is by grace you have been saved. And God raised us up with Christ and seated us with him in the heavenly realms in Christ Jesus. (Ephesians 2:5–6 NIV)

It is widely held that one has to keep the moral law of Moses, in order to be saved. That is why the idea that people can know in this life that they have been saved, are presently saved, and most certainly will be saved, is often rejected as self-evidently absurd. As they say, salvation depends on keeping the moral law; and one cannot know whether one has done enough in that direction to qualify for salvation until the final judgment. For anyone to claim to be already saved, they think, is like a student claiming to have passed final exams before even having taken them.

Now it is true that some elements in salvation are spoken of as being future. The redemption of our physical bodies is one such element (Phil 3:20–21). And so is salvation from the wrath of God: 'we shall be saved from the wrath of God through him,' says Paul (Rom 5:9 DWG). But, futurity does not imply uncertainty. In this very passage Paul points out that, because of the consistent character of the love of God, once we have been justified by faith, salvation from the coming wrath of God is even more certain than Christ's dying for us when we were still sinners (5:8–9).

We wait for Christ as our deliverer from the coming wrath; and as we wait for him to come again we are to know that God has not appointed us 'to suffer wrath, but to receive salvation through our Lord Jesus Christ, who died for us' (1 Thess 5:9–10 DWG). A believer whose life's work for Christ is substandard, and does not survive Christ's judgment, will suffer incalculable loss; but he will not lose his salvation. 'He himself will be saved' (1 Cor 3:15), because his salvation was never conditional upon his works, and therefore never uncertain.

Moreover, though some elements in salvation are necessarily future for the believer, others can rightly be spoken of as having already taken place. Justification and the receiving of eternal life are two such elements, so that Paul can inform his converts: 'By grace you *have been* saved' (Eph 2:8 emphasis added). The formula may be old, but it is nevertheless true: the believer has been saved from the penalty of sin, is being saved from the power of sin, and one day will be saved from the very presence of sin.

David Gooding, *True to the Faith: The Acts of the Apostles—Defining and Defending the Gospel*, 269

19th September

JUDGMENT THAT FELL ON THE SACRIFICE

Reading: Isaiah 53:5–12

Then the fire of the Lord fell and consumed the burnt offering and the wood and the stones and the dust, and licked up the water that was in the trench. (1 Kings 18:38)

God made Israel so that he could talk to them and speak the message of his love and mercy to their hearts, but they had run away after their false gods. Now he will speak to them through Elijah his servant, but what on earth will he say? Consider how they've run away from God; how they've abandoned him. They have left off talking to God for ages and gone after empty nonsense. Will there be some thundering rebuke, some terrible announcement of judgment upon them for their apostasy?

No such thing. God spoke to them that day by means of a sacrifice. Elijah placed the sacrifice upon the altar and doused it with water and cried to the living God in the name of Israel, 'so these people will know that you, Lord, are God, and that you are turning their hearts back again' (1 Kgs 18:37 NIV). God responded by fire from heaven, and accepted the sacrifice on behalf of guilty Israel. God spoke: what a moment in the history of that erring and apostate nation, to discover that God was still waiting to speak to them and make himself known. Not in his judgment upon them, but in his judgment upon that sacrifice.

Who could read the story of Mount Carmel without thinking of another mountain? Can the living God be heard to speak—will he speak to me? Where can I hear him and what will he say? If there is a living God you'll hear him on the mount called Calvary. You'll hear him speak in the voice that is heard from the central cross, 'My God, my God, why have you forsaken me?' (Matt 27:46). The answer is that the judgment you deserve has fallen upon God's own Son. This is God incarnate dying for you.

Does that speak to your heart? Is that what God is really like? Ponder it, friend. The Bible says that God makes himself known through the preaching of the cross of Christ (1 Cor 1:18). It is there that you see he loves you. This is who his Son died for. What a message!

David Gooding, *Faithful Service to a Rebellious People: Four Studies from 1–2 Kings on the Life of the Prophet Elisha*, 10–11

20th September

THE SACRIFICE THAT CLEANSES

Reading: 1 Corinthians 6:9–11

*How much more will the blood of Christ, who through the eternal
Spirit offered himself without blemish to God, purify our conscience
from dead works to serve the living God? (Hebrews 9:14)*

Israel's sacrifices, insofar as they did any good at all, provided priests and worshippers with ceremonial cleansing for their bodies. For people still in their spiritual infancy such ceremonial cleansing was not without its value. It began at a lowly level to teach Israel concepts of defilement and cleansing that later on could be applied at a much higher level. One ceremony in particular is referred to as the ashes of a heifer, which, sprinkled on those who are ceremonially unclean, sanctify them so that they are outwardly clean (Heb 9:13). It had to be applied to anyone who had touched a dead bone or body (see Numbers 19). It made the Israelites feel that physical death is abhorrent to the living God and defiling to man. We can only imagine the abhorrence and distress felt by our Lord as he stood at the open grave in which his friend Lazarus's stinking corpse lay (John 11:34–39).

But if physical death is bad, spiritual death and corruption are worse. And that is our real problem. To worship and serve the living God acceptably nowadays, we must approach not some earthly shrine made of wood and granite with stained glass windows in Jerusalem or in any other place; we must come direct to the living God in heaven. God is spirit, and our Lord taught us that he must be worshipped in spirit and according to truth (John 4:21–24). The unregenerate person is dead; not physically, but spiritually dead in their transgressions and sins (Eph 2:1); so obviously they cannot serve and worship God acceptably in that state. They need cleansing. Not ceremonial cleansing of the body, effected by holy water mixed with ashes, but spiritual cleansing of their conscience and spirit. This is what Christ provides—

> How much more will the blood of Christ, who through the eternal Spirit offered himself without blemish to God, purify our conscience from dead works to serve the living God?

David Gooding, *An Unshakeable Kingdom: The Letter to the Hebrews for Today*, 174–5

21st September

THE PERFECT SACRIFICE

Reading: Psalm 40: 6–8

*Sacrifices and offerings you have not desired,
but a body have you prepared for me. (Hebrews 10:5)*

In Psalm 40 a voice is speaking, which the people to whom the letter to the Hebrews was written would recognize as the voice of the coming Messiah. The psalmist has read the heart of God. He realizes that, although all down the centuries sacrifices were offered at the command of God and served his intended purpose, God's heart was never satisfied with them. How could it be, when it is impossible for the blood of bulls and goats to take away sins (Heb 10:4)?

What do animals know about sin? They are never haunted by that characteristically human thing, a guilty conscience. Law and morality mean nothing to them. Maintaining true moral and spiritual values is not something they worry about. When they were offered to God to make atonement for sin, and came stalling and kicking at the smell of the blood at the altar, they never knew what sin had been done, how God felt about it, why he must judge it, nor why they had to suffer. How then could the sacrifice of animals ever satisfy God?

So now the voice of Messiah is heard as he enters the world announcing an altogether different kind of sacrifice. First comes the statement that the animal sacrifices commanded by the law did not satisfy God. And in their place is to be put Messiah's sacrifice, in obedience to the will of God. The first is taken away, the second is put in its place.

His sacrifice is infinitely superior to the sacrifice of animals because he did know about sin, yet he was utterly sinless himself. His conscience was never once blurred or blunted by so much as one wrongdoing or compromise. He saw the evil and horror of human sin as no other man has ever seen it. And, being God incarnate in a human body, he understood how God in his holiness felt about sin as no other human being could possibly understand it. He understood perfectly what God willed him to do about it: it was God's will that he should sanctify us through the offering of his sinless body (see 10:9–10).

He did the will of God. He offered his body. We were sanctified. And his one act of offering has so completely satisfied God that he has never needed, nor will ever need, to offer his body again. God has what he always wanted; animal sacrifices are obsolete and irrelevant.

David Gooding, *An Unshakeable Kingdom: The Letter to the Hebrews for Today*, 189–90

22nd September

FAITH'S BASIC DOCTRINE OF SACRIFICE

Reading: Genesis 4:1–16

By faith Abel brought [God] a better offering than Cain did. By faith he was commended as righteous, when God spoke well of his offerings. (Hebrews 11:4 NIV)

This is a fallen world, and the first major question after creation was, how may we approach God acceptably? Cain made a fundamental mistake. His works, John tells us, were evil (1 John 3:12). He thought he could carry on sinning and yet keep himself right with God by formally bringing an offering to keep God happy, while he himself unrepentantly persisted in his sinful way of life. Impossible! Sacrifice is not a bribe, nor a cover up, nor a licence to sin. God rejected Cain's offering and eventually Cain himself.

Abel offered a better sacrifice than Cain, and God accepted it, which showed that Abel was righteous. Not sinless—but right with God and living a life pleasing to God. But notice what the verse does not say. It does not say that by faith Abel did righteous works, and on that ground his sacrifice was accepted. It says: 'By faith Abel offered God a better sacrifice.' To do something by faith, you must do it in response to, and according to a word from God. And what Abel is said to have done by faith was to offer his sacrifice. It was by faith because he brought it in response to God's word, whether in response to the example God set his parents in Eden (Gen 3:21), or in response to some other word of God which Genesis does not record.

It was not that Abel simply 'had great faith in his sacrifice', or felt that his works were so good that he could be sure that God would accept his sacrifice. Many people conceive strong convictions like this in their hearts. But that is not faith, it is presumption, because their conviction is simply their own subjective idea. It is not based on anything that God has said.

Nowadays, if we are true believers, we will show it first by shunning any and every attitude tainted by Cain's mistake, and then by making sure that the sacrifice by which we approach God is the sacrifice described in his word—and nowhere more fully than in our epistle. Now that God has said that all other sacrifice is finished, to persist in offering sacrifices for sin would raise a query whether we were true believers at all.

David Gooding, *An Unshakeable Kingdom: The Letter to the Hebrews for Today*, 204–5

23rd September

JUSTIFICATION BY FAITH APART FROM THE LAW

Reading: Acts 13:26–43

Through him everyone who believes is set free from every sin, a justification you were not able to obtain under the law of Moses. (Acts 13:39 NIV THROUGHOUT)

After a careful introduction Paul came to his major point: 'God has brought to Israel the Saviour, Jesus' (v. 23). He pressed home on his congregation that this salvation was actually being offered to them—'to us that this message of salvation has been sent' (v. 26). Moreover, as he reached the climax of his sermon he indicated that by 'salvation' he meant something that was not possible through the law of Moses; yet it was offered by God to all simply on the grounds of faith in Christ, namely, forgiveness of sins and complete justification (vv. 38–39).

Even before he started to speak, Paul must have known what the result would be of such a direct, aggressive, unambiguous presentation of the superiority of Christ over Moses; of justification by faith over justification by attempting to keep the law; and what the reaction might be when he told these religious people that, in spite of their religious endeavours, they still needed to be saved. It might well stir up a hornet's nest.

If he had vigorously denounced their sins and urged everybody to a renewed effort to keep the law of Moses more strictly, there may have been little or no opposition. After all, that is what most religious congregations expect preachers and prophets to say, and Jewish preachers in general could be very direct and express themselves very strongly. But to preach that people can never expect to be justified by the law of Moses, however hard and honestly they try to keep it, seems to many to make a mock of sincere human effort to be good. And they resent it. To preach that people can be justified without works, simply by faith in Jesus, strikes them as liable to undermine moral effort altogether, and they reject it as morally irresponsible antinomianism.

Paul therefore spent the whole introduction to his sermon pointing out that the doctrine of justification and salvation by faith is not some strange novelty invented by the Christians: it is a doctrine testified to by the Law and the Prophets of the Old Testament (cf. Rom 3:21).

David Gooding, *True to the Faith: The Acts of the Apostles—Defining and Defending the Gospel*, 249

24th September

PENTECOST AND THE PARABLE OF THE VINEYARD

Reading: Acts 2:14–36

'He will come and kill those tenants and give the vineyard to others.'
When the people heard this, they said, 'God forbid!' (Luke 20:16 NIV)

If it is true that Jesus Christ was the son of the owner of the vineyard, and in addition heir to the whole universe; and if in fact he was thrown out of his own vineyard and crucified by his own creatures; then what happened at Pentecost expresses a mercy that almost passes belief. A more easily credible story would have been that the 'tongues as of fire' (Acts 2:3) that descended from heaven on that occasion were sent to lick up and consume the very stones of Jerusalem and all it contained.

As it was, those tongues of fire came to announce to the murderers of Jesus that he was risen from the dead and had ascended to God's right hand; to argue the case that the Jesus they had killed was therefore demonstrated to be both Lord and Messiah; and that now therefore—and here comes the incredible bit—pardon and forgiveness were offered to them and to all mankind, together with a hitherto unparalleled gift of new life and a new relationship with God.

That is not to deny that fire of a very different kind will fall one day. Throwing out God's Son and heir has not turned the earth into a self-contained apartment; still less an impregnable fortress where mankind can effectively barricade themselves against all invasion, or even interference, from outside. People may live as if they own the world, but they are still only tenants and the landlord has plans for redevelopment. He will not wait for ever before his Son and heir takes over the property and restores the earth to what he intended it to be. God makes no secret of his glorious designs. Nature's subjection to frustration, corruption and pain is only temporary: nature shall eventually be released and brilliantly reconstructed (Rom 8:20–21).

But since it would be as pointless as it would be impossible to release nature from her bondage to corruption and leave her still in the control of sinful, rebellious men, there will first have to come what Scripture refers to as 'the day of the Lord' (2 Pet 3:10). Preceded by cosmic convulsions on a grand scale, that day will launch cataclysmic judgments on all unrepentant and recalcitrant tenants, destroying their opposition and removing them.

David Gooding, *True to the Faith: The Acts of the Apostles—Defining and Defending the Gospel*, 64

25th September

TRYING TO EARN GOD'S SALVATION AT THE EXPENSE OF OTHERS

Reading: Luke 14:1–6

*'Of how much more value is a person than a sheep!
So it is lawful to do good on the Sabbath.' (Matthew 12:12 DWG)*

This dispute concerned nothing less than the attitude of God towards man's need and man's salvation. The Pharisees' position was that the honour due to God meant that no work might be done on the Sabbath. That was what Scripture said. They added, however, that healing a man on the Sabbath was work, and therefore God's honour and obedience to his law demanded that the man's need however great must not be attended to on the Sabbath. It must wait.

Christ pointed out that if their son or ox fell into a well on the Sabbath, any one of them would run and pull them out at once. Yet here was a man whose body was morbidly filling up with water and soon—none of them knew how soon, it would prove fatal. Why make him wait to be rescued, when they would not make even their animals wait? The answer had nothing to do with God's honour, but everything to do with their pride and self-interest. They held that by keeping God's law they gained merit; and upon their merit depended acceptance with God and eventual entrance into his kingdom.

So they added regulations to the law of Sabbath, which made it not just a day of rest and delight in God, but a rigorous test of ability to keep endless strict regulations. Their interpretation allowed them to pull their ox out of a well on the Sabbath, because if their animal drowned they lost money. But they enforced their rule against a man being healed on the Sabbath, for if he died they lost nothing. It was not God's honour nor man's good, but their own self-interest and pride of attainment that concerned these Pharisees.

According to Christ, their merit was useless. Their bloated sense of religious attainment was a spiritually pathological state more dangerous than the physical dropsy which threatened the patient's life. In the first place, acceptance with God and entrance into his kingdom do not, cannot, and never will depend upon a person's merit. Worse still, their rules amounted to a slander on the character of God. His honour and due never demand that man's salvation must wait. If man is in desperate need and danger, God will always give that need priority, and Calvary has subsequently shown us to what extreme he is prepared to go.

David Gooding, *According to Luke: The Third Gospel's Ordered Historical Narrative*, 277–8

26th September

CHRIST'S REFUSAL TO RETALIATE BRINGS US TO REPENTANCE

Reading: 1 Peter 2:21–24

When they hurled their insults at him, he did not retaliate; when he suffered, he made no threats. Instead, he entrusted himself to him who judges justly. (1 Peter 2:23 NIV)

Because he trusted God, that one day God would see justice done, it set our Lord free. No archangel or some angel amongst the millions of them was ordered to take our place, he did it himself—'He himself bore our sins in his body on the tree' (1 Pet 2:24). They made a wreck of that body, didn't they? It wasn't simply the impertinence of the men who blindfolded him and then struck him and said mockingly, 'Prophesy! Who is it that struck you?' (Luke 22:64). Such sheer ignorance is beyond pity. It wasn't the pain of the lash; it was the envy of the high priests that smarted most. It wasn't just the sins of the unconverted that he bore; it was the sins of the cowards amongst his own disciples that hurt. Why did he not retaliate? Because this gave us an opportunity to reflect on what we have done, and for God's Spirit to bring us to repentance.

Christ deliberately did not 'revile in return' (1 Pet 2:23). Why not? So 'that we might die to sin and live to righteousness' (v. 24)—turn away from unrighteousness, reflect on what our sins have done to Christ and live for God. He found the strength to do it; and opened up for us the possibility of repentance and new life, from the conviction that there is a God who cares for justice.

We are told that we must forgive one another, as God in Christ has forgiven us (Eph 4:32). Tell me, on what terms did God through Christ forgive you? Did he say, 'You are already forgiven; you needn't trouble too much'? No, he did not! When you came to Christ, you had to repent. 'Do not repay evil for evil or reviling for reviling, but on the contrary, bless, for to this you were called, that you may obtain a blessing' (1 Pet 3:9). We must not avenge ourselves; we must behave like Christ behaved. He did not retaliate; he left it to God to judge, which gave us an opportunity of repentance before the coming of the final judgment. We are not asked to forgive those who refuse to repent, but to not retaliate, to treat them kindly and pray for God's mercy on them. We should be willing to forgive those who do repent.

David Gooding, *The Implications of the Sufferings of Christ: Three Studies on Major Themes in 1 Peter*, 8

27th September

DELIVERANCE FROM A GREATER BONDAGE THAN ISRAEL'S

Reading: John 8:14–29

'I came from the Father and entered the world; now I am leaving the world and going back to the Father.' (John 16:28 NIV)

The redemption of Israel out of Egypt was but a primary run through, an elementary lesson. There remains the great problem of the redemption of the world—the redemption of mankind, not from bondage to a pharaoh but from bondage to 'the god of this world' and all his infernal designs (2 Cor 4:4). And how should it be done? How should I be delivered from the slave mentality of thinking that this world is all there is?

It was done this way. Down into our world came our Lord Jesus Christ, telling us that he had been sent from God, 'I came from the Father and have come into the world.'

On that very last occasion before he went to the cross, when he stood to say his farewell words, he called his apostles around him and made it abundantly clear what lay at the heart of all he had been saying. 'I will no longer speak in parables to you, I will tell you plainly. My significance as Jesus Christ of Bethlehem is that I have come from the Father. As you see me standing here with my two feet on your planet, do you believe that I did not begin in that manger where Mary bore me, but that I am the pre-existent Son of God and one with God? I have come down from that world, sent by the Father into your world. Do you believe it, gentlemen? I have come from God and presently I shall go back to the Father. You will see me impaled on a cross and your hearts shall have sorrow. But then I shall rise again and return to the Father and you will have joy, exceeding joy that no one will take from you. Do you believe there is another world for anybody to come from, or for anybody to go to? Do you believe that I am the Apostle of God, sent from the Father into this world as the great Passover lamb to bring you not only forgiveness of sins but to lead you back to that glorious inheritance from which I came?' (see John 16:25–33).

Still today that is the primary message that Jesus Christ brings us. He talks to us about the forgiveness of our sins, but there is no point in having forgiveness if this world is all there is.

David Gooding, *No Longer Bondmen: Thirteen Studies from Exodus on the True Meaning of Freedom*, 27–8

28th September

DELIVERANCE FROM THIS WORLD

Reading: Exodus 5:1–9

[Christ] gave himself for our sins to deliver us from the present evil age. (Galatians 1:4)

Let me remind you what Pharaoh had done to the Israelites. Think of God in the past with all his wonderful purposes, his covenant with Abraham, and his great and glorious promises for Israel stretching right on into the far distant future. Then think of how Pharaoh put a cage around Israel and got them to work morning, noon and night. Life was nothing other than working, eating and sleeping—that was Pharaoh's interpretation of this world.

But Moses came and said, 'No, that isn't what life is. It is a far bigger thing. Life is to be lived against the background of God's great eternal purpose. In the present it's to be lived in the worship of God, and it's to be lived for God's great and glorious future.'

But Pharaoh said, 'Don't talk such drivel, Moses, and as for you and all your miracles, our scientists can produce the same thing in their laboratories anyway. So get back to your own work, because we don't believe this God. Life for your Israelites is just what I make it in the here and now, and that's that.'

It required the coming of Moses to break that prison, and to lead Israel out of it. I'll scarcely need to apply the parable, for the prince of this world has set up such a cage for mankind as a whole. He has persuaded multitudes that this life is all there is and they live for this world. As for God's purposes in the past and his purposes in the future, they're ignorant of them, and in no sense intend to cooperate with him. They know nothing but this world.

As Christians we are in this world, but for us the prison house has been broken. We've believed that the Lord Jesus is the Son of God who came from the eternal beyond into our world, and has gone back again. He has given to us eternal life, not merely in the future, but in the present. We know God and share the life of God even now. And as we journey on through life, we're living with our eye on the goal of God's eternal purpose.

David Gooding, *Is Hell a Reality? One Study on the Christian Doctrine of the Final Judgment*, 26–7

29th September

THE BEAUTY OF FORGIVENESS

Reading: Isaiah 44:21–23

As far as the east is from the west, so far does he remove our transgressions from us. (Psalm 103:12)

There's scarcely a more beautiful subject in the whole of God's Bible than this matter of forgiveness. God labours long to assure our hearts of the boundless forgiveness that he's prepared to offer us.

His prophets declare that he hides the sins of those who repent in the thick cloud through which none can see (Isa 44:22); he casts their sins into the depths of the sea (Mic 7:18–19); he casts all their sins behind his back (Isa 38:17).

Our Lord reminded us that the forgiveness God gives is free. In the parable of the Two Debtors, our Lord said that the debtors were forgiven when they had nothing to pay with (Luke 7:42). God made them a gift, so to speak, of their debts. The New Testament uses two words to describe forgiveness. There is this word that indicates it was a *gift*, an act of grace on God's part; something we don't deserve or can't buy. The other word indicates that it is a *release* from the guilt of sin that chains us on the inside.

Modern psychology shows the physical damage that unforgiven sin can do. Do you remember the occasion when the man was let down through the roof of the house on a bed (Luke 5:17–26)? There may well have been a link between some unforgiven sin and the paralysis from which he suffered. He was paralysed; but our Lord did not say first of all, 'Rise and walk'. He said, 'Man, your sins are forgiven you.' His gracious but penetrating eye may have seen into the depths of the man's personality to a submerged sense of guilt, maybe, which bound his physical frame in paralysis. Forgiveness casts off those shackles and sets men and women free.

We should not forget too, that God has the ability not only to forgive but to forget. We do not resemble him in that. Very often, when we've been deeply wounded and are prepared to forgive, we find it virtually impossible to forget. God assures the repentant heart that he not only forgives, but, using his omnipotent power, he deliberately forgets. He says, 'I will remember their sins and their lawless deeds no more' (Heb 10:17).

David Gooding, *Christian Foundations: Ten Studies on Key Biblical Concepts*, 29–30

30th September

TRUE FORGIVENESS MEANS THAT WE KNOW WE ARE FORGIVEN

Reading: Luke 24:44–49

'To him all the prophets bear witness that everyone who believes in him receives forgiveness of sins through his name.' (Acts 10:43)

I have a friend, a very active Christian worker among young people, who came to know God's salvation as a lad. He himself had a school teacher who frequently stressed to the children that it was impossible for anyone to know that their sins were forgiven. But the Apostles were in the habit of *preaching* in these terms: 'Let it be known to you therefore, brothers, that through this man forgiveness of sins *is proclaimed* to you' (Acts 13:38 emphasis added).

The word means to preach as a herald preaches it: a public proclamation. God is anxious that people should know that there's forgiveness of sins, and he wants to give it the widest publicity.

That, of course, was the nature of the dispute between our Lord and the Pharisees. They had the idea that we must wait until the final judgment for the verdict. The thing that most concerned them was to have a young preacher of some thirty years of age going around the countryside telling people outright, 'Your sins are forgiven' (Luke 5:20). They thought it savoured of presumption and bordered on blasphemy. And yet, when Christ spoke those words to a person, there was no doubt in their mind about it.

In fact, the joy of forgiveness is that we know it. David is quoted in the New Testament to this effect, 'Blessed are those whose lawless deeds are forgiven, and whose sins are covered; blessed is the man against whom the Lord will not count his sin' (Rom 4:7–8; cf. Ps 32:1–2). David's future was clear and he lived in the certainty that God would never count his sin against him, which made that stately king burst out in joyful happiness.

When we consider the forgiveness that God has given us, and the knowledge and certainty of it, I sometimes wish our Christianity were not quite so stately and we had more room for the spontaneous. In fact, I'd go so far as to say that it wouldn't be forgiveness unless we could know it. Would you call it forgiveness if, in your heart, you forgave someone who'd sinned against you, but you said to yourself, 'I shan't let him know'? To leave the fetters of his guilt in place and make him think that he's still chained, is the very opposite of forgiveness. The very word itself demands that the person who's forgiven shall know it.

David Gooding, *Christian Foundations: Ten Studies on Key Biblical Concepts*, 30–1

1st October

GOD'S OFFER OF FORGIVENESS DRAWS US TO HIM

Reading: Luke 7:36–38

*'For the Son of Man came
to seek and to save the lost.' (Luke 19:10)*

A fallen woman was saved and made fit company for God's own Son. But when exactly did it happen? We cannot tell. Little is told us about her, except that by the time our Lord called Simon's attention to her, she had already been forgiven, so that Simon's objection to our Lord's reception of her was groundless.

She had been immoral; she no longer was. We can only guess when the change took place. But this we know, it had not been produced by the kind of religion that Simon followed. His preaching against immorality was perfectly correct, biblical in fact, and necessary. But it had not produced a change in this woman. Once she had fallen, it simply drove her deeper into despair. How could the past be wiped out, even if she lived morally for the rest of her life? And if the past could not be wiped out, how could she ever get back into decent society? And if she couldn't do that, what other way was left open to her of making a living in the world in which she lived, except by continuing in her sin? And when Simon and his ilk, both by their preaching and their behaviour, made it obvious that they despised her and regarded themselves as infinitely superior, her despair probably deepened into cynicism.

But one day she heard a different kind of preacher. He likewise preached against immorality, though with this difference: his teaching included the synagogue goers too as morally bankrupt before God. But then he said that God was prepared to receive, welcome and utterly forgive all who came in true repentance. As God, he had authority in the here and now to receive them just as they were; to forgive, cleanse and sanctify them, and to admit them into personal fellowship with him.

On these terms he invited sinners to 'come to him', and in her simplicity she had taken him literally. She had accepted his invitation, braving the contempt, disgust and anger in almost every face at the table. But no sooner had she come than she knew his word was true. She was forgiven and received, and oblivious of her surroundings she had given vent to her relief and joy.

David Gooding, *Windows on Paradise: Scenes of Hope and Salvation in Luke's Gospel*, 13–14

2nd October

LOVE FOLLOWS FORGIVENESS, NOT THE OTHER WAY ROUND

Reading: Luke 7:36–50

*'Therefore, I tell you, her many sins have been forgiven—
as her great love has shown.' (Luke 7:47 NIV)*

Simon was very sceptical about this young preacher, and particularly concerned about this novel idea that people could know that their sins were forgiven. He said to himself, 'If this Jesus were a prophet, he wouldn't let a sinful woman like that touch him.'

Our Lord's reply was, 'Simon, she isn't a sinner any longer. Her many sins *have been* forgiven.'

Simon would have been disposed to challenge that statement, 'How do you know her sins have been forgiven?'

Said our Lord, 'Look at her love, and that will show you that she's been forgiven. You've admitted that when a man who's been burdened with a big debt is forgiven, he begins to love his creditor (v. 43). On that same evidence, I hold this woman's love up before you as proof that she's been forgiven.'

Observe which way round it is—the love follows the forgiveness. We don't need to work up some love for God to make us sure that God has forgiven us. But rather, in our bankruptcy we lay hold upon the forgiveness God provides, and the knowledge that we're forgiven will work in us the gratitude which God looks for.

We may be grateful to God that his forgiveness isn't a will-o'-the-wisp emotion—neither for us nor for him. Even between human beings, forgiveness isn't a matter of feelings at all.

I borrow my friend's car, go out and smash the thing up. My friend feels indignant, but his Christianity rises to the surface and in his heart he forgives me. All the while I haven't yet seen my friend. In addition to my aching bones, my stomach is churning: if only I knew what he's feeling, what he's already said and what's in his heart. But I haven't heard that yet. All I know are my feelings, which are strictly irrelevant, of course, because it's his feelings that are going to count.

There are people who have done some grievous sin and they've never been able to remove the remorse from their consciences. Sometimes they confuse that with the knowledge of forgiveness, and imagine that if only they were truly forgiven they'd cease to have any feelings of remorse. Our feelings are irrelevant. Once God has said 'I forgive you', we have the forgiveness, whatever our feelings.

David Gooding, *Christian Foundations: Ten Studies on Key Biblical Concepts*, 32–3

3rd October

THE RESULTS OF FORGIVENESS

Reading: Luke 8:1–3

For we are [God's] workmanship, created in Christ Jesus for good works, which God prepared beforehand, that we should walk in them. (Ephesians 2:10)

To recur to the woman in Simon's house (Luke 7:36–50), Luke could scarcely have chosen a more appropriate example to place at this point in his narrative. Forgiveness is that aspect of salvation that most of all raises the question of its validity. Is it more than a condoning of sin? And of all the types of sinner who call for forgiveness, is not a woman of this kind one whose repentance people are most likely to doubt; whose return to her former ways people most readily expect; and whose conversion they are most likely to regard as bogus? Her kissing and anointing of our Lord's feet, her wiping of his feet with her hair, could it not be merely fleeting emotionalism? Or worse?

But let Luke tell his full story. 'Soon afterwards,' he says, 'as Christ went on his preaching tours through villages and towns up and down the country, certain women followed him. They spent their time, money and energy looking after Christ and his band of apostles' (see 8:1–3). Socially they were a very mixed group, and at least one of them came from a privileged background. But what they all had in common was gratitude to Christ for having saved them from evil spirits and diseases. Not content to let their gratitude spend itself in mere emotionalism, they had voluntarily undertaken this tiresome unromantic work at their own expense.

Together then, these two stories have made their common point. Although salvation is, and must be, not by works, but by grace through faith; nonetheless, where it is genuinely experienced it will lead to love and gratitude to the Saviour. And love and gratitude will in turn lead to devotion and practical good works.

David Gooding, *According to Luke: The Third Gospel's Ordered Historical Narrative*, 140–1

4th October

DELIVERANCE EVEN FOR THE OPPRESSORS

Reading: Luke 4:16–21

The Spirit of the Lord GOD is upon me, because the LORD has anointed me to bring good news to the poor, he has sent me to bind up the brokenhearted, to proclaim liberty to the captives . . . (Isaiah 61:1)

It was a dramatic gesture; Jesus was indisputably claiming to be the Messiah. He was claiming to have come in order to relieve the oppressed and to liberate the prisoners. But equally emphatically he was declaring that at this stage he was not going to institute God's judgment on the oppressors. It was not that he did not believe in the execution of judgment: on other occasions he spoke with great solemnity of the universal judgment that will accompany his second coming.

But at Christ's first coming he was as much concerned to liberate the oppressors as he was to liberate the oppressed. Men like the tax collector doubtless oppressed and swindled the widows in their district. But they did so because they themselves were slave-driven by lusts and complexes that they could not control. Saul of Tarsus hounded people into literal prisons, because he himself was imprisoned in the infinitely worse prison of religious bigotry. To have instituted the day of God's vengeance would certainly have relieved one class of prisoner, but it would have put the other class beyond the hope of deliverance forever. Moreover, when compassion for the widow has made all legitimate allowances, it must be admitted that the widows themselves were not sinless. Their sins, though less lurid, imprisoned them as much as the tax-collectors' imprisoned them. It was best even for the widows that Christ did not at once institute the day of judgment.

This delay in the coming of the day of judgment, however, must sorely try the faith of those who are actually then obliged to endure outrage and injustice. Indeed, the bitterest element in their suffering could well be the doubt that might arise whether there was after all a God who cared for justice, or whether their suffering was simply the meaningless product of a materialistic and fundamentally amoral universe. But this trying of faith is not a disaster; it is not even an awkward but unavoidable consequence of God's determination to save as many sinners as possible. If we are to believe Peter (1 Pet 1:6–9), it is a necessary process in the strengthening of that faith, to the point where it will enable believers to enjoy to the maximum the inheritance that lies before them in the age to come.

David Gooding, *Windows on Paradise: Scenes of Hope and Salvation in Luke's Gospel*, 33

5th October

FORGIVENESS AND PERFECTION

Reading: Hebrews 8:8–12

In order that the righteous requirement of the law might be fully met in us, who do not live according to the flesh but according to the Spirit. (Romans 8:4 NIV)

Some will object that if the covenant guaranteed forgiveness so that we could be sure of it in advance, it would be nothing better than the old mediaeval scandal in which you could buy indulgences in advance for sins you had not yet done but intended doing, and could so proceed to commit the sins with the certainty of being forgiven with virtual impunity.

The answer to the objection is that it forgets what the first clause of the new covenant says. That clause expresses God's determination to write his laws on the heart of the believer, so that, as Paul would put it, 'the righteous requirements of the law might be fully met in us, who do not live according to the sinful nature but according to the Spirit'. That is, the new covenant does not simply provide forgiveness; rather the very first clause announces that its prime objective is to make us holy by the progressive work of the Holy Spirit in our hearts, and guarantees that God will not give up until he has made us perfect, whatever it costs (see 1 Cor 11:31–32).

Only in this context does the third clause assure us that God's acceptance of us does not depend on our spiritual progress, and certainly not on our attaining to perfection. We will have many difficult lessons to face in the school of progressive holiness, and our mistakes and failures will be numerous. But we may find courage and comfort in God's guarantee of complete forgiveness, in the knowledge that we can never lose our acceptance with God, and that the goal of perfection will at last be attained.

David Gooding, *An Unshakeable Kingdom: The Letter to the Hebrews for Today*, 164–5

6th October

GOD'S LAW WITHIN

Reading: Ezekiel 11:16–20

*I will put my laws into their minds,
and write them on their hearts. (Hebrews 8:10)*

The new covenant is radically different from the old in other respects as well. Look at the first thing God covenants to do: 'I will put my laws in their minds and write them on their hearts.' The point of this promise can be seen if we remember that the ten commandments of the old covenant were written on two tables of stone. That is why they were so ineffective in getting people to do God's will. They were simply external commands written on stone. They told people what to do, but they could not give them the strength to do it; they told them what not to do, but could give them no power to refrain from doing it. They were in themselves perfectly good and reasonable commands, and if people could have kept them, they would have produced in them most noble characters. But no one could keep them. As the Old Testament puts it, our hearts are weak and sinful, deceitful above all things, and desperately sick (Jer 17:9).

Before one could have any hope of keeping God's law in a manner that would satisfy God, one would need to be given a completely new heart, a new nature, a new power. And therefore it is precisely this that the first clause in the new covenant provides for. God's undertaking to write his law on our hearts means far more than helping us to remember it so that we could if necessary repeat if off by heart. It means nothing less than the implantation within us of a new nature, the very nature of God in fact (see 2 Pet 1:3–4). For, as the letter to the Romans puts it, 'the mind of the flesh is enmity against God; for it is not subject to the law of God, neither indeed can it be' (Rom 8:7 RV). If, therefore, we are going to fulfil God's law, God must create within us a new life that by its very nature does the law of God. John the apostle calls the process by which it is done a 'new birth'; the new covenant calls it 'the writing of God's law on our hearts'.

David Gooding, *An Unshakeable Kingdom: The Letter to the Hebrews for Today*, 161–2

7th October

THE NEW COVENANT

Reading: Jeremiah 31:31–36

For I will forgive their iniquity,
and I will remember their sin no more. (Jeremiah 31:34)

The stupendous thing about this magnificent clause is that here we have forgiveness of sins written into the terms of the covenant. Consider its significance. You may well be thinking, 'Yes, since I was converted I have found that I do love to do God's will and I instinctively think about his word; it is so different from what it used to be before I got converted. Then I loathed doing certain things that God said and now I love to do them. But still I don't always manage to do God's will, so what happens then? What happens when I fail, in spite of all my good intentions? Is everything done for?'

Of course not, for the final clause of the covenant is this: 'I will forgive their wickedness and will remember their sins no more' (Heb 8:12 NIV) Thank God for the order of this covenant. Drawn up as it is by the most exact lawyer in the universe, its very order is significant. He does not say, 'First, I will forgive their iniquities and then I will write my law in their hearts.' He says, 'First, I will write my laws in their hearts and in their minds. And in spite of all that, if they fail shall I do with them what I did with Israel and turn away from them? No! This covenant is different: I will be merciful to their iniquities, and their sins I will remember no more.'

Now, here is a very interesting thing, which is quite the opposite of what you might expect. When believers in Christ discover this limitless grace of God towards them, and the function of the Lord Jesus as their priest to save them to the uttermost, and the unbreakable terms of the new covenant, they don't feel that they want to take advantage of it all in order to go and sin and do as they like. Not if they really belong to Christ. It makes them feel that they want to go out and live always and ever for Christ; that to sin against him would be the biggest ingratitude they could ever be capable of. They are determined always to seek the aid of the high priest, so that they may not sin and displease him.

David Gooding, *An Unshakeable Kingdom: The Letter to the Hebrews for Today*, 164

8th October

GOD CAN JUSTLY FORGIVE AND FORGET

Reading: Hebrews 9:15–22

For I will forgive their wickedness
and will remember their sins no more. (Hebrews 8:12 NIV)

'Remember' is a legal term. It means 'to recall to the mind and take due legal action'. When Revelation 18:5 says of Babylon, 'her sins are heaped high as heaven, and God has remembered her iniquities', there follows a description of the judgments that fall on her as God reviews her sins and passes judgment on them. The new covenant, therefore, is saying that God will never bring up believers' sins against them in the legal sense, and will never execute upon the believer the penalty that those sins deserve.

This is not because God has grown sentimental about the sins of believers, nor because he treats them as favourites whose sins are to be indulged. It is because Christ has himself paid the penalty. That is why, when he instituted the covenant, he handed a cup to his disciples, saying that the wine in it symbolized his blood of the new covenant, which is poured out for many for the forgiveness of sins (Matt 26:28).

God's forgiveness is never anything less than just. Take for example people like King David, Isaiah and Jeremiah who lived under the terms of the old covenant. Like the rest of us, they were sinners and therefore incurred the penalties of that old covenant. How then could they be forgiven and saved? Someone will say, 'Could they not be transferred, so to speak, from the old covenant and given the benefits of the new?' The answer is, they could. Indeed, according to Hebrews 9:15, that is precisely what God has done for them. But he has not done it by deciding to break the old covenant himself, dishonour its terms and disregard the very sanctions to which he had pledged himself.

God is not like Adolf Hitler, who was in the habit of solemnly concluding treaties and covenants with other nations when it suited him, and then, when it ceased to suit him, tore them up and conveniently forgot all about them. Before God could transfer people from their obligation to the old covenant and introduce them to the benefits of the new, all the debts that they had contracted under the old covenant had to be paid. And so says Hebrews 9:15, 'a death' [i.e. the death of Christ] took place 'that redeems them from the transgressions committed under the first covenant', that those 'who are called may receive the promised eternal inheritance.'

David Gooding, *Windows on Paradise: Scenes of Hope and Salvation in Luke's Gospel*, 92–3

9th October

NEW LIFE AS A GIFT

Reading: Ephesians 2:6–18

*For as by the one man's disobedience the many were made sinners,
so by the one man's obedience the many will be made righteous. (Romans 5:19)*

The Bible stresses that salvation isn't by human works. It is very unkind to teach people to work out salvation by their own efforts. You might as well tell my crab apple tree to bear Braeburns—or at least try. But what mockery that would be. My tree will never grow that variety of apple unless somebody is able to graft into it the kind of nature that grows Braeburns.

In a much more wonderful sense, that's precisely what God offers the human race. God can graft into them a completely new life, with a new nature and a new power. God's answer to the fall of the human race is to start a new race from a new man who shall spread his life through all the members of this new race. This new man is our Lord Jesus Christ. The obedience that our verse refers to is that one great act of obedience that he performed when he faced *sin*, bearing its penalty for those who had failed. All that Christ did, and the power with which he did it, can be transmitted in its value to us men and women, so that a new life is grafted in.

Admittedly, this new creation may be exceedingly small, but then life has a way of starting small. The vast complex of the human body starts from an infinitesimally small cell. A new-born baby possesses all the qualities and powers to direct its development. In a few years' time, the first teeth will drop out and new teeth will come; the body will grow and certain chemicals will presently cease to be needed; nature will shut them off and supply other chemicals.

You say, 'It must be extraordinarily difficult to be a baby. How on earth does it know what to do at the right time?'

Well, of course, the baby doesn't worry its head. It got this marvellous life as a gift, and the life inside is just working itself out. It's a perfect miracle; complicated in one sense, but utter simplicity.

No less a miracle is God's great work of the new beginning that he offers to us all, without exception. We are asked to come and take this implantation of new life as a free gift. It's as easy as that.

David Gooding, *Christian Foundations: Ten Studies on Key Biblical Concepts*, 7–9

10th October

THE CERTAINTY OF ETERNAL LIFE

Reading: 1 John 5:13–21

And this is how we know that he lives in us:
We know it by the Spirit he gave us. (1 John 3:24 NIV)

This life is a much bigger thing than just going to work and coming home; eating your meals; getting married and setting up a home; being successful in business and ending in a grave. This life itself is bigger, for it is in this life, Christ says, that we can begin a relationship with God that is eternal life.

Let me use a simple illustration. This Christmas time you may go into a home, and see a father with his ten-year-old boy on the carpet playing with his Christmas present, which is a train set. As they play with those trains on the floor, something else is happening. There is a relationship now beginning to build up between that boy and his father. The boy is coming to understand his father, coming to love his father, coming to know his father; and the father is getting to know the boy. And, please God, that growing relationship with his father that was formed then will last through the whole of life, long after the boy wants to play with trains.

This is what Jesus Christ is saying to every one of us men and women. Let death focus your attention on what this life is about. I say it reverently: God has come down to our earth to 'play trains' with us on our very carpet, so that life's experience in the here and now will begin to be the basis upon which we may find God and enter into a personal relationship with him. To receive eternal life now—to have it and to know it, so that when this life is done the relationship remains eternally.

If I were to ask you husbands how you know your wife will be faithful to you until death, as she promised, you wouldn't be able to prove it to me logically. You would reply, 'I know my wife.' And if you asked me how I can be sure of life after death with God in God's heaven, I would say that I can't prove it to you, but I know it because I know God through Jesus Christ. I have received that relationship—that very life of God that Christ has brought into being, and I know him.

David Gooding, Can We Be Certain About Life After Death? One Study on the Biblical Doctrine of Resurrection, 10–11

11th October

GOD HIMSELF WITNESSES TO US THAT WE HAVE ETERNAL LIFE

Reading: 1 John 5:6–12

I write these things to you who believe in the name of the Son of God that you may know that you have eternal life. (1 John 5:13)

How can I be sure that I have eternal life? If I am going to face the rigours of life in serving the Lord, and face the responsibilities of being a servant of God who one day will be called to account for his service, I shall need an absolute certainty in my heart that I have eternal life.

I want to go to London, so I ring up British Airways and say, 'When is the next plane to London?' And I'm told, '10.30, sir'. I take it as God's absolute truth, in spite of the fact that I have sometimes been misled by such charming voices at the end of a telephone.

'If we receive the testimony of men' like that, and we do, 'the testimony of God is greater', says John (v. 9). So much so that if God ever tells you anything, you ought to believe it the moment he says it. 'This is the testimony of God that he has borne concerning his Son' (v. 9), and who should know about God's Son if God doesn't?

But now consider what verse 10 says: 'Whoever does not believe God has made him a liar, because he has not believed in the testimony that God has borne concerning his Son.' Isn't it curious that what we would never think of doing to the British Airways attendant, we not only do to almighty God, but we think it's a mark of humility and godliness on our part? God says that the believer can be sure of eternal life; and then many folks say, 'Oh, I don't think you can be sure. I mean, I think it's more humble not to be sure.'

The question resolves itself, therefore, into what you think of God. Does God tell the truth? My dear friend, we have an eternity to spend somewhere. None of us will exist in God's heaven if we can't believe implicitly what God says. To live in a heaven with a God whom you couldn't trust, what kind of a heaven would it be? Ultimately this matter of faith rests not on some sentiment, but on a deep-seated conviction about the very character of God. And if I don't believe him the moment he speaks, I'm implying that he is a liar.

David Gooding, *Life in the Family of God: Fourteen Studies from 1 John on Life in the Family of God*, 80–2

12th October

ASSURANCE OF SALVATION

Reading: Joshua 6:8–14

Because God wanted to make the unchanging nature of his purpose very clear to the heirs of what was promised, he confirmed it with an oath. (Hebrews 6:17 NIV)

Rahab had shown covenant faithfulness, kindness (ḥesed in Hebrew) to them; but would they return covenant faithfulness to her? Where could she find a guarantee of loyalty? She'd not asked that of any of her lovers recently. But now, with the judgments of God facing her, this became the supreme question. As for these men and their God, what was their God like? If she could get an oath from them in the name of their God, would it stand? 'I have shown you covenant kindness,' she said; 'show covenant kindness to me. Swear an oath by your God, the Lord of heaven and earth, and give me a token of truth' (see Josh 2:11–12). It's nice when people brought up to tell lies start concerning themselves about truth. And they bound the scarlet cord in the window and the spies slithered down the rope, and off they went back to the camp.

Do you suppose the days that followed were a little anxious? How many times must she have said to herself, 'Will that oath stand? Will the Lord of heaven and earth honour the oath taken in his name?' Oh, let's trust him, my brothers and sisters; thereby do we guilty sinners find our way back to God and discover the security against all judgment. The Creator is loyal even to his sinful creatures—not only to save us and pardon us but to swear an oath about our security.

> *His oath, his covenant, his blood,*
> *Support me in the whelming flood;*
> *When all around my soul gives way,*
> *He then is all my hope and stay.*[1]

You worship the merciful God of heaven. To this fickle woman who had yet to learn the true meaning of love, even she knew that love means loyalty. She'd come to know a God who loved her while she was still a sinner; and though she couldn't yet know it, he loved her so much that he would give his only Son for her, lest she perish.

---

1 Edward Mote (1797–1874), 'My hope is built on nothing less.'

David Gooding, *Entering the Inheritance: Four Studies on Major Themes in Joshua 1–12*, 18–19

13th October

THE CERTAINTY OF OUR INHERITANCE

Reading: Joshua 4:15–24

For one who has died has been set free from sin. Now if we died with Christ, we believe that we will also live with him. (Romans 6:7–8)

In this story we hear Joshua talking to the priests, 'Come up out of the Jordan' (Josh 4:17). So up they came, and the stones that they had taken from the middle of the river were set up at Gilgal. What for this time? To remind Israel that not only was the living Lord once down there, but they had been too. That would be a difficult concept for some of them to get, wouldn't it? Four generations on, the people would say, 'Yes, our fathers came through the river, but what's that got to do with us?' Being a member of that corporate body meant that when Israel came through Jordan, every descendant came through Jordan too.

Our blessed Lord died on Calvary two thousand years ago—but what's that got to do with me? How did you get into your inheritance? Not being saved merely from dying and death; you were saved *through* death, weren't you? You died with Christ; you were buried with Christ and have been raised with Christ. And what are the implications? 'Well, if you have died with Christ, why do you carry on behaving as though you are living in the world?' says Paul. 'And if you are risen with Christ, come up and set your mind on things that are above, where Christ is, seated at the right hand of God' (see Col 2:20–3:3).

Granted, you've a lot more fighting to do. But, my brother, my sister, the inheritance that God has given you is actually already beyond the reach of death. The gifts of forgiveness and eternal life are the gifts of eternity: your inheritance is already beyond the wasting effects of death. Don't set your affection on things in the earth, for you are dead and your life is hidden with Christ in God. 'When Christ who is your life appears, then you also will appear with him in glory' (Col 3:4).

David Gooding, *Entering the Inheritance: Four Studies on Major Themes in Joshua 1–12*, 23

14th October

THE CONQUEST OF THE FEAR OF DEATH

Reading: Hebrews 2:10–18

That through death he might destroy the one who has the power of death, that is, the devil, and deliver all those who through fear of death were subject to lifelong slavery. (Hebrews 2:14–15)

Death is still an enemy. Say what we will, we shrink from it, and from the pain and sorrow, disease and disgust that so often accompany it. It is not the process of dying that holds the most terror, but what happens afterwards; for death carries its real sting in its tail. Ever since the devil induced mankind to disobey God, and through that one man's disobedience sin entered the world, and death through sin, the *sting* of death has been sin, for after death comes the judgment (Rom 5:19; 1 Cor 15:56; Heb 9:27). Scripture affirms it and conscience inwardly knows it and fears it, whatever people say outwardly.

When someone has died as he lived—unbelieving, unrepentant, unforgiven—it is no use pretending that sin does not matter and all will be well. 'The power of sin is the law,' Scripture adds (1 Cor 15:56), and God's law will never say that sin does not matter, either here or in the world to come. How could it? Death is not some kind of fairy wand that magically transforms the impenitent sinner into a glorious saint. If you die an unforgiven sinner, you remain an unforgiven sinner for ever (Rev 22:10–11).

The only way Christ could save us was by first becoming human like us, so that he could die. And then not by miraculously coming down from the cross and escaping death, but by deliberately remaining on it and dying. For by death he suffered the penalty of our sin to set our conscience free from guilt, and therefore free from the fear of facing God's wrath after death. By dying and rising again he showed us that his sacrifice for us was accepted, and we who trust him are accepted in him; the reign of sin and death is broken, and the devil is robbed of his power. Believers may know with absolute certainty that to die is to depart and to be with Christ, which is far better (Phil 1:23); that to be absent from the body is to be immediately at home with the Lord (2 Cor 5:6–8); that at the resurrection they will have new and glorious bodies, like the body of the risen Saviour (Phil 3:20–21); and that one day death itself will be done away with for ever (1 Cor 15:26).

David Gooding, *An Unshakeable Kingdom: The Letter to the Hebrews for Today*, 91–3

15th October

WHAT HAPPENS WHEN A BELIEVER DIES?

Reading: Philippians 1:19–26

But we do not want you to be uninformed, brothers, about those who are asleep, that you may not grieve as others do who have no hope. (1 Thessalonians 4:13)

Let's take the man or woman who has received Christ personally, in true repentance and faith, what happens to them when they die? The Bible describes what happens to their body as a *sleep*. That's all, they fall asleep. It's a lovely word, isn't it? When children get too tired and they become fractious and difficult to deal with, a wise parent puts them to bed and they go to sleep.

But what happens to that person's *soul* or *spirit*? Well, the Bible is very clear. When a believer dies physically, the real inner person goes to be with Christ that very moment. The Apostle Paul says, when we are at home in the body, in that sense we are absent from the Lord; but to be absent from the body is to be at once and immediately present with the Lord (2 Cor 5:6–8). You will remember that that is what our Lord told the dying thief, who in true repentance turned toward Christ and said, 'Remember me when you come into your kingdom'. Our Lord said to the man, 'This very day you will be with me in Paradise.' (see Luke 23:42–43)

That is a glorious thing. Talk about taking away death's sting! It positively puts a radiance around death, because to be immediately absent from the body is to be present with the Lord. I had occasion to feel it when my own father died, as we, his family, gathered round his bed and watched him come to the end of his days and enter into the Father's home above. Yes, we sorrowed at the thought of him leaving, and the actual physical suffering he was going through. But what a thrill it was to see the old man's face light up with joy, when we bent over and said, 'Dad, you're going home!'

Then, finally, the Bible says that for believers there comes the very resurrection of their bodies. For the Bible declares that when Christ comes again the dead in Christ shall rise first, and the living Christians will be caught up together with them to meet the Lord in the air. And with bodies like the glorious body that our Lord now has, we shall forever be with the Lord (see 1 Thess 4:16–17).

David Gooding, *Can We Be Certain About Life After Death? One Study on the Biblical Doctrine of Resurrection*, 12

16th October

A GREATER THAN JOSHUA BRINGS US INTO OUR INHERITANCE

Reading: Hebrews 4:1–10

Now the promises were made to Abraham and to his offspring. It does not say, 'And to offsprings', referring to many, but referring to one, 'And to your offspring', who is Christ. (Galatians 3:16)

Not until the coming of the Saviour was the promise of the seed finally fulfilled. In that same promise to Abraham in Genesis 15, God promised him not merely a seed, but he promised him an inheritance. It was nothing short of the whole land of Canaan with much more besides, and one day they would come into that glorious inheritance. God said that in the interval they would spend some time in Egypt, and so they did. And then God said that he would bring them out with great substance, and so he did. We rejoice in the story, for he sent Moses to bring the people out of Egypt and teach them the law of God and the rudiments of redemption. Moses led them out of Egypt towards their great inheritance that had been promised to them by God via Abraham.

But if Moses could bring them out of Egypt, there was one thing that Moses could not do. Moses could not bring them into their promised inheritance, and he died before they entered in. Poor old Moses; for all his wonder, there were things that Moses could not do, and Israel would have been outside their inheritance still had not God in his wisdom raised up Joshua the saviour. What Moses could not do, that Joshua did: he brought the people finally into their inheritance that God had promised to Abraham.

We as Christians listen with both our ears pricked up. Was it Joshua, then, who brought them into their inheritance? Yes, and no, says the Epistle to the Hebrews. He brought them in, but the land was never fully subdued; 'For if Joshua had given them rest, God would not have spoken of another day later on' (Heb 4:8). What rest is that, and who shall bring us into that rest?

You start with Abraham once more. Justification, yes; redemption from Egypt, yes; but how would Israel ever come into their full inheritance? Not until the 'greater than Joshua' came, died and went down into his Jordan, and came up again in resurrection life to lead the people clean over Jordan into their full inheritance.

David Gooding, *Entering the Inheritance: Four Studies on Major Themes in Joshua 1–12*, 9

17th October

CHRIST SUSTAINS OUR FAITH

Reading: John 21:15–19

*'But I have prayed for you that your faith may not fail.
And when you have turned again, strengthen your brothers.'* (Luke 22:32)

The relationship between God and the person who is saved is a relationship of faith. It has to be: all personal relationships involve faith between the persons concerned, and this one supremely so. 'Without faith it is impossible to please him' (Heb 11:6). No wonder then that Satan makes it his chief aim to attack and destroy a believer's faith. And it would be a hopeless situation if believers were left at this weakest point to face the fury and subtlety of Satan by themselves, uncertain of the outcome. But God, who has provided all the other elements in our salvation, has not overlooked our need at this critical point. He has provided an utterly indestructible defence for our faith in the person of our King–Priest who always lives to make intercession for us.

It goes without saying that all the credit for the survival of Peter's faith belongs to Christ and his intercession; and therefore it is not surprising to learn from Christ's remarks that the issue was never in doubt. '*When* you have turned again, Peter,' he said—not *if* you return, but when you have returned to me—'strengthen your brothers.' There was no doubt whether he would recover or not. Christ had prayed that his faith should not fail; and Christ never yet prayed a prayer that did not secure its objective, and he never will. Granted there were some hours in the courtyard of the high priest when anyone who knew Peter only superficially might well have concluded that he perhaps had never been a genuine believer at all; or if he had, his faith must have now disappeared permanently. But in spite of all appearances to the contrary, the underlying fact was that his faith had not, and did not, fail.

And we can be sure that where there has once been true and genuine faith exercised in Christ, Christ will maintain that faith. Battered as it may be at times, and compromised as it may appear from the person's outward behaviour, he will maintain it and bring it through to ultimate triumph. And therefore God would have every believer in Christ know, and grow strong in the knowledge, that 'he is able to save to the uttermost those who draw near to God through him, since he always lives to make intercession for them' (Heb 7:25).

David Gooding, *Windows on Paradise: Scenes of Hope and Salvation in Luke's Gospel*, 107–8

18th October

THE GROWTH OF PETER'S FAITH AFTER HIS FAILURE

Reading: Luke 22:54–62

He is able to save to the uttermost those who draw near to God through him, since he always lives to make intercession for them. (Hebrews 7:25)

Peter's mental picture of himself was shattered, and he himself reduced to a gibbering coward by a sliver of a girl and the jeers and threats of a few common soldiers. He couldn't understand it. He felt he was falling into a chasm, and try as frantically as he might he could get no grip of himself or anything else. It was nightmarish.

What was that? Oh, only a cock crowing. Then suddenly he remembered. He looked up and in that very moment he saw Christ turn and look straight at him. Nothing was said, but at once Peter remembered what Christ had said about him in the upper room. And to think he had dared to contradict him! What must Christ think of him now? It was too much; he couldn't face any more; he got up and made for the door.

But in his mind that cockerel wouldn't leave off crowing and he relived the whole thing over again in all its shameful detail. Presently it seemed to crow once more, but this time it was different. It was as though a dark cloud was lifting and light was shining through again.

'So that was what Christ was trying to say to me as he looked at me from the other end of the room (Luke 22:31–34). When the cock crowed the second time, I looked up and he deliberately turned and looked at me. So he wasn't reproaching me, he was wanting to remind me that he had known all about it before it happened. I had only then discovered what a failure I was; but he had always known it. When I first came to him and he said that I was Simon but that he was going to make me into a living stone (John 1:42; 1 Pet 2:5), he must have known exactly what I was like and yet he made the promise. And what else did he say? "When you have recovered, strengthen your brethren." So Christ not only knew I should fall, but wanted me to know beforehand that he would see me through and back again. He wanted me to know that he still had a use and a future for me.'

David Gooding, *Windows on Paradise: Scenes of Hope and Salvation in Luke's Gospel*, 109–10

19th October

SEALED WITH THE HOLY SPIRIT

Reading: Ephesians 1:11–14

You were sealed with the Holy Spirit of promise, which is an earnest of our inheritance, unto the redemption of God's own possession, unto the praise of his glory. (Ephesians 1:13–14 RV)

Firstly, Paul says, 'on believing you were sealed with the Holy Spirit.' It's a delightful metaphor that is used of the gracious gift of the Holy Spirit: the sealing by God. In the ancient world, a book's seal was an indication of its ownership: you sealed it with your seal. Or it was a question of security: you were sealing it as your property and therefore defying anybody to misappropriate it.

When this metaphor is used of the gift of the Holy Spirit, it's enough to make a man's or a woman's heart bubble over with joy, isn't it? Can you imagine it? Upon her believing, God says, 'That woman is mine, let all the universe know it. I have given her the Holy Spirit, and in so doing I have sealed her for my own property. I defy anybody to rob me of her.'

And secondly, the apostle says, 'which is an earnest of our inheritance'. *Earnest* is an Old English word we don't often use in our part of the world. It means in modern terms a deposit, or a part payment.

Perhaps you hadn't thought of buying a new coat this November but you go down to the city and there is such a lovely model of a thing that you cannot possibly say no to! It costs one hundred and fifty pounds maybe, and you just haven't got the spare cash with you. It's the only one they have in the shop and you want to make sure that nobody comes in and buys it before you have time to get the whole amount, so you ask the assistant if he would be prepared to take a deposit. You pay the deposit and this secures it as yours against the day you pay the whole sum into the shop.

And isn't it glorious that God gives us the Holy Spirit? He is God's deposit. One day, God will give us the whole of the glorious inheritance he has promised to those who love him (Jas 2:5). In the meanwhile, we have the deposit, the earnest. Our wildest imaginations can scarcely cope with it, but *already* the Holy Spirit is in the believer's heart as the part payment, the deposit of what one day we shall enjoy in glory.

We've got that straight, haven't we? This happens the moment a person believes in the Lord Jesus. We don't have to pray for the *sealing* of the Holy Spirit, nor for the *earnest* of the Holy Spirit; they're given as a gift the moment we believe on the Lord Jesus.

David Gooding, Obtaining the Goal of Salvation: Three Studies on the Work of the Holy Spirit, 15–16

20th October

THE SEALED

Reading: Revelation 7:1–8

Do not harm the earth or the sea or the trees, until we have sealed the servants of our God on their foreheads. (Revelation 7:3)

Is there salvation for anybody against the judgments of God? It tells us that there are two groups of people who experience the salvation of God: those who are sealed (Rev 7:4), and those who have been saved (v. 14). The sealed, and then the saved: two sides of salvation.

Before the seventh seal is opened (ch. 8), the four angels are commanded 'Do not harm the earth or the sea or the trees, until we have sealed the servants of our God on their foreheads' (7:3).

The six seals were but preparatory warnings, like the plagues on Pharaoh. The seventh is different; it introduces the great day of God's wrath. That's a very different thing. The plagues under Pharaoh were meant to lead Pharaoh to repentance, but when he finally hardened his heart and wouldn't repent, there came the last plague, the tenth. There was no salvation from that.

Before the great day of wrath comes, 'Wait a minute,' says God, 'seal these. Nothing must touch them.'

Who are they? That is an important question. You must decide who they are; but at the basic level, it illustrates a vast and beautiful principle of salvation. They're sealed against any suffering of the wrath of God. Whoever these 144,000 are, my brothers and sisters, don't you feel a kindred spirit in your heart with them? The principles of salvation are common to all God's people of all times. We've been sealed against suffering the wrath of God, and no child of God, no believer in God, shall ever suffer the wrath of God.

That's basic gospel: you shall not come into judgment (John 5:24); 'For God has not destined us for wrath, but to obtain salvation through our Lord Jesus Christ' (1 Thess 5:9). When you start thinking about prophecy, 'put on . . . for a helmet the hope of salvation' (v. 8), for God has not appointed you to wrath. Not one iota of the wrath of God shall ever touch a genuine believer, and that's true of all believers of every dispensation. Do say 'Amen!'

David Gooding, The Past, Present and Future Revealed: Eight Comparative Studies on Daniel and Revelation, 96–7

21st October

THE SAVED

Reading: Revelation 7:9–17

These are the ones coming out of the great tribulation. They have washed their robes and made them white in the blood of the Lamb. (Revelation 7:14)

Coming victoriously through the great tribulation, this great multitude cry with a loud voice, 'Salvation belongs to our God who sits on the throne, and to the Lamb!' (v. 10). What is the ground of their salvation, and what will their salvation involve? Well, let's read it once more:

> These are the ones coming out of the great tribulation. They have washed their robes and made them white in the blood of the Lamb. Therefore they are before the throne of God . . . (vv. 14–15)

That is the basis of their standing. You say, 'But they're not in heaven, are they? This is an earthly people.' Whether they're on earth or in heaven, notice their theological standing. They are 'before the throne'. It's not just a question of local position, being before him and standing in his presence. As distinct from those who call upon the rocks to cover them, these stand before the throne, accepted.

Now some lovely things are said relevant to creation: 'they . . . serve him day and night in his temple [so they're in his temple]; and he who sits on the throne will shelter them with his presence. They shall hunger no more, neither thirst any more; the sun shall not strike them, nor any scorching heat' (vv. 15–16). What a marvellous promise.

You'll notice that the description is in terms of the created powers of the universe—no hunger, no thirst, neither shall the sun strike them, nor any scorching heat. It's no good hiding our eyes from the fact that creation has hurt a lot of people, and not merely by physical sunstroke. This is a broken creation, and it's not just physical thirst that has tormented people, but a deeper thirst. Nature cries out to have its proper desire satisfied, but when life doesn't satisfy it creates an almost intolerable thirst. Wind and wave and sun cause death and disablement and disease. Creation has hurt people, for it's a broken world.

Salvation will not only protect us from the wrath of God, but one day he who sits on the throne will shelter his redeemed people with his presence. The sun won't hurt them any more; neither shall they thirst any more. The one who made the universe will gear it towards their blessing and none of the powers of the universe will hurt them.

David Gooding, *The Past, Present and Future Revealed: Eight Comparative Studies on Daniel and Revelation*, 97–8

22nd October

THE GOSPEL TO THE GENTILES

Reading: Ruth 3:8–18

For he himself is our peace, who has made us both one and has broken down in his flesh the dividing wall of hostility. (Ephesians 2:14)

Naomi is a personification of Israel, and her memory was stirred about the vow of ancient promise and the great redeemer who was to come. She eventually told Ruth to go down to the threshing floor and make herself known to Boaz.

So down the Gentile girl went and approached this very kind and gracious man and said, 'You are our kinsman: would you not redeem us?'

And he said, 'Yes, I will, but there is a kinsman who has first rights. I will test him out tomorrow and, so long as he's not willing to redeem and passes on the rights to me, I will redeem you and I will marry you.'

And Ruth went home. What a conversation they had again that night!

'How did you get on, my dear?' said Naomi, as Ruth came through the door staggering under six whole measures of grain. I suspect it was as much as the sturdiest of young women could have carried in those days. For Boaz had said, 'Now, bring your shawl here,' (or was it a cloak?) 'and let me put some barley in it. Don't go back to your mother-in-law empty-handed.'

God makes us eat our words sometimes! This was the woman who came back to Bethlehem and said to her neighbours, 'I went out full and the Lord has brought me home empty.'

Now here comes Ruth, staggering under this gift: 'Boaz said I wasn't to come to you empty.' Oh, what a gospel message and what a testimony the Gentile Ruth had to preach to that woman of Israel! She said to Naomi, 'Tomorrow he will redeem me, and he will marry me.'

So that was new, and we move forward in time to the early Christians testifying to the Jews that they had come to believe in the true and living God, for they had discovered the Jesus of Bethlehem. What a story of grace it is, of how he would welcome even the Gentile. Then they heard the almost incredible message, that this great Redeemer–Saviour loved the church, which was being formed not only of Jews but of Gentiles. He loved it as a man loves his wife; and when his redemption is complete, there will come the marriage of the Lamb, and Gentiles shall be part of that bride.

David Gooding, *A Story of True Love: Three Studies on Understanding the Book of Ruth*, 30

23rd October

THE SCOPE OF OUR SALVATION

Reading: Genesis 41:37–57

*And he who was seated on the throne said, 'Behold,
I am making all things new.' (Revelation 21:5)*

The salvation that God has provided for us in Jesus Christ our Lord is gloriously large. It meets the needs of individuals, and indeed it is as individuals that we must enter into the benefits of God's salvation. We cannot enter in as families, nations, or groups of people; we must enter into the good of God's salvation as single individuals and there is enough in Christ to meet our every need.

But then God's salvation is concerned with even bigger things than the salvation of the individual person. God has designs in Christ to fill this world to overflowing with the glory of his light, peace and salvation. That is why Jesus Christ our Lord taught us to pray:

> Our Father in heaven,
> hallowed be your name.
> Your kingdom come,
> your will be done,
>   on earth as it is in heaven. (Matt 6:9–10)

All true Christians who pray this prayer find their hearts leaping within them, for the very fact he told us to pray is a guarantee that God shall fulfil our prayers and his will shall be done on earth as it is in heaven. I must leave to your imagination what a glorious thing it will be when God's will is done on our sorry old planet, as it is done at this moment in heaven. It shall be glory that defies description.

At the end of Genesis, when the story for the moment reaches its initial climax, we shall find God's great saviour and deliverer, Joseph, rescuing the then known world from famine and economic difficulties. He is one of God's prototypes of what Jesus Christ our Lord will do on a vastly bigger scale when he comes again. He shall take over the economics of our world, the problems of its currency and pollution and growing shortages, and deal with the root problem, which is sin in the hearts of men and women. He shall dismiss those who are unfit to rule and institute his own government. By that means he shall bring in a period of unparalleled blessing to this world, as he demonstrates how it can and should be run to the glory of God and the blessing of mankind.

David Gooding, *The God of New Beginnings: Eighteen Studies on God's Programme of Salvation in Genesis*, 147

PART 15

The God whose Great Salvation Changes our Thinking

24th October

THE PATH TO SALVATION

Reading: 1 Timothy 1:12–16

*Formerly I was a blasphemer, persecutor, and insolent opponent. But
I received mercy because I had acted ignorantly in unbelief. (1 Timothy 1:13)*

Explaining God's strategies for the eventual conversion of his beloved Israel, Paul wrote to the Gentile Christians at Rome:

> For just as you were at one time disobedient to God but now have received mercy because of their disobedience, so they too have now been disobedient in order that by the mercy shown to you they also may now receive mercy. (Rom 11:30–31)

The word he uses for disobedience means not so much the breaking of a commandment but rather the withholding of the obedience of faith. When he reminds the Gentiles that they were once disobedient, he is thinking of what he said earlier; that God originally revealed himself to the nations but that they did not like what they saw of God and refused to accept or believe it (1:18–28).

Now God has revealed more of himself in Jesus, and this time the Jews have not liked it, and have refused to accept or believe it. It is a disaster; and yet God is determined to turn it to their eventual good. 'God has consigned all to disobedience,' Paul concludes, 'that he may have mercy on all' (11:32).

The first indispensable step to true faith, and thus to salvation, is to discover that one has so far been an unbeliever. For religious people that can be very difficult. It was so with Saul of Tarsus. For some years he fought against admitting it; but on the Damascus road he caved in and confessed that, for all his sincere faith in God, in the only sense that really mattered he had never yet believed. And in that moment he found faith, mercy and salvation. The same applies to us all, whether pagan, Jew, or nominal Christian.

David Gooding, *True to the Faith: The Acts of the Apostles—Defining and Defending the Gospel*, 188

25th October

THE WRONG WAY—
THROUGH OUR OWN EFFORTS

Reading: Genesis 16

For the mind that is set on the flesh is hostile to God, for it does not submit to God's law; indeed, it cannot. (Romans 8:7)

How should we fulfil God's great purposes? Abraham, finding Sarah was barren, at her suggestion took Hagar, the slave girl, thinking that by his own strength he would fulfil the great promises of God. But he learned that the power of the flesh is insufficient and unable to please God.

When Hagar found that she was to have a child, she treated her mistress with contempt—the slave girl was taking the centre of the home. Finding her nose out of joint, Sarah said, 'This slave is putting on airs and graces, and refusing to obey me. It is insufferable, Abraham. May the Lord judge between you and me.' Sarah asked God to judge the matter and he did, but it wasn't very pleasant.

Eventually Hagar ran away. The angel of the Lord met her in the wilderness, and said, 'Return to your mistress and submit to her'. He also said, 'You will have a child and he will be a wild donkey of a man.'

I'd say it wasn't very easy in Abraham's home for the next few years. I imagine that quite frequently there were what I euphemistically call 'scenes' in the house, with Sarah saying, 'Abraham, this is impossible. Look what the boy did. My best china! Look at the furniture! And as for that hussy of a girl . . .' And Abraham saying, 'Yes, it's terrible, but you can't turn her out. The angel of the Lord has sent her back and we will have to put up with it.'

I can understand why the angel of the Lord sent her back like that. It was the only way to teach Abraham the lesson, 'that which is born of the flesh is flesh' (John 3:6). You may see me on my knees praying and studying my Bible, but it remains true that that which is born of the flesh is flesh. I've a wild donkey inside me that 'does not submit to God's law; indeed, it cannot'. Its energies could never be recruited to fulfil the lovely law of God. So Abraham was saddled with this difficult lesson—the impossibility of ruling this boy with any success for many long years until the promised offspring was born.

David Gooding, *King of kings and Lord of lords: Four Studies Exploring God's Sovereignty Over Various Spheres*, 26–7

26th October

OUR PRAYERS REVEAL HOW WE THINK ABOUT SALVATION

Reading: Luke 18:9–14

But the tax collector, standing far off, would not even lift up his eyes to heaven, but beat his breast, saying, 'God, be merciful to me, a sinner!' (Luke 18:13)

It is all too easy for people, particularly if they have suffered some injustice or other—and even if they haven't—to regard themselves as the innocent and good, and to take it for granted that it is other people who are wicked. We need therefore to watch the stance we take before God in our prayers. If our persistence in prayer shows what we think of God's character, our prayers also reveal what we think of ourselves, sometimes without our realizing it. And that could be disastrously wrong.

The Pharisee in the parable was a very religious man, and doubtless he and his friends had often been unjustly treated by tax-collectors. This led him therefore to take his stand before God on the ground of his own good deeds, and to point out to God how much better he was than the loose-living men around him. Especially, of course, the tax-collector over the way. This was misguided indeed. By the relative standards of human justice, he might perhaps have been better than the tax-collector. But he was forgetting that judged by God's absolute standards of justice he stood condemned as a sinner who fell short of God's glory in common with everyone else, religious and irreligious, cheated as well as cheaters, persecuted as well as persecutors. Taking his stand on his own merits, therefore, the Pharisee went home from the temple, unaccepted, unjustified and still under God's displeasure.

The tax-gatherer took a different stance. He stood at a distance, like the lepers in Luke 17:12. He owned the gulf that his sins had put between himself and God, and made no attempt to bridge it by any talk of what good deeds he had to his credit. Feeling himself unworthy even to look up to God's heaven, he confessed the absolute justice of God's condemnation of his sin, and in his utter spiritual bankruptcy simply cast himself on the mercy of God. On those grounds God accepted him. He didn't have to wait until the second coming to know it: he went home from the temple justified. All distance between himself and God was gone forever and he could await the coming of the Lord in confidence and peace.

David Gooding, *According to Luke: The Third Gospel's Ordered Historical Narrative*, 309

27th October

FAITH'S REASONS AND COMMITMENT

Reading: Luke 4:22–29

*'Elijah was sent to none of them but only to Zarephath,
in the land of Sidon, to a woman who was a widow.' (Luke 4:26)*

As Messiah, Christ claimed to be able to free people from their slavery to evil habits, complexes and sin. His physical miracles gave evidence that his claims were to be taken seriously. For any individual the final proof that Christ could effect such deliverance would only come as they personally committed themselves to Christ and allowed him to do his work of deliverance within them. But that act of faith would have to come before they could have the final proof that Christ's claim was true. Why were the people at Nazareth not prepared to take that step of faith?

The story of the Sidonian widow can throw a light on the problem (1 Kings 17:8–16). When she met Elijah, she had only enough food left for one more meal, and then she was going to lie down and die. Elijah told her that if she would first make him a meal from that food, God would then miraculously maintain her food supply until the end of the famine. It was a tremendous test. If she took Elijah at his word and he then turned out to be a fraud, she had lost her last bite of food and imminent death would stare her in the face. What made her stake all she had on Elijah's word?

The fact is that it was easier for her than might appear at first sight. She was utterly without resources. Even if she refused to trust Elijah and kept her food for herself, it was such a minute quantity that death was still imminent. If, however, she gave the food to Elijah, and he then turned out to be a fraud, she had lost very little. Death would come a few hours sooner, that was all. But if she dared to commit herself to Elijah and he turned out to be true, she was saved. She had virtually nothing to lose but everything to gain.

If, however, she had not been a widow, or if she had had slightly more food—say a basketful instead of a handful—she might well have been tempted to trust her own resources in the hope that somehow they would see her through the famine. But then, because she was depending on her own meagre resources, she may well have been afraid to take the step of faith and give Elijah anything.

David Gooding, *Windows on Paradise: Scenes of Hope and Salvation in Luke's Gospel*, 34–5

28th October

EVIDENCE FOR OUR FAITH

Reading: John 20:24–29

*Jesus said to him, 'Have you believed because you have seen me?
Blessed are those who have not seen and yet have believed.' (John 20:29)*

Thomas may well have said, 'Yes, I'm the man who doubted. But I was also the one who said, "Let us also go, that we may die with him" (John 11:16). I was prepared to die for the Saviour. But when they told me that Jesus was risen from the dead, I just couldn't believe it. I mean, what evidence was there? I need evidence if I'm going to believe.'

And the Bible would agree (Heb 11:1). Yes, of course you need evidence. Faith in Christ is not a leap in the dark, you know. Evidence comes first, and then, on believing this evidence, you take the next step and believe in his name to get eternal life. The trouble is that many people don't believe because they haven't spent any time reading the evidence or thinking about it.

'Anyway,' says Thomas, 'I said to them, "I can't believe unless I see the print of the nails in his hands and where the spear was thrust into his side." The next Sunday the Lord suddenly appeared, and said, "Thomas, put your finger here; see my hands. Reach out your hand and put it into my side." How did he know what I'd said? The other apostles have gone and told tales about me, I suppose. But wait a minute: if he wasn't risen from the dead, how could they tell him any tales? I daresay they'd prayed about it. But then, it's because the Lord is alive that he hears our prayers!'

What a marvellously gracious thing it was. Our Lord didn't say, 'Foolish man, you should not have doubts!' He said, 'Thomas, you wanted evidence, didn't you? Here's evidence, so stop doubting and believe.' And in that moment Thomas discovered a risen Lord who's not only alive but knew the very thoughts that Thomas had been thinking.

Then our Lord said to him: 'Because you have seen me, you have believed; blessed are those who have not seen and yet have believed.' There's a something more reliable than sight, and that is the conscience and the heart, and the communication of God's Spirit directly to our hearts. When he gives us the evidence, we shall know it.

Do you dare to seek it sincerely? For God says, 'if you seek me, you shall find me' (see Prov 8:17; Jer 29:13).

David Gooding, *Understanding the Trinity: Six Studies on God's Revelation of Himself*, 12

29th October

TRUSTING IN WHAT CANNOT SAVE

Reading: Exodus 12:33–36

For its maker trusts in his own creation when he makes speechless idols! (Habakkuk 2:18)

The Israelites had once been slaves in Egypt and Pharaoh had mightily oppressed them. God in his mercy had brought them out. There is a tremendous testimony in Scripture to the heart of God and the divine protest against all exploitation of labour. To grind workers down and give them a mere pittance, to have people in factories and keep their wages low, or slave labour camps with just a survival diet—the God of heaven will not have it.

When Israel came out of Egypt by God's deliverance, God made the Egyptians pay them their back wages. After all the long years in which they'd been cheated of their wages, now the Egyptians were obliged to give them back. The Israelites took the gold and the silver and the clothing and much else.

That was all very good. But now a sad thing happened. They're now saying that the gold, which was the by-product of their redemption, is the source of their salvation—'These are your gods, O Israel, who brought you up out of the land of Egypt!' (Exod 32:4). It was a sad mistake, but then it has happened many, many times.

When I was living in the North East of England, opposite my lodging was a gentleman who had gone on the convoys to Russia. He had seen life and death and he came back from those convoys a hard boiled atheist. He was listening one night to his radio when Billy Graham came on to preach the gospel. As he sat in his own living room, the Holy Spirit of God moved in his heart and made him aware that there was a great spiritual salvation which was being offered to him. Should he refuse it, nothing else could save him; so he knelt there by his radio and received Christ.

Presently he went back to the church where he was brought up. He told them that he had found the Saviour; he had been saved. They looked at him coldly and said, 'What nonsense, we don't believe in being saved.' They believed in social good work, in education, in psychological counselling, and in many other good things that help people, but all of them combined cannot save.

Here were those Israelites worshipping a golden calf in the name of God. They called it Jehovah—the one who had brought them out of Egypt—but they were worshipping something that could not save them.

David Gooding, *Standing on the Other Side: One Evangelistic Study on Making a Decision About Christ*, 6–7

30th October

SECURITY IN GOD ALONE

Reading: Genesis 22:15–19

By faith Abraham, when he was tested, offered up Isaac. (Hebrews 11:17)

God did not say, 'Abraham, if you are really a believer, be a bit kinder to those Philistines, and look after the poor.' I suspect Abraham was kind to the poor. But this was a bigger test than that, for God was now asking him, who had received the promises (Heb 7:6), to deliver up Isaac in whom all the promises were invested.

What was it demonstrating? It was demonstrating that Abraham's faith was in God alone. God asked him to surrender Isaac, so that all Abraham's hope and confidence for the future should be in God. Sometimes God will lead us as believers to that same kind of mountaintop, where all he has given us seems to be taken from us and we are left with God alone. It is a painful but a blessed place: to find yourself bereft of all but God is to be made conscious of his promises.

Having endured and come through the test, and shown by his works that his faith in God was genuine, Abraham received the promise, 'because you have done this and have not withheld your son, your only son, I will surely bless you, and I will surely multiply your offspring as the stars of heaven' (Gen 22:16–17). And on that occasion God not only gave the promise but he confirmed it with an oath, saying, 'By myself I have sworn, declares the LORD' (22:16)

Says the writer to the Hebrews,

> God . . . guaranteed it with an oath, so that by two unchangeable things, in which it is impossible for God to lie, we who have fled for refuge might have strong encouragement to hold fast to the hope set before us. We have this as a sure and steadfast anchor of the soul, a hope that enters into the inner place behind the curtain. (Heb 6:17–19)

There is security for you! If our faith is like an anchor in God himself, then let the world collapse, let the whole universe collapse, and the galaxies go to nothing. And what are you left with then? You are left with God and God's unbreakable word for now and for eternity.

David Gooding, *Three Creation Stories and Three Patriarchs: Eight Studies on Understanding the Major Sections of Genesis*, 64–5

31st October

THE RIGHT WAY—THROUGH TRUSTING IN THE LIVING CHRIST

Reading: Colossians 2:8–12

In him also you were circumcised with a circumcision made without hands, by putting off the body of the flesh, by the circumcision of Christ. (Colossians 2:11)

Many of us spend years of our lives struggling with the flesh, until we come to realize that the fulfilment of God's holy law is not in the power of my flesh desperately trying to subdue sin, but in knowing another kind of power. 'Walk before me,' says God to Abraham, 'and be blameless' (Gen 17:1). Then God asked him to observe the covenant of circumcision, a covenant in which the flesh was cut off (vv. 9–11).

Similarly, the new birth is an event which cuts the roots of my personality. No longer are believers 'in the flesh'. The flesh is still evident in us, but the roots of our personalities are now in Christ and in the Spirit (Rom 8:9)—a wonderful reality, mysterious though it is. As I think, then, of my charge to walk before him and be blameless, I may know that there is a power adequate to my responsibility.

It may take me years of uneven experience and progress to learn how that power is to use me. I may have to be taught by uncomfortable methods that my flesh is still impossibly bad and remains flesh. God's Spirit will progressively teach me, if I let him, that the fulfilling of God's way of life for me is not a question of my fleshly powers and determination to try to accomplish his will. Rather it is despairing of myself altogether, and trusting the living Christ to live and work in me.

I shall inevitably fail if I try to do the will of God in the power of my flesh. I'll be tempted to say, 'Well, it's all impossible. What's the good of pretending to live up to a full Christian standard?' That leads to insincerity and disillusionment, and even to loss of faith. Or it is possible that, in attempting to live a godly life in the power of my flesh, I shall conveniently forget the glaring moral failures in my life and compensate by concentrating on the fulfilment of certain tiny little rules, like the Pharisees did.

Let me honestly face my inabilities. Let me learn constantly and consistently to go on abandoning all faith in the flesh, and remember that for those who have no confidence in the flesh there is an inimitable path to follow with our living Lord in whom and by whom we are saved.

David Gooding, *King of kings and Lord of lords: Four Studies Exploring God's Sovereignty Over Various Spheres*, 27–8

1st November

CHRIST IS NOT ASHAMED TO BE KNOWN AS ONE OF RAHAB'S DESCENDANTS

Reading: Matthew 1:1–6

By faith Rahab the prostitute did not perish with those who were disobedient, because she had given a friendly welcome to the spies. (Hebrews 11:31)

As we think of God's great longsuffering, the story we shall now consider will warm our hearts. It is the delightful record of a woman who, amidst all that carnage, was saved by God, protected from the judgment and brought through alive and safe.

Not only was this woman saved, but as we go through the New Testament we discover that she was given the inestimable honour and privilege of becoming an ancestress of Christ. Her name was Rahab, her profession the oldest in the world. Yet the amazing fact is that when you open the first page of the New Testament to read the genealogy of Jesus Christ our Lord, there it is for everybody to see. In the ancestry of Jesus Christ himself there was this colourful character. I fancy if some of us had such a woman in our past we wouldn't be so keen on tracing our ancestry or parading it in our family tree, but the Saviour doesn't mind you knowing that one of his ancestors was the harlot of Jericho.

What can any of us say? As Paul said to the Christians in Corinth, 'And such were some of you. But you were washed, you were sanctified, you were justified in the name of the Lord Jesus Christ and by the Spirit of our God' (1 Cor 6:11). He was reminding them of their colourful, not to say lurid, past.

This is the gospel of a God whose judgments must fall upon sinful men and women. A God who not only delights to save, but has a salvation devised in his heart that would make us all princes and princesses in the royal house of Jesus Christ his Son. A gospel that assures us not only of forgiveness and pardon for the past; but for everyone who trusts Christ this present life is leading on to an exhibition of God's grace that will stagger the wildest imagination. We shall reign with Christ, says the Bible (see 2 Tim 2:12); we are heirs of God and joint-heirs with Jesus Christ his Son (see Rom 8:17). As the heir of all things, the heir of this vast universe, he will share that incalculable wealth with every man, woman, boy and girl who has repented of sin and come for salvation through his atoning death, suffered at Calvary.

David Gooding, What Moses Could Not Do: Nine Studies on the Major Sections in the book of Joshua, 15

2nd November

REPENTANCE AND CONVERSION

Reading: Acts 2:36–42

And in the same way was not also Rahab the prostitute justified by works when she received the messengers and sent them out by another way? (James 2:25)

The writer to the Hebrews tells us that Rahab really got converted, despite that little bit of a fib, or rather that big whopper, she told. 'She meant it well,' says James; 'it was all in the interests of her new found faith.' She saw so vividly that if ever she was to be saved from the impending judgment, it would mean a complete transfer of her loyalties. Conversion is nothing less than that.

You say, 'It was treachery of the first order for her to receive those spies and give them comfort and consolation.' But, ladies and gentlemen, when the judgments of God are at hand it will ultimately be every man for himself. People won't stand in batches before the great white throne. Then all loyalties must be tested and judged in the light of the supreme loyalty, as each human heart is asked, 'Whom do you love, and what evidence is there?'

So Rahab decided to take a stand in loyalty against Jericho, in favour of the living God, the Creator. That's repentance, you know, and let us not forget to preach it either. Listen to Peter on the day of Pentecost when he preached his sermon that Jesus Christ was risen from the dead and God had made him both Lord and Christ. The crowd came around, pricked in their very hearts.

'What shall we do?' they said to Peter.

'I'll tell you,' said Peter. 'You'll get baptized in the name of Jesus.'

They said, 'Peter, you don't understand. We're convinced by what you said, and of course we want forgiveness. But at this moment, to stand away from our society would be a cultural difficulty for us—some of us are members of the Sanhedrin. Besides, you should be preaching salvation by faith, not by works! Why can't we believe on the Lord Jesus and just carry on as we were before?'

'You can't do that', says Peter. 'You tell me you've professed faith in Christ, and you've come in repentance to the living God. Then you will show the genuineness of your repentance by standing clear of the nation that has murdered his Son. Save yourselves from this crooked generation' (see Acts 2:36–40). They could not be loyal both to the Sanhedrin that murdered Jesus and to Jesus himself.

David Gooding, *Entering the Inheritance: Studies in Joshua 1–12*, 17–18

3rd November

SALVATION MAY INVOLVE STRUGGLE

Reading: Luke 14:25–33

*'Whoever does not bear his own cross
and come after me cannot be my disciple.' (Luke 14:27)*

I'm sure someone will say to me, 'I thought you Christians believed that salvation is a free gift. You don't have to struggle for it, do you? You cannot deserve it, and you don't earn it; it's not a prize given for those who succeed in the battle.'

Well, of course that is absolutely true. 'By grace', says Paul, 'you have been saved through faith. And this is not your own doing; it is the gift of God, not a result of works, so that no one may boast' (Eph 2:8–9). Salvation is free; you cannot earn it. Eternal life is the free gift of God, and if we will have salvation we take it as a gift.

Well then, what's all that about it being a struggle? To get salvation some of you may have to go through a struggle. Suppose I've got a pen in my hand, and I were to say, 'If you would like this pen, I'll give it to the first person who comes forward', I think most of you would say to yourselves, 'I don't want a pen anyway, but even if I did I wouldn't go out in front of everybody and humiliate myself to take a pen.'

Yet that is how it is with salvation. There are many folks who see salvation as a gift, but when they think of coming to Christ and receiving it all sorts of obstacles suddenly appear in the way. 'What will my friends think?' 'Do I *need* to be saved—am I not good enough as I stand now? I'm not going to humiliate myself.'

For some people in many countries it's a very big struggle. From time to time my colleagues and I do work in Russia and in the countries to the south of it. Once we received a letter from a student in Tajikistan, who had been a Muslim and had trusted the Saviour. He wrote to us saying, 'When I trusted the Saviour my brothers beat me unmercifully. My father took a knife and carved into my back, trying to persuade me to give up Christ.'

Yes, some people suffer the loss of all things. It doesn't buy salvation; but if it were to cost you everything to come to Christ and receive the free gift of salvation, would you come?

David Gooding, *Life's Struggles and God's Judgment: Two Evangelistic Studies from Revelation*, 5–6

4th November

OUR CLAIM TO BE FORGIVEN REQUIRES THE EVIDENCE OF A CHRISTIAN WALK

Reading: Mark 2:1–12

'I say to you, rise, pick up your bed, and go home.' (Mark 2:11)

Our Lord was teaching, and some decidedly critical theologians were present. Suddenly there was a commotion as the roof opened. Then four men began lowering a friend of theirs on his bed through the hole and down to the feet of our Lord. Because there were so many people present, this was the only way for them to get him anywhere near the Saviour.

The Lord saw at once that he was paralysed, but instead of saying, 'Be healed,' he said, 'Son, your sins are forgiven.' The theologians murmured among themselves and muttered, 'This is sheer blasphemy! Who can forgive sins but God alone?'

They had a point. For instance, if someone injured you, and I came along as a complete outsider saying, 'Stop all that, for I forgive the man', you would turn round to me and say, 'What on earth have you got to do with it? It's not within your power or authority to forgive my enemy's sins.' And since each one of us has sinned against God, there is only one who can pronounce divine forgiveness.

When our Lord said, 'Your sins are forgiven,' he was implicitly claiming to be God incarnate, but his critics were not to be persuaded if he simply said so. So he answered their criticisms by saying, 'Which do you think is the easier thing for me to say, "Your sins are forgiven", or, "Rise, take up your bed and walk"?'

They didn't attempt to reply, and so, to prove that he had the authority to forgive sins because he was God incarnate, he said to his critics, 'But that you may know that the Son of Man has authority on earth to forgive sins,'—he said to the paralysed man—'Rise, pick up your bed, and go home.' The man rose up and walked, supplying the necessary evidence to the theologians that our Lord's claim was true.

We who claim to have been forgiven will be required by our critics, and they are many, to demonstrate the evidence that we are in fact forgiven. The evidence that can convince them is that we do possess the power to rise up and walk in true Christian grace and courage and holiness and practicality; and if that kind of evidence is missing in our lives, any claim to have been forgiven will convince very few people.

David Gooding, *Rise Up and Walk: Two Studies on Living Faithfully for God in a Hostile World*, 3–4

5th November

THE BASIS OF OUR FORGIVENESS REQUIRES US TO FORGIVE OTHERS

Reading: 1 John 2:7–12

I am writing to you, little children, because your sins are forgiven for his name's sake. (1 John 2:12)

As I come to these verses, I would like to ask what forgiveness has got to do with loving one another. 'I am writing to you, little children, because your sins are forgiven for his name's sake'—what's that got to do with loving one another?

And my reasoning is like this. How did you get into the family at all? When you were converted, born again, when you became a child of God and entered the family of God, anybody would tell you that the basic initial experience was the forgiveness of sins. Everyone in the family of God knows the delight of having their sins forgiven. From Mary, the woman out of whom the devils had gone, and those many others who came to the Lord Jesus, they all in that first moment of their believing in him heard the delightful message, 'Your sins are forgiven.' Let's notice what it says, 'your sins are forgiven for his name's sake.' For the sake of the Lord Jesus, our sins are forgiven. What a delightful thing that is. When as prodigals we come home, the Father forgives us for Christ's sake.

'Now, I'm supposed to love you,' says John. Isn't that what he's been saying in the previous verses? 'But you've done something against me and I don't love you. You seek my forgiveness and I'm not prepared to forgive you.' But wait a minute! My sins are forgiven for his name's sake. I get my forgiveness, not because I deserve it but because Christ deserves it. Having regard to the worth of the Lord Jesus, the Father has forgiven my sins.

Then you come along. You've done something wrong—maybe even against me; you confess it and your sins are forgiven for his name's sake. But I'm not prepared to forgive them. Does that mean that I refuse to acknowledge the value of Christ—I repudiate 'his name's sake'? How can that be?

How can I be in the family of God and owe my place in it to the fact that I've been forgiven for the sake of the Lord Jesus, and then not be prepared to forgive my brothers and sisters for his name's sake?

David Gooding, *Life in the Family of God: Fourteen Studies from 1 John*, 33

6th November

THE FAITH THAT OVERCOMES THE WORLD

Reading: 1 John 5:1–5

Who is it that overcomes the world except the one who believes that Jesus is the Son of God? (1 John 5:5)

Shall we notice what it doesn't say? It doesn't say, 'This is the one that overcomes the world: the man or woman who believes that God has forgiven their sins.' The overcoming of the world lies in the fact that we believe Jesus is the Son of God. If he isn't the Son of God, there isn't such a thing as forgiveness anyway, and there's nothing in the gospel. So this matter is fundamental because everything else depends on it.

To understand it, we should perhaps go back to John's Gospel, where our Lord said, 'I came from the Father and have come into the world, and now I am leaving the world and going to the Father' (John 16:28).

'We believe that,' said the disciples.

'Do you really believe it?' said our Lord. 'Let me tell you, gentlemen, the time is coming very soon when you will see me hanging upon a cross, rejected, tortured, crucified. When that happens, your faith that I am the Son of God is going to be sorely tested. You will in fact desert me, and you will be scattered each to his own home, and will leave me alone (16:31–32). You'll wonder if there's nothing in it after all. Some of you are going to be very frightened to stand with me, for you could lose everything you have in this world, your life included. Then it will become exceedingly important whether I am the Son of God or not. If I'm not the Son of God, you'd be fools to lose anything, wouldn't you? If I am the Son of God, you'd be foolish not to sacrifice everything for my sake.'

In times of testing the question remains: is he, or is he not the Son of God? My young fellow Christians, you've got a career before you. How will you decide it? When the world puts its pressure on and frightens you with the way it acts, if you're going to obey the Lord you've got to make great sacrifice. How will you overcome? The vital thing is this: is Jesus the Son of God or isn't he? If he is, then no matter what you're called upon to sacrifice for him, it's worthwhile. If he isn't, kick the lot out of the window.

David Gooding, *Life in the Family of God: Fourteen Studies from 1 John*, 76–7

7th November

FAITH WITHOUT WORKS

Reading: James 2:14–24

So also faith by itself, if it does not have works, is dead. (James 2:17)

Perhaps it will help us if we recall the delightful parable the Lord Jesus told of the Good Samaritan. There was this poor fellow who had been attacked by brigands and left half dead on the road. There came by two exceedingly religious gentlemen, a Levite and a priest, men whose task in life was especially religious. One came and looked and passed on. The other didn't even bother to look. I suspect he had it in his head that his task of singing hymns and songs of praise was so important that he needn't bother with lending a practical hand to the down-and-out. How about us?

There is one area especially where we evangelicals need to be very careful not to deceive ourselves with religion, and that is the glorious doctrine of justification by faith without works.

Let nobody be left in any doubt about what I personally believe: 'For by grace you have been saved through faith. And this is not your own doing; it is the gift of God, not a result of works, so that no one may boast' (Eph 2:8–9). This is the glorious doctrine that broke the tyranny of religion in the Middle Ages and set free the ancient world by the preaching of the gospel; and it has set our hearts free too. God give us the grace in these modern days never to let it go.

That said, however, there could lurk a danger here. As James now proceeds to warn us, we could deceive ourselves by our very theology and argue that because, after all, salvation is by grace and is not of works, then it doesn't really matter whether we behave like Christians or not. It doesn't really matter whether we have works to back up our profession, or not. Reading what James says here, multitudes of people have thought James was contradicting Paul and denying the gospel that we are justified without works. But that is not true; James says the same as Paul and Paul says the same as James.

Take one little test. Referring to Abraham, James observes, 'You see that faith was active along with his works, and faith was completed by his works' (Jas 2:22). Faith active with his works. We are justified by faith, but the mark of genuine faith is that it leads to works.

David Gooding, A Vision of the Perfect Man and Woman: Seven Studies on Major Themes from James, 17–18

8th November

FAITH EVIDENCED BY A WILLINGNESS TO SACRIFICE

Reading: Genesis 22:9–14

And Abraham called the name of that place Jehovah Jireh: as it is said to this day, 'In the mount of the LORD it shall be seen.' (Genesis 22:14 KJV)

James quotes Abraham, who was certainly justified by faith but he was also justified by works—'and the scripture was fulfilled that says, "Abraham believed God, and it was counted to him as righteousness"' (Jas 2:23). It was fulfilled on Mount Moriah when Abraham offered his son to God.

My dear brothers and sisters, there will come a time in our lives when God will call upon us to show by our works that our faith is genuine. He may bring us to a point where he will ask us to offer all and be left standing with nothing except God. Are we ready for that? You say, 'My heart is willing, but I don't know if I would be able to bring the knife down on the sacrifice. What if, in the end, I couldn't go the whole hog and faltered?' Courage, my brothers and sisters, God sees your heart.

You remember in that lovely story, when Abraham took the knife and showed God that he was ready to justify his faith by his works, the angel interposed and the sacrifice was stopped. But the sacrifice wasn't aborted in that moment. Once Abraham had demonstrated what was in his heart, God removed Isaac and in his place put the sacrifice of the ram. Abraham came down the mountain and he called the place *Jehovah Jireh*. He didn't call it 'The mountain of my tremendous sacrifice for God,' for everyone to see it. No, indeed not! He said, 'In the mount of the Lord, it shall be seen.' What shall be seen? 'It shall be seen that, when I came to my test and it was almost more than flesh and blood could stand, I was prepared to do it. Then God came in and provided the shortfall by the sacrifice of a ram.'

We may be sure that God will test us, and who among us would dare to say that we shall come through one hundred percent with flying colours? You say, 'What if I come short and my sacrifice is not what it should be?' Ah, my friend, it is precisely there that God has the sacrifice of his glorious Son, which more than makes up for the shortfall of our devotion. But be assured, God will want to see by the attitude of our hearts and in the action of our lives that our faith is genuine.

David Gooding, *A Vision of the Perfect Man and Woman: Seven Studies on Major Themes from James*, 20–1

9th November

THE MESSIAH'S FAITH IN JEHOVAH

Reading: Isaiah 49:1–7

And he said to me, 'You are my servant, Israel, in whom I will be glorified.' (Isaiah 49:3)

Remember the joy—and if I dare use the word of God himself, the excitement—with which God could not refrain himself, but tore the heaven apart on more than one occasion to announce his pleasure in his Son. He was the first man on earth ever, who truly and without exception and without sin did the will of God perfectly.

But now listen as Messiah speaks: 'But I said, "I have laboured in vain; I have spent my strength for nothing and vanity; yet surely my right is with the Lord, and my recompense with my God"' (Isa 49:4). As he served the Lord so impeccably and gloriously, bringing forgiveness and ease of soul, rest and satisfaction to men and women, he met with enormous official opposition. The nation, particularly through its theologians and priests, opposed him and the vast majority in Israel rejected him.

Do you suppose our blessed Lord had no feelings about it personally? We cannot suppose that he said, 'Well, that's okay. Poor little people, I don't take much notice of them whether they like me or don't like me.' Can we? No, no! To have preached and gone about doing good, to have shown the magnificent grace of God and then be rejected, called a blasphemer and betrayed by the nation and put on a cross, how he must have felt at the end of his labours. Had he laboured for nothing; humanly speaking had it all been in vain?

Amidst his agonies it was not only the rejection of Israel, but the falseness of Judas. And the band of men that he had spent so much time personally discipling, they had proved to be such a poor, broken, feeble, weak lot of cowards. What must he have felt like? How could that kind of result have satisfied him?

'My judgment is with the Lord, and my recompense with my God' (49:4 RV). He had not the slightest quaver of a doubt in God, nor complaint against him. He trusted in God: God would see that true justice was done and his recompense would be with God. There was no doubt in his mind about God, and he reports to us the assurance the Lord gave to him.

David Gooding, *Satisfaction in Serving the Lord: One Study on Three Life Principles from Isaiah*, 5–6

10th November

PAUL'S RESPONSE OF FAITH TO THE LORD'S CALL ON HIS LIFE

Reading: Acts 9:20–31

For to this end we toil and strive, because we have our hope set on the living God, who is the Saviour of all people. (1 Timothy 4:10)

Another evidence of the genuineness of Saul's conversion was his response to the Lord's commissioning. Before his conversion he was convinced that he ought to do all that was possible to oppose the name of Jesus of Nazareth (Acts 26:9). Now as he lay blinded in a room in Damascus, Ananias brought him the Lord's commission. He was to carry the name of Jesus before the Gentiles and their kings and before the people of Israel; and he was to suffer severely for that name (9:15–16). At once, says Luke, he began to preach in the synagogues that Jesus is the Son of God (v. 20), and to prove that Jesus is the Christ (v. 22).

Of course we can say that Saul's case was special. And so it was, for he was an apostle. But what applied to him at his exalted level applies in principle to us all. No true conversion has (as yet) taken place unless the person concerned is ready at once to confess the full deity of the Lord Jesus. We know that many people take a long while to come to full faith in Christ. Like the blind man of John's famous story, they begin by believing something before they eventually believe everything (John 9). But no one is genuinely and fully converted, no one is a true Christian, until they believe in and are ready to confess the full deity of Jesus. If Jesus is not God incarnate, he has no salvation for us. Morality, yes, and example and exhortation—all of it very exalted, but no salvation. If he were merely God's Suffering Servant, but not God's Son, his death could not atone for our sins. Nor could he impart the Holy Spirit to anyone, nor incorporate all the millions of his believers into himself.

Finally, Saul was prepared not only to publicly confess the deity of Jesus, but also to suffer for that confession. Opportunity was not long in coming; and when it came, it arose not in a worldly but in a religious and theological context. It is often so. But still today readiness to suffer for the Name is an indispensable hallmark of a genuine conversion.

David Gooding, *True to the Faith: The Acts of the Apostles—Defining and Defending the Gospel*, 185–6

11th November

FAITH IN CHRIST'S ENTIRE PROGRAMME OF SALVATION

Reading: Luke 7:18–23

*'Are you the one who is to come,
or shall we look for another?' (Luke 7:20)*

At this time John was in prison and it was reported to him that Jesus was doing marvellous miraculous things, which fitted in exactly with half of John's expectations of what the Messiah would do. But Jesus was apparently making no attempt to fulfil the other half of his expectations. He had not even made the slightest move to get John out of prison, nor to execute God's judgment on the evil Herod who had put him there. Why not? When was Jesus going to start abolishing evil rulers like Herod, put down the Roman tyranny and give Israel her political independence under a just government once more? How could Jesus convincingly claim to be the answer to the world's problems if he merely contented himself with saving individuals?

John is not the only one to have felt the problem. To this very day there are many who feel that they cannot believe in Jesus if he is interested merely in the saving of individuals and not in putting right the great political, economic and social evils of the world.

The Lord's reply (7:21–23) was not to deny that he would ever execute God's judgment on evil men and governments. His reply was to do a number of miracles, such as Isaiah had prophesied Messiah would do (see Isa 35:3–6; 61:1–3), and to send John the story of them, so that he might see beyond doubt that Jesus was fulfilling part of the programme that the prophets had laid down. And if he was already fulfilling one part, he would fulfil the other part later on.

Christ insisted that the preaching of the gospel to the individual must take precedence over the executing of God's judgment on the wicked in general and on unjust governments in particular (see Luke 7:22). It would be a sorry thing for us all if that were not so. The day of the Lord will certainly come, and it will come too soon for many people. The reason it waits is that 'The Lord . . . is longsuffering . . . not willing that any should perish, but that all should come to repentance' (2 Pet 3:9 KJV). We may feel that by delaying to right the world's wrongs, Jesus is putting his own reputation as Messiah at risk. But we serve a Messiah who in his compassion for men and women puts the salvation of the individual before his own reputation.

David Gooding, *According to Luke: The Third Gospel's Ordered Historical Narrative*, 135–6

12th November

FEAR OF MAKING OUR FAITH KNOWN

Reading: Luke 12:4–12

'Why, even the hairs of your head are all numbered. Fear not;
you are of more value than many sparrows.' (Luke 12:7)

Christ began to teach them that first they must confess him publicly, however frightening it might be to have to do so; and secondly how to cope with their fear and overcome it. He began by warning them against hypocritically trying to hide what they really believe; and the ground of his warning was that in the end it is impossible to hide it anyway. 'Nothing is covered up that shall not be revealed, or hidden that will not be known' (see 12:1–3).

But how can anyone overcome the fear that tempts them to keep their faith dark? We can never totally eliminate fear (true, healthy fear, that is; not the neurotic kind). We were never meant to; fear is a protective mechanism that the Creator himself has put within us. Christ therefore does not simply tell us not to fear, but rather to make sure we fear the things that ought to be feared the most; and fearing them will deliver us from lesser fears. It is an undeniably frightening thing to be threatened by men who have power to kill the body; but when they have done that, they can do no more. It would therefore be very short-sighted to let fear of human persecution lead us to deny God, for God has infinitely more that he can do. 'But I will warn you whom to fear: fear him who, after he has killed, has authority to cast into hell. Yes, I tell you, fear him!' (v. 5). And this bigger fear will deliver us from the smaller fear.

But fear of God's power is only one element in our cure; the other is faith in God's sense of comparative values (see vv. 6–7). God is aware of the odd sparrow that is thrown in for nothing if you buy four others, and even the hairs on our head are numbered. Whether we live or die, therefore, God is aware of what is happening to us at every moment. If that is so, the only other thing we need to know is how much he values us. 'You are of more value than many sparrows,' says Christ. And his cross tells us how much more.

David Gooding, *According to Luke: The Third Gospel's Ordered Historical Narrative*, 248–50

13th November

THE SERIOUS BUSINESS GOD CALLS US TO DO

Reading: Isaiah 55:1–5

I counsel you to buy from me gold refined by fire, so that you may be rich, and white garments so that you may clothe yourself. (Revelation 3:18)

They don't know that they're wretched, pitiable, poor, blind and naked (Rev 3:17). 'Blind?' you say. Yes. Here they are in a world overflowing with the good benefits God has given to them, and they can't see that there's a hand behind it. The loving God our creator stands behind it, offering the gifts hoping they will lead them to open their eyes. But they don't see it. It's as if there is no God.

Says the Lord Jesus, 'I could give you sight, I could open your eyes. I could give you clothing to cover your shame, so that you might stand cleansed before God, forgiven, justified and certain of his acceptance.'

'How shall I get it?' you say.

'Well,' says Christ, 'I want you to come, and buy from me gold refined by fire, and fine linen, white and clean, that the shame of your nakedness may not be seen' (Rev 3:18).

You say, 'There it is again—he says 'buy', but isn't it free?'

Yes. That's an apparent contradiction, isn't it? Why does God talk like that? Salvation is free, absolutely free; but if you want it, you'll have to come and do real business with the living Christ. We must come to him in our need, and say, 'Lord, how can I have this gift, and how can I be sure of it?' He says, 'Come buy of me that gold which is eternal, those values that are eternal.'

Oh, what lovely things they are: the life with God, eternal life; membership of the family of God; heirs of God and joint heirs with Christ. One day we shall sit with him upon his very throne (Rev 3:21), welcomed into his eternal heaven with all its joys. Oh, what valuables there are! 'Come and get them,' says Christ. 'Come and do dealings with me.'

And you ask, 'How much will I have to pay?' Nothing! But you can't just sit and do nothing; you must come to Christ. Come and get the garments that are pure white; the righteousness that God gives us freely through the redemption that is in Christ Jesus. Then we can come into the presence of God, clothed with this spotless garment that is not of our works, but of the righteousness, the forgiveness and the holiness that Christ has bought for us at the cost of his death.

David Gooding, *Life's Struggles and God's Judgment: Two Evangelistic Studies from Revelation*, 8–9

Part 16

The Holy God who Makes us Holy

14th November

THE BEAUTY OF HOLINESS

Reading: Exodus 40:1–5

One thing have I asked of the LORD, that will I seek after: that I may dwell in the house of the LORD all the days of my life, to gaze upon the beauty of the LORD and to enquire in his temple. (Psalm 27:4)

When the tabernacle was formed and God graciously deigned to dwell in it, then he called to Moses out of the tabernacle and invited him and the people to draw near. As they came to that small but exquisitely designed and exceedingly expensive shrine, they learned about the holiness of God.

There were ascending degrees of holiness. First, you would pass through the gate, which was one area of holiness; then the door, an even greater area of holiness; then the veil at last, and you were in the very presence of God, in a holiness that could not be exaggerated or increased here on earth. The holiness was symbolic of the very holiness of the thrice-holy God in heaven itself.

As the people came near, they were not only struck by the holiness of God; as they saw the rich colours on the gate and on the door and on the veil, they were struck by the beauty of that holiness. As the priests surveyed the cherubim on the veil, it reminded them of the wonderful mysterious beauty of the glory of God who dwelt there.

Therefore, the offerings they were to bring to God were to be the very best they could find. They would be made awesomely aware of that holiness, of its standard and of its right demands. As that glory reflected on them, they would come to see how inadequate their gifts were, how far short their devotion came, how compromised their holiness was, and their own sinfulness in personality and character and deed. So, as they learned of the holiness of God, God graciously put into their hands offerings of substitution that would cover their inadequacies and be the ground upon which they drew near to God.

Moreover, as those offerings were offered, the priests in Israel were charged with the inspection of the animals. They had to be cut into their parts, examined and carefully laid on that altar. The priests would be responsible for seeing that those sacrifices were healthy sacrifices, fit to take the place of the people and die in their stead in this sacred ministry to God.

David Gooding, *Prepared for Glory: Five Studies from Leviticus on Approaching a Holy God*, 16

15th November

HOLINESS AND SINCERITY

Reading: Matthew 26:17–29

Let us therefore celebrate the festival, not with the old leaven, the leaven of malice and evil, but with the unleavened bread of sincerity and truth. (1 Corinthians 5:8)

Were the disciples sincere as they sat in the Upper Room with our Lord, when three times he told them that he would not take another glass of wine until everything was fulfilled?

Wine was something you drank two or three times a day with meals in Palestine. Could the cross be so near that he would not drink another glass of wine with them? They thought they were sincere, but the disciples could not have dreamt it was so near. They had been disputing about who should be first and chief; then our Lord said, 'One of you will betray me!' They could not grasp that. Surely their hearts could not be so evil?

Evil is nearer than we think! From their experience we too must learn not to trust our own judgment. It is bad enough to tolerate malicious gossiping over dinner tables, but it is a fearful thing to sit at the Lord's Supper having spread or about to spread some malice about a fellow Christian. We are worse than we think we are, so may he make us realists and sincere. We can but tell the Lord that we want to serve him. He will search us, prove our hearts and see if there is any wicked way in us; and there is enough in his love, grace and power to help us.

Was our Lord sincere? Let us listen to him as he approached the cross to accomplish our redemption. 'And he said, "Abba, Father, all things are possible for you. Remove this cup from me. Yet not what I will, but what you will"' (Mark 14:36). It was no superficial tide of excitement that carried our Lord to the cross. He prayed with all the sincerity of his heart that the cup might pass; but just as emotions are not our final guide, neither were they his. Having looked at the very last degree of what it would mean, he said, 'Nevertheless, not my will, but yours, be done' (Luke 22:42).

We are saved because in him and in his life there was no leaven; nothing but absolute sincerity and complete truth. May God make us like him. May he take his word and purify our hearts, and lead us yet more to discover his grace, love and power, so that as freeborn children we may journey resolutely towards home.

David Gooding, *Patterns of Praise: Four Studies from Leviticus 23 on the Feasts of the Lord*, 22

16th November

THE PERFECT BALANCE OF THE HOLINESS OF THE LORD JESUS

Reading: Leviticus 4:14–17

For there is one God, and there is one mediator between God and men, the man Christ Jesus. (1 Timothy 2:5)

In the primitive parts from which I come, if you lived in the country you kept chickens in a chicken run. They would fly away from time to time, but we had a way of coping with that. We cut one wing short so that it was unbalanced and the chicken couldn't fly. It flapped down on the ground again and that taught it to stay where it should. But left to itself, the secret of its flight is that its wings are so beautifully balanced.

Here's a bird on the altar, and I say, 'Bird, do you know that you needn't have been on this altar? If only you'd kept singing your lovely song up in the tree the priest would never have got you. Why did you use your lovely wings to come down, near enough so that the priest could get you and bring you to that end?'

As I see our blessed Lord with open arms nailed to Calvary, I say, 'Lord, whatever made you come down? Caiaphas would never have seized you if you hadn't. And when you came down, why did you let them take you and put you on a tree?'

The answer would be in his wings, wouldn't it? He was absolutely balanced. He loved the Lord his God with all his mind, heart, soul and strength. Yes, but he loved his neighbour as himself. God's holiness demanded that no sin could be in heaven. He loved his Father and loved his holiness. But God's holiness must forever have kept us out of heaven, and he loved us as he loved himself. There could be no compromise—if he was going to love God with all his heart, mind, soul and strength, and love us as himself—those two 'wings' brought him inevitably and at last to Calvary, and you and I are eternally safe because of it.

Would anyone say, 'That's marvellous! Now I'm free to go and do as I please'?

No, I think not, for I know what's springing up in your heart. You are saying, 'Oh, wretched man, wretched woman, that I am, how could I ever have taken my redeemed life and trivialized it by doing my own will and seeking my own thing? May God help me from now on and forever to present my body as a living sacrifice, holy and acceptable to God' (see Rom 12:1).

David Gooding, Prepared for Glory: Five Studies from Leviticus on Approaching a Holy God, 24–5

17th November

PREPARING FOR US A PLACE OF PERFECT HOLINESS

Reading: 1 Thessalonians 4:14–17

'And if I go and prepare a place for you, I will come again and will take you to myself, that where I am you may be also.' (John 14:3)

When Christ ascended and sat down on the right hand of the majesty on high, he was but 'ascending to where he was before' (John 6:62). As the Son of God, he resumed his rightful position; the Father glorified him alongside of himself with the glory which Christ had with the Father before the world was (17:5).

And yet it is also true that when the man Christ Jesus ascended into heaven, it changed the face of heaven. Never before had there been in the immediate presence of God a human being with a glorified human body. We are not told what adjustments will be necessary in those glorious realms when the millions of Christ's redeemed people follow him into the eternal tabernacle of God's presence, not as disembodied spirits but as truly and fully human beings with glorified bodies. But of this we can be sure, Christ will have prepared accommodation suited to our redeemed humanity, ready to welcome all his people, including Peter who once denied him.

Christ's phrasing is significant. He could have said, 'I shall come again and take you to heaven where there will be no more crying, sorrow or pain, and no more curse'—and that would have been perfectly true. But he expressed himself differently, for he was thinking of his second coming as the event that shall finally perfect the holiness of his people. 'I will come again', he said, 'and take you to myself, that where I am there you may be also.'

Here is the first and foremost purpose for which Christ is preparing a place for us in the Father's house. It is so that one day we shall be forever with him where he is, and never again wander from him. Never again shall weakness lead Peter to deny him, nor fear panic the other disciples into forsaking him. It will be a temple from which, as Revelation 3:12 puts it, 'Never shall [we] go out of it.' Our devotion will be complete.

David Gooding, *In The School of Christ: Lessons on Holiness in John 13–17*, 80–1

18th November

THE BREAD OF THE PRESENCE

Reading: Exodus 25:23–30

He chose us in him before the foundation of the world, that we should be holy and blameless before him. (Ephesians 1:4)

God had come down to Israel. How would they entertain him? It's bad enough, so I'm told, to have the preacher come to stay with you sometimes, but fancy having God always! How would you entertain God? So Israel were instructed to put loaves on a table before the Lord.

I turn to my New Testament and enquire as to what the goal of my salvation is. The Epistle to the Ephesians tells me that it is God's electing good pleasure to have chosen me in Christ before the foundation of the world to be holy and blameless before him. That's why he has chosen me! Forever I shall be before him and he will be able to look upon me with delight and satisfaction and enjoyment. That's why he made me in the first place, and now that he has redeemed me he wants to set me before his face.

I say to myself, 'Yes, that's all right, God. One of these days, when your work is finished and I am home at last with the Lord, perhaps you will find satisfaction in me.'

Then the word comes, 'No, long before that! While you are still on the desert sand I want you to be before me.'

And I say, 'How is it possible, Lord?'

The answer comes back, 'I've already done it. It was my intention that you should be before me, and the thing is done. Even as I chose you, I have blessed you in Christ. I have raised him from the dead and set him at my right hand; in raising him and putting him there, I have put you there.'

I can scarcely believe it—can you? Yet it is true. As true as that table took those loaves and presented them before God to his satisfaction, so the Saviour has taken those who trust him and he presents them before God. He holds them up before him to the satisfaction of almighty God now and forever. So, in Christ, God's great purpose is being done here and now. This humble believer and that believer, presented in the gold of the person and the character and the worth of his Son, is held before God and God can already accept me and find something to delight in while we journey towards home.

David Gooding, *No Longer Bondmen: Thirteen Studies from Exodus on the True Meaning of Freedom*, 127–9

19th November

THE FOUNDATION OF HOLINESS

Reading: Acts 10:34–48

*In every nation anyone who fears him and does what
is right is acceptable to [God]. (Acts 10:35)*

Is that how you preach the gospel—that 'in every nation anyone who fears him and does what is right is acceptable to God'?

You say, 'But surely all our righteousnesses are as filthy rags?' Yes, of course they are, and the prophet who confessed that on behalf of his nation was being very honest. He said, 'You know, we [Jews] have all become as one who is unclean and our righteous deeds are like a polluted garment' (see Isa 64:6).

When we see ourselves as we really are, every one of us would admit our righteousness comes short. But don't let that lead us to give the unconverted a wrong impression that God doesn't like good works, for that's nonsense. God is for good works; and if you're going to turn people into saints they've got to become people who will be full of good works that are pleasing to God.

What then is the secret of a truly holy life? Here is this Gentile Cornelius. He wants to please God, and God has noticed and approved. The man will never be saved by those works, but he's telling God that he wants to please him. God reads men's hearts, and has prepared Peter to come and preach the gospel to Cornelius, so that he might get saved. Listen then to how Peter preached it.

'I used to think we Jews were better than you Gentiles, but I discovered that it isn't so. You're interested in good works, so let me tell you about Jesus Christ. He was anointed with power and the Holy Spirit; he went about doing good and healing all who were oppressed by the devil, for God was with him.'

'That's marvellous; where's he now?' says Cornelius.

'I have to tell you that we Jews murdered him.'

'What, you Jews, with all your fancied holiness?'

'Yes, we murdered God's Son. That exposed our holiness as bogus, didn't it? Now he's raised from the dead, it's Jesus Christ who is going to be judge. It's not a question of whether I as a Jew am better than you, or you as a Gentile are better than me; it's a question of how we stand before Jesus Christ. He's the judge and we Jews are sinners. Are you Gentiles not sinners too? The marvellous thing is that God has declared that everyone who believes in him receives forgiveness of sins through his name.'

That is foundation number one of true Christian holiness: Jew and Gentile saved solely through the death and resurrection of Jesus Christ our Lord.

David Gooding, *Daring to be Different: Seven Studies from Acts on Defining and Defending Christianity*, 41–2

20th November

HOLINESS REQUIRES A NEW NATURE

Reading: 2 Peter 2:17–22

He saved us, not because of works done by us in righteousness, but according to his own mercy, by the washing of regeneration and renewal of the Holy Spirit. (Titus 3:5)

The Apostle Peter, in his kind but firm manner, reminds us that it is by failing to understand, and then by failing to experience this personal, internal, spiritual regeneration, that some people who profess to be Christians eventually get themselves into trouble.

He uses a vivid illustration to illustrate what he means. He reminds us of the ancient Greek fable entitled 'The sow that took a bath'.

A sow had been watching the ladies of the city attend the public baths. It had seen them emerge all pink and beautiful in their flowing dresses and decided to follow their example and be a lady itself. So it went to the baths and had itself scrubbed all over, and came out all pink and smelling of scent. Then it dressed itself up in a beautiful dress and put a jewel in its snout and pranced up the main street on its hind legs, doing its best to behave like ladies behave.

For a while it more or less succeeded, until it came across a pool of dirty muddy water and forgot all about trying to be a lady, dived into the water and wallowed in the mud. That ruined its whole attempt to act like a lady.

The important thing to notice is why its attempt failed. It failed because the sow made the mistake of thinking that in order to be a lady it had simply to try to do the things that ladies do. So it got itself cleaned up outside, but alas it had never been changed inside. If the sow were to have any hope of ever becoming a lady, the first essential would be that it would have to be changed inside and receive the life and nature of a lady; in other words, to be born again. Without that internal regeneration, all hopes of behaving as a lady would be in vain.

David Gooding, *In The School of Christ: Lessons on Holiness in John 13–17*, 26–7

21st November

THE ASSURANCE OF GOD'S LOVE ENABLES US TO FACE OUR FAILINGS

Reading: Romans 5:1–5

God's love has been poured into our hearts through the Holy Spirit who has been given to us. (Romans 5:5)

The work of making us holy is not the work of a moment, is it? We shall not wake up one Monday morning and say to ourselves, 'I feel a bit different this morning and I don't know what it is. Oh, I think I've become holy overnight.'

Genuine holiness will mean that, as we can bear it, God will have to make us face ourselves and our wrong attitudes, our sinful actions and our bad tempers, our bitterness, our pride and all the rest of that ugly brood. But being made to face ourselves is painful, and God will require us to repent. Repentance is not only a thing we do the very first moment we get converted, for, as we can gather from our Lord's letters to his churches in the book of Revelation (chs 2–3), he is constantly calling on his people to repent. The process of sanctification will not all be unpleasant—of course not. The gracious Holy Spirit knows what we can bear. But if we're going to be holy, then we shall have to be prepared to face the unpleasant experience of getting to know ourselves and repenting and persevering.

How can we find the courage to face that? That is why this lovely chapter in Romans comes here in this position. After we know ourselves justified, now we're facing the long period of sanctification. Watch the masterliness of the Holy Spirit as he pours out the love of God into our hearts. He gives believers the confidence that they are already accepted, they already have peace with God. You see, if we don't have that confidence, we can fall into a grievous misunderstanding that our acceptance with God depends upon our progress.

And then, when folks get to middle age and find their progress hasn't been as much as they hoped, if they thought their acceptance with God depended on their progress they would despair, wouldn't they? And if they weren't sure to start with that they're accepted with God, psychologically there would be a temptation with many to hide it and make out they're better than they really are.

It is of the utmost importance; it is the foundation of true holiness that we know 'God's love has been poured into our hearts through the Holy Spirit who has been given to us.'

David Gooding, *Obtaining the Goal of Salvation: Three Studies on the Work of the Holy Spirit*, 8

22nd November

THE HOLY SPIRIT CHANGES OUR DESIRES

Reading: Romans 8:1–5

Those who live according to the Spirit set their minds
on the things of the Spirit. (Romans 8:5)

The Bible clearly says that Christians do not go about trying to live as Christians ought to live because they are afraid of the penalty. With the coming of God's Holy Spirit into their lives, old desires are changed and new desires and powers spring up that were not there before.

I remember asking a young man what had led him to Christ. The question was very pertinent because he was studying theology and had been about to enter Holy Orders, even though he frankly confessed that he was not saved.

I said, 'What made you first think that you were not right?'

He said, 'There's a group of students composed of all sorts of people and they meet together every Saturday to study the Bible. I have found that a profound mystery. I can understand reading the Bible as something you have to do in your studies, but it baffles me that anybody should study it in their spare time. And when I went along to some of the meetings, they obviously enjoyed the stuff! I didn't enjoy it.'

He tried to make himself love God a bit more. He went on a pilgrimage to Rome but gave up before he got there. He hitchhiked his way back over the continent, and in England he was given a lift by a man who turned out to be a Baptist pastor, who asked him to lunch in a hotel.

'To my horror,' he said, 'he tipped the waiter with the Gospel of John! I thought that I would never get away from these people who seem, somehow, to love this Bible.'

He found the answer to it all when he too, as a bankrupt sinner, received not only forgiveness, but the Holy Spirit with all his new power and new life. He has new interests now, and he doesn't have to try to love the Bible; it comes naturally to him.

He had been honest to express what a good many people feel. There are many men and women, and they find this book absolute boredom. It's double Dutch to them, and yet it is God's word. If we don't love God's word, how shall we love God's heaven? How can we pretend to be Christians if we don't love his word and the God who wrote it? It's no good trying to make ourselves love it.

David Gooding, *Christian Foundations: Ten Studies on Key Biblical Concepts*, 45

23rd November

THE CONSTANT BATTLE BETWEEN THE SPIRIT AND THE FLESH

Reading: Galatians 5:16–23

For the desires of the flesh are against the Spirit, and the desires of the Spirit are against the flesh, for these are opposed to each other, to keep you from doing the things you want to do. (Galatians 5:17)

I am not saying that men and women will never sin again when they come to Christ and receive the Holy Spirit. The Bible is very real and down-to-earth. It says that, when a man or woman receives God's Holy Spirit, a battle starts within them that will never cease while this life on earth lasts. Our verse explicitly describes it: 'For the desires of the flesh are against the Spirit, and the desires of the Spirit are against the flesh, for these are opposed to each other, to keep you from doing the things you want to do.' Those old desires are there still, and this new power begins to strive against the old. There will be times when the old gets the mastery, but the winning of the final war will always be on the side of God's Holy Spirit.

You say, 'If the Holy Spirit comes into a man when he is saved and he still sins, does God shut a blind eye to them?'

No, indeed not. But do you not see the realism and the extent of God's salvation? Christ died on the cross to deliver us from the curse of his law we have broken. He has paid the expense of the whole thing, and now for the person who trusts Christ the penalty of God's law over his sins has been paid permanently.

Like a father teaching his son to work with very precious glass, he knows that if he gives the young man his beautiful cut-glass work to finish, the unskilled hands may smash the whole thing. The father is so keen to teach his son to do it properly that he's prepared to pay all the expenses for breakage; not intending to encourage his son to be careless, but that's the only way of doing it.

God has a marvellous salvation through the death of Christ on the cross for those who trust him. The penalty of all their sins is paid in full while they develop under the leading of God's Holy Spirit.

I pause therefore, and suggest that we ask ourselves on what principle we are living. Are you living as a child of God? Have you received God's Holy Spirit? Or perhaps you don't know what that means. You know this is Christianity, but it is so easy to be content with something less.

David Gooding, *Christian Foundations: Ten Studies on Key Biblical Concepts*, 45–6

24th November

THE NECESSITY OF GROWTH

Reading: Ephesians 4:7–16

. . . until we all attain to the unity of the faith and of the knowledge of the Son of God, to mature manhood, to the measure of the stature of the fullness of Christ. (Ephesians 4:13)

According to Paul, the most pressing need for members of the body of Christ is that each member shall grow. It is important that we do some work for the Lord, but what work we do will depend on whether we grow.

A little baby in his cot has got all the potential, but what a tragedy it would be if he didn't grow. Through the early years, through the teenage years, and even when you are over seventy, you will have to grow.

Why is it so important to grow up to 'the full stature'? How do you measure it? The measurement is Christ. We have to grow so that the whole body will be fully grown in all its members to match the head. Some growing! But it is the most pressing need: 'until we all attain to the unity of the faith and of the knowledge of the Son of God.' If we are going to function as members in his body, then it is vitally important that we get an ever enlarged and more correct concept of who the head is.

The head is that same Son of God through whom the universe was planned and made; that same one who made the principalities, powers, mights and dominions. When the Apostle John, who leaned on his breast at the Last Supper, saw him in his glorified state, he temporarily fell at his feet as dead. 'Fear not, John,' he said (Rev 1:17), and his heart is still the same. What then will it be to see him in his glory? Listen to what Paul says: 'For this light momentary affliction is preparing for us an eternal weight of glory beyond all comparison' (2 Cor 4:17). We need to grow up, for in the coming eternity we have to bear a colossal weight of glory.

Just imagine being in the body of the Son of God! We need to have some notion in our heads and hearts of who this Son of God is. He is the one for whom the universe was made. He has chosen to make us part of his body; not merely treating us like slaves, giving us commands, but graciously sharing his very life. With his life within us, we respond to the head. We will need to grow up to get to know the head, so that he might operate efficiently within us.

David Gooding, *Where Does God Dwell Today? Two Studies on the Purpose and Nature of the Church*, 17–18

25th November

TRIALS BRING US CLOSER TO OUR DESTINATION

Reading: Exodus 15:22–27

But rejoice insofar as you share Christ's sufferings, that you may also rejoice and be glad when his glory is revealed. (1 Peter 4:13)

So God allowed Marah, and a bitter experience it was. Look at the text and just notice that Marah is on the map (Exod 15:23). These passages are a kind of map of Israel's way from Egypt to Canaan. And how kind of God to provide us too with a map of our way from salvation to glory!

You know how it is when you go on holiday and you've got a map with you. It's a difficult job, because it says that you'll see a signpost, and when you get there there's no signpost. But how nice it is when at last you see the signpost. What does it say? 'Broken down old tower'! It looks broken down enough, but we're right here and the map said it would be here!

It's like that in God's holy Word. It says, 'Shout for joy at this juncture,' and they praised him. Another mark on the map says, 'Weep for the sheer bitterness of the road here.' I'm glad it's there, because when I strike the bitter path sometimes I feel I must be lost. Why don't I have the joy I once had? Then I look at the map and it says, 'Around about here you will know bitterness.' Well that's pretty tough, but I know then that I'm on the right road and I'm not lost after all.

Shall I tell you something? It was marvellous when the children of Israel were standing by the Red Sea and singing the praise of God—they felt they were nearly in Canaan. But when they got to Marah and were sad and bitter, they were nearer Canaan than they were when they were singing!

You mustn't think that just because now you have struck a difficult patch you necessarily have lost your way. You are probably nearer glory now than you were down the road before. And not merely nearer in time chronologically, but perhaps nearer in spirit. When you stood singing, it was delightful and wonderful; but there was just that little bit of excitement in it and you were saying words that were a little bit too big for you. Never mind—you meant them. But now you are facing some of the realities and God is putting you through his discipline. Even though it doesn't seem like it, you are more ready in spirit now than you were before.

David Gooding, *No Longer Bondmen: Thirteen Studies from Exodus on the True Meaning of Freedom*, 87–8

26th November

DISCIPLINE THROUGH TRIALS

Reading: Hebrews 12:4–12

He disciplines us for our good, that we may share his holiness. (Hebrews 12:10)

What a softening and a soothing of my troubled spirit it is, when I come to see that God's ways with me are not punishments and rejections.

'I will not bring on you any of the diseases I brought on the Egyptians, for I am the Lord, who heals you' (Exod 15:26 NIV). Never will one drop of wrath fall on my head, for there is no condemnation (Rom 8:1). Pains there will be, but the pains of love's chastening; and when I begin to see that, another healing comes into my life.

In some great tragedy or trial it is easy to become embittered, and difficult sometimes to resist being bitter even towards God himself. 'Why did he allow it? Why has he singled me out for this and not allowed it for somebody else?'

But the bitterness only makes the trouble worse.

I used to get fearful headaches as a child. I still remember the kind parent who used to stand over me and say, 'Don't cry!' But how could I stop crying? 'The crying will make it worse,' she said. And so it did!

When I see that these things are love's chastisement, and I hear his voice saying, 'Those whom I love, I reprove and discipline' (Rev 3:19), there begins to be an inner healing of the spirit and I say, 'It's all right; it shall be well.'

And so said the writer of the Epistle to the Hebrews. They had been asked to stand by as their furniture was smashed and their homes ruined, their loved ones carted off to jail by their persecutors (Heb 10:34). Their knees were beginning to sag, their hands hung down, and they felt like giving up. They believed in God's Son, yet here was God allowing them to suffer these tremendous atrocities. The writer explained that, whatever the enemy intended, God meant it for their education. Afterwards it would yield its harvest of pleasant fruit.

> Therefore lift your drooping hands and strengthen your weak knees, and make straight paths for your feet, so that what is lame may not be put out of joint but rather be healed. (Heb 12:12–13)

Some of our wounds will leave scars as long as life shall last, but a scar is a sign of a wound that's healed! 'I am the Lord, who heals you.'

David Gooding, No Longer Bondmen: Thirteen Studies from Exodus on the True Meaning of Freedom, 91–2

27th November

FOCUSING ON CHRIST'S PERFECTIONS RATHER THAN ON OUR SIN

Reading: Hebrews 12:1–3

We have seen his glory, glory as of the only Son from the Father, full of grace and truth. (John 1:14)

When I listen to a piece of music I feel that delight peculiar to an innocent who doesn't know much about the difficulty of actually playing it. You who are experts know how difficult it is. So, when you hear a master playing it, and the way he makes even that difficult phrase seem easy, you are open-mouthed in your admiration. And only those who are trying to live a holy life will begin to appreciate fully the marvellous expertise of Jesus Christ our Lord, going through life and its difficult patches in a way that somehow made it look easy, and our hearts are drawn out in admiration and worship of him.

And therein lies another reason that makes the worship of our Lord an exceedingly wholesome as well as a practical thing. We all fall and fail, and feel miserable with ourselves. Therefore, we turn to reflection about it and to humble confession before God.

That is good, but it can be taken to extremes. If the devil cannot trip us up by worldliness and carelessness, then he will spoil us by pushing us over the edge of some extreme or other in our spiritual exercises. He commonly does it with younger believers. Like all of us they fail, and then they feel miserable about it. They start to confess their sins before the Lord until their exercises before God are one long series of ugly things, telling God at length how bad they are. In the end it leaves them worse than when they started, for it's what you constantly think about that you become like.

God's way is better. As we approach the divine presence, aware of our faults he puts into our hands, as it were, that great sacrifice for sin, points us back to our sinless Lord and says, 'Please now, I've had enough of listening to all your badness. I know it and I don't like it. Talk to me about the excellence of Jesus Christ your Lord. Have you not seen that where you failed, he was perfect, and do you not admire him for it?'

As we change the centre of our preoccupation from our sinful selves to the perfect Christ, our hearts begin to respond in admiration to him, and presently little by little we find ourselves becoming more like the one we constantly think about and the one we admire.

David Gooding, *The Adoration of Christ: Six Studies on the Nature and Practice of Worship*, 35

28th November

WE ARE TO BE IMITATORS OF CHRIST

Reading: Ephesians 5:1–21

Therefore be imitators of God, as beloved children.
(Ephesians 5:1)

Sometimes when we come into the presence of the Lord and see his glory, we perceive how wretched we are. And before we know where we are, we've concentrated so much on our horrible thoughts that almost every prayer is a confession of our faults. And if we're too much occupied with our failures, we shall become like them and push ourselves down in the mud more and more.

But God's way is healthy. He points us to the blessed Lord Jesus, the one who died for us, and also to all the marvellous detail of his personality that equipped him to do it. As we contemplate his beauty we begin to admire him, and from admiring him we worship him, and from worshipping him we aspire to be like him and to imitate him.

When I use the word 'imitate', I don't mean it in a bad sense. We can have imitation coffee, but don't drink it, it's horrible! It isn't the real thing. That's imitation in a bad sense, but there's a good sense of imitation, isn't there?

In my day, the great footballer in England was Stanley Matthews. It was not an uncommon sight to be going round the corner of some poor run down street, and there was a little chap with a football, and in his eyes he was Stanley Matthews. He was lining himself up like Stanley Matthews and kicking the ball like Stanley Matthews. As far as he could, he was imitating Stanley Matthews. He'd be a great footballer when he grew up.

God shows us his Son. 'Look at my Son,' he says; 'don't you think he's marvellous?' We admire him and we worship him, and before we know where we are we're trying to imitate him. 'Carry on,' says God. 'Be imitators of God, as beloved children. And walk in love, as Christ loved us and gave himself up for us, a fragrant offering and sacrifice to God' (Eph 5:1–2).

As we behold the glory of the Lord we become aware of our sinfulness; and yet, as we penetrate further and watch it more closely, we find that our very sinfulness makes us more aware of his wonder. We admire him and worship him and think of his offering, and then begin to imitate him. In that way, we are vessels of mercy prepared for glory.

David Gooding, *Prepared for Glory: Five Studies from Leviticus on Approaching a Holy God*, 14–15

29th November

OVERCOMING THE LURE OF THE FORCES AROUND US

Reading: Ephesians 4:7–13

You ascended on high, leading a host of captives in your train and receiving gifts among men. (Psalm 68:18)

Paul's great aim was that the Ephesian believers would grow up into Christ, who is the head, and become spiritually mature. As he thought of that, he perceived that there were great forces in Ephesus pressurizing them to conform to the Gentile way of living.

As he saw the pressure against them, he came upon Psalm 68 that begins by talking about how God had delivered his people in the days of Deborah. Then he came across this phrase: 'You ascended on high, leading a host of captives in your train and receiving gifts among men' (Ps 68:18). He said to himself, 'What can it mean, "You ascended on high"? How could God ever ascend anywhere? He is supreme.'

Then, illuminated by the Holy Spirit, he saw that if God ascended, it must be that he would first have to descend. The supreme Lord, who could go no higher, first descended. We think of it with awe, especially at the Lord's Supper. He not only came down to our earth, he became human. For our sake he first descended, to fight our battle, to deliver us from the authority of darkness and translate us into his glorious light.

When Barak was told to rise up and face the enemy, he descended Mount Tabor. The Lord had gone out before him, so Barak overcame the enemy and, as Deborah said, he 'led captivity captive' (KJV – Judg 5:12; Ps 68:18). The people that had once held Israel in captivity, now Barak took them captive.

Our blessed Lord first descended. He led captivity captive and turned the tables on his enemies. Now risen, he distributes the spoils of his victory in the form of gifts to people. What kind of gifts? Paul enunciates them, 'apostles, prophets, evangelists, pastors and teachers' (Eph 4:11). Why do we need them? Because we are involved in the battle: it is the knowledge of the true God versus idolatry. And here are gifts from the risen Lord, empowered by him to build us up, so that we in turn will become strong to serve and to do the job that God has given us. In spite of all the pressures of our contemporary Gentile society, we are to grow in grace, become mature believers, and 'grow up in every way into him who is the head' (4:15).

David Gooding, *God's Great Salvation: Four Old Testament Character Studies*, 20–2

30th November

THE RIGHT ATTITUDE TO EVIL POWERS

Reading: Matthew 5:17–20

Do not rejoice in this, that the spirits are subject to you,
but rejoice that your names are written in heaven. (Luke 10:20)

I once was invited to preach in a church that began its life as a Spiritist Church, though it hadn't been that for many a long year. Their leader, now an elderly and delightful Christian, told me when I asked what it was that first made him think that the spiritism in which he was engaged was evil. He said, 'Well, I will not tell you some of the experiences we had, but what I noticed was that in all those experiences, there was never any moral progress. It was spiritism and power, but no moral progress. The thing that first made me see the difference was reading the Sermon on the Mount, with all its moral imperatives and the matter of sin and guilt and the need for repentance and personal salvation.' He found the Saviour and abandoned his spiritism.

And if we know our job as Christian preachers, we will certainly see to it that we keep the gospel at the very centre of all our preaching: a personal relationship with Jesus Christ our Lord and his glorious salvation.

It seems to me a very important thing to observe how little is said in the Acts of the Apostles about turning out evil spirits. Paul turned many out in Ephesus, for instance, but we are told very little about it (Acts 19:12).

What a tremendous book trade Luke could have had if he had seen the possibilities, commercial and otherwise, of writing Christian thrillers all about demons and Satan and witches! They would have sold in their thousands.

It is so perilously easy to minister to bad taste and unspiritual appetites seeking excitement, and playing into the hands of Satan by concentrating people's minds on spirit things when they ought to be concentrated on the Lord. My brother and sister, would you permit a little word of advice from a man whose hair grows grey? If you find it much more interesting to read books about witches and casting out demons than to read the Gospel of John, something has gone wrong with your spiritual taste. Notice how little is said in the book of the Acts on that business of casting out evil spirits and learn to have true, healthy proportions in the work of the Lord.

David Gooding, Daring to be Different: Seven Studies from Acts on Defining and Defending Christianity, 64–5

1st December

ACCEPTING CHRIST AS LORD

Reading: Romans 14:5–9

And being made perfect, he became the source of eternal salvation to all who obey him. (Hebrews 5:9)

We should notice the term: not simply 'to all who believe him', but 'to all who obey him'. From the very start we are called to yield Christ 'the obedience of faith' (Rom 16:26). It is not that we are to obey a code of laws in order to be saved, but we are saved on the condition that we receive him as Lord. He is the author and source of eternal salvation, so there is no insecurity or doubt. Salvation cannot be cut short half way: it is an eternal salvation. But he requires all who desire the eternal salvation to commit themselves utterly and without question to him as their Lord as well as their Saviour. To all who do so he is prepared to accept total responsibility for their eternal salvation. He will do all and will save them for ever.

Some will object that we are making things too hard, and imperilling the doctrine of salvation by grace. They urge that all we have to do to be saved is to believe in Jesus as our Saviour. Do that and we are eternally secure. Then after that we can make up our mind whether we wish to go further and become loyal disciples of Christ by receiving and obeying him as Lord.

That is not true. The gospel preached to the ancient Israelites in Egypt was not, 'If you want to escape from Egypt and enter the promised land, all you have to do is to shelter behind the blood of the Passover lamb. After that you can decide whether or not you wish to commit yourself to Moses as your captain and follow him and God across the desert.' No salvation was offered to Israel that did not require them to commit themselves unconditionally to Moses' captaincy right from the start.

And so it is with us. We are required right from the very start to yield ourselves to the complete lordship of Christ. Certainly it is altogether by grace and through faith in Christ, who was 'lifted up' on the cross for us, that we are born again. But we are not born again into the kingdom of God on the understanding that once we are inside the kingdom, we shall still be free to make up our minds whether we intend to obey the king or not.

David Gooding, *An Unshakeable Kingdom: The Letter to the Hebrews for Today*, 122–3

2nd December

THE MOTIVATING POWER FOR CHRISTIAN BEHAVIOUR

Reading: John 13:1–15

For I have given you an example, that you also should do just as I have done to you. (John 13:15)

Here we have the heart-secret of Christian ethics. True believers will increasingly feel impelled to treat others as Christ has treated them. Has Christ forgiven them? Then they will stand ready to forgive others. Has Christ laid down his life for them? Then they ought to lay down their lives for others.

That will mean serving others in practical ways; but in spiritual things as well. And it becomes clear that we can help others only to the extent that we have experienced the help of Christ ourselves.

If you notice that a fellow-believer whom you know well is behaving in a way that is unbecoming for a Christian, you may feel it your Christian duty to help him recognize his faults, and to 'wash his feet', so to speak. But do be careful how you go about it. You can only do effectively for him what you have first experienced Christ do for you. Remember how you too need Christ to wash your feet. Remember how he goes about it; and as you come to correct your friend, imitate his method. For if you come in some superior manner and sternly rebuke your friend, you will find that all their psychological defensive mechanisms will come into play, and they will steel their heart against you, and not allow you to proceed with your intended mission. Indeed, you may well be fortunate if they do not start accusing you of arrogance and pride, because your criticisms, though true, have humiliated them, and made them feel miserable and worthless.

You would do better to approach them as the Lord approached his apostles. He let them sit up on their couch, and he kneeled at their feet. That made them feel important, almost embarrassingly so. But it was not a mere gimmick: he meant them to feel important, for he loved them individually, and to him they were so important, in spite of their present faults and failings that he was about to go to Calvary and give his life for them. Sensing that he loved them, and that in his eyes they were individually dear, they found the courage to open their hearts to his gentle teaching, and even to his rebukes. And in finding the courage to face their failings, they took the first step towards overcoming them and towards Christian maturity and holiness of life.

David Gooding, *In The School of Christ: Lessons on Holiness in John 13–17*, 41–2

3rd December

LIVE IN LOVE AND WALK IN THE LIGHT

Reading: 1 John 2:9–11

Whoever loves his brother abides in the light, and in him there is no cause for stumbling. (1 John 2:10)

What does it mean, 'cause for stumbling'? If I hate my brother, that very attitude of heart will trip me up and lead me into doing all sorts of sinful things. Not only so, but I'll be a cause of stumbling to other people. As the world looks on and sees Christians tearing each other to pieces vitriolically, what a stumbling block it is to them. If I allow myself to be driven by anger or jealousy, it perverts my judgment and trips me up into doing all sorts of harmful and foolish things. Loving keeps me in God's light, and helps me see things as he sees them.

Then verse 11 tells us in terrifying language of the opposite extreme. 'But whoever hates his brother'—that is, as a practice he constantly lives in hatred of his brother—'is in the darkness.' He has no fellowship with God, he walks in darkness and in consequence he can't see where he's going. And finally, 'the darkness has blinded his eyes' and perverts his moral judgment.

And we can experience that, even as believers. From time to time we get tripped up and temporarily feel ourselves blown with passions of rage. When we're in our temper we feel it right to go and do something, and then afterwards we feel ashamed of ourselves. That temporary burst of temper blinded our eyes and made a thing feel right when it was, in fact, fearfully wrong. Thank God that we can come and walk in the light (1 John 1:7). Thank God for the light that will expose us and show us ourselves; and then there is forgiveness and cleansing from all unrighteousness (1:9).

Sometimes temper, hatred and wrath represent themselves to us as our protector. 'It protects our rights,' we say, and so we cling to it. Whereas, when the light of the Lord Jesus shines into our dungeon, we can see it, not as our protector, but as our jailer. When the truth and the light of God show us what the reality is, we see our lust, our hatred and our anger for what it is. Seeing it is the first step to going free, and we have the exhortation then to love one another and not to live in hatred.

David Gooding, *Life in the Family of God: Fourteen Studies from 1 John*, 32

4th December

RECOGNIZING THE SOURCE OF TEMPTATION

Reading: James 1:13–18

Let no one say when he is tempted, 'I am being tempted by God,' for God cannot be tempted with evil, and he himself tempts no one. (James 1:13)

When we are tempted it is exceedingly important to recognize the source of the temptation. Among the ancient Greeks, if a man felt the strong passions of sexual desire within him, that was a goddess; they called her Aphrodite. And if he felt the urgings of aggression within his heart, they said it was the god of war. Very often the result was that he felt perfectly justified in destroying you, your house, your family, your children and thousands of others in cruel wars. It was the gods that were moving him to war, he would say. We have still not completely got beyond that, even in this present day.

Here is a bright young woman and she has just seduced her boss, ruined his marriage and broken up his family. You ask her why she did it. 'I couldn't help it. *Love* made me do it,' she says. Now love has become a goddess; you have to obey her every prompting and it is enough excuse to say, 'Love made me do it.'

In that sense our modern world is becoming increasingly like the ancient world. True Christians would never take that view, would they? I hope not!

What would you say to a man who let it slip that he was thinking of joining the Freemasons, with all their old idolatry? He says, 'I was out of work and desperately needing a job, and I believe the Lord opened the way for me to enter this firm. They said that I would have to join the Freemasons. I knew it wasn't for the best, but if the Lord opened the way it must be right.' We should need to say, firmly and lovingly, 'Don't be deceived, my brother; God never leads anybody, or lures them, into sin.'

Joseph believed with all his heart that it was God who had overruled that he should be put down into the pit and then find himself in Potiphar's house as his chief steward. That was the Lord's leading. But when Potiphar's wife made her advances, Joseph did not say, 'Well it was the Lord who put me into this situation. He must know about it, and perhaps it is OK because the Lord led me.' Be not deceived, God does not tempt us.

David Gooding, *A Vision of the Perfect Man and Woman: Seven Studies on Major Themes from James*, 15

5th December

DEFINING WORLDLINESS

Reading: John 12:4–11

They themselves did not enter the governor's headquarters, so that they would not be defiled, but could eat the Passover. (John 18:28)

The assembled Jews wanted to keep the Passover; so, lest they became defiled, they refused to go into Pilate's hall to accuse Christ and further his execution. They kept it, but the Passover had become an utterly empty and meaningless thing. When their forefathers had been in Egypt under the domination of a cruel Pharaoh, God had broken their chains and set them free, but now these responsible leaders hugged their chains to themselves.

Coming to the closing section of his Gospel, as the cross drew near, John records our Lord's conversation with his disciples. Three times he repeated the phrase, 'the ruler of this world' (John 12:31; 14:30; 16:11). Satan was the cruel master over so many of those who kept the Passover. Think of Caiaphas, so enamoured of his place in society as high priest and his comfortable occupation under the Romans that he would choose his career and position in this world rather than God's Christ. Think of Judas, whom the ruler of this world claimed as his slave for only thirty pieces of silver, dangled so close to his eyes that they blotted out God's divine Son and all that went with him. And what do you think of those disciples who were sitting around when Judas began complaining about the money being spent on Christ? Did the ruler of this world perhaps think of insinuating himself into their hearts a little? He is always up to his tricks. It is not always in great things like wealth or exalted position that he gets his grip on our hearts, but often by little things here and there. He will move us from 'using' this world, until we love it; and whatever we say with our lips, when given the choice we will choose things rather than Christ.

That is *worldliness*. We can be worldly with very respectable things. Satan can get us to adopt an attitude of heart towards things that are good, lovely, legitimate, or even God-given, until we just take them without allowing them to lead us eventually to God. Our only protection is to live constantly near our Lord and near in spirit to his cross. Rules and regulations will never deliver us from worldliness. What a sad mistake some have made, when, with all goodwill, they have tried to save themselves and their fellow Christians by inventing all sorts of rules.

David Gooding, *Patterns of Praise: Four Studies from Leviticus 23 on The Feasts of the Lord*, 18–19

6th December

A GENTILE ATTITUDE TO OUR WORK

Reading: 1 Thessalonians 2:6–12

*Whatever you do, work heartily, as for the Lord
and not for men. (Colossians 3:23)*

Why do you go to work? 'What a stupid question!' you say. 'I go to work to get food and clothes.' Is that your prime motive? I thought you were regenerate! That is what the Gentiles do (Matt 6:32). When they go to work their prime motivation is food and clothes; what power comes from it, I suppose, and what toys. But surely the prime motivation for a believer to go to work is not to get food and clothes. Eight hours a day are not to be so thrown down the drain.

If I am a believer in Christ, my first-level motivation is that I seek the rule of God in my daily work and the practical righteousness that results from that. The prime purpose in daily work is not merely getting food and clothes. They shall perish—don't we know how soon they perish, and how soon we want some more. What a waste of time, if eight hours a day are given simply and primarily to get things that perish so quickly.

Daily work is the school where I learn to seek the kingdom of God, and his rule in my life. I have learnt in the Bible that I ought to be honest. But learning it in my study is one thing; where shall I practise what I have learned about the need for honesty? 'You will go to work,' says God. 'If you are not inclined to do so, the stomach I have given you will get hungry and then off to work you will go!' In its disciplines we learn to behave honestly, justly, compassionately, unselfishly and caringly for other people. As we work through the hours of the days and the years, the rule of God begins to form in us a Christian character. If I listen to the Lord Jesus, that's why I go to work.

Sometimes the whole motive for going to work can be lost. Here's a Christian man—nobody can deny that he needs clothes, so he goes to work and there comes a temptation to do a shady deal. The worldly man does it, why shouldn't he? He does the shady deal, gets a dozen coats, but has lost the very thing for which the Lord sent him to work—to develop the rule of God in his life. What a tragedy.

David Gooding, *The Lord Saves His People: Fourteen Studies on Understanding the Major Sections of Judges*, 61

7th December

THE BEAUTY OF OUR LORD'S PERFECT SELF-CONTROL

Reading: Matthew 26:36–46

'Watch with me . . . Watch and pray that you may not enter not into temptation. The spirit indeed is willing, but the flesh is weak.' (Matthew 26:38, 41)

They could not watch, and they could not pray. Their eyes were heavy; they struggled and lost control of their bodies and went off to sleep. Suddenly the armed soldiers were upon them. Peter had one sword. Christ had forbidden him to use it, but he could not resist the temptation to try to stop the soldiers; in fact, to try to stop our Lord being killed! It was a natural reaction, but if Peter had succeeded we would all have been lost. He went to cut the man's head off and missed. He just got his ear. It is very difficult to use a sword if you are not used to it, and especially when you have just wakened up!

Against this background, see the beauty of self-control in our Lord. 'Put your sword back into its place. . . . Do you not realize, Peter, that if I had asked my Father, this very moment he would send me more than twelve legions of angels?' (see 26:52–53). Twelve legions of swords, and every one of them superhuman! Was there any temptation to use them? Peter only had one sword and he could not stop himself from using it. What would have happened if he had had twelve legions of them? Our Lord had the self-control to have every one of them sheathed. He could have defended himself against those ungodly and wicked men; but if he had, 'how then should the Scriptures be fulfilled?' (v. 54). That must move our hearts!

As we watch our Lord overcome that temptation in the garden and go on and die for us, we remember that there are Scriptures that we too must fulfil. The danger is that we forget the flesh is weak. If our bodies are to be brought under the control of the Holy Spirit, we must watch and pray (v. 41). 'Be sober-minded; be watchful. Your adversary the devil prowls around like a roaring lion, seeking someone to devour' (1 Pet 5:8).

We may intend to fulfil God's Word, but to do so we shall require the vigorous discipline of prayer to bring our bodies under control. A little sleep, nodding off, becoming careless will mean that before we know where we are temptation is upon us, and we cannot resist it.

David Gooding, *The Battle in Gethsemane: One Study on the Lord Jesus Submitting to His Father's Will*, 5

8th December

BRINGING OUR EMOTIONS UNDER GOD'S CONTROL

Reading: Mark 14:32–36

And he said to them, 'My soul is very sorrowful, even to death. Remain here and watch.' (Mark 14:34)

Emotions are difficult things to control. Peter had told the Lord Jesus, 'If I must die with you, I will not deny you' (v. 31). He probably thought he meant it, but he had not a clue as to the preparations necessary to face it.

How different our Lord was. He did not come running into the garden saying, 'God, I am ready for anything you want. This cup—yes, I will drink it; I will do anything you ask!' In that cup was the wrath of God against our sins. Did he want to do it? Certainly not! The very thought caused sweat to run down his cheeks until it dropped off heavily like drops of blood. All the emotions of his being were against doing it. It was with honesty that he prayed in the garden, 'Abba, Father, all things are possible for you. Remove this cup from me' (v. 36). He meant it. Emotionally he did not want to do it, but the will of God meant that he must do it. So he prayed, 'Not what I will, but what you will' (v. 36). That is how we should handle our emotions. We thank God for giving us all the lovely tasks we enjoy doing, and there would be something wrong with God if his service were always some agonizing experience. But there are tasks to be done that are not pleasant. We must learn to cope with them and control our emotions.

Some of us are very easily put off. We serve the Lord if we feel like it, and if we do not feel like it we do not do it. Instead of being spiritually motivated we become merely emotionally motivated. At the Lord's Supper we know that we should thank the Lord for dying for us, but because we do not really feel like doing it we may feel that it would be a little hypocritical. So we do not do it! How would we feel if we sent someone a present and did not hear from them? They did not thank us because they did not feel like doing so—they didn't know what to say!

There are times when we must learn to go against our emotions. We must obey God's will when we feel like doing it, and when we do not.

David Gooding, *The Battle in Gethsemane: One Study on the Lord Jesus Submitting to His Father's Will*, 6

9th December

CONTROL OF THE WILL

Reading: Luke 22:47–53

*'Father, if you are willing, remove this cup from me.
Nevertheless, not my will, but yours, be done.' (Luke 22:42)*

When they came to arrest him, our Lord Jesus said, 'This is your hour, and the power of darkness' (Luke 22:53). The people who came to arrest him were under the power of Satan. How does Satan maintain his power over people? He tells them that God is a tyrant, and having their own way is freedom.

Listen to the crowd shouting around Pilate. He asks, 'What wrong has he done?' In the end their shouts prevailed. Pilate released Barabbas and handed Jesus over to their will (23:22–25). On the way to Calvary there were women who saw the terrible state of the abused Jesus—his back bleeding, his head crowned with thorns. They mourned and wailed for him: 'But turning to them Jesus said, "Daughters of Jerusalem, do not weep for me, but weep for yourselves and for your children"' (23:28). Did they realize the final result of having their own way? 'Then they will begin to say to the mountains, "Fall on us," and to the hills, "Cover us"' (23:30).

That is where having our own way will lead to. Many people remain unsaved because they think that if they were to be saved they would have to give up their own way. And so they would! 'Let the wicked forsake his way, and the unrighteous man his thoughts; and let him return to the LORD, and he shall have compassion on him' (Isa 55:7).

See Jesus Christ our Lord, the King of kings, on his way to God's throne. He kneels prostrate in prayer, saying, 'Not my will, but yours, be done' (Luke 22:42). He is now exalted, and has gone there in obedience to God by suffering death for our sins. Why should we obey him? Because he never asks us to do anything he has not done himself: 'Son though he was, he learned obedience through what he suffered' (Heb 5:7 DWG).

There may come days of great crisis for us, when to stand for the Lord will be to face great persecution and suffering. But let us resolve before God to control our bodies, our emotions and our wills, and be prepared to do his will—whatever it may be. 'Whoever does the will of God abides for ever' (1 John 2:17).

David Gooding, The Battle in Gethsemane: One Study on the Lord Jesus Submitting to His Father's Will, 6–8

10th December

BRINGING THE GIFT OF SPEECH UNDER THE CONTROL OF CHRIST

Reading: James 3:1–6

He who loves purity of heart, and whose speech is gracious, will have the king as his friend. (Proverbs 22:11)

What a magnificent gift the faculty of speech is. It immediately puts mankind supreme over all the known animals. It is one of the most godlike things about you. It makes us like him who is *the Word* and capable of communion with him.

Hence, the human faculty of speech is one of the highest things in the human personality. Even now that it is injured through sin, what a magnificent gift it is; from the mother cooing to her baby and building up marvellous bonds of love and affection that will last a lifetime, to a Churchill rallying a whole nation in time of war. What a marvellous gift God has given to the evangelist. Power, life and death are in the tongue, when a word spoken can lead a soul to Christ and save that soul for eternity.

It was a cruel thing that Satan did when in a sense he made humans mute; still with the faculty of speech, but estranged from the one who gave it to them. So today we have millions of men and women endowed by the Creator with this glorious faculty of speech, but as far as God is concerned they are absolutely mute. They never speak to him; they never pray to him and they have never known the highest function of speech. Physical muteness is like a prison where the human personality wants to express itself and can't; but the spiritual muteness that Satan has induced in the human race towards its creator is an astounding tragedy. What a magnificent moment it is when you sit beside somebody who has never used the faculty of speech to speak to the Lord, and for the first time a creature uses his godlike gift and talks to the Saviour.

But our troubles are not at an end when first we come to the Saviour. Being one of the highest gifts, the faculty of speech has suffered one of the biggest ruinations. James tells us that, even for a redeemed person, it is one of the most difficult things to bring back under control. Because it is such a high gift, when used right it is full of blessing, but when used wrongly it can be lethal; so he talks to us particularly about the need, if we are to be mature believers, to set about bringing it under the control of Christ.

David Gooding, *A Vision of the Perfect Man and Woman: Seven Studies on Major Themes from James*, 44–5

11th December

HOW DO WE CONTROL THE TONGUE?

Reading: James 3:7–12

For every kind of beast and bird, of reptile and sea creature, can be tamed and has been tamed by mankind, but no human being can tame the tongue. (James 3:7–8)

I have no hope of controlling my tongue by my own unaided human effort; my only resource is in the Saviour and the Holy Spirit. If I realized that more, I should be more on my knees, saying, 'Lord, today I must speak; help me tame my tongue.'

What is the trouble? Our divided nature is the trouble. A fountain can't put out sweet and salty water simultaneously; a fig tree won't produce grapes; a thorn bush won't produce figs. Yet when we speak it is evident that there are very curious contradictions within us still. One minute our tongues are blessing the Lord with all sorts of holy phrases and beautiful songs, the next minute you should hear us when we get bad-tempered, frustrated and jealous. The same tongue that blessed the Father, in bitterness curses our fellow men and women.

Why is it? Facing up to that question could be the beginning of controlling the tongue. We are believers, yet inside we still have those unworthy motivations and emotions. If they are not kept under by the grace of God, they will capture and use our tongues. Hence James finishes his chapter by reminding us that we need *wisdom*, not just *knowledge*.

You can't stand for and preach the truth, if all the while you are being motivated by false motives like pride and party spirit. You can use the truth not merely to state what the word of God teaches, but then to go further and in pride of heart bitterly to denounce any other believer who doesn't yet grasp the truth exactly like you have grasped it. You can train believers to be proud instead of loving their fellow-believers; to introduce harsh differences and loveless attitudes to dear fellow believers in Christ. We must stand by the truth, but may God give us wisdom to know how to use and how to speak that truth.

Says James, 'a harvest of righteousness is sown in peace by those who make peace' (Jas 3:18). If our teaching is guided by unworthy wisdom that comes from below and we use our preaching to foster animosities and strife towards fellow-believers, we may be successful as orators, but one thing we shall never produce is a harvest of righteousness. The fruit of righteousness can only be grown in the soil of peace when it is tended by teachers who aim to make peace.

David Gooding, A Vision of the Perfect Man and Woman: Seven Studies on Major Themes from James, 51–2

12th December

WHEN AND HOW TO SPEAK

Reading: 1 Peter 3:10–12

Let your speech always be gracious, seasoned with salt, so that you may know how you ought to answer each person. (Colossians 4:6)

The law says that I am to love my brothers and sisters as myself. Suppose one of you had fallen into some fault, would you like somebody to be your free advertising agent? If we really loved one another as we should, we wouldn't say more about it than absolute necessity forced us to say.

James discusses the matter of worldliness; and there seems to me to have been few topics where believers speak against each other more than on the question of worldliness. In particular, criticizing what pleasures they allow themselves. Have you noticed that?

I think I can tell you how it comes about! Here is a good man and before he got converted he was head-over-heels into tennis. He had no time for God or anything else. Sometimes after the match he ended up in the pub the worse for wear. When he got converted he came to see that he had wasted his life. From then on he wanted to live for the Lord and he wasn't going to waste his time on tennis, so he decided he wasn't going to play any more tennis. He will give himself full time to the Lord.

Then, over the garden fence, he suddenly sees another brother playing tennis! He decides there is something seriously wrong with his spirituality: he must be worldly. 'I gave that kind of thing up when I got converted,' he says. Then he proceeds to spread it around the earth, 'I saw Mr So-and-So the other day playing tennis!' And so it goes on and someone says, 'He will never preach here again!' Several of us may have been tempted to talk against a brother like that.

Read the inspired apostle's lesson: 'You are not to speak against a brother like that' (see Jas 4:11). But what if he is doing wrong? Well, suppose he is, the Bible says you are not to speak against him; you are to love him. And if you start speaking about him all over the place you are doing worse than ever he could; you are now positively breaking a straightforward commandment. The law says that you shall love your neighbour and that means you will not go around speaking against him. If you don't take the law seriously, you are saying by your behaviour that you are superior to the law.

David Gooding, *A Vision of the Perfect Man and Woman: Seven Studies on Major Themes from James*, 67–8

13th December

HOW WE SHOULD PRAY FOR OUR FELLOW CHRISTIANS

Reading: Ephesians 3:14–19

For this reason I bow my knees before the Father . . . that according to the riches of his glory he may grant you to be strengthened with power through his Spirit in your inner being, so that Christ may dwell in your hearts through faith. (Ephesians 3:14, 16–17)

What Paul is praying for is not some sudden experience but for a process: 'that you may be strengthened with power through his Spirit in your inner being.' God is interested in carrying out a process in my heart, steadily strengthening my inner being by his Spirit. What for? Well, so that Christ may dwell in my heart.

Somebody says, 'But that's curious, because the moment I trusted Christ, Christ came and dwelt in my heart. Why does Paul need to pray for me now that Christ will dwell in my heart?'

The simple answer is this: Paul means here, not merely that Christ should have come in, but that he should take up his residence in every part of your being. Now, for that to happen it will require a process and there are no short cuts to it that I know of. You see, it's one thing to know with my head that Christ is actually in me—I can grasp that. It's another thing to know it so that I am conscious of it in everything I do, every moment of the day,

Have you arrived there yet? I haven't. I get talking with a fellow believer about a difficult passage of Scripture. We're discussing Scripture, so I am indeed very spiritual. Suddenly he disagrees: 'You've got it wrong,' he says. So he must be told the truth, and the stupid man can't see the truth! And then he has a view of his own, and before I know it I get steamed up. I'd quite forgotten for the time being that Christ is meant to be dwelling in my heart as well as his. We've been discussing theology, but Christ is meant to dwell even among theology, let alone when it comes to clearing away the breakfast things or something like that.

It's lovely to have exciting meetings and marvellous feelings. Well, let's hope Christ is in them. It's also good if Christ is in your feelings on a Monday morning and when the business is difficult.

'So that Christ may dwell in your hearts through faith' (v. 17)—to come to that position it will mean my inner self being strengthened. That is a long drawn out process; but God does perform it in the hearts of his people bit by bit, by bit.

David Gooding, *Christ Living in You: One Study on the Gift and Gifts of the Holy Spirit*, 8–9

PART 17

The God of Revelation who Wants to be Known

14th December

GOD IS HIS OWN EVIDENCE

Reading: John 5:31–47

'And the Father who sent me has himself borne witness about me.' (John 5:37)

We should always remember that *God is his own evidence*. That is to say, since he is the Creator, he is the ultimate source of everything. There is no being in the universe who is altogether independent of God and able to give us an independent assessment of God's claims to be God! Neither is there anyone able to provide us with evidence that did not ultimately originate with God himself. God is self-evident; and true faith on our part is our response to God's self-revelation.

And so it is with the Son of God. He is his own evidence. If you wish to provoke faith in him, proclaim him himself. Preach his person, repeat his words and sermons. Relate his deeds and miracles; tell out his virgin birth, his cross, his death, his resurrection. Relay the interpretation that he himself gave of these great events. It is this that creates and draws out people's faith. Of course, like John the Baptist we can each give our own personal testimony to Christ and to what he has done for us. That is certainly valid and helpful, and the Lord will use it to lead other people to himself and to salvation.

But as our Lord himself pointed out, at the ultimate level he does not accept human testimony as though it were some independent source of validation for his claims (5:33–34). There is no such independent evidence, nor can there be. The divine persons themselves are the source of all the evidence that draws out our faith in the Father, the Son and the Holy Spirit.

Perhaps the Samaritans spoke more wisely than they knew, when they said to the woman, 'It is no longer because of what you said that we believe, for we have heard for ourselves, and we know that this is indeed the Saviour of the world' (4:42).

David Gooding, *An Unshakeable Kingdom: The Letter to the Hebrews for Today*, 20–1

15th December

GOD'S REVELATION OF HIMSELF CULMINATING IN CHRIST

Reading: Hebrews 1:1–5

In these last days he has spoken to us by his Son. (Hebrews 1:2)

In the past, God's revelation of himself was piecemeal and progressive. But in Christ it is full and final. In Abraham, for example, God showed how he was prepared to justify anyone who 'believed God' (Rom 4:3–5). But it remained a secret how God could possibly be just and righteous himself and yet declare sinners like Abraham, and us, to be right with God and accepted by him. In Christ and in his death as an atonement for sin, that long-kept secret is now fully revealed (3:25–26).

To cite another example, through the law of Moses God indicated the standard of behaviour he required from mankind. Moses never showed us how such fallen, sinful people could possibly keep that law and meet its requirements. But Christ did (8:2–4). In Christ God says everything he has to say. Christ is God's last word to man and beyond him God has nothing more to say. Nothing more needs saying.

So God's revelation was not only piecemeal, it came in different forms. God showed us something of his sympathetic heart in appointing priests in Israel, and something else about himself and his purposes by instituting kingship. He raised up judges to be the people's deliverers and saviours (Judg 2:18). Then he spoke through sacrifices, rituals and ceremonies. But the priests were at best weak and failing men. The kings were often disobedient to God and tyrannical towards the people. The saviours and deliverers were never totally free from the slavery of sin themselves. The sacrifices, rituals and ceremonies were only symbols, and they could not effect the inner spiritual cleansing which they outwardly symbolized.

But one and all these different modes of revelation pointed forward to Christ, and in him they all unite. What they said partially and indistinctly, he expresses to perfection. He is the perfect priest and the ideal king because he was the unfailingly obedient subject, the sinless Saviour and the supremely effective sacrifice.

David Gooding, *An Unshakeable Kingdom: The Letter to the Hebrews for Today*, 25

16th December

MANIFESTING GOD'S NAME

Reading: Deuteronomy 32:1–4

For I will proclaim the name of the LORD;
ascribe greatness to our God! (Deuteronomy 32:3)

This is not a poem of fiery denunciation. If you only listen to it, it's like a refreshing rain, a gentle dew. Not some avalanche or tornado uprooting everything, but a gentle rain to nurture the tender grass.

What a blessed occupation it is for any preacher of the word to 'proclaim the name of the Lord'. That took Moses back to his initial ordination as he stood by the burning bush and God came down and told him to deliver his people from Pharaoh and bring them to the promised land. Quaking in his shoes, Moses said,

> 'If I come to the people of Israel and say to them, "The God of your fathers has sent me to you," and they ask me, "What is his name?" what shall I say to them?' God said to Moses, 'I AM WHO I AM.' And he said, 'Say this to the people of Israel, "I AM has sent me to you."' God also said to Moses, 'Say this to the people of Israel, "The LORD, the God of your fathers, the God of Abraham, the God of Isaac, and the God of Jacob, has sent me to you." This is my name for ever, and thus I am to be remembered throughout all generations.' (Exod 3:14–15)

As Christians, we can't read it and not remember our blessed Lord as he accounted for his ministry to his Father, a few steps away from Gethsemane and the cross: 'I have manifested your name to the people whom you gave me out of the world' (John 17:6). In our poor perverted world, amongst even Israel that soon would put him to a cross, he came to declare the marvellous, delightful name of God. Having begun his prayer that way, he finished with the same remark: 'I made known to them your name, and I will continue to make it known, that the love with which you have loved me may be in them, and I in them' (17:26).

What an important thing it is for you preachers, pastors, shepherds of God's people and Sunday school teachers to declare the name of God and tell people what God is like. Has it dawned yet on my dull heart that the love with which God loved the Lord Jesus is the love that God has for me?

David Gooding, *With Moses on the Plains of Moab: Six Studies from Deuteronomy on Going Forward with God*, 46

17th December

THE LORD MANIFESTS HIMSELF TO US

Reading: John 21:1–14

That disciple whom Jesus loved therefore said to Peter, 'It is the Lord!' (John 21:7)

He manifested himself to Mary. She was standing broken-hearted at the Lord's empty tomb, when a man she thought was the gardener began to speak to her. It was, of course, the Lord. In this appearance he announced to her the new relationship that he had formed: 'I am ascending to my Father and your Father, to my God and your God' (see John 20:11–17). So real, so vibrant with the energies of eternal life did that relationship become to Mary from that moment onwards, that she abandoned the tomb for ever. She had discovered the reality of the living Lord and the truth of his statement, 'Because I live, you also will live' (14:19). As a result, she and all the other Christian women abandoned any idea of turning the tomb of Christ into a shrine, since people do not make a shrine to somebody who is living.

Simon and some other disciples had been out all night fishing and had caught nothing (21:3). As dawn broke, they saw a stranger standing on the shore. He called across the water and asked if they had any fish. When they shouted back, 'No,' he told them to cast their net on the right side of the boat, and when they did they took an enormous catch. Eventually John realized who the stranger was. 'Peter,' he said, 'it is the Lord!' And it was indeed. The Lord had come to them in the course of their work, and through the success that had attended his guidance he manifested himself to them.

He does the same for us still. We don't see him, and it does not happen every day of the week, or every time we read the Scriptures or on every occasion that we do some work for him. But from time to time in the midst of our studies, life's griefs and duties, true to his promise he comes to us and manifests himself in a way that is overwhelmingly real to our hearts. We sense the glow of his presence, the vibrancy of his life. We hear with the heart's inner ear the rustling of the Shepherd's robes beside us, and we say with deep conviction, 'It is the Lord!'

David Gooding, *In The School of Christ: Lessons on Holiness in John 13–17*, 101–2

18th December

KNOWING GOD

Reading: John 10:1–16

*'I am the good shepherd. I know my own and my own know me,
just as the Father knows me and I know the Father.'* (John 10:14–15)

At the spiritual level knowing God denotes a personal, direct, intimate relationship with God. Other people may help us a great deal to understand things about God; but in order to experience salvation, to have God's law written in our hearts, we must know God personally and directly ourselves. A woman may first come to know of her husband-to-be through the glowing reports of some friend, and the friend may after a while introduce the couple to each other. But if ever the woman is to become the man's wife, there must come a point when the friend gets out of the way and the woman enters a direct and personal relationship with the man.

Moreover, failure to enter such a personal relationship with God is spiritually fatal. Our Lord has himself warned us that when at last he rises up and closes the door, and has to bid those on the outside to depart from him, the reason why they will have to depart will be given in these words, 'I never knew you' (Matt 7:23).

Conversely, of the true believer Christ says, 'I am the good shepherd. I know my sheep and my sheep know me, just as the Father knows me and I know the Father.' And again, 'My sheep hear my voice, and I know them, and they follow me. I give them eternal life, and they will never perish, and no one will snatch them out of my hand' (John 10:14–15, 27–28).

Now the glorious thing about this personal knowledge and relationship with God is that it is not something we have to work up and qualify for by long and rigorous preparatory disciplines. The new covenant offers it as a gift. It is effected by the Holy Spirit in the very heart of every one who trusts Christ. Listen to Paul: 'And because you are sons, God has sent the Spirit of his Son into our hearts, crying, "Abba! Father!"' (Gal 4:6).

When we first trust Christ and become children of God, we are still very immature. We are not yet spiritual adults or even full-grown strong young people; we are nothing but spiritual little children. Yet John says of such, 'I write to you, dear children, because you have known the Father' (1 John 2:13 NIV).

David Gooding, An Unshakeable Kingdom: The Letter to the Hebrews for Today, 162–3

19th December

KNOWING THE 'I AM' IS THE SECRET OF DELIVERANCE

Reading: Exodus 3:7–15

God said to Moses, 'I AM WHO I AM.' And he said, 'Say this to the people of Israel, "I AM has sent me to you."' (Exodus 3:14)

Moses said to God, 'When I go to my people in Egypt and tell them, "The God of your fathers has appeared to me, and has come down to bring you out of Egypt," and they say to me, "Yes, but what is his name?" What might I say?'

What is the personal name of God that tells out his very character and *himself*; and when he divulges it to us it sets up an intimate fellowship, as it is with friends? It's like this. Do you know a Mrs Smith? Yes, there are thousands of Mrs Smiths! But it's when she says to you, 'You may call me by my personal name,' that you count it a privilege and it sets up a relationship.

May I call God by his personal name? That's what is afoot: God's self-revelation of his name, 'I AM THAT I AM'. Knowledge of God as the great I AM—constant, always faithful, who never changes as to his character, who has come now to honour his covenant with Abraham, to bring out his people, set them free and lead them to their inheritance. That name and belief in it would be essential if ever Israel were to break free of Pharaoh. They would need great faith in Moses for him to challenge the almighty Pharaoh, and they would need greater faith in the I AM and the reality of God if they were to escape the claws of the Egyptian monarch. 'Tell them,' says God, 'that my name is I AM THAT I AM.'

Didn't our Lord himself use the same tactics? In the Gospel of John we hear him talking to us about another sinister prince. 'The prince of this world' (KJV), he calls him, who holds people enslaved (see John 12:31; 16:11). What will be the secret of delivering them from his grasp? Among other things, it will be the declaration of the personal name of God. As he gives account of his ministry, our Lord says, 'I have manifested your name to the people whom you gave me out of the world' (17:6). And he says it once more at the end of his prayer, 'I made known to them your name, and I will continue to make it known, that the love with which you have loved me may be in them, and I in them' (17:26).

David Gooding, *Genesis to Joshua: Seven Studies Introducing the Old Testament*, 14

20th December

REAL WORSHIP REQUIRES KNOWLEDGE OF GOD

Reading: Philippians 3:7–11

. . . that I may know him and the power of his resurrection, and may share his sufferings, becoming like him in his death. (Philippians 3:10)

It would seem that adoration of the divine persons proceeds not merely from his gifts, but from those revelations that come from time to time to our spirits when we perceive something about the divine persons. In the Bible when we read of people worshipping, we should notice that they are generally worshipping as a response to some specific glory of God. They are not merely content to say that God is glorious; we all know that. It is some special feature about God that has gripped their hearts and is promoting their worship.

Who am I to criticize, but sometimes one of the reasons our worship is weak is because we are content with *generalisms*. 'How wonderful God is!' Well, we know that, but what were you meaning when you said *wonderful*? Wonderful, in what respect? It would help us to worship more if you specified what it is.

If I may for a moment descend from high levels to low, it could happen that I remark to my friends, 'You should have seen Mr Ponsonby's car this morning, it was a . . . well it was—well it was wonderful!'

They might ask me, 'What was it about the car that was wonderful?'

'Well, it was marvellous. I mean to say, it had four wheels and a steering wheel.'

That doesn't get you very far, does it? The ladies would do better than that. They would say, 'It's a wonderful car. You should have seen the colour tones: a delightful powder blue and seats to match of real leather, and the carpets on the floor were this deep!'

Now they're telling you something about the car, aren't they? Why it is wonderful. And a sixteen-year-old gentleman would have done better than I could. He wouldn't have said it had four wheels; he would have said it has fuel injection and goes from nought to sixty in minus ten seconds, and its rating was this, and so on! Why couldn't I say all those things, and only manage 'it was wonderful'? Because I don't know much about cars, that's the answer.

Why is it that sometimes I can't manage more than to say, 'God is wonderful'? Could it be that I don't live quite near enough to him to see any more detail?

David Gooding, *The Adoration of Christ: Six Studies on the Nature and Practice of Worship*, 11–12

21st December

MYSTERIES REVEALED TO CHILDREN

Reading: Luke 10:21–24

'I thank you, Father, Lord of heaven and earth, that you have hidden these things from the wise and understanding and revealed them to little children.' (Luke 10:21)

The Lord did not feel the slightest sense of disappointment or shame that, after all his immeasurable sacrifice, so far his converts were not even the wise and intelligent of this world but only those who at best could be called intellectual infants. Quite the reverse: it filled him with joy that God in his sovereignty had hidden 'these things' from the intellectual and wise. Christ was observing that the knowledge of God and of his salvation is not one of those things that must yield up its secrets to anyone if only they have sufficient intellectual power to analyse them. Atoms and molecules for instance and all things physical do belong to that lowly level. Granted they are very complicated, and it takes intellectual powers bordering on genius to penetrate their secrets; but that is all it takes, precisely because physical things belong to such a lowly level. Move a little up the scale of things to the level of personhood, and then not all the giant intellects in the world could fully get to know a person simply by using their brains, if that person was unwilling to open up and let themselves be known by communicating their thoughts and feelings.

How much more it is with God. The high mysteries of his person, his mind, his heart, his salvation are infinitely too exalted and wonderful to be penetrated and understood simply by submitting them to a sufficiently powerful intellectual analysis. By God's own choice and decree they remain hidden to the wise. And yet impenetrably mysterious though they are, the next thing that moved Christ to holy joy was his Father's ability and willingness to reveal them to intellectual infants. This was not exclusivism: anyone with the sense to do it can take the position of an infant before God's great mysteries. Nonetheless God's ability and willingness to reveal himself to the humblest of people is an exhilaratingly joyous thing to behold in action. Those of giant intellect often find it virtually impossible to communicate their profound philosophical insights to people of humble intellects. Not God. Take, for instance, the twelve apostles, all of them humble men. On Christ's own admission they were intellectual infants. Yet not only had they grasped profound things about God, and his Son and his salvation, but they had recently been out communicating these things successfully to many of their fellow-men.

David Gooding, *According to Luke: The Third Gospel's Ordered Historical Narrative*, 208–9

22nd December

HOW THE LORD MADE HIMSELF KNOWN AFTER HIS RESURRECTION

Reading: Luke 24:28–35

Then they told what had happened on the road, and how he was known to them in the breaking of the bread. (Luke 24:35)

'He took the bread and blessed and broke it and gave it to them' (Luke 24:30). That inevitably called attention to his hands, and maybe they would have seen the nail marks in his wrists. But afterwards it was not the nail marks which they cited to the apostles as the means by which they had known him, but rather the action of breaking the bread itself. They related how he was known to them 'in the breaking of the bread'.

On two exceedingly significant occasions the Lord had broken bread and distributed it to his disciples. The first was at the feeding of the five thousand (see Luke 9:16). The disciples would never have forgotten the astounding sight as the bread multiplied itself in those hands. What is more, the miracle was subsequently used by the Lord as a parable of the giving of his flesh and blood for the life of the world (see John 6:32–59). Now the stranger, who had just completed a long survey of the Old Testament showing that the divine plan was for Messiah to give his body for his people's sins, took the bread into his hands, blessed, broke and distributed it to them. At once they knew him, for it was an inimitable gesture of self-revelation.

The second occasion had been in the upper room at the celebration of the last Passover and the institution of the Lord's Supper. Cleopas was not present on that occasion; he may not have been present at the feeding of the five thousand either. He would certainly have heard of both. The mysterious talk on both occasions of Christ's giving of his body and blood had obviously not made sense to the apostles let alone to Cleopas, not even after he died, until just now the stranger had demonstrated that the Old Testament was full of prophecies, ceremonies, types and prototypes of Messiah's destined sacrificial self-giving. Now as the stranger once more broke the bread and gave it to them, it all came together and made sense. 'Their eyes were opened and they knew him' (Luke 24:31).

Still today, though at a deeper level, we recognize the authentic Saviour of the world by that same gesture: none other in the world of human history offered up his body for our personal redemption.

David Gooding, *According to Luke: The Third Gospel's Ordered Historical Narrative*, 374–5

23rd December

MAKING CHRIST KNOWN TO OTHERS

Reading: Luke 9:46–50

*'Whoever receives this child in my name receives me,
and whoever receives me receives him who sent me.' (Luke 9:48)*

There was another lesson which Christ had to teach them. When Christ had sent them out on their mission, he had given them power and authority and had impressed on them that it was very important how people received them (see 9:3–5). To reject them was to stand in danger of the judgment of God.

Perhaps it was this, coupled with the degrees of success achieved by the different apostles in their mission, or perhaps the fact that only three of them had been allowed to accompany Christ on the mount of transfiguration, or perhaps it was all these things and more besides—whatever it was, it led them to think that they themselves were important, and then to argue among themselves which of them was the most important.

Christ cured their mistake by pointing out that if he sent a mere child as his representative on some mission or other, it would be equally important whether people received the child or not, as it would be whether they received an official apostle or not. The importance did not reside in the child itself or in the apostles themselves, but in the fact that they represented Christ and Christ represented God.

In this sense there were no degrees of importance. Even the least among them was great, if he represented Christ and the Father. Nor could anyone ever attain to a more magnificent greatness than to represent 'the Majestic Glory' (2 Pet 1:17)—never mind in what lowly mission.

David Gooding, *According to Luke: The Third Gospel's Ordered Historical Narrative*, 180–1

Part 18

The True God who is the God of Joy

24th December

THE LORD'S JOY

Reading: Luke 15:1–7

'I tell you, there will be more joy in heaven over one sinner who repents than over ninety-nine righteous persons who need no repentance.' (Luke 15:7)

To the critics of Christianity, the Lord appeared as too joyful to be truly religious. It was not so much that he was personally jovial, but rather that his religious activities were accompanied with a joyful spirit, almost bordering upon excitement. 'This man', they said in dismay, 'receives sinners and eats with them.' And our Lord did nothing to dispel the thing that seemed to grieve them so much.

This joy that centred around his evangelical activities, he pressed home on the dismayed Pharisees with such parables as the Prodigal Son. He described the return home of the prodigal, not accompanied by him singing and praying, but by singing and dancing and a banquet! This wasn't the way a Pharisee was accustomed to take his religion. Our Lord seemed surprised that they could not perceive what it was that gave him such a great joy.

He said, 'Suppose one of you, being a farmer, lost a sheep. You would go out over the mountains after the lost one, and when you found it and brought it home you would hold a celebration and say, "Rejoice with me for my lost sheep has been found." You would do it if it were your business and your cash. How is it that your joy doesn't carry over into religion? Why do you count it strange that to me it is a joyful thing to sit by the side of a prostitute or tax-collector, and little by little bring them back to God and watch the joy of their spirit as they become reconciled to him?'

Yet they did count it strange, for there was very little room in the religion of the Pharisees for that kind of joy. They were accustomed to the art of proselytizing, but that was merely a matter of changing from one form of religion to another: from being a Greek to becoming a Jew. Pharisees on the whole were strangers to the joy of leading someone personally to God. In consequence, they missed what was one of the chief delights of religion; indeed one of the chief delights of heaven. 'There is more joy in heaven', said Jesus, 'over one sinner who repents than over ninety-nine very religious people who have no need of repentance.'

David Gooding, *The Unexpected Christ: Four Studies on the Person and Character of Jesus*, 31–2

25th December

WHERE WE FIND THE SECRET OF JOY

Reading: John 2:1–11

When the wine ran out, the mother of Jesus said to him,
'They have no wine.' (John 2:3)

Our Lord's first miracle was at a wedding feast in a village called Cana of Galilee, and halfway through the wine ran out. What he did about it was certainly a miracle, but it was evidently meant to be a parable as well. For the wine does run out, and not only at weddings but when it comes to a good many other experiences too. Human relationships that were meant to yield pleasant joys do sometimes break up. Often people find that the goal they were chasing, when at last it is within their grasp, somehow loses its charm. The joy, the wine, runs out.

Our Lord's whole mission would concern itself with human lives from which the joy had run out, and his concern would be to bring that joy back in even greater measure than before. It is interesting to see his way of accomplishing it. He took the water pots that had previously been used in the religious service of the Jews. They were there for religious cleansing. The Lord ordered them to be filled with water, and then turned that water into wine. His gesture is exceedingly significant. At the minimum, what he is saying is that the secret of true joy in life, and in its relationships, is that we should put religion central. It is from true religion that a person's principal joy should spring.

For many people this is a startling thing, for we don't commonly regard religion as life's principal joy. These people at the wedding had been through the religious ceremony, the marriage was solemnized and the time for religion was over. Now they were at the wedding breakfast, so bring on the wine and let joy be unconfined. And it does seem to me that Christ is putting his finger on that very attitude.

It ought not to be that religion is the solemn part, and after that comes the fun and games and the joy. It ought to be that the religious part is the fountain of the principal joy. We notice that those water pots were there for purifying. It wasn't the thing to do, to remind your guests at a wedding breakfast that they needed cleansing and that they needed personally to get right with God. Yet it was precisely the water pots that were there for cleansing that our Lord took, and turned them to the source of the party's greatest joy.

David Gooding, *The Unexpected Christ: Four Studies on the Person and Character of Jesus*, 35

26th December

THE SECRET OF JOY AND THE KNOWLEDGE OF GOD'S ACCEPTANCE

Reading: Psalm 103:1–12

But I have trusted in your steadfast love;
my heart shall rejoice in your salvation. (Psalm 13:5)

Is it not true that our joys in life run out sometimes because of the quirks of our character—our little envies, spites and revenges? Our hidden neuroses, maybe, which we inflict upon our friends until our relationships are strained? Thus it is that the joy of many a marriage runs out, and likewise in many other relationships.

If, therefore, we are to find religion enjoyable, we must face this matter of personal cleansing and what Christ has to say about how salvation can begin to affect our relationships. At Cana, Christ turned the water of cleansing into the wine of enjoyment. He tells us that he has not come to criticize, judge or find fault with us (John 3:17, 12:47). He has come to die for us, that through his sacrifice he might offer God's complete unreserved forgiveness here and now in this life, so that we might discover that God has accepted us as we are, and never will reject us.

It was this that sent the early Christian missionaries around the Roman Empire. They often didn't stop to preach long diatribes against sin, for most of their fellow men and women knew that they were sinners. What they preached was, 'We have found God's Christ: he has died for us, risen again, and God has commanded us to tell people that in his name they may receive absolute forgiveness of sins.' The message was that God loves us while we are yet sinners and receives us just as we are. On the basis of Christ's sacrifice God grants us his acceptance, which is unconditional and undeserved, and independent of our subsequent strivings. When a person grasps that, it begins to set loose the wells of joy within them.

To know that they are accepted by God; to be assured from the Saviour himself that, because of his sacrifice they shall never come into judgment. To know that Christ's sacrifice has cleansed their guilt and that God can receive them in all realism. To be sure that because God still loves them and Christ has died for them, they shall never be rejected. To know, therefore, that God's love for them does not even depend on their spiritual progress; that they are accepted by God, and will forever remain accepted. Thus it is that when people first discover it, it sets their hearts aflame with joy.

David Gooding, *The Unexpected Christ: Four Studies on the Person and Character of Jesus*, 37

27th December

JOY THAT DEATH IS NOT THE END AND ADVENTURE AWAITS

Reading: Revelation 21:15–27

You have come . . . to the assembly of the firstborn who are enrolled in heaven. (Hebrews 12:22–23)

Life has an unhappy way of introducing us early to its pains and frustrations. When we see what life could be if only it were not for human pig-headedness and stupidity; if only it were not for disease; if only it were not for sin. When I see what life could be, then the idea that this majestic thing must end in the grave is a depressing thought.

It would surely be supreme among the joys of life, if a person could be sure that there was a life to come. If they knew that there was indeed some scheme worthy of all their powers and ambitions; a divine programme that would make this life meaningful as a preparatory school to qualify us for the subsequent enjoyment. 'In this rejoice,' said our Lord, 'that your names are written in heaven' (see Luke 10:20). There is such a future and your part in it is guaranteed.

It was one of the early Christians' principal joys. In the midst of persecution under Nero the Christian church comforted themselves with this consideration, that their future not only held joy, but it held no ultimate terror. They looked with calmness at the prospect of the final great judgment, for they were taught that the thing that shall determine a person's destiny is whether or not their name is written in the Lamb's Book of Life. It was our Lord himself who told us that we could be utterly certain in this life that our names are in that book. Therefore, the future held no terror for them, but rather joy.

It was a certainty and a joy that gave meaning not only to the joys of this life, but to its sorrows too. For if there is an eternity of glorious achievement and adventure with God; if there is a destiny worthy of God for redeemed humanity; then even life's pains are worth enduring. In the good hand of God, if those pains could be turned to teach us valuable lessons and shape the development of our characters, then might we not even find cause for thankful rejoicing in our suffering?

David Gooding, *The Unexpected Christ: Four Studies on the Person and Character of Jesus*, 38–9

28th December

WHY SOME PEOPLE MISS THE JOY

Reading: Matthew 11:11–19

'We played the flute for you, and you did not dance;
we sang a dirge, and you did not mourn.' (Matthew 11:17)

You will remember our Lord's conversation with the Pharisees when he likened them to children sitting in the market place, shouting to their playmates. He said to them, 'John came to you preaching his stern gospel of repentance and hell fire, and you didn't like that. Then I came along with my delightful message of God's love and forgiveness, and you didn't like that either.' How strange it was! Christ was likening himself, therefore, to the piping and the dancing. A lovely description of our Lord's ministry.

He came with a message of forgiveness so full and so free that it was like the piping of children for sheer exuberant enjoyment of life—their shoulders didn't yet carry any cares. That's what Christ's gospel was like, a thing of sheer joy. 'I came to you with this glad message of God's forgiveness and the gift of eternal life; the certainty of God's acceptance and the glory and majesty of the destiny of the redeemed; and you didn't want it.'

Why didn't they want it? The question is relevant even now. Why is it that so much religion still will not have it that a person can be certain that they are right with God and sure of God's heaven? Perhaps the answer is the same now as it was then. The Pharisees could not altogether see that they had any need of such salvation. Had they not been circumcised at eight days old? Hadn't they been dedicated in their lives according to their Jewish religion? They rejected the implications of John's preaching that they too, along with the prostitute, needed to repent and be saved. They would have admitted to the odd minor sin here and there; but surely nothing serious enough to warrant God's wrath?

And therefore, not granting the first part, they saw no need for the second—the gift of personal salvation and eternal life. So they missed its joy and gladness and were content with the round of religious tradition. In Christ's estimation, for all their excellent self-discipline, they had but the shell of true religion without its life. They had its external image, but they had missed the fountain of its true joy.

David Gooding, *The Unexpected Christ: Four Studies on the Person and Character of Jesus*, 39–40

29th December

THE OLDER BROTHER STANDING AWAY FROM THE CELEBRATION

Reading: Luke 15:11–32

And he said to him, 'Son, you are always with me, and all that is mine is yours.' (Luke 15:31)

The older brother's grievance was that he had worked like a slave for his father for many years and had never got anything out of it to rejoice over with his friends, not even so much as a young goat. Yet his brother, who had wasted his father's resources in disgraceful debauchery, had only to come home to be given the calf which the family kept fattened up ready for a special celebration. That was to reward sin and selfishness, and to penalize honest endeavour.

The Pharisees felt the same about Christ's gospel of forgiveness and salvation by grace. They had honestly toiled hard to keep God's commandments. Like the elder brother they were proud of their record; but it had never brought them any joy, sense of acceptance with God or any assurance of salvation. How could it? Salvation and acceptance with God can never be enjoyed on those terms. Yet here were some of these tax-gatherers and sinners who had broken practically every commandment, and now through simple repentance and faith they were enjoying the welcome of Christ, and sensed the very kiss of God's acceptance in their hearts. It made the Pharisees angry and they had to brand it as bogus.

The parable conveys another answer to the Pharisees' criticism. Astonished at his elder son's sense of grievance the father pointed out that in welcoming home the prodigal, he had not penalized the elder son in any way or robbed him of what was his. 'All that I have', he said, 'is yours.' But that did not pacify him. 'All these years I have slaved for you,' he said, and he had a slave's mentality. He had no feeling of being the heir to all the father had, simply because through no merit of his he was the son of his father. Like a slave he thought only of earning everything for himself by his own hard work. Generosity to a bankrupt but repentant prodigal was to him not an expression of his undeserved wealth as the heir of all the father had, but the squandering of hard-won earnings which he could not afford to give away. He would not join in the joy of a banquet provided at such expense.

For similar reasons, many still intentionally shut themselves out of the possibility of sharing with God the joys of redemption both now and hereafter.

David Gooding, *According to Luke: The Third Gospel's Ordered Historical Narrative*, 285–6

30th December

FACING TRIALS WITH JOY

Reading: Matthew 13:3–9, 18–23

Count it all joy, my brothers, when you meet trials of various kinds, for you know that the testing of your faith produces steadfastness. (James 1:2–3)

James's advice must sound exceedingly strange, when you first hear it. When you fall into trials so severe that they will penetrate to the depths of your heart and show whether you are a believer or not, how could you possibly count it all joy?

I have often come down to an examination hall in my university and outside were hundreds of students about to face their final examination with all that would depend on that. This was finals and nobody that I have known has counted it all joy. How could they? For the simple reason that they couldn't have known whether they would pass until the examiners pronounced their verdict.

Listen to James, 'Count it all joy . . . for you *know* . . .' Mark the verb for this is the secret of facing such a trial with joy. We can face it, knowing on God's authority that the trying, the proving of our faith produces endurance, perseverance. It doesn't simply mean that it turns us into persevering men and women. This is the word that the Lord Jesus used in that famous parable in Luke 8, 'But the *seed* in the good soil, these are the ones who have heard the word in an honest and good heart, and hold it fast, and bear fruit with perseverance' (Luke 8:15 NASB). With perseverance—not with patience, as distinct from impatience. Some of God's good saints are horribly impatient! We are talking here about the good seed that grows and brings forth fruit with perseverance, endurance.

There is only one way known in this life to bring forth fruit in a plant. That is, if the plant persists in growing through the rainy days and the sunny days, through the wind and the calm, in the end it brings forth fruit. The same forces that would destroy a plant that had no root contribute to the maturing and the fruitfulness of a plant that has a root.

As we face trials that will test whether we are believers or not we are to count it all joy, for we have it on the authority of God himself that trials produce endurance and in that confidence we can go through the storm. Those students wouldn't have looked so worried if they could have been sure that they would come through the test with flying colours!

David Gooding, A Vision of the Perfect Man and Woman: Seven Studies on Major Themes from James, 7–8

31st December

A NEVER FAILING SOURCE OF JOY

Reading: John 14:28–31

'I am going away, and will I come to you. If you loved me, you would have rejoiced, because I am going to the Father, for the Father is greater than I.' (John 14:28)

We must ask in what sense his going could possibly prove a source of joy, and what he meant when he said, 'The Father is greater than I.' The two things are linked.

As to his essential nature, our Lord was equal with the Father; but during his life on earth our Lord was not on equal terms with the Father. He had voluntarily subjected himself to the limitations of a human body, which could only be in one place at any given time. The Father is not thus limited. Moreover, Christ could not be in his disciples while he was confined to the body of flesh and blood that he had then. The Father had no such limitation.

The glory of the new situation would lie in two things.

One, our Lord was going to the Father with all that that would mean in terms of the glorification of his human body and release from the limitations of earthly life.

Two, he would come to them and he would no longer be tied to one place at a time, or to one person at a time. Like the Father, he would be able to be present in all his people everywhere, at every moment and in every circumstance.

Sometimes we may feel that it would be better for us if we could have the Lord physically with us, as he was with the apostles during his life on earth. But that feeling is mistaken. It is no insult to the apostles to remember that while the Lord was physically with them on earth their behaviour at times left very much to be desired. For instance, Peter's grossest failure occurred not after the Lord had left the apostles and gone back to heaven, but while he was still with them on earth. We are now in fact in an infinitely better situation than the apostles were then. For, having gone to the Father and come to us by his Spirit, the Lord is nearer to us than ever he could have been to the apostles before Calvary. He is constantly with us in a way that was impossible when he was physically present on earth. And this is, by definition, a source of joy that can never be taken from us.

David Gooding, *In The School of Christ: Lessons on Holiness in John 13–17*, 109–10

Index of Daily Readings and Key Verses

Note: Page numbers for daily readings are shown in **bold** type, key verses in **grey bold** type. All other references (excluding those found within the daily reading) are shown in *italic*.

OLD TESTAMENT

Genesis
1   *137*
1:5   **62**
1:26–31   **61**
1:26–30   *236*
1:26   *61*
1:27   **60**
2:17   *137*
2:18   *269*
3:4–5   *258*
3:5   *172*
3:15   *174*
3:21   *299*
4:1–16   **299**
8:9   *7*
8:15–22   **75**
12:1–9   **238**
12:1   *238*
12:3   *251*
15   *323*
15:6   *129*
16   **334**
17:1   *340*
17:9–11   *340*
22   *129*
22:1–8   **21**
22:5   *21*
22:9–14   **348**
22:14   *348*
22:15–19   **339**
24:10–27   **110**
24:26–27   *110*
28:10–22   **86**
28:17   *86*
32:10   *196*
37:1–11   **271**
37:12–20   *271*
40:14, 23   *271*
41:37–57   **330**
41:52   *271*
49:10   *280*

Exodus
2:1–10   **278**
2:2   *278*
3:1–6   **279**
3:2b   *279*
3:7–15   **394**
3:8   *206*
3:14–15   *391*
3:14   *394*
4:11   *66*
4:1–19   **52**
5:1–9   **305**
12:33–36   **338**
14:10–28   **150**
14:19–20   *150*
15:22–27   **368**
15:26   *369*
17:16   *101*
25:21–22   *45*
25:22   *118*
25:23–30   **361**
28:36–38   *221*
32   **157**
32:4   *338*
32:26   *157*
34:6   *194*
40:1–5   **357**
40:17–38   **10**

Leviticus
2:4–13   **183**
4:14–17   **359**
16   **118**
19:18   *121*
26:11–13   *147*
26:13   *82*

Numbers
6:22–27   *145*
14:39–15:2   **288**
19   *297*
22–24   *145*

Deuteronomy
4:7   **240**
5:12–15   *82*
6:7   *140*
11:26–28   *239*
12:5   *46*
20:11   *156*
32:1–4   **391**
32:3   *391*

Joshua
2:11–12   *319*
2:12–21   **155**
2:12   **155**
4:15–24   **320**
6:8–14   **319**
6:15–25   **192**
9:3–27   **156**
10:11   *281*
10:16–28   **281**
24:2   *238*
24:15   *134*

Judges
2:18 390
4:14 **173**
5 **173**
5:12 372
6:11–24 **47**
6:24 47
6:25–32 **134**
7:15–25 **165**
11:13 187

Ruth
1:16 **125**
2 **125**
3:8–18 **329**
4:13–22 **280**
4:14 280
4:18–22 155

1 Samuel
1:6–8 97
1:11 97
1:21–28 **231**
2:1–10 **97**
2:22–25 **222**
2:35 96
4:21 231
5 231
6:10, 12 231
9:1–24 **99**
10:8 100
13:5–7 **100**
13:8–14 100
13:14 74, 106
15:1–23 **101**
15:22 101
17:4–24 **179**
17:45 179
20 74
20:5–23 **178**
27:1–4 179

2 Samuel
1:5–16 **87**
2:10–28 **70**
6:1–7 **54**
6:13–23 154
6:22 154
7 273
7:1–16 **147**
7:6 147
9:1–11 **74**
9:1 74
10:1–6 **187**
10:2 187
12:1–14 **106**
14:12–21 **119**
19:9–24 **158**

1 Kings
1:1–10, 33–34 275
1:38–53 **275**
6 46
7:21 198
8:1–10 **43**
8:13 273
12:4, 16 81
12:25–33 **46**
17:8–16 336
18 245
18:18–39 **53**
18:21 117
18:37 296
18:38 296

2 Kings
17:22–23 46
18:9–16, 32–35 **198**
19:15 198

1 Chronicles
2–3 266
6:31–50 **266**
11:1–9 **40**
11:2 151
11:3 39
13:6 43
15:2 154
15:13 54
15:15 154
15:16–28 **253**
17:13 11
21:1–17 **166**
21:15–22:1 **167**
21:24 167
22:5 180, 256
22:10 256
29:1–9 **256**
29:20 **266**
29:23 98, 237

2 Chronicles
6:1–11 **273**
6:6 241
6:12–42 274
6:18–21; 7:1–4 **11**
6:41–42 274
6:41 273
10:1–11 **81**

Ezra
3:11–4:4 **227**

Nehemiah
2:17–20 **228**
13:1–9 187

Job
1:6–12 **107**
38:12–21 **62**

Psalms
2:9–12 177
8 **60**
8:4–6 9
8:4–5 146
8:5 236
13:5 **403**
16:11 226
20:7 99
22:22 221
23 216
23:2–3 67
27:4 357
32:1–2 307
40:6–8 **298**
42 **18**
42:1 **18**
45 33
45:1–9 **191**
45:4 191

INDEX OF DAILY READINGS AND KEY VERSES

Psalms (cont.)
51   106
68:18   372
75:3   52
94:3–11   **117**
96   **293**
96:11–13   293
98:8–9   293
103:1–12   **403**
103:12   306
103:13–22   **194**
110   **242**
137:2   216
139:23–24   102

Proverbs
3:6   108
8:17   337
11:2   179
21:3   100
22:11   383

Isaiah
6:1–8   **218**
6:1   218
6:9–12   218
25:6–9   244
35:3–6   351
38:17   306
40–48   51
40   218
40:3   250
41:8   51
43:1–4   **51**
43:1   51
43:13, 21   51
44:21–23   **306**
45:20–25   **240**
45:22   53
46:1–7   **55**
46:4   55
46:5–13   **235**
49:1–7   **349**
49:3   349
50:4–8   **8**
51:12–16   **65**
51:13   65

53   218
53:1–5   **14**
53:3–5   148
53:5–12   **296**
53:6   149
53:12   146
55:1–5   **353**
55:7   382
61:1–3   351
61:1   311
62:3   289
64:6   362
65:17–25   **57**

Jeremiah
9:23–24   **176**
15:16   **163**
17:9   313
29:13   109, 337
31:31–36   **314**
31:31   193
31:34   314

Ezekiel
11:16–20   **313**
28:14   166
34:11–16   **108**

Daniel
3:16–30   **283**
3:28   283
4   216
8:12   197
10:1   241
11:28–35   **241**
12:5–13   **282**
12:13   282

Hosea
11:8   216

Joel
2:25   66

Micah
4:1–5   145
5:2   145

6:1–8   **145**
7:18–19   306
7:20   **145**

Habakkuk
2:18   338

Haggai
1:1–15   **224**
1:9   224
2:1–9   **262**
2:3–4   262
2:9   227
2:10   224
2:20–23   **90**
2:20   224
2:23   90

Zechariah
1:1–6   **229**
1:5   229
1:16   287
2:1–13   **287**
2:5   44
3:1–4   **219**
3:1   220
3:2   220
3:3   219
3:4   220
3:5–10   **220**
3:5   221
3:7   221, 222
3:8   289
4:1–10   **223**
4:6   164
4:9   223
5:1–4   **230**
6:13   68
6:9–14   **289**
7:8–14   **216**
8:11–13   **215**
9:9   68
10:6   216
11:13   69
12:10–13:3   **69**
12:10–13:1   148
12:10   **14, 69, 255**

Zechariah (cont.)
14:5–11 **217**
14:16 *69*
14:20 **217**
14:21 **217**

Malachi
1:6–14 **136**
1:6 **136**
2:7, 13–14 *136*
4:5 *255*

NEW TESTAMENT

Matthew
1:1–6 **341**
1:5–6 *155*
3:13–17 **7**
4:3–4 *139*
4:9 *87*
4:10 *87*
5:17–20 **373**
5:19 *101*
5:45 *5*
6:9–10 *330*
6:19–24 **276**
6:26–34 **137**
6:32 *379*
7:13–14 *84*
7:23 *393*
10:30 *70*
11:1–10 **116**
11:11–19 **405**
11:17 **405**
11:29–30 *81*
11:30 *81*
12:12 **302**
13:3–9, 18–23 **407**
14:8 *72*
14:22–36 **22**, **94**
14:33 **22**
16:13–20 **92**
16:18 **92**
16:24–17:9 **265**
16:25 **265**
17:1–8 *94*
17:1–5 **6**
17:15–19 *94*
17:24–27 **23**
18:15 *23*
18:20 *45*
19:27–30 **277**
19:28 *284*
19:29 **277**
20 *104*
22:37–40 *121*
22:37–38 **133**
23:37–38 *44*
25:30 *285*
25:31 *284*
25:46 *141*
26:17–29 **358**
26:24 **178**
26:28 *315*
26:36–46 **380**
26:38, 41 **380**
26:47–56 **72**
26:52–54 *380*
27:4, 24 *72*
27:46 *296*
28:18 *67, 81*

Mark
1:8 **25**
2:1–12 **344**
2:11 **344**
2:16 *114*
9:12 *255*
10:35–45 **161**
10:41–45 **68**
14:31 *381*
14:32–36 **381**
14:34 *381*
14:36 *358*

Luke
3:1–6 *250*
3:16–17 *116*
3:22 *7*
4:4, 8, 12 *209*
4:16–21 **311**
4:18 **116**
4:22–29 **336**
4:26 **336**
5:10 *26*
5:17–26 *306*
5:20 *307*
5:33–39 **20**
5:33 **20**
7:6 *243*
7:18–23 *116*, **351**
7:20 **351**
7:28 *250*
7:36–50 **309**, *310*
7:36–38 **308**
7:42 *306*
7:47 **309**
8:1–3 **310**
8:15 *407*
8:40–56 **243**
9:3–5 *398*
9:10–17 **244**
9:16 *397*
9:27 *294*
9:28–36 **245**
9:31 *294*
9:46–50 **398**
9:48 **398**
10 *104*
10:16 *200, 203*
10:17–23 **131**
10:20 *131*, **373**, *404*
10:21–24 **396**
10:21 **396**
12:1–3 *352*
12:4–12 **352**
12:7 **352**
12:35–40 **33**
12:42–48 **88**
12:45–46 *205*
13:1–5 *59*
13:4–5 *59*
13:10–17 **82**
13:16 **82**
13:31–35 **148**
13:34 *148*
14:1–6 **302**
14:25–33 **343**
14:27 *343*
15:1–7 **401**
15:7 **401**

INDEX OF DAILY READINGS AND KEY VERSES

Luke (cont.)
15:11–32 **406**
15:31 **406**
16:1–13 **286**
16:19–31 **270**
16:23 *141*
16:26 **261**
17:12 *335*
17:20–21 *159*
18:1–8 *71*
18:9–14 **335**
18:11–12 *129*
18:13 **335**
18:15–17 **159**
18:16 *159*
18:35–43 **71**
18:38 *71*
19:1–10 **129**
19:9 *129*
19:10 *206, 308*
19:11–19 **93, 284**
19:20–27 **285**
19:26 **285**
20:16 **301**
22:16 *245*
22:19–23 **39**
22:19–20, 22 *74*
22:25 *161*
22:26 *161*
22:28–34 **248**
22:29–30 *33*
22:31–34 *325*
22:31 *107*
22:32 *225, 324*
22:42 *69, 149, 358, 382*
22:47–53 **382**
22:54–62 **325**
22:64 *303*
23:22–25 *382*
23:28 *382*
23:30 *382*
23:42–43 *322*
24:13–27 **132**
24:15 *132*
24:28–35 **397**
24:35 **397**
24:36–39 *152*
24:39 **152**
24:44–49 **307**
24:46–47 *195*
24:47 *241*
24:50–52 *22*

John
1:1–9 **3**
1:1–3 *45*
1:1 **3**
1:12 *181*
1:14–18 **45**
1:14 *6, 10, 114, 370*
1:18 *4, 13*
1:29 *117*
1:32–34 *7*
1:42 *325*
2:1–11 **402**
2:3 **402**
3:17 *403*
3:6–7 *181*
3:6 *334*
4 *135*
4:21–24 *297*
4:42 *389*
5:16–20 **4**
5:19 **5**
5:21–30 **5**
5:24 *327*
5:31–47 **389**
5:37 *389*
6:25–40 **115**
6:32–59 *397*
6:37 *128*
6:38 **115**
6:45 *203*
6:62 *360*
7:37–44 **19**
7:37 **19**
8:14–29 **304**
8:32 *84*
8:42–47 **30**
8:46 *191*
9 *350*
9:1–12 **66**
10:1–16 **393**
10:14–15 *393*
10:27–28 *393*
10:28–29 *150*
11 *243*
11:9–10 *62*
11:16 *337*
11:34–39 *297*
12:4–11 **378**
12:24 **271**
12:31 *378, 394*
12:47 *403*
13:1–15 **375**
13:6–11 *225*
13:15 **375**
13:16–20 **205**
13:20 *200, 203, **205***
13:34 *121*
13:36–14:3 **225**
14:1–3 *254*
14:1 *36*
14:3 *12, **253**, **360***
14:6 *199*
14:8–10 *24*
14:12 *94*
14:15–22 **12**
14:16–17 **12**
14:19 *27, 392*
14:21 *27*
14:23–27 **27**
14:28–31 **408**
14:28 *408*
14:30 *378*
15:1–8 **32**
15:5 *160*
15:7 **32**
15:9–17 **123**
15:12 **123**
15:14 **124**
15:15 *160*
15:16 *51*
16:1–4 **210**
16:2 **210**
16:11 *378, 394*
16:13–14 *12*
16:19–28 **130**
16:19–22 *20*
16:25–33 *304*
16:27 **130**

INDEX OF DAILY READINGS AND KEY VERSES

John (cont.)
16:28   304, 346
16:31–32   346
16:33   *151*
17:5   *360*
17:6–12   **24**
17:6   *391, 394*
17:7–8   **205**
17:8   *132*
17:11   **24**, *132*
17:20–26   **17**
17:21   **17**
17:22–24   *24*
17:26   *391, 394*
18:28   *378*
18:37–38   *191*
18:37   **196**
19:10   *191*
19:20   *241*
19:30   *246*
19:34   *45*
20:10–18   **247**
20:11–17   *392*
20:17   **247**
20:24–29   **337**
20:29   *337*
21:1–14   **392**
21:7   *392*
21:15–19   **324**

Acts
1:1–11   **152**
1:5   *250*
1:11   *253, 254*
2:1–13   **250**
2:3   *301*
2:14–36   **301**
2:36–42   **342**
3:21   *217*
4:12   *195*
4:32   *106*
5:1–16   **44**
6:15   *153*
7:2–3   *251*
7:44–53   **195**
7:40–56   **153**
7:56   **153**
8:26–39   *206*
9:1–19   **251**
9:3   *251*
9:5   *206*
9:10–22   **207**
9:15–16   *350*
9:15   *251*
9:19b   **207**
9:20–31   **350**
10:34–48   **362**
10:35   **362**
10:43   *307*
12:1–18   **252**
13:23   *300*
13:26–43   **300**
13:38–39   *83*
13:38   *307*
13:39   **300**
15:1–11   **83**
15:10   *83*
16:11–15   **109**
16:16–40   **73**
17:30–31   *177*
19:5   *209*
19:12   *373*
19:13–20   **209**
19:15   **209**
19:23–37   **204**
19:37   **204**
20:17–27   **141**
20:22–23   **141**
20:28   *56*
21:10–14   **184**
21:13   *184*
22:25   *184*
26:9   *350*
26:12–23   **206**
27:13–38   **56**
28:1–10   **59**

Romans
1:1, 3   *195*
1:18–28   *333*
1:23   *259*
3:21   *300*
3:21–31   **294**
3:25–26   *390*
3:26   *294*
4:3–5   *390*
4:4–25   **239**
4:7–8   *307*
5:1–5   **364**
5:5   *364*
5:6–11   **113, 128**
5:6–10   *123*
5:6   **128**
5:8–9   *295*
5:8   **113**
5:19   *316, 321*
6:1   *84*
6:5   *162*
6:7–8   **320**
7:18   *225*
8:1–5   **365**
8:1   *103, 150, 369*
8:2–4   *390*
8:4   *312*
8:5   **365**
8:7   *177, 313, 334*
8:9–11   **41**
8:9   *340*
8:13–15   *105*
8:15   **105**
8:17   *181, 284, 341*
8:18–22   **269**
8:19   *290*
8:20–21   *301*
8:21   *217*
8:28   **225**
8:33–34   *35*
8:38–39   *56*
10:17   *209*
11:26   *69*
11:30–32   *333*
12:1   *97, 231, 283, 359*
14:5–9   **374**
14:5–8   **139**
14:8   **139**

Romans (cont.)
16:26 *374*

1 Corinthians
1:2 *207*
1:4–17 **34**
1:8 **34**
1:9 **33**
1:10–20 **175**
1:12–13 *176*
1:18–31 & Eph
  2:19–22 **180**
1:18 *296*
1:20–24 *174*
1:25 **174, 179**
1:27 *164*
1:30–31 *175*
2:4–6 *186*
2:4–5 **175**
2:6–8 *173*
2:7 **186**
2:9–16 **186**
2:9 **287**
3:1–9 **164**
3:10 *164*
3:15 *295*
3:16–17 *250*
3:16 *43*
4:1–7 **176**
4:6–13 **138**
5:7 *246*
5:8 *358*
6:2–3 *284*
6:9–11 **297**
6:11 *341*
6:19–20 *172*
6:19 *250*
10:1–2 *150*
10:13 *282*
10:17 *39*
11:3 *8*
11:27–32 **102**
11:28 **102**
11:31–32 *312*
12:11–13 **25**

12:13 *207*
12:27–31 **122**
13 **121**
14:1 **122**
14:12 *89*
15:12–17 *200*
15:20–28 **9**
15:26 *321*
15:28 **9**
15:56 *321*

2 Corinthians
1:3–11 **48**
1:3 **48**
2:12–17 **185**
2:14 **185**
2:17 *150*
3:12–18 **13**
3:17 **13**
3:18 *18*
4:4 *304*
4:6 *165*
4:7 **165**
4:10–11 *165*
4:13–18 **182**
4:17 **182,** *367*
4:18 **270**
5:6–8 **321,** *322*
5:8 *249, 286*
5:14–15 *156*
5:17 *51, 150*
10:17 **138**
11:2–3 *275*
11:2 *155*
11:13, 26 *205*

Galatians
1:4 **305**
2:4 *205*
2:20 *31, 72, 132*
3:10–14 **295**
3:16 *323*
4:1–7 **31**
4:6 *393*
4:8–11, 28–31 **105**

4:26 *287*
5:13 **156**
5:16–23 **366**

Ephesians
1:3–10 **268**
1:4 **361**
1:10 **269**
1:11–14 **326**
1:13–14 **326**
1:13 *126*
1:15–23 **89**
1:18 **268,** *290*
1:20–23 *9*
1:22–23 *91*
2:1–6 *150*
2:1–5 **261**
2:1–2 *40*
2:1 *297*
2:5–6 **295**
2:6–18 **316**
2:7 *93*
2:8–9 *343, 347*
2:8 *295*
2:10 *51,* **310**
2:13–15 *40*
2:14 **329**
2:18 *153*
2:19–22 & 1 Cor
  1:18–31 **42, 180**
2:21–22 **256**
2:22 *42*
3:7–13 **171**
3:10 **171**
3:14–19 **386**
3:14, 16–17 **386**
3:16–17 *42*
3:17–19 *43*
4:7–16 **367**
4:7–13 **372**
4:11–16 **95**
4:13 *367*
4:15 *372*
4:32 *303*
5:1–21 **371**

Ephesians (cont.)
5:1 **371**
5:1–2 **135**
5:25–27 **131**

Philippians
1:1 *160*
1:6 *223*
1:19–26 **322**
1:23 *321*
2:5–12 **146**
2:5–7 *8*
2:6–8 *174*
2:7–8 *9*
2:9–10 *149*
2:12–18 **274**
3:3 *239*
3:5 *251*
3:7–11 **395**
3:10 *395*
3:12–21 **272**
3:12–14 *228*
3:14 **272**
3:20–21 *295, 321*
3:20 **252**
3:21 *152, 288*
4:14–20 **135**

Colossians
1:12–17 **58**
1:16 *58, 91*
1:17 **235**
1:18–20 **36**
1:18 *91*
1:20 *9, 57*
1:21–23 **177**
1:21 **177**
1:24–29 *91*
1:27 *41*
2:8–12 **340**
2:9 *11*
2:11 *340*
2:13–19 **151**
2:13–15 *281*
2:18–23 *272*
2:20–3:4 *320*

3:5 **281**
3:11 **40**
3:22–25 *277*
3:23 **379**
4:1 *88*
4:6 *385*

1 Thessalonians
2:6–12 **379**
4:13–17 *243*
4:13 **322**
4:14–18 *254*
4:14–17 **360**
4:14 *243*
4:16–17 *322*
4:16 *150*
5:9–10 *295*
5:8–9 *327*

2 Thessalonians
1:7–10 *116*
2:1–4 **197**
2:4 *258, 259*
2:5–12 **259**
2:8 **197**
2:9 *202*
2:13–17 **160**
2:14 *160*

1 Timothy
1:12–16 **333**
1:13 **333**
2:4 *75*
2:5 **359**
3:15 *53*
4:10 *350*
6:12 *274*
6:15 *275*
6:17–19 *286*
6:17 *137*
6:19 *286*

2 Timothy
1:13–18 **104**
2:8–13 **290**
2:12 *284, 341*

4:1–5 **199**
4:2 *199*
4:7 *158*
4:10 *265*

Titus
1:2 *192*
3:1–8 **76**
3:5 *76, 363*

1 Peter
1:6–9 *311*
1:6–7 *183*
1:17 *103*
1:20 **245**
2:5 *325*
2:9–12 **96**
2:9 *160*
2:21–24 **303**
2:21 *181*
2:23 *303*
2:24 *23, 103*
2:25 **276**
3:9 *303*
3:10–12 **385**
3:13–21 **77**
3:18 *73, 119*
4:1 *229*
4:13 *368*
5:8 *380*
5:10 **215**

2 Peter
1:3–8 *284*
1:3–4 *313*
1:5–7 *228*
1:10–11 *284*
1:11 *228*
1:17 *398*
2:1–10 **203**
2:1 *205*
2:6 *59*
2:12–16 **84**
2:17–22 **363**
3:9 *351*
3:10 *301*

2 Peter (cont.)
3:13 *58*

Hebrews
1:1–5 **390**
1:1–2 *257*
1:2–3 *10*
1:2 *256, 390*
1:3 *57, 90*
1:8–9 *33*
2:1–4 **85**
2:3 *85*
2:5–10 *284*
2:5–9 **236**
2:7–9 *61*
2:8–9 *269*
2:8 *236*
2:9 **242**
2:10–18 **321**
2:10 *36*
2:11 *162*
2:14–15 **321**
2:14 *162*
2:17 *114*
3:1 *74*
4:1–10 **323**
4:12 *230*
5:1–10 *130*
5:2 *219*
5:7–10 **98**
5:7 *382*
5:8 *98*
5:9 *374*
6:1 *95*
6:17–19 *339*
6:17 *319*
7:11–18 **221**
7:17 *289*
7:20–28 **249**
7:20–25 *130*
7:21 *249*
7:25 *248, 274, 324, 325*
7:6 *339*
8:1 *249*
8:7–13 **193**
8:8–12 **312**
8:10 *313*
8:12 *314, 315*
9:11–14 **246**
9:12 *45*
9:13 *297*
9:14 *297*
9:15–22 **315**
9:21–22 *118*
9:23–10:7 **237**
9:23 *237*
9:24 *222*
9:27 *321*
9:28 *254*
10:4 *298*
10:5 *298*
10:9–10 *298*
10:10 *69*
10:14 *222*
10:16–17 *39*
10:16 *102*
10:17 *306*
10:19–25 **254**
10:34 *369*
10:37–38 *254*
11:1 *337*
11:4 *299*
11:6 *324*
11:17 **339**
11:31 *341*
12:1–3 **370**
12:1 *228*
12:3 *256*
12:4–12 **369**
12:10 *369*
12:12–13 *369*
12:18–29 *222*
12:22–23 **404**
12:29 *54*
13:1 *121*

James
1:2–3 *407*
1:5–8 **211**
1:5 **211**
1:13–18 **377**
1:13 *377*
1:14 **212**
1:22 *212*
2 *277*
2:1–13 *159*
2:1–4 **162**
2:1 **162**
2:5–9 **163**
2:5 *326*
2:8–13 **103**
2:8, 10–11 *121*
2:13 **104**
2:14–24 **347**
2:17 **347**
2:21 *129*
2:23 *348*
2:25 **342**
3:1–6 **383**
3:7–12 **384**
3:7–8 **384**
3:18 *384*
4:1–4 **212**
4:6–10 **226**
4:8 **226**
4:10 **166**
4:11 *385*
5:1–6 *293*
5:7–11 **181**
5:13–20 **255**
5:17 *255*

1 John
1:1–4 **26**
1:1–3 *3*
1:2 *35*
1:3 **26**
1:7 *376*
1:9 *225, 376*
2:1–6 **208**
2:3 *208*
2:7–12 **345**
2:9–11 **376**
2:10 *376*
2:12–17 **140**
2:12 *345*
2:13 *140, 393*
2:15 *137*

INDEX OF DAILY READINGS AND KEY VERSES

1 John (cont.)
2:16   137, 138
2:17   382
2:18–21   **200**
2:18   257
2:19   200
2:22–27   **202**
2:22   202
2:28   275
2:29   28
3:1–3   **28**
3:1–2   30
3:1   28, 30
3:2   35
3:3   18, 29
3:4–10   **29**
3:9   29
3:10   30
3:12   299
3:16–24   **127**
3:18–19   127
3:24   317
4:1–6   **201**
4:2   201
4:5   203
4:6   203
4:7–21   **120**
4:7–17   **126**
4:7–12   **114**
4:7   120
4:9   6, 114
4:12   126
4:13   31, 126
4:14   4
4:15   31
4:16   18

5:1–5   **346**
5:5   **346**
5:6–12   **318**
5:6   117
5:13–21   **317**
5:13   318

2 John
4–11   **124**

3 John
9–10   205

Jude
6–7   59
11–23   **257**
20–25   **35**

Revelation
1–3   223
2–3   364
1:5–6   **149**
1:17   367
2:10   107
2:26–27   284
3:7   **107**
3:12   360
3:14–22   **133**
3:17   353
3:18   353
3:19   369
3:20   44
3:21   98, 353
4–5   149
4   **149**
4:3–4   75

4:6   76
5:1–10   **267**
5:2   149, 267
5:5   280
5:6   67
5:9   172
5:9–10   77
5:11–14   **67**
7:1–8   **327**
7:3   **327**
7:9–17   **328**
7:14   327, 328
7:17   67
8   327
12   **174**
12:10   220
13   174
13:1–18   **258**
13:1–17   **172**
13:4   **258**
13:13–15   259
18:5   315
19:10   35
19:11–16   **196**
19:9   **244**
20:11   260
21:1–4, 15–20   **260**
21:2   **260**
21:3   41, 42
21:4   67
21:5   **330**
21:12   260
21:15–27   **404**
21:25–26   260
22:3   **93**
22:10–11   321

Publications by David Gooding

Doctoral dissertation
'The Greek Deuteronomy', PhD thesis, University of Cambridge, 1954, unpublished. Deals with the textual problems raised by the Chester Beatty Papyrus VI (963), Dublin.

Books
Recensions of the Septuagint Pentateuch. Tyndale Lecture 1954. Cambridge: Tyndale Press, 1955.

The Account of the Tabernacle: Translation and Textual Problems of the Greek Exodus. Texts and Studies: Contributions to Biblical and Patristic Literature, ed. C. H. Dodd, no. 6. Cambridge: Cambridge University Press, 1959.

edited *The Text of the Septuagint: Its Corruptions and Their Emendation* by Peter Walters (formerly Katz). Cambridge: Cambridge University Press, 1973.

Studies in Luke's Gospel. Bible Study and Discussion Papers 1–3. Dublin: Biblical Studies Institute, 1973.

An Unshakeable Kingdom: The Letter to the Hebrews for Today. Scarborough, Ontario: Everyday Publications, 1975; rev. edn Leicester: Inter-Varsity Press/Grand Rapids: Eerdmans, 1989; repr. Port Colborne, Ontario: Gospel Folio Press, 1989, 2002; repr. Coleraine, N. Ireland: Myrtlefield House, 2013; also available for Logos (Bellingham, Wash: Faithlife), and Kindle; repr. African Christian Textbooks, 2014; Audible audiobook, 2021.

    [in Bulgarian] *Посланието към Евреите*. Sofia: Нов човек (New Man), 1995;

    [in Chinese] 1975.

    [in German] *Ein unerschütterliches Reich: 10 Studien über d. Hebräerbrief.* Dillenburg: Christliche Verlagsgesellschaft, 1987; rev. edn *Ein unerschütterliches Reich - Felsenfeste Wahrheit in unsicheren Zeiten - Kommentar zum Hebräerbrief.* CMVH, 2013.

    [in Hungarian] *Rendíthetetlen királyság*. Stuttgart: Evangéliumi, 1991; *A Zsidókhoz írt levél mai üzenete: Rendíthetetlen ország*. Evangéliumi, 2017.

    [in Polish] *Niewzruszone Królestwo: list do Hebrajczyków dzisiaj*. Wydaw. Ewangeliczne, 1990, 1994.

    [in Romanian] *Epistola către Evrei. O împărăție ce nu poate fi clatinată*. Cluj, Romania: Editura Logos, 2006.

    [in Russian] *Осуществление Ожидаемого: Посланце к Евреям*. Moscow, 1996, 1998.

    [in Swahili] *Ufalme Usiotetemeka: Magundisho juu ya Barua kwa Waebrania*. Bunia, Zaire: Editions Evangeliques.

    [in Spanish] *Según Hebreos: Un reino inconmovible*. Barcelona: Publicaciones Andamino, 1990, 2008; Belfast: Myrtlefield Español, 2022.

    [in Vietnamese] *"Vương Quốc Không Hề Rúng Động": Thơ Hêbơrơ Cho Thời Hiện Đại*. Leicester: IVP, 2003, 2014.

Relics of Ancient Exegesis: A Study of the Miscellanies in 3 Reigns 2. Society for Old Testament Study Monograph Series, 4. Cambridge: Cambridge University Press, 1976.

According to Luke: A new exposition of the Third Gospel. Leicester: Inter-Varsity Press, 1987; repr. Port Colborne, Ontario: Gospel Folio Press, 2002; repr. Eugene, Origen: Wipf and Stock, 2005; repr. as *According to Luke: The Third Gospel's Ordered Historical Narrative*. Coleraine,

N. Ireland: Myrtlefield House, 2013; also available for Logos (Bellingham, Wash: Faithlife), and Kindle; repr. African Christian Textbooks, 2014.
- [in Dutch] *Volgens Lukas*. Royal Jongbloed, 1995.
- [in German] *Das Evangelium nach Lukas: Botschaft, Aufbau und Ziel*. Christliche Literaturverbreitung, 2012.
- [in Hungarian] Budapest: Evangéliumi Kiadó, 1987.
- [in Polish] *Według Łukasza: nowe spojrzenie na Trzecią Ewangelię*. tr. Witold Gorecki. Wydawnictwo Ewangeliczne, 1992.
- [in Spanish] *Según Lucas: una nueva exposición del tercer Evangelio*. Editiorial Clie/Publicaciones Andamio, 1996; *Según Lucas: La narración histórica ordenada del tercer Evangelio*, Belfast: Myrtlefield Español, 2022.
- [in Russian] *Новый взгяд на Евангелие от Луки*. Duncanville, USA: World Wide Printing, 1997.
- [in Vietnamese] *Theo Thánk Lu-ca*. 2015.

True to the Faith: A fresh approach to the Acts of the Apostles. London: Hodder & Stoughton, 1990; repr. Port Colborne, Ontario: Gospel Folio Press, 1995; repr as *True to the Faith: Defining and Defending the Gospel*. Coleraine, N. Ireland: Myrtlefield House, 2013; also available for Logos (Bellingham, Wash: Faithlife), and Kindle; repr. African Christian Textbooks, 2014.
- [in Hungarian] *A krisztusi hithez hűen: Az Apostolok Cselekedetei könyvének új megközelítése*. Budapest: Evangéliumi, 2000, 2017.
- [in Portuguese] *Permanecendo fiel à fé: Atos dos Apóstolos Definindo e Defendendo o Evangelho*. Porto Alegre, Brazil: Editora Verdade, 2015.
- [in Romanian] *Faptele Apostolilor. Credincioși adevărului*. Cluj, Romania: Editura Logos, 1995.
- [in Russian] *Верные вере: Новый подход к Деяниям святых Апостолов*. 1994; & Duncanville, USA: World Wide Printing, 1998.
- [in Spanish] *Según Hechos: permaneciendo fiel a la fe*. Editiorial Clie/Publicaciones Andamio, 1990, rev. edn 2008.
- [in Vietnamese] *Sống Đúng Đức Tin*. 2016.

In the School of Christ: A Study of Christ's Teaching on Holiness. John 13–17. Port Colborne, Ontario: Gospel Folio Press, 1995, 2001; repr. as *In the School of Christ: Lessons on Holiness in John 13–17*. Coleraine, N. Ireland: Myrtlefield House, 2013 ; also available for Logos (Bellingham, Wash: Faithlife), and Kindle; repr. African Christian Textbooks, 2014.
- [in Bulgarian] В училището на Христос. Sofia: Veren, 2000, 2017.
- [in Burmese] 2013.
- [in Dutch] *In de School van Christus. Johannes 13-17*. Royal Jongbloed, 1997.
- [in German] *In der Schule des Meisters: Eine Betrachtung der Lehren Christi über Heiligkeit – Johannes 13–17*. Christliche Literaturverbreitung, 2015.
- [in Hungarian] *Krisztus iskolájában*. Budapest: Evangéliumi Kiadó, 1996.
- [in Polish] *W szkole Chrystusa: studium nauczania Chrystusa na temat świętości, Ewangelia Jana 13-17*. tr. Adam Mariuk. Areopag, 2010.
- [in Portuguese] *Na Escola de Cristo: Lições sobre a santidade em João 13-17*. Porto Alegre, Brazil: Editora Verdade, 2017.
- [in Russian] *В Школе Христа (Учение Христа о святости)*. Newtownards, N. Ireland: Myrtlefield Trust, 1997.
- [in Spanish] *Según Juan: En la escuela de Cristo. Juan 13-17*. tr. Roger Marshall. 1995; Barcelona: Publicaciones Andamino, 2012; *En la escuela de Cristo:*

    Lecciones sobre la santidad en Juan 13–17, Belfast: Myrtlefield Español, 2022.

Windows on Paradise. Port Colborne, Ontario: Gospel Folio Press, 1998, 2001; Coleraine, N. Ireland: Myrtlefield Trust, 2013; Coleraine, N. Ireland: Myrtlefield House, 2014, 2018.
- [in Albanian] *Dritare në parajsë*, Myrtlefield House, 2018.
- [in Bulgarian] *Прозорец към рая*. Sofia, Bulgaria: Veren, 2011, 2014.
- [in Burmese] Myrtlefield Trust, 2012.
- [in Hungarian] *Mennybe nyíló ablakok*. tr. Péter Vohmann. Budapest: Evangéliumi, 1991.
- [in Malay] *Jendela Syurga*. 2008.
- [in Russian] *Окно в рай. Исследование Евангелия от Луки*. Newtownards, N. Ireland: Myrtlefield Trust, 1993.
- [in Spanish] *Ventanas al paraíso: Estudios en el evangelio de Lucas*. Terassa, Barcelona: Talleres Gráficos de la M.C.E. 1982.
- [in Thai] Myrtlefield Hosue, 2013.
- [in Vietnamese] *Những Cửa Sổ Trên Trời*, Myrtlefield Trust, 2013

The Riches of Divine Wisdom: The New Testament's Use of the Old Testament. Coleraine, N. Ireland: Myrtlefield House, 2013; also available for Logos (Bellingham, Wash: Faithlife), and Kindle; repr. African Christian Textbooks, 2014.
- [in Hungarian] *Isten sokféle bölcsessége: Hogyan használja az Ószövetség az Újszövetséget*. Budapest: Evangéliumi, 2010.
- [in Russian] *Христианикая интерпретация Ветхого Завета* [= Christian Interpretation of OT]. Belfast: Myrtlefield House, 2008, rev. edn 2016.
- [in Spanish] *La Multiforme Sabiduría de Dios: El uso que hace el Nuevo Testamento del Antiguo Testamento*. Belfast, N. Ireland: Myrtlefield Español, 2020.

Books published with John Lennox

Christianity: Opium or Truth? Port Colborne, Ontario: Gospel Folio Press, 1997; rev. edn Coleraine, N. Ireland: Myrtlefield House, 2014; also available for Kindle; repr. African Christian Textbooks, 2014; repr. 10 of Those, 2019.
- [in Bulgarian] *Християнството: опиум или истина?* Sofia, Bulgaria: Veren, 2004; 2nd edn, Sofia: Veren, 2014.
- [in Czech] *Křesťanství – opium, nebo pravda?* Brno, Czechia: Myrtlefield House/ALEF Křesťanské sbory, 2014; repr. 2020.
- [in French] *Le christianisme: opium ou vérité?* Valence, France: Éditions LLB, 2023.
- [in German] *Opium fürs Volk?* Bielefeld: Christliche Literatur-Verbreitung, 2012.
- [in Hungarian] *Kereszténység: illúziók vagy tények?* Budapest: Evangéliumi, 1998; *Kereszténység: Ópium vagy Igazság?* Budapest: Evangéliumi, 2013.
- [in Portuguese] *Cristianismo: Ópio do Povo?* Porto Alegre, Brazil: Editora Verdade, 2014.
- [in Russian] *Христианство: опиум или истина?* Moscow: Myrtlefield Trust, 1991 & Duncanville, USA: World Wide Printing, 1998.

Worldview I: The Human Quest for Significance: Forming a Worldview. rev. English edn published in *The Quest for Reality and Significance* series.
- [in Hungarian] *Küzdelem az élet értelméért: Világnézetünk alakítása*. Budapest: Evangéliumi, 2001.
- [in Russian] *Мировоззрение. Для чего мы живем и каково наше место в мире*. Том 1. Minsk: Yaroslavl, 1999, 2001;

The Definition of Christianity. Port Colborne, Ontario: Gospel Folio Press, 1997, 2001; rev. edn Coleraine, N. Ireland: Myrtlefield House, 2014; also available for Kindle; repr. African Christian Textbooks, 2014.

    [in Bulgarian] *Дефиниция на християнството*. Sofia, Bulgaria: Veren, 2004, 2014.

    [in French] *Le sens du christianisme*. Valence, France: Éditions LLB, 2022.

    [in German] *Christentum definitiv!: Der Unterschied zwischen christlicher Botschaft und Christenheit*. Hammerbrücke: Germany: Jota Publikation, 2003.

    [in Hungarian] *A keresztyénség meghatározása*. tr. Peter Vohmann. Budapest: Evangéliumi.

    [in Polish] *Definicja chrześcijaństwa*. tr. Przemysław Janikowski. Areopag, 2001.

    [in Portuguese] *A Definiçao Do Cristianismo*. Porto Alegre, Brazil: Editora Verdade, 2014.

    [in Russian] *Определение Христианства*. Duncanville, USA: World Wide Printing, 1997, 2005 and Minsk: Myrtlefield Trust, 1999.

    [in Spanish] *Una definición del cristianismo para el siglo XXI : un estudio basado en los hechos de los Apóstoles*. Barcelona: Editiorial Clie, 2001; 2nd edn, *La definición del cristianismo*, Belfast: Myrtlefield Español, 2022.

Key Bible Concepts. Port Colborne, Ontario: Gospel Folio Press, 1997, 2007; repr. Coleraine, N. Ireland: Myrtlefield House, 2013; also available for Kindle; repr. Bible Educational Services, 2013; repr. African Christian Textbooks, 2014.

    [in Arabic] Belfast: Myrtlefield House, 2016.

    [in Bulgarian] *Ключови библейски Понятия*. Sofia, Bulgaria: Veren, 1997, 2004.

    [in Burmese] Coleraine, N. Ireland: Myrtlefield House, 2013.

    [in Chinese] Hong Kong: CCL, 2002, 2014, 2019.

    [in French] *Concepts bibliques clés*. Valence, France: Éditions LLB, 2022.

    [in German] *Schlüsselbegriffe der Bibel*. Bielefeld: Christliche Literatur-Verbreitung, 2013.

    [in Korean] 성경의 핵심용어 해설. Korea: BrethrenHouse, 2017

    [in Malay] *Konsep Utama Dalam Alkitab*. Myrtlefield Trust, 2004.

    [in Norwegian] Kristiansand, Norway: Bibelsk Bibliotek, 1997.

    [in Polish] *Kluczowe koncepcje biblijne*. Areopag, 2001.

    [in Portuguese] *Conceitos-Chave da Bíblia*. Porto Alegre, Brazil: Editora Verdade, 2013, 2016.

    [in Russian] *Ключевые понятия Библии*. Myrtlefield Trust, 1997.

    [in Spanish] *Conceptos bíblicos fundamentales: para comprender y enseñar la Biblia a la sociedad de hoy*. Barcelona: Editorial Clie/Publicaciones Andamio, 1995, 2001; 2nd edn, *Conceptos bíblicos fundamentales*, Belfast: Myrtlefield Español, 2022.

    [in Swahili] *Lulu za Biblia*. Dodoma, Tanzania: Kanisa la Biblia, 2014.

    [in Vietnamese] *Khái Niệm Nền Tảngthánh Kinh*. Hanoi, Vietnam: Tôn Giáo, 2013.

Worldview II: The Search for Reality (1). rev. English edn published in *The Quest for Reality and Significance* series.

    [in Hungarian] *Küzdelem az élet értelméért II. Világnézetünk alakítása*. Budapest: Evangéliumi, 2011.

    [in Russian] *Мировоззрение: Человек в поисках истины и реальности шь*. Том 1. Minsk: Yaroslavl, 2004;

Worldview III: The Search for Reality (2). rev. English edn published in *The Quest for Reality and Significance* series.

    [in Hungarian] *Küzdelem az élet értelméért III. Világnézetünk alakítása*. Budapest: Evangéliumi, 2012.

    [in Russian] *Мировоззрение: Человек в поисках истины и реальности*. Том 2. Minsk: Yaroslavl, 2004;

    [in Ukrainian] Kiev: Myrtlefield Trust/Ukrainian Bible Society, 2005.

The Bible and Ethics: Studies for Group and Individual Work. Coleraine, N. Ireland: Myrtlefield Trust, 2011; repr. Port Colborne, Ontario: Gospel Folio Press, 2011; India, Bible Educational Services, 2013; rev. English edn Coleraine, N. Ireland: Myrtlefield House, 2014; also available for Kindle.

    [in Burmese] 2015.

    [in French] *L'éthique selon la Bible*. Valence, France: Éditions LLB, 2023.

    [in Hungarian] *Bibliai és etikai nevelés*. tr. Péter Vohmann. Budapest: Evangéliumi, 2019.

    [in Portuguese] *A Bíblia e a Ética*. Porto Alegre, Brazil: Editora Verdade, 2020.

    [in Spanish] *Fundamentos para una ética bíblica: La Biblia y la educación ética para un mundo en transición*. Barcelona: Andamio Editorial, 2001, 2015. *Fundamentos para una ética bíblica*, Belfast: Myrtlefield Español, 2022.

    [in Russian] Библия и нравственное воспитание [= The Bible and Ethical Education]. Newtownards, N. Ireland: Myrtlefield Trust, 1997 and Duncanville, USA: World Wide Printing, 1999.

Being Truly Human: The Limits of our Worth, Power, Freedom and Destiny. The Quest for Reality and Significance. Vol. 1. Belfast, N. Ireland: Myrtlefield House, 2018; also available for Kindle.

    [in German] *Was ist der Mensch?: Würde, Möglichkeiten, Freiheit und Bestimmung*. Die Suche nach Wirklichkeit und Bedeutung. Buch 1. Christliche Verlagsgesellschaft, 2020.

Finding Ultimate Reality: In Search of the Best Answers to the Biggest Questions. The Quest for Reality and Significance. Vol. 2. Belfast, N. Ireland: Myrtlefield House, 2018; also available for Kindle.

    [in German] *Was können wir wissen?: Können wir wissen, was wir unbedingt wissen müssen?* Die Suche nach Wirklichkeit und Bedeutung. Buch 2. Christliche Verlagsgesellschaft, 2020.

Questioning our Knowledge; Can we Know What we Need to Know? The Quest for Reality and Significance. Vol. 3. Belfast, N. Ireland: Myrtlefield House, 2019; also available for Kindle.

    [in German] *Was sollen wir tun? Was ist das beste Konzept für Ethik?* Die Suche nach Wirklichkeit und Bedeutung. Buch 3. Christliche Verlagsgesellschaft, 2021.

Doing What's Right: Whose System of Ethics is Good Enough? The Quest for Reality and Significance. Vol. 4. Belfast, N. Ireland: Myrtlefield House, 2019; also available for Kindle.

    [in German] *Was dürfen wir hoffen? Antworten einfordern - Den Schmerz des Lebens ertragen - Was ist Wirklichkeit?* Die Suche nach Wirklichkeit und Bedeutung. Buch 4. Christliche Verlagsgesellschaft, 2021.

Claiming to Answer: How One Person Became the Response to our Deepest Questions. The Quest for Reality and Significance. Vol. 5. Belfast, N. Ireland: Myrtlefield House, 2019; also available for Kindle.

Suffering Life's Pain: Facing the Problems of Moral and Natural Evil. The Quest for Reality and Significance. Vol. 6. Belfast, N. Ireland: Myrtlefield House, 2019; also available for Kindle.

Books published posthumously

Bringing Us to Glory. Edited by Helen Crookes. Belfast: Myrtlefield House, 2020; also available for Kindle.

Journeys with Jesus: True Stories of Changed Destinies in John's Gospel. Edited by Joshua Fitzhugh. Belfast: Myrtlefield House, 2021; also available for Kindle.

The Letters of David W. Gooding: Answering Questions Related to the Christian Faith. Belfast: Myrtlefield House, 2024.

Published lectures and booklets

Recensions of the Septuagint Pentateuch. Cambridge: Tyndale Press, 1955.

How about God? Four broadcast talks. Belfast: Graham & Heslip, n.d.

The inspiration and authority, canon and transmission of Holy Scripture. Edinburgh: Darien Press, 1961.

How to Teach the Tabernacle. Dublin: Merrion Press, 1970; repr. Port Colborne, Ontario: Everyday Publications, 1977; rev edn *Drawing Near to God: Lessons from the Tabernacle for Today.* Belfast, Myrtlefield House, 2019

    [in Burmese] 2015, 2020.

    [in Hungarian] *Az eljövendő árnyéka: hogyan tanítsuk a bibliai Szent Sátort?* [= The Shadow of the Future: How to Teach the Holy Tent of the Bible]. Budapest: Evangéliumi, 2018.

    [in Russian] 1992.

    [in Spanish] *Cómo enseñar el tabernáculo.* Port Colborne, Ontario: Everyday Publications, 1977.

Current Problems and Methods in the Textual Criticism of the Old Testament. Belfast: Queen's University, 1979.

How? The Search for Spiritual Satisfaction. Leicester: Inter-Varsity Press, 1980. Reprinted in *Christianity: Opium or Truth?* (ch. 8).

    [in Italian] *Essere soddisfatti... e continuare ad esserlo.* Fondi, Italy: Unione Cristiana Edizione Bibliche, 1984.

Freedom under God. Bath: Echoes of Service, 1988.

Modern Myths.

    [in Bulgarian] Модерните митове. Sofia: Veren, 2019.

Unfettered Faith: The Promotion of Spiritual Freedom. Coleraine, N. Ireland: Myrtlefield Trust, 1986.

    [in Bulgarian] Освободената вяра: По-голяма гуховна свобога. Sofia, Bulgaria: New Man, 1995.

    [in Croatian] *Raskovana Vera: Unapređenje duhovne slobode.* Bački Petrovac, Serbia: Hristova crkva braće, 1989.

    [in Polish] *Wiara wyzwolona z Więzów.* Poznań, Poland: Wydawnicto Ewangeliczne, 1990.

Wer glaubt muß denken. Bielefeld: Christliche Literature-Verbreitung, 1998.

The Bible: Myth or Truth. Reprinted in English in *Christianity: Opium or Truth?* (ch. 2).

    [in Bulgarian] Библията: мит или истина. Coleraine, N. Ireland: Myrtlefield Trust, 2001; Sofia, Bulgaria: Veren, 2008.

    [in German] *Die Bibel—Mythos oder Wahrheit?* Dillenburg: Christliche Verlagsgesellschaft, 1993; *Die Bibel—Mythos oder Wahrheit? Gibt es eine echte Erfüllung?* 2nd edn Bielefeld: Christliche Literature-Verbreitung, 2001.

Chapters and major articles

'The Text of the Psalms in two Durham Bibles.' *Scriptorium* 12:1 (1958): 94–6.

Articles in *New Bible Dictionary* on 'Bezalel, Bezaleel'; 'Capital' [in tabernacle]; 'Censer'; 'Gershom, Gershon'; 'Kaiwan'; 'Kohath, Kohathites'; 'Merari, Merarites'; 'Oholiab'; 'Rephan'; 'Snuffers'; ' Tabernacle'; 'Texts & Versions 2. The Septuagint'; 'Trays'. Leicester: Inter-Varsity Press, 1962.

'Aristeas and Septuagint Origins: A review of recent studies.' *Vetus Testamentum* 13:4 (1963): 357–379.

'Ahab According to the Septuagint.' *ZAW* 76 (1964): 269–80.

PUBLICATIONS BY DAVID GOODING

'Pedantic Timetabling in 3rd Book of Reigns.' *Vetus Testamentum* 15:2 (1965): 153–66.

'The Septuagint's Version of Solomon's Misconduct.' *Vetus Testamentum* 15:3 (1965): 325–35.

'An Impossible Shrine.' *Vetus Testamentum* 15:4 (1965): 405–20.

'Temple Specifications: A Dispute in Logical Arrangement between the MT and the LXX.' *Vetus Testamentum* 17:2 (1967): 143–72.

'The Septuagint's Rival Versions of Jeroboam's Rise to Power.' *Vetus Testamentum* 17:2 (1967): 173–89.

'The Shimei Duplicate and its Satellite Miscellanies in 3 Reigns II.' *Journal of Semitic Studies* 13:1 (1968): 76–92.

'Problems of Text and Midrash in the Third Book of Reigns.' *Textus* 7 (1969): 11–13.

'Text-Sequence and Translation-Revision in 3 Reigns IX 10 – X 33.' *Vetus Testamentum* 19:4 (1969): 448–63.

'Observations on Certain Problems Connected with the So-called Septuagint.' *TSF Bulletin* 56 (1970): 8–13.

'Jeroboam's Rise to Power: A Rejoinder.' *Journal of Biblical Literature* 91:4 (1972): 529–33.

'Two possible examples of midrashic interpretation in the Septuagint Exodus' in *Wort, Lied, und Gottesspruch: Festschrift für Joseph Ziegler* (ed. Josef Schreiner; Echter Verlag: Katholisches Bibelwerk, 1972), 39–48.

'On the use of the LXX for dating Midrashic elements in the Targums.' *Journal of Theological Studies* ns 25:1 (1974): 1–11.

'A Recent Popularisation of Professor F. M. Cross' Theories on the Text of the Old Testament.' *Tyndale Bulletin* 26 (1975): 113–32.

'An Appeal for a Stricter Terminology in the Textual Criticism of the Old Testament.' *Journal of Semitic Studies* 21 (1976): 15–25.

'Traditions of Interpretation of the Circumcision at Gilgal', in *Proceedings of the Sixth World Congress of Jewish Studies, held at the Hebrew University of Jerusalem, 13–19 August, 1973, under the Auspices of the Israel Academy of Sciences and Humanities, Division A* (ed. A. Shinan; Jerusalem: World Union of Jewish Studies, 1977), 149–64.

'Structure littéraire de Matthieu 13:53 à 18:35.' *Revue biblique* 85:2 (1978): 227–52.

'Demythologizing, Old and New, and Luke's Description of the Ascension: A Layman's Appraisal.' *Irish Biblical Studies* 2 (1980): 95–119.

Articles in *Illustrated Bible Dictionary* on 'Septuagint'; 'Tabernacle'. Leicester: Inter-Varsity Press, 1980.

'The Literary Structure of the Book of Daniel and its Implications' (The Tyndale Old Testament Lecture, 1980). *Tyndale Bulletin* 32 (1981): 43–79.

'Demythologizing the Ascension: A Reply by D. W. Gooding.' *Irish Biblical Studies* 3 (1981): 45–54.

'A Sketch of Current Septuagint Studies.' *Proceedings of the Irish Biblical Association* 5 (1981).

'The Composition of the Book of Judges.' *Eretz-Israel*, H. M. Orlinsky Volume. Jerusalem: 1982.

Articles in *New Bible Dictionary* on 'Bezalel, Bezaleel'; 'Capital' [in tabernacle]; 'Censer'; 'Gershom, Gershon'; 'Kaiwan'; 'Kohath, Kohathites'; 'Merari, Merarites'; 'Oholiab'; 'Rephan'; 'Snuffers'; 'Tabernacle'; 'Texts & Versions 2. The Septuagint'; 'Trays'. 2nd edn Leicester: Inter-Varsity Press, 1982.

'Philo's Bible in the *De Gigantibus* and *Quod Deus*.' in *Two Treatises of Philo of Alexandria: A Commentary on De Gigantibus and Quod Deus Sit Immutabilis*, with V. Nikiprowetzky (ed. D. Winston and J. Dillon; BJS 25; Chico, Calif.: Scholars Press, 1983), 89–125.

'The Problem of Pain.' *Journal of the Irish Christian Study Centre* 1 (1983):63–9.

'An Approach to the Literary and Textual Problems in the David-Goliath Story', in *The Story of David and Goliath: Papers of a Joint Research Venture* by Dominique Barthélemy et al.; Orbis Biblicus et Orientalis, no. 73 (Fribourg: Éditions Universitaires, 1986; Göttingen: Vandenhoeck & Ruprecht, 1986), 55–86.

'David-Goliath Project: Stage Four', in *The Story of David and Goliath: Papers of a Joint Research Venture* by Dominique Barthélemy et al.; Orbis Biblicus et Orientalis, no. 73 (Fribourg: Éditions Universitaires, 1986; Göttingen: Vandenhoeck & Ruprecht, 1986), 145–154.

The Bible and Moral Education for Schools, with John Lennox. Moscow: *Uchitelskaya Gazeta* (Newspaper for Teachers), 1993–5; repr. as *The Bible and Ethics*.

Articles in *New Bible Dictionary* on 'Bezalel, Bezaleel'; 'Capital' [in tabernacle]; 'Censer'; 'Gershom, Gershon'; 'Kaiwan'; 'Kohath, Kohathites'; 'Merari, Merarites'; 'Oholiab'; 'Rephan'; 'Snuffers'; 'Tabernacle'; 'Texts & Versions 2. The Septuagint'; 'Trays'. 3rd edn, Leicester: Inter-Varsity Press, 1996.

'The tabernacle: no museum piece' in *The Perfect Saviour: Key themes in Hebrews* (ed. Jonathan Griffiths; Nottingham: Inter-Varsity Press, 2012), 69–88.

Review articles

Review of Ilmari Soisalon-Soininen, *Der Charakter der asterisierten Zusätze in der Septuaginta*. *Gnomon* 33:2 (1961): 143–8.

Review of Joost Smit Sibinga, *The Old Testament Text of Justin Martyr. Journal of Theological Studies* ns 16:1 (1965): 187–92.

Review of Ilmari Soisalon-Soininen, *Die Infinitive in der Septuaginta. Journal of Theological Studies* ns 18:2 (1967): 451–5.

Review of James Donald Shenkel, *Chronology and Recensional Development in the Greek Text of Kings viii*. *Journal of Theological Studies* ns 21:1 (1970): 118–31.

Review of Adrian Schenker, *Hexaplarische Psalmenbruchstucke: Die hexaplarischen Psalmenfragmente der Handschriften Vaticanus graecus 752 und Canonicianus graecus 62, Journal of Theological Studies* ns 27:2 (1976): 443–5.

Review of Raija Sollamo, *Renderings of Hebrew Semiprepositions in the Septuagint. Journal of Semitic Studies* 25:2 (1980): 261–3.

Review of John W. Olley, *"Righteousness" in the Septuagint of Isaiah: A Contextual Study. Journal of Theological Studies* ns 32:1 (1981): 204–12.

Review of J. H. Charlesworth, *The Pseudepigrapha and Modern Research. Irish Biblical Studies* 4:1 (1982): 46-49.

Review of Anneli Aejmelaeus, *Parataxis in the Septuagint. Journal of Semitic Studies* 28:2 (1983): 369–71.

Short Notice on M. K. H. Peters, *An Analysis of the Textual Character of the Bohairic of Deuteronomy. Journal of Theological Studies* ns 34:2 (1983): 693.

Review of Homer Heater, *A Septuagint Translation Technique in the Book of Job. Journal of Theological Studies* ns 35:1 (1984): 169–77.

Review of Roger Beckwith, *The Old Testament Canon of the New Testament Church. Irish Biblical Studies* 8:4 (1986): 207-211.

Review of George Alexander Kennedy, Duane Frederick Watson (eds.), *Persuasive Artistry: Studies in New Testament Rhetoric in Honour of George A Kennedy. Evangelical Quarterly* 64 (1992): 264–8.

Popular articles

'The True Peacemaker and Benefactor of the People.' *Precious Seed* 3:7 (1950).
'Modern Translations—Their Use and Abuse.' *Precious Seed* 7:8 (1956).
'New Testament Word Studies.' *Precious Seed* 12:1–4 & 13:1–6 (1961–62).
'El portal de la eternidad.' *Edificación Cristiana* (Madrid, Spain) 74 (Jul/Aug 1978).
'Symbols of Headship and Glory.' *The Word* (Belfast, 1980);
> [in German] 'Symbole oder Zeichen von Autoritat und Herrlichkeit' tr. von G. Giesler. *Verlegerbeilage zu Die Wegweisung* 6/87. Dillenburg, Christliche Verlagsgesellschaft, 1987.

A series of 34 articles in *The Question Box*, answering questions from readers. Japan, 1986–88.
'Questions People Ask About the Bible', a series of 10 articles published in *The Word* (Belfast, 1987–90).
'The Use of the Old Testament by the New.' [in Spanish] *Edificación Cristiana* (Madrid, Spain) (1995?).
'How do you relate and reconcile the teaching on women in 1 Corinthians 11 and 14?' *The Word* (Belfast, 1994).

Sermons and lectures

Many sermons and lectures are available from the Myrtlefield House website in audio and digital text formats.

WWW.MYRTLEFIELDHOUSE.COM

Our website contains hundreds of resources in a variety of formats. You can read, listen to or watch David Gooding's teaching on over 35 Bible books and 14 topics. Our website is optimized for both computer and mobile viewing, making it easy for you to access the resources at home or on the go.

For more information about any of our publications or resources contact us at: info@myrtlefieldhouse.com

MYRTLEFIELD DEVOTIONALS

The first of these 365 one-page readings focuses on the work of Christ as the one who brings us through life's journey to the destination of becoming like him. The second volume aims to deepen our understanding of some of the characteristics of our God in the assured hope that such understanding will renew our minds and, consequently, the way we live our lives.

Bringing us to Glory
Daily Readings for the Christian Journey

Changing us for Glory
Daily Readings on God's Transforming Power

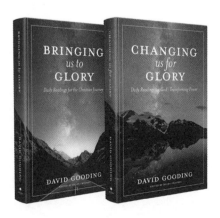

MYRTLEFIELD EXPOSITIONS

Myrtlefield Expositions provide insights into the thought flow and meaning of the biblical writings, motivated by devotion to the Lord who reveals himself in the Scriptures. Scholarly, engaging, and accessible, each book addresses the reader's mind and heart to increase faith in God and to encourage obedience to his Word. Teachers, preachers and all students of the Bible will find the approach to Scripture adopted in these volumes both instructive and enriching.

The Riches of Divine Wisdom
The New Testament's Use of the Old Testament

According to Luke
The Third Gospel's Ordered Historical Narrative

True to the Faith
The Acts of the Apostles: Defining and Defending the Gospel

In the School of Christ
Lessons on Holiness in John 13–17

An Unshakeable Kingdom
The Letter to the Hebrews for Today

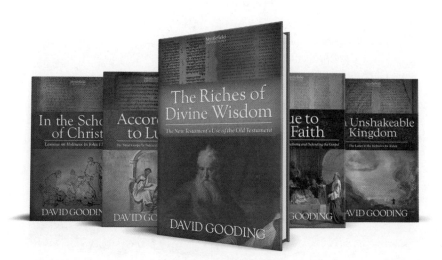

MYRTLEFIELD ENCOUNTERS

Myrtlefield Encounters are complementary studies of biblical literature, Christian teaching and apologetics. The books in this series engage the minds of believers and sceptics. They show how God has spoken in the Bible to address the realities of life and its questions, problems, beauty and potential.

Key Bible Concepts
Defining the Basic Terms of the Christian Faith

Christianity: Opium or Truth?
Answering Thoughtful Objections to the Christian Faith

The Definition of Christianity
Exploring the Original Meaning of the Christian Faith

The Bible and Ethics
Finding the Moral Foundations of the Christian Faith

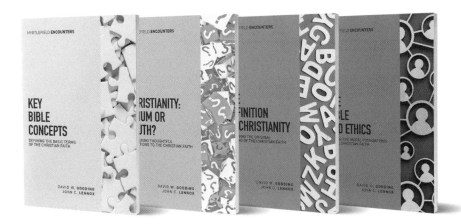

MYRTLEFIELD DISCOVERIES

Myrtlefield Discoveries combine depth of insight with accessible style in order to help today's readers find the Bible's meaning and its significance for all of life. Covering whole books of the Bible, themes or topics, each book in this series serves as a guide to the wonders of God's word. The material is intended to prepare readers to share what they have learned. Study groups, teachers and individual students will all benefit from the way these books open up the biblical text and reveal its application for life.

Drawing Near To God
Lessons From the Tabernacle for Today

Windows on Paradise
Scenes of Hope and Salvation in the Gospel of Luke

Journeys with Jesus
True Stories of Changed Destinies in John's Gospel

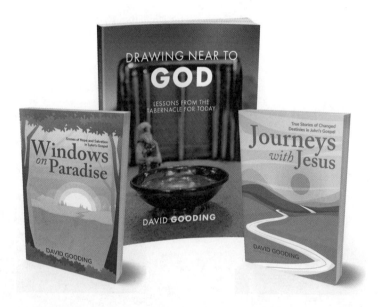

Also available.

The Letters of David W. Gooding
Answering Questions Related to the Christian Faith

THE QUEST FOR REALITY AND SIGNIFICANCE

We need a coherent picture of our world. Life's realities won't let us ignore its fundamental questions, but with so many opposing views, how will we choose answers that are reliable? In this series of books, David Gooding and John Lennox offer a fair analysis of religious and philosophical attempts to find the truth about the world and our place in it. By listening to the Bible alongside other leading voices, they show that it is not only answering life's biggest questions—it is asking better questions than we ever thought to ask.

Book 1—Being Truly Human
The Limits of our Worth, Power, Freedom and Destiny

Book 2—Finding Ultimate Reality
In Search of the Best Answers to the Biggest Questions

Book 3—Questioning Our Knowledge
Can We Know What We Need to Know?

Book 4—Doing What's Right
Whose System of Ethics is Good Enough?

Book 5—Claiming To Answer
How One Person Became the Response to our Deepest Questions

Book 6—Suffering Life's Pain
Facing the Problems of Moral and Natural Evil

The Lord changes us for his glory as we look upon him. What I love about David Gooding's latest devotional is its constant focus upon the Lord, drawing my eyes upward to him through clear explanations of biblical passages. Seeing God's beauty, his power, his joy and his holiness is what the church needs today. I highly recommend this book to help you draw near to Christ and become more like him.

Dr Todd Bolen
Professor of Biblical Studies, The Master's University

If you have ever struggled to comprehend all that the gospel gives you, this year-long devotional will unveil the fullness of it. You will gain a new understanding of the glory of God, the oneness of the Trinity, forgiveness, God dwelling in us, the love and humility of God, his commitment to make us like himself—and so much more. I look forward to reading it day by day.

Judy Douglass
Global Director—Cru's Women's Resources
Author, Speaker, Podcaster

Living our lives as followers of Jesus in today's fast-paced world, with its unique challenges and opportunities, demands we should be well equipped. This exciting new book offers a rich resource for this very purpose.

Professor Gooding was 'a man after God's own heart' who invested his life in the teaching of Scripture and the encouragement of God's people. This book draws on the deep well of his Scriptural knowledge and scholarship, together with spiritual insight from his own pilgrimage as a faithful servant of God. The style is compelling and clear, reflecting his wonderful gift as a teacher.

I look forward to engaging daily with this helpful and thoughtfully curated book. I heartily recommend it to readers of all ages, but especially to young people, as an important, relevant and very accessible guide in contemporary Christian life.

Dr Sharon Jones
Stranmillis University College, Belfast

When we fix our gaze upon the Lord Jesus through his word, we not only get to know him, but we are also transformed into his likeness. In his book, *Changing us for Glory*, Dr David Gooding gives us a wonderful guide as we read God's word, granting greater understanding and insight into God's character, relational nature and desire to be known.

Steve & Donna Gaines
Bellevue Baptist Church, Memphis, TN

Having extensively used the first volume of daily readings, *Bringing us to Glory*, I was eagerly looking forward to this new collection. And what a gift it is! Each day is an open door, calling us to a deeper understanding of the sheer glory of God's character, full of insight to feed the soul, excite the imagination and stimulate the desire to discover more and to be changed in the discovery. Helen Crookes deserves both our congratulations and our thanks for her dedicated and skilful work in the production of this second volume, which along with the first will now become an essential part of my daily life and which I will recommend without hesitation.

Gilbert Lennox
Bible teacher, Chair of New Horizon Ministries and friend of David Gooding

Dr Gooding's devotional – *Changing us for Glory: Daily Readings on God's Transforming Power* – stirs the heart and stimulates the mind as he expounds profound truth understandably and applicably. The reader will find this treasure to be overwhelmingly biblical, richly theological and warm-heartedly evangelistic. May this classic work prove to be spiritually transformative to all who love the Lord Jesus Christ.

Richard Mayhue, Th.D.
Research Professor of Theology Emeritus, The Master's Seminary

In this well-written exploration of the 'Christ-likeness' journey, Professor Gooding seeks to make known a practical roadmap for our daily transformation through what the Apostle Paul referred to as the 'unsearchable riches' (Romans 11:33). Of great significance are the author's challenging insights related to intra-trinitarian love between Father, Son and Holy Spirit, along with various personal implications for our living out the mystery of Christ in us, our only hope of glory (Colossians 1:27).

Dr. David Ferguson
Executive Director, GreatCommandment.net

As a man, husband, father and pastor, the perpetual need of my life is to abide day by day in the presence of the Lord. Thankfully our heavenly Father, who provided daily manna for Israel and fresh oil for the first believers, has now given us a treasure trove of help and hope through Dr Gooding's *Changing us for Glory*. You will find this resource both timeless and timely. May the daily meditations land on you in your specific time of need, just as they have for me.

Jeremy Morton
Lead Pastor, First Baptist Church, Woodstock, Georgia

I don't usually use daily reading notes, preferring to spend time reading through whole books of the Bible, but these notes are a joy to use. They range through the riches of both the Old and the New Testament: through the Law and the Prophets, meditations on the Psalms and Wisdom literature, the Gospels and the Epistles. As you read through these glorious texts, you are accompanied by the writings of David Gooding with his depth of understanding, wealth of experience and deep love of the Lord. As you read God's word, it is a privilege to be encouraged by this teaching from a faithful brother who has gone before us.

Karen Soole
author of Liberated: How the Bible exalts and dignifies women *and* Unleash the Word